CHILDREN'S RIGHTS AND TRADITIONAL VALUES

Programme on International Rights of the Child
Series Editor: Geraldine Van Bueren

Children's Rights and Traditional Values

Edited by
GILLIAN DOUGLAS
Cardiff University
LESLIE SEBBA
Hebrew University of Jerusalem

DARTMOUTH

Aldershot • Brookfield USA • Singapore • Sydney

© Gillian Douglas, Leslie Sebba 1998

Published by
Dartmouth Publishing Company Limited
Ashgate Publishing Limited
Gower House
Croft Road
Aldershot
Hants GU11 3HR
England

Ashgate Publishing Company
Old Post Road
Brookfield
Vermont 05036
USA

British Library Cataloguing in Publication Data
Children's rights and traditional values. - (Programme on
   international rights of the child)
   1.Children's rights 2.Children - Legal status, laws, etc. -
   Great Britain 3.Children - Legal status, laws, etc. - Israel
   I.Douglas, Gillian II.Sebba, Leslie
   323.3'52

Library of Congress Cataloging-in-Publication Data
Children's rights and traditional values / edited by Gillian Douglas
   and Leslie Sebba.
         p.   cm. – (Programme on International Rights of the Child series)
      Papers originally presented at a symposium held at the Faculty of
Law of the Hebrew University of Jerusalem in March 1996.
      Includes bibliographical references.
      ISBN 1-85521-956-5 (hb)
      1. Children–Legal status, laws, etc.–Congresses. 2. Children's
   rights–Congresses. I. Douglas, Gillian. II. Sebba, Leslie.
   III. Series: Programme on International Rights of the Child series.
   K639.A55   1998
   346.01'35–dc21   97-51289
                                                                              CIP

ISBN 1 85521 956 5

Printed in Great Britain by Galliard (Printers) Ltd, Great Yarmouth

Contents

List of Contributors

Andrew Bainham is a Fellow of Christ's College, Cambridge.

Leora Bilsky is a Lecturer in Administrative Law, Feminist Theories and Child Law at the Faculty of Law, Tel Aviv University.

Gillian Douglas is a Reader in Law at Cardiff Law School, University of Wales.

William Duncan is Professor of Law and Jurisprudence at Trinity College, University of Dublin.

Ze'ev W. Falk is Professor Emeritus at the Faculty of Law, the Hebrew University of Jerusalem.

Stephen Goldstein is Professor of Law at the Faculty of Law, the Hebrew University of Jerusalem.

Yehiel S. Kaplan is Lecturer in Family Law and Jewish Law at the Faculty of Law, University of Haifa.

Michael King is Professor and Co-Director at the Centre for the Study of Law, the Child and the Family, Law Department, Brunel University.

James Michael is a Senior Lecturer in Law at University College, London.

Wayne Morrison is a Lecturer in Law at Queen Mary and Westfield College, University of London.

David Nelken is Distinguished Professor of Sociology and Head of the Department of Social Change, Legal Institutions and Communication at the University of Macerata in Italy. He is also a Distinguished Scholar of the American Sociological Association; Distinguished Research Professor of Law at Cardiff Law School, University of Wales; and Visiting Professor of Law (Criminology) at University College, London.

Katherine O'Donovan is Professor of Law at Queen Mary and Westfield College, University of London.

His Honour Judge David Pearl is the Chief Adjudicator, Immigration Appeals and a Circuit Judge. He is also Visting Professor of Law at King's College, London, Honorary Professor of Law, University of East Anglia, and a Life Fellow of Fitzwilliam College, Cambridge.

Ya'ir Ronen is a Child Advocate. He has an MA in Educational Counselling from Tel Aviv University and is a Dr.Juris. student at the Faculty of Law, Hebrew University of Jerusalem.

Leslie Sebba is Associate Professor at the Institute of Criminology, Faculty of Law, the Hebrew University of Jerusalem.

Nadera Shalhoub-Kevorkian is Lecturer at the Faculty of Law (Institute of Criminology) and the School of Social Work of the Hebrew University of Jerusalem.

Varda Shiffer is a graduate of the School of Educational Leadership, and a doctoral candidate in the Political Science Department of the Hebrew University of Jerusalem.

Geraldine Van Bueren is a Reader in Law and Director of the Programme on International Rights of the Child in the Department of Law of Queen Mary and Westfield College, University of London.

Series Preface

The concept of international children's rights has come of age, and the Programme on International Rights of the Child Series is the first series of volumes dedicated to exploring specific aspects of international children's rights. The series comprises both sole authored and edited volumes, and single disciplinary and multi-disciplinary monographs, all considering issues which are at the rapidly expanding boundaries of international children's rights.

This volume could not have been published without the generosity of John Levy and the Academic Study Group, which enabled the Programme on International Rights of the Child and the Hebrew University of Jerusalem to organise a symposium in Jerusalem on children's rights and traditional values.

Geraldine Van Bueren
Series Editor
Programme on International Rights of the Child
Queen Mary and Westfield College
University of London

Acknowledgements

This collection of papers grew out of a symposium on the theme of Children's Rights and Traditional Values held at the Faculty of Law of the Hebrew University of Jerusalem in March 1996 and co-hosted by Israel's Centre of the Child and Law, National Council for the Child. The symposium was organised by Leslie Sebba, with Geraldine Van Bueren of Queen Mary and Westfield College, University of London, and Tami Morag, of the National Council for the Child. It brought together scholars from England and Wales, Eire, Israel and Palestine. The Academic Study Group on Israel and the Middle East, which promotes study tours to Israel, provided generous funding for the participants from the UK and Eire to attend, and we gratefully acknowledge their assistance, and in particular, the efforts of John Levy, their Director. The Faculty of Law at the Hebrew University showed the visitors wonderful hospitality and an excellent opportunity was given to discuss the topics which form the subject-matter of this collection. Staff of the National Council for the Child, Defence for Children International, Israel, and Al-Haq all gave generously of their time to explain their work to the symposium participants, and provided valuable insights into the challenges facing children's rights and human rights activists in Israel and Palestine.

Professor David Nelken, who did not take part in the symposium, was nevertheless kind enough to provide an afterword to the ideas and issues raised by the contributors and we wish to express our gratitude to him.

The bulk of the preparation of the copy for the publishers was carried out by Ann Bladen at Cardiff Law School, and we wish to record our enormous thanks to her for taking on the task. We also acknowledge the help and consideration shown by the publishers.

Editors' Introduction

The relation between law and tradition is highly complex. On the face of it, traditional values and practices constitute an obstacle to the adoption or recognition of 'progressive' legal rights, and the two are thus in a constant state of potential conflict. This potential for conflict has acquired an enhanced significance with the 20th century movement in favour of the adoption of international normative standards. One of the more recent sets of standards to be adopted has been the United Nations Convention on the Rights of the Child, which gives expression to this conflict in Article 24.3, where it is stated that 'States Parties shall take all effective and appropriate measures with a view to abolishing traditional practices prejudicial to the health of children'. Other provisions in the Convention, however, reflect a greater tolerance of tradition. Thus, Article 30 guarantees to a child belonging to an ethnic, religious or linguistic minority the right 'to enjoy his or her own culture, to profess and practise his or her own religion, or to use his or her own language'.

The agonising attempts to reconcile universal and traditional norms in the context of human rights have been documented by Alston[1] and Van Bueren.[2] Moreover, we have now entered an era in which the move towards the recognition of universal human rights, in particular as appertaining to hitherto oppressed groups such as women and children, is encountering head-on an ideology which holds that traditional communities and cultures be allowed to retain their identities - and even be encouraged to prosper. While international documents have sought to adopt formulae which will reconcile these conflicting pressures, there is a need for in-depth studies of the issues arising, conducted in societies with differing characteristics in terms of the extent and nature of the traditional values and practices adhered to. In this respect, the present volume may be seen as a case-study (or collection of case-studies), focusing on Britain, with its increasingly culturally and socially diverse population, and moving rapidly from 'glorious isolation' to a European-oriented standardisation; and Israel, with its mix of ancient traditions, religious conservatism (sometimes extremism), cultural variety and western modernism.

The issues arising, however, go beyond the question of the extent to which legal norms should take account of traditional values. Additional thought must be given to possible varieties in the inter-relationship between the concepts involved - and the possible naiveté of our opening assumption which perceived traditional norms and practices as phenomena extraneous to the law, and subject to manipulation by it. Can traditional practices in fact be expected to give way to legal enactments? Legal sociologists tend to be sceptical of the positivist assumptions regarding the power of law to change human behaviour;[3] legal norms are seen as following in the wake of social norms (traditional or otherwise) or of functioning independently of them.[4]

On the other hand, adherents to the historical school of jurisprudence perceive the legal norms themselves as an inevitable reflection of traditional cultural norms of the society to which they apply.[5] Cultural norms being diverse among different societies, this analysis lends little encouragement to modern attempts at laying down universal standards - and the recognition of universal rights.

Further confusion is contributed to these debates by the uncertainty as to when traditional norms or customs are to be themselves perceived as having the status of 'law'. This uncertainty derives partly from substantive anthropological differences as to the binding nature of customary norms,[6] but mainly because of semantic differences as to how law should be defined and, in particular, how far law is a pluralistic concept.[7] In this context it may be pointed out that for religious traditionalists (e.g., orthodox Jews or Muslims) 'the law' may refer to their traditional normative system rather than the prevailing secular one. Thus, for Jewish communities in the diaspora a major issue over the centuries was the extent to which it was appropriate for the Jewish law (which they applied within the community) to take account of prevailing secular legal norms.[8]

Another approach is for the law to appropriate traditional norms by recognising them as a *source* of law. To some extent this approach was maintained in England throughout the centuries during which the common law was held to be superior to statute - and in a modern case in which the breach of (or conspiracy to corrupt) commonly-held 'public morals' was seen as a basis for the imposition of criminal responsibility.[9] This seems inappropriate in contemporary Britain where the concept of a traditional national value system is having increasingly to defer to a more pluralistic approach whereby recognition is granted to the traditions of minority groups.

The Israeli legal system (against the background of which several of the papers in this volume were written) has been more explicit in referring to extraneous cultural norms. The Ottoman Mejelle, which used to apply to certain areas of civil law, specified custom as a source of law. In other respects, however, gaps ('lacunae') in the law were to be filled by reference to English law.[10] This principle was abolished in 1980, when the Foundations of Law Act specified that gaps in the law were to be governed by 'the principles of Israel's heritage - liberty, justice, equity and peace'.[11] The significance of this expression was, of course, controversial. Moreover, the Basic Laws which were adopted in 1992/94 provided that the human rights enshrined therein were to be respected according to the principles of the Declaration of Independence, and with the aim of maintaining the values of the State of Israel as a 'Jewish democratic state', thus further ensuring that the role of Jewish traditional religious values in the legal system would be an enduring source of academic ferment.

This variety of conceptual inter-relationships between legal rights and traditional values forms the backdrop to the present volume of essays, which explores the extent to which recognition of the concept of children's rights is affected by adherence to religious, cultural and ethnic traditions. It seeks first to illuminate the interface between, on the one hand, internationally-agreed norms of conduct regarding children and, on the other, national and cultural determination to preserve and inculcate distinct teachings and attitudes towards children. Secondly, it is intended to offer a reflection upon the conflicts within societies between different cultural and religious groups in their attempts to determine whether liberal/secular or conservative/religious norms will predominate in attitudes to children and their upbringing.

The contributors to this volume were given a free hand to write about any aspects of the title which interested them. The collection is therefore a mix of contributions, some examining international aspects of the subject (see, for example, Geraldine Van Bueren's essay at Chapter 2 and William Duncan at Chapter 3), while the majority discuss issues of interest and concern within the municipal legal context, though influenced by the general global debate about children's rights. There are inevitable varieties in focus, interest and approach, reflecting the different cultural and political contexts in which the authors are writing.

While most of the contributors write from a perspective which accepts the significance and value of children's rights, the concept itself does not go unchallenged. Both Michael King at Chapter 1, and David Nelken in his Afterword, express scepticism at its value from a theoretical perspective, while Ze'ev Falk, at Chapter 7, offers a criticism of its utility as an operating principle in court proceedings. His essay champions the (perhaps now too traditional and insufficiently modern?) concept of the best interests of the child, while Leora Bilsky, at Chapter 9, offers a further critique by suggesting that the individualistic liberal emphasis in rights discourse may be ill-adapted to embrace either family, or community, values. Yehiel Kaplan, too, at Chapter 4, and Yai'ir Ronen at Chapter 14, explore the tension between children's rights and best interests, the former comparing the Israeli rabbinical courts' approach, informed by religious teachings, with that of the civil courts, and the latter considering how those purporting to act as advocates for children can come closer to providing a voice which reflects their rights rather than their welfare.

Some contributors have chosen to focus upon similar issues, albeit adopting different, or contrasting, approaches; thus, a number of the Israeli contributors write about education (see e.g., Stephen Goldstein at Chapter 8, Leora Bilsky at Chapter 9 and Leslie Sebba and Varda Shiffer at Chapter 10), while two of the British contributors write about juvenile offenders (Gillian Douglas at Chapter 15 and Wayne Morrison at Chapter 16). This concentration of attention on certain topics in the different jurisdictions underscores the extent to which children's rights issues will be determined by political and social pressures and concerns operating at the local level, perhaps lending some strength to King's critique based upon his conception of law as an autopoietic system.

The symposium and the theme of this collection also sought to address the additional complication of considering the significance of 'traditional values' for the children's rights debate. One might tentatively define a traditional value as adherence to a belief in a particular conception of a good, handed down from one generation to the next. But there is an essential difficulty in determining what such traditional values might consist of in different cultures. The phrase is not quite the same as *community* values, although some of the contributors do consider issues of multi-culturalism, ethnic diversity and universalism. In the secular 'modern' Britain under New Labour, or a post-modern western world to which (some) segments of Israeli society might wish to belong, the continuing identification and relevance of, let alone adherence to, 'traditional values' might seem problematic (as Andrew Bainham suggests in Chapter 6). For some contributors, (see for example, James Michael at Chapter 11 and Katherine O'Donovan at Chapter 12), such values are demonstrated in the long-held, rarely questioned, assumptions of what is 'good for' children - which brings us back to the best interests/children's rights dichotomy mentioned above. For others, especially the Israeli authors, traditional values may be synonymous with the religious precepts and practices perceived by some to be the *raison d'être* of the Jewish state.

It would have been a major oversight to have held a symposium in Israel which ignored the Palestinian and Arab dimension. Notwithstanding political difficulties, the discussions held in Jerusalem were informed by the experiences and reflections of a number of Palestinian and Arab-Israeli lawyers and scholars, and this collection includes two contributions which explore the Islamic (David Pearl at Chapter 5), and Palestinian (Nadera Shalhoub-Kevorkian at Chapter 13), dimensions to children's rights. The latter in particular brings together a number of perspectives - feminist, Palestinian and children's rights - in discussing the personal and individual ramifications of the political events which occurred during the *Intifada*.

The aim of the editors is to offer a variety of perspectives on the theme, with the hope that the particular blends of social, cultural and religious diversity in both the United Kingdom and Israel/Palestine, mingled with the political factors operating as well, will render these jurisdictions of particular interest as case-studies in the reception of western, or liberal, norms and values as epitomised by the concept of 'children's rights', without necessarily discarding certain 'traditional' values.

Notes

1   See Alston, P., (ed), *The Best Interests of the Child: Reconciling Culture and Human Rights*: Clarendon Press, Oxford: 1994.
2   See Van Bueren, G., *The International Law on the Rights of the Child*, Martinus Nijhoff, Dordrecht: 1995.
3   See Allott, A., *The Limits of Law*, Butterworths, London: 1980; Cotterrell, R,. *The Sociology of Law*, 2nd ed., Butterworths, London: 1992, Ch 2.
4   The theory of autopoiesis is consistent with this approach.
5   Cf. Cotterrell, op.cit., pp. 20-22.
6   Cf. Freeman, M.D.A., *Lloyd's Introduction to Jurisprudence*, 6th ed., Sweet and Maxwell, London: 1994, pp. 791-2.
7   See Cotterrell, op.cit., pp 39-40.
8   See Shilo, S., 'Influences of the European Legal Tradition on Jewish Law', in Rabbello, A.M., (ed.), *European Legal Traditions and Israel*, Hebrew University, Jerusalem: 1994, pp. 27-38.
9   See *Shaw v DPP* [1962] AC 220, HL (the 'Ladies' Directory' case).
10 Art. 46 of the Order-in-Council, 1922.
11 See Barak, A., 'The Tradition and Culture of the Israeli Legal System', in Rabbello A.M., (ed.), op.cit., at pp. 473-492.

1 'You Have to Start Somewhere'

MICHAEL KING

I

In today's world of moral uncertainty one needs to raise questions about the justice-seeking activities of lawyers. How is it possible to be a moral lawyer and how is it possible to be a lawyer and a moral being? These questions tend to be answered by invoking political realities. What constitutes injustice or immorality is likely to relate to reference points along a political continuum where democracy is being denied, power abused, rights ignored or overridden. From the legal perspective, the role of law becomes in essence one of rectifying such irregularities and, where appropriate, punishing such illegality and preventing and deterring its future occurrence. Legal morality for those active in the field of human rights is seen to proceed, therefore, through a process of *redressing unlawful imbalances of power* and so of promoting or restoring the world to a state of *equilibrium and legality*. As with retributionist justifications for making immoral acts crimes, law and morality are seen as reinforcing each other with law reinforcing and intensifying the opprobrium with which the immoral act is regarded.[1]

The difficulty for lawyers engaged in such balance-restoring activities who wish to claim the moral high ground is that critical observers of law and politics may well situate the endeavours of both law and lawyers on one side of a distinction rooted in political difference, whether this difference is based on party politics, gender politics, racial politics or cultural politics. In itself this would not create problems for law's moral objectives if there could be some guarantee that legality would always correspond to the positive side of the chosen political distinction. Unfortunately, there can be no such guarantee. Lawyers who claim justice (and not just law) is on their side might welcome being seen as a thorn in the flesh of governments, big business and state bureaucracies, but may well be unhappy to be presented with an image of themselves as the oppressors of minorities or destroyers of cultural heritage and traditional values or of Habermas's 'life world'. From within the legal system the only method of avoiding the risk of attracting such a negative image is to draw a distinction between those practices (of ministers, civil servants, minority groups, cultures, traditions etc.) which may be classified as valid, normal, healthy or lawful and those which infringe some *fundamental principles*. These fundamental principles may be based on 'natural law', human rights, children's welfare, according to the particular circumstances. It may be that invoking these higher authorities may rescue individual lawyers from a crisis of confidence in the moral righteousness of their enterprise, but it may also plunge the legal system into an even deeper crisis, as the search intensifies to discover exactly where law should mark out these fundamental principles and on what basis they are to be justified?[2]

Why then may not society simply elevate morality to the status of final arbiter, for such a move would clearly remove the paradox of the oppressive seeker-after-justice or the destructive redresser of power imbalances? Such a possibility would depend upon communications based upon the moral distinction between good and evil being or becoming functional for all society's operations. In other words it would be conditional upon society's acceptance of a moral code as capable of generating the knowledge and shared meanings necessary for all social performance. When in the past society was able to present itself as a collective version of individual consciousness, governed by obedience to God's precepts or loyalty to the king or the flag, such a possibility did indeed seem probable. To insist today, however, that an authoritative evaluation of social events could be determined by individuals following some universally acceptable moral code, which could then be enforced by law is to suggest that what was possible in pre-modern societies is still possible today. It is unlikely that even the most optimistic contemporary moral philosophers would not wish to be associated with this suggestion,[3] for society has evolved in ways which appear to construct an impenetrable barrier between moral codes and social performance.

The important difference between modern society and traditional, archaic or primitive societies, which may account for this barrier, lies in the organisation of social structures. In modern society this takes the form predominantly of *functional differentiation*.[4] It is the simultaneous existence of these different function systems, such as politics, economics, law, religion, and science, which produce communications capable of providing meaning for social interaction and so allow society to exist in its modern form. The structure and operations of these subsystems reflect their specific functions within society. They consist, not of people or ideologies, but of communications organised in such a way that they always refer back to previous communications of the same kind.

Within this vision of society, therefore, the difficulty for a moral code, existing at the level of individual consciousness, to operate as a system of communications at the social level lies in the fact that there can be no guarantee that moral principles will be translatable into social action. Despite the efforts of some sociologists, social psychologists, and moral philosophers to convince us to the contrary, all their attempts to present today's society as an aggregate of individual consciousnesses necessarily create a belief that social imperfection is a direct product of human imperfection and that the way to a better world is to produce better people. According to this view, if society is defective, only bad motives or perhaps insufficient self-knowledge stands between us and the creation of a perfect society.[5] The autopoietic view of society as a system of social communications, by contrast, draws a clear distinction between individuals and society, with the latter consisting of communications and nothing but communications. Attempts to transfer moral precepts, which have served the individual well in his or her interpersonal relationships, to the level of social performance, result invariably in these precepts being reconstituted as legal, political, religious, scientific or economic communications, which refer back, not to morality, but to law, politics, religion, science, economics etc. for their authority and legitimacy.

This relatively new theoretical perspective also offers a very different vision of the relationship between social systems than that which most moral philosophers and legal theoreticians would accept. In the particular case of law and morality, it does not see these two systems as involved in some kind of collective endeavour to make people behave in desirable ways, the systems sometimes overlapping and at other times in conflict one with the other.[6] Instead, autopoietic theory regards each of these two systems' normative operations as quite independent of the other. Each, on the other hand, is quite capable of reconstructing information from the other system, but always on its own terms. Now the important questions no longer revolve around issues of what is law and what is morality and whether or not the one reflects the other, but regard rather the ways that law makes use of moral communications and morality of legal communications.

Using this perspective any solution to problems is necessarily a product of one society's communicative subsystems, and not of 'people' or 'society' since neither people nor society can know of the existence of problems except in terms generated by social subsystems.[7] This does not mean that what are referred to as 'social problems' are always either exclusively legal or exclusively political - they may also be moral or interpersonal, but what appears as a social problem at any one time must owe its existence to the unique coding of one among several co-existing, self-referring communicative systems. These may include law, politics, science, religion, interpersonal relations and economics. Furthermore, within the conditions of functional differentiation pertaining in modern society there is no possibility of deliberately appointing any one of these systems to a position of supreme authority over all the others and, therefore, no possibility of knowing what has 'really' caused the problem or where the 'right' solution may be found. Even though judges, ethics committees or evangelists may sometimes talk as if they had access to universal truths, there is nothing to prevent critical observers from remarking that these truths are in fact falsehoods or that their application is relative only to particular cultures or ideologies. Consequently, the solutions to ongoing problems which these 'truths' are expected to offer will continue to be contingent in nature, in the sense that there are unforeseen possibilities which lie beyond the formulation of both the problem and its solution, beyond the horizon of the system's experience and action. The presence (invisible to the system) of these possibilities indicates that things may turn out differently than expected and that appearances given form by and within the system may turn out to be deceptive.[8]

II

There was nothing inevitable about the emergence of children's rights as a category within international law with the creation of the United Nations Convention. Philip Alston attributes the appearance of this 'most detailed and comprehensive of all the existing international human rights instruments' to an unlikely sequence of political events which started with an attempt by Poland to 'seize at least some of the human rights initiative from Jimmy Carter'.[9] Yet, for such an event to take place within the arena of international politics, one needs to acknowledge a pre-existing set of concepts which situated the enforcement and protection of 'rights' within the realm of attainability and another set of which presented children as a distinctive group, separate from other adults, and having their own particular needs and interests which could be converted into rights. To an observer of international politics this combination of children with rights may seem as unlikely and as fortuitous as the political events identified by Alston. And yet, it led eventually, as we all know, to the creation of the Children's Rights Convention and to its widespread ratification.

Historically, children, at least in the context of European society, had before the latter half of this century been defined by their *lack of rights,* reinforced by a legal system, which went out of its way to emphasise the *rights of others* (particularly fathers) to make decisions or veto the decisions of those who had not reached an age when they were legally competent to own property.[10] It is true that from the 18th century onwards the incompetence of age also carried with it some benefits, such as that of not being accountable contractually for debts relating to non-necessaries and not having to suffer the upper range of criminal penalties,[11] but these could hardly have been seen and were certainly never referred to as 'rights'.

Why then should society have wanted to grant children, meaning all people under eighteen years old,[12] special rights which it does not accord to adults? Observers of social movements might want to explain the emergence of children's rights as the product of some inexorable, universal victim-rescuing crusade, which once it had exhausted the available supply of oppressed groups, the poor, indigenous people, women, psychiatric patients, prisoners, animals etc. turned its attention to the plight of children. Such an explanation, however, does not address the particular issues either of children or of rights.

Ever since the European romantic movement of the late eighteenth and early nineteenth centuries, it has been fashionable to regard children as a special group, having special interests. While beliefs about the nature of childhood tended at this time to be rooted in the romantic Rousseauesque notion of children as 'noble savages', needing protection against the corrupting adult world, those who seek actively to protect children are more likely to look for the foundations of children's rights in the realms of the human and medical sciences. Here children, both during and way beyond infancy, make their appearance as impressionable creatures in the process of formation, whose future may be blighted by insensitivity, ignorance or irresponsibility on the part of adults.[13] The influences of Freud and, to a lesser extent, Piaget on modern psychological ideas concerning what children are and how they should be brought up are everywhere. Yet the shift towards the end of the last century from Rousseau's unnatural or Darwin's natural evolution of the child towards today's 'psychology of child development' did not represent simply a change in notions of childhood. What was of particular importance was the fact that the formation of children rapidly became a scientific enterprise. In Foucault's terms, the technologies were put in place for a discipline of child development to operate effectively through the medium of expert systems. Today, we now believe that we know or have the means of knowing *scientifically* what is good or bad for children and that knowledge provides the panoply of techniques and practices for protecting children and promoting their welfare.

In a recent development in the philosophy of science, however, theorists who see themselves as post-modern have rejected any possibility of applying science to identify what children need psychologically and what causes them psychological harm. For them 'the psychological child', as well as childhood itself, is a product of social conditions and changes in response to changes in the social world. The identification of the needs of and harms to the 'psychological child' are to be found in such contemporary phenomena as compulsory schooling, small family units, the organisation of work, and restricted expressions of sexuality.[14] This, as we shall see, is likely increasingly to represent a serious challenge to the efforts of international children's rights lawyers to ground their claims for fundamental principles in scientific knowledge. It may also throw serious doubts on the ability of moral philosophy to extricate lawyers from their dilemma, for any attempt to transform morality into legal formulae relating to the interests of and harms to children may itself depend upon 'scientific truths'.

III

If we turn now to the 'legal child' and more particularly to children's legal rights, it does not seem too outrageous to claim from the outset that rights cannot be anything but a product of decisions. You cannot have rights without some notion that whatever is in issue can be resolved through decision-making. It would make no sense, for example, to talk of rights against God, or against the weather, since neither are seen as directly subject to decisions.[15] In the same way, where children are concerned, it was not possible for eighteenth century judges to conceptualise the possibility that children had rights, when the only decisions that law recognised were those which protected a father's property interests.[16] Children could be seen as having rights only after their well-being was conceived, not as the result of God's will or 'the luck of the draw' or even 'a matter for the family', but as the consequence of decisions which were open to public scrutiny. Moreover, where legal rights are concerned, these decisions had to be based on the belief that children's 'interests should be protected by the imposition of duties upon others'.[17]

While children may since the time that Isaac was rescued from sacrifice (and probably before) have been presented to the world as innocent victims, the possibility of them becoming victims *with rights* arose only after it was accepted that there were reliable ways of rescuing them from those people or those social conditions that were 'victimising' them. Before children could have rights, society had to abandon the belief that the suffering of children, as well as the ending of such suffering, was beyond the boundaries of social control. Children's needs and the failure to meet those needs had to be seen as attributable to decisions. To think that children have legal rights, therefore, is to assume that there are decisions capable of being taken by law which will have the effect of making life better for them. At the time when Blackstone was commenting on the Laws of England, the failure to enforce a moral duty against a neglecting eighteenth century parent was a matter, not for legal decision making, but for self-improvement, for 'the father's interest in educating his children is but an extension of his own self-interest'.[18] Today, however, as we all know, each serious incident of child neglect may give effect to a complex process of decision taking in which evidence is accumulated, risks assessed, and the effects of alternative solutions predicted. Not only are legal decisions taken, but those whom society designates as decision-makers, are seen as being responsible for any harm that may befall the child. Children's rights may now be invoked to protect children's interests, and the duties that Raz emphasises as necessary for the existence of rights, will fall, not only on the parent(s) of the child, but also on the social workers, doctors, judges[19] and, even in some situations, members of the government. Risks to children become formulated in such a way as to make it seem that much of the responsibility lies with those professionals who are appointed specifically to minimise those risks and maximise the protection of children.

IV

While most legal campaigners for the promotion of children's interests see law's eventual recognition of rights for children as belated progress and as such a cause for celebration,[20] the same phenomenon may be interpreted rather differently from the perspective of autopoietic systems theory. From this position, the legal system may be seen as constructing a 'semantic artefact' of 'the child' as a person who has rights; who has, that is, interests to be protected by law.[21] This construction is in itself neither positive nor negative, but, once created, it may be used by law to make lawful/unlawful attributions to a wide range of social events.

Although on a superficial reading these two interpretations, that of children's rights campaigns and autopoietic theory may appear to be saying roughly the same thing, in fact the two conceptual frameworks on which they rely could hardly be further apart. The first invokes a universal moral principle that children *should have rights* and that law was wrong in the past to deny or ignore this principle, while the second sees law as a normatively closed system responding in legal ways to irritations in its social environment, i.e. society. These irritations may come from communications generated from many different sources, but law can recognise them only as legal communications, and in this case, only in the restricted terms of rights, interests and duties.

It is true that both these conceptual frameworks recognise the particular difficulties posed by the fragmentation of modern society, but what is seen as being fragmented is very different. For the children's rights campaigners, it is authority that is fragmented as the result of cultural, political or religious differences. Hence the call for some uniting force to bind different interest groups together in an international campaign to make the world a better place for children. For autopoietic theory, the fragmentation that causes problems concerns society's self-referring function systems and their inability to relate to one another except in an indirect manner. This form of fragmentation means that, however effectively campaigns designed to promote children's welfare appear to be in resolving conflicts of authority arising from cultural, political or religious differences, by invoking the kind of fundamental principles that we discussed earlier, their resolutions will operate authoritatively only *within the boundaries of the particular system used in the resolution process.* Legal solutions will, for example, hold good only for law, political solutions for politics, moral solutions for morality etc. What an autopoietic analysis is doing, therefore, is to define the limits of meaning for each of these systems of communication in a manner that is only possible from outside the system. While law in its attempts to resolve a variety of conflicts may act as a first-order observer of political interests, moral principles or cultural traditions, autopoietic observations provide second-order accounts of law's efforts and, in particular of the reconstruction of morals, cultures, politics etc. as capable of being formulated into conflicts resolvable by law.

Indeed, from the position of this second-order observation, the situation is even more complex than that already described, for the second order observer may see law's evocation of fundamental principles as attempts to justify or legitimate what are in essence *legal decisions, that is decisions which have meaning for law,* and not as the universal norms or consensual values that law holds them out to be. While other systems will certainly recognise them as legal decisions, there is absolutely no guarantee that they will invest them with the overriding authority that law optimistically proposes. Rather than being fundamental principles of morality or developmental psychology, they are likely to be interpreted by non-legal systems as law's version of moral principles or law's selection from psychological evidence. The conflicts that law claims to have resolved through its application of fundamental principles may appear to the second order observer as no closer to resolution than they were before the issue entered the legal arena.

If we now return to the post-modern critique of child psychology, mentioned briefly at the end of the second section of this essay, it becomes only too clear that if law is to continue with its invocation of psychological principles to reinforce its decisions about what is lawful or unlawful behaviour for or towards children (in general or at different ages) it has to close its eyes to such unsettling criticisms. If law is to call upon the assistance of psychology (or psychiatry), it must be as 'psychological science', able to provide definite answers to questions concerning what is good or bad for children. The legal system cannot handle and cannot be expected to handle, therefore, the post-modern 'discovery' that psychological science no longer presents truths or reality about children in any absolute or universal sense, but is itself a product of social conditions (including those which law has helped to construct). Despite the post-modernist revolution, therefore, law and psychology are likely to continue to co-evolve *within the legal system* in what Teubner refers to as 'a hypercycle' - a closed system within which legal and psychological experts on children continue to exchange realities and construct norms in a reciprocal manner, both of these groups systematically excluding from their joint sights any critical observations of the relative or suspect nature of psychological knowledge.

If law takes the alternative strategy of abandoning psychology altogether, it could turn to moral or political philosophy for those fundamental principles necessary for evaluating legally conduct towards and by children. Such a solution, however, is likely only to postpone the crisis, rather than avoid it. For neither moral nor political theory has anything to say about what is good or bad for children, except in the most general moral or political terms. In other words, moral and political philosophers today are obliged to seek their knowledge about what is good or bad for children, what is in favour of or contrary to their interests, in areas of specialist scientific expertise, such as child psychology and psychiatry. So we are back again with the same problem.

At one time it seemed that it might have been possible for the legal system largely to avoid these problems of children and their welfare by renouncing 'epistemic authority' over children's issues to mediation or family group conferences.[22] But any chance of law retreating into the background has been brought to an abrupt halt by the emergence of children's rights, and in particular by the UN Convention and the constitutions of several countries which have adopted the whole or parts of the Convention.[23] Now law, as well as would-be moral lawyers, is faced with a crisis of how to remain 'good for children' while at the same time reconciling the political, cultural and religious differences over what is and what is not in children's interests. The next section examines the attempts by promoters of children's rights to find solutions to the crisis.

V

Seen from *within law* the task that children's rights charters present for law is that of protecting the rights of children, enshrining universally-agreed upon minimum standards while at the same time remaining sufficiently flexible to accommodate a wide range of different family and cultural structures and values.[24] Yet as our second-order observations of law have revealed, it is this notion of 'sufficiently flexible minimum standards' that creates such problems for law. Alston states the issue as follows:

> On the one hand, the norms must be sufficiently clear, comprehensive and *inflexible* to provide the international community with some basis on which it might seek to constrain a government which undermines or circumvents minimum standards of decent behaviour. On the other, any enterprise which is avowedly universalist in its aspirations and aims to address a very wide range of issues, *must be characterised by a sufficient degree of flexibility and adaptability.*[25]

Rather than allowing indeterminacy to lead to paralysis, however, Alston sees it as a virtue, serving 'to emphasise the importance of institutions as a means through which to pursue the interpretive enterprise and a need to develop a better understanding of the different cultural dimensions of the relevant norms'.[26] Quite where this 'interpretive enterprise' and 'better understanding' is to develop is unclear, but, like other international children's rights lawyers before him, he appears to be referring to the existence of a world community capable of being unified by the motivation of promoting the welfare of children. For the moral enterprise of children's rights law to succeed, therefore, in its task of reconciling cultural diversity, it has to be assumed that the world community is amenable to a learning process which will eventually lead to an acceptance of legal decisions as to what is and what is not good for children carrying universal authority. Van Bueren also has no doubts about the existence of such a world community. According to her analysis, there is something called 'international political will' upon which 'reforms depend'; this, apparently, 'can be increased if the successes of human rights strategies are highlighted'.[27]

The vision of law that shines through these and other accounts by international children's rights lawyers is essentially a political one, with law operating as a political instrument for good in the world. It achieves this either directly by imposing 'minimum standards' and so eliminating child-harmful conduct or indirectly through increasing awareness and serving symbolically as a beacon to throw light on what could be achievable, given sufficient 'political will'. This may well be how children's rights activists see the legal system and would want the legal system to project itself, but their ambitions for law create enormous difficulties, which go far beyond practical problems of enforcement. They concern, as we have seen, the task of producing authoritative legal communications - that is communications which are able to distinguish between what is lawful and what is unlawful in such a way as to carry conviction throughout the world.

Michael Freeman's 'cultural pluralist' solution to this task is to assess the values that underlie various practices that may affect children's well-being by 'appealing to some reasonable ranking of the values in question'.[28] This, he argues, is distinguished from relativist approaches which ask 'whether they are sanctioned by the relevant social understanding of the cultures within which they are practised'. In preference to a permissive solution of allowing practices derived from the conflicting values of different cultural traditions to co-exist, Freeman's cultural pluralism obliges law to 'subject [each] practice to an internal critique, in deconstructing the arguments that are used to support it'. In such a way, he tells us, the arguments in favour of female circumcision will be comprehensively rejected, while those in favour of male circumcision, 'namely cultural (or religious) identity ... would prevail'.

Thus a cultural pluralist approach would apparently enable law to distinguish between lawful and unlawful practices, not by imposing universal norms, but by ensuring that rationality triumphs over irrationality in a contest between harms and benefits to children.

This solution may appear particularly inviting to those moral lawyers who balk at any suggestion that they might be guilty of inflicting Western (or Northern) values on the cultures and traditions of 'the South' or on aboriginal communities. Yet Freeman's solution relies upon the belief, firstly, that the kind of deconstructionist rationality that he invokes is itself free from cultural contaminants, and secondly, that the essential task of weighing cultural harms against cultural benefits, the 'internal critique', is unproblematic. From the autopoietic observation point, however, what is interesting is Freeman's overriding assumption that the results of a contest between three different philosophical traditions - namely monism, cultural pluralism and relativism - will be able to provide solutions to problems that have been constructed by law and the need to code events in terms of their lawfulness and unlawfulness.

None of this means that law should never decide upon issues involving evaluations of different cultural practices concerning children. Contrary to what some people believe, there is no normative agenda in the autopoietic analysis. All the theory tells us is that in the modern world it is unrealistic to expect that law's evaluations will be treated outside law as anything other than legal decisions. The children's rights movement may have pushed the legal system into believing that it has the capacity to take decisions concerning events and situations which it had previously declared beyond its competence. For autopoietic observers, however, the effects and effectiveness of such decisions outside law's boundaries will not depend upon the construction within law of a vision of a world subjected directly or indirectly to legal order or of a world where something called 'international political will' is amenable to legal influence. Nor will it depend upon how persuasive has been a court's weighing of the psychological evidence or of the conflicting moral principles. What will happen will happen rather as the result of contingent events which are not only beyond the control of law, but even beyond what can be known by the legal system. For the autopoietic observer the possibilities that are achievable by international children's rights lawyers appear much more constrained than they believe and would have us believe. Rather than accepting their own self-image of being involved in the mammoth task of creating a better world for children, the autopoietic observer sees them as engaged in the much more modest process of persuading the legal system to adopt their particular vision (whether moral or political) of what is good and bad for children and with justifying that vision in ways which have meaning for law's normative operations. Even if they are successful in their task, there can be no guarantee that these operations will change the world, and if the world does change, that it will be in the direction that they would have wanted. But, as they themselves would tell us, 'You have to start somewhere'.

Notes

1   See Smith, K.J.M. (1988) *James Fitzjames Stephen: Portrait of a Victorian Radical* Cambridge: Cambridge University Press, p.56.

2   See, for example, *Alhaji Mohamed v Knott*, [1969] 1. Q.B. 1; *Wisconsin v. Yoder*, [1972] 406 US 205.

3   As Margaret M. and C.A.J. Coady emphasise in an essay entitled, 'There Ought to be a Law against it: Reflections on Child Abuse, Morality and the Law', when they write - 'When there is lacking a rational consensus on the empirical or moral data or even rudimentary agreement on the theoretical framework within which such data can be understood, then the assumption that the law embodies a communal wisdom about morality is unwarranted.' (p.138) (in

Alston, P., Parker, S. and Seymour, J. eds. (1992) *Children, Rights and the Law* Oxford: Clarendon.

[4] This is the account of society offered by contemporary theorists of social autopoiesis. See Luhmann, N. (1990) *Essays on Self Reference* New York: Columbia University Press; King, M. and Schütz, A. 'The Ambitious Modesty of Niklas Luhmann' (1994) 21 *Journal of Law and Society*, p.261.

[5] For a general discussion of these issues see chapters one and eight of King, M. *A Better World for Children? Explorations in Morality and Authority* (1997) London: Routledge.

[6] See Coady and Coady, n 3 above.

[7] See Luhmann above n 4.

[8] ibid, ch. 2.

[9] Alston, P. 'The Best Interests Principle: Towards a Reconciliation of Culture and Human Rights' (1994) 8 *Int J of Law and Fam* 1 at p 6.

[10] Eekelaar, J. 'The Emergence of Children's Rights' (1986) *Oxford Journal of Legal Studies* p.161; Pollock, F. and Maitland, F.W. *The History of English Law* (1968 edition).

[11] But see Douglas at Chap. 15 below who argues that the *doli incapax* presumption should be seen as a right.

[12] This is the definition of 'a child' given in Article 1 of the UN Convention on the Rights of the Child.

[13] The philosopher C.A.J. Coady writes, for example: 'One of the most important facts about childhood, particularly early childhood, is the degree to which the child's experiences and the treatment he or she receives is so profoundly formative of the child's future as adolescent and adult.' Coady (1992) 'Theory Rights and Children', in Alston et al, above n 3, p.49.

[14] See, for example, Stainton Rogers, *Stories of Childhood. Shifting agendas of child concern* (1992) Hemel Hempstead, UK: Harvester Wheatsheaf.

[15] In these days of global warming and the influence that the use of fossil fuels may have on this process, one could perhaps refer to the rights to a particular climate or against damaging changes in climatic conditions.

[16] Pollock and Maitland (above n 10) write: 'The law had not even been careful to give the father a right to the custody of his children; on the other hand, it had given him a right to the custody of his heir apparent, whose marriage he was free to sell. It had looked at guardianship and paternal power merely as profitable rights, and had only sanctioned them when they could be made profitable' (vol. ii, p.44).

[17] Raz, J. 'Legal Rights' (1984) *Oxford Journal of Legal Studies* p.13.

[18] Blackstone *Commentaries on the Laws of England* (1775: 7th ed) vol. i:16.

[19] This is more true for civil law countries on the Continent of Europe than for common law jurisdictions, such as the United Kingdom, the Commonwealth or the United States. This is because several civil law jurisdictions make specialist

children's judges personally responsible for the well-being of children who are the subject of a court order.

[20]   See, for example Eekelaar, J. (1986) above n 10; Freeman, M.D.A. 'Taking Children's Rights More Seriously' in (1992) Alston et al (eds), above n 3.

[21]   Teubner, G. 'How the Law Thinks: Toward a Constructivist Epistemology of Law' *Law and Society Review* vol. 23, no. 5, pp. 727-56.; King, M. and Piper, C. (1995) *How the Law Thinks about Children* (2nd edition) Aldershot, U.K.: Arena.

[22]   King and Piper, op. cit., p.32

[23]   For example, South Africa and Bulgaria.

[24]   This adapts Van Bueren's account of the task of international law 'to protect the rights of all family members'. (Van Bueren, G. 'The International Protection of Family Members as the 21st Century Approaches' (1994) *Human Rights Quarterly* 732 at p.734).

[25]   Alston, P. above n 9 at pp. 17-18, emphasis added.

[26]   ibid at p.17.

[27]   Van Bueren above n 24, at p.765.

[28]   Freeman, M.D.A. 'The Morality of Cultural Pluralism' (1995) 3 *The International Journal of Children's Rights* 1.

2 Children's Rights: Balancing Traditional Values and Cultural Plurality

GERALDINE VAN BUEREN

Introduction

Although it is still accepted by some that national laws may be neutral instruments of policy, international human rights law has never made claim to such a fallacy. Instead of impartiality, international human rights law is goal-oriented. The principle expressed in *Tyrer v. United Kingdom* makes it clear that the *raison d'être* of international human rights law is to raise the value of the individual in the state's eyes and to improve the quality of individual daily life by the progressive implementation of human rights standards.[1] However, although human rights law has never sought to be perceived as impartial in its goals, its claim to a pedigree derived from universal sources is contentious.[2] Specific instruments and approaches have been justifiably criticised as being under the influence of the industrialised west but this criticism is inappropriate when applied to many of the international children's rights standards.[3] This is also evidenced by the almost universal ratification of the United Nations Convention on the Rights of the Child 1989 even by states who are not party to other human rights treaties.[4] This is because there is no longer any significant disagreement at governmental levels over the existence of such legal rights; it is the content and extent of these rights which is the subject of disagreement.[5]

Culture, Traditional Values and Children's Rights

Procedural universality may well have been achieved by almost universal ratification of the Convention on the Rights of the Child and the passing of some of its articles into customary international law,[6] but if international

15

children's rights are to be more than a universal symbol then the disputes over universalist, traditional values and traditionally plural approaches need urgent resolution.

The notion of different cultural approaches is implicitly enshrined in the Charter of the United Nations[7] but as the Vienna Declaration, adopted by the Second World Conference on Human Rights, makes clear, '[w]hile the significance of national and regional particularities and various historical, cultural and religious backgrounds must be borne in mind, it is the duty of States, regardless of their political, economic, and cultural systems to promote and protect all human rights and fundamental freedoms.[8] Some in the West deny that there is even a problem. Judge Higgins,[9] for example, observes that the culturally relativist approach is 'rarely advanced by the oppressed who are only too anxious to benefit from perceived universal standards'.[10] This, however, only takes us so far. Although it may be true that there is global recognition that the attaching of electrodes to children in detention in Turkey amounts to torture, there is not universal agreement when one moves away from the more extreme forms of direct state action, particularly when one considers practices, for which the state may be liable, initiated within the family.[11] In particular the concept of the child's consent, which lies at the heart of child self-determination and parental responsibility debates, raises questions of the extent to which states ought to interpret their responsibilities in line with the prevailing traditional values of the community. Is it possible to apply the international rights of the child in a way which is consistent with cultural plurality but which abides by the universal principles enshrined in the Convention on the Rights of the Child or was Herodotus correct when he observed that

> if one were to offer men to choose out of all the customs in the world such as seemed to them the best, they would examine the whole number and end by preferring their own.[12]

The concepts of culture and tradition are broad, embracing not only indigenous but also religious, customary practices and traditions, and perhaps institutional values. Traditional values and cultural practices do not match recognised state boundaries. Within one country there may be many tribal differences, and these may also be practised across boundaries arbitrarily drawn during colonial periods. According to the World Health Organisation the traditional practices of societies are 'closely linked with the living conditions of the people and with their beliefs and priorities'.[13] The traditional values of any society are significant, as An-Naim observes, because whilst 'cultural legitimacy may not be the sole or even primary determinant of compliance with human rights standards, it is ... an extremely significant one'.[14]

Contrary to popular perception, neither tradition nor culture is static. They are constantly evolving, albeit often imperceptibly. This has important implications because, although the traditional approach has conceived of culture as based on geographic location, there are also child and adult cultures. Yet with the exception of the preambular paragraph 'Taking due account of the importance of the traditions and cultural values of each people for the protection and harmonious development of the child' and article 5's reference to 'the extended family or community as provided for by local custom',[15] there is little express reference to culture as a positive value in the Convention on the Rights of the Child. The reference which has attracted most attention is the prohibition of 'traditional practices prejudicial to the health of the child'[16] which focuses on eliminating the negative aspects of tradition. Such a prohibition highlights the role of international human rights law, which seeks to protect and preserve traditional values consistent with the human rights of the child whilst seeking to prohibit those inconsistent traditions. Hence the African Charter on the Rights and Welfare of the Child refers to the duties on Member States of the Organisation of African Unity to 'take all appropriate measures to eliminate harmful social and cultural practices affecting the welfare, dignity, normal growth and development of the child'.[17]

Although it is the role of law to set standards aimed at eliminating all harmful traditional practices, it is questionable whether such a prohibition alone is sufficient. Certain traditional practices by their very nature reach down into the heart of a community and may even be regarded by members of that community as important in defining that community's identity. Some traditional practices, such as female circumcision, may perform a social role, making it difficult in some societies for girls who are not circumcised to marry.[18] Therefore alternatives have to be organically developed. To implement children's rights in one culture is not simply a matter of translation;[19] attention has to be paid to the functions they perform in different traditions. Children's rights have a better prospect for implementation if they reflect local cultural beliefs. A 'homeomorphic equivalent' has to be found.[20] A similar approach has been advocated in interpreting Islamic primary sources. An-Naim urges that the sources ought to be placed in their historical context, thus permitting an interpretation 'consistent with a new understanding of what is believed to be the intent and purpose of the sources'.[21] One such application of this approach was in Tunisia, where the former President, Bourgiba, abolished polygamy on the basis that Mohammed only permitted polygamy if all the wives were treated equally. Bourgiba argued that only the prophet was able to offer such equal treatment and therefore no other man would be permitted more than one wife.[22]

Few cultures, however, have adopted a culturally egalitarian approach. In seeking to place a practice in its context it may also be necessary to ascertain whether children's rights are in fact being exploited in ideological battles which obscure their original legal significance to the detriment of their beneficiaries. There are, however, genuine issues of cultural differences, not all of which are designed as masks to deflect criticism of regimes. Particularly problematic is the child's right or freedom to adopt or choose a religion of his or her own choice.[23] In discussions about this right we are witnessing a clash of traditional values, although one, human rights, is a newer tradition. The tradition of human rights is an essentially anthropocentric tradition with the human being at the centre, whereas religious approaches have divinity at its centre. As Cover observes in relation to Judaism, 'while it created room for the diffusion of authority it did not have a place for individualism'[24] and it is therefore a challenging task to create sufficient space within Judaism for the recognition of children's rights.

Even if the homeomorphic equivalent is sought, as helpful as it is, it cannot be regarded as the elusive golden key. The problem was recognised in the statement of the American Anthropological Association in 1947 that '[R]espect for differences between cultures is validated by the scientific fact that no technique of qualitatively evaluating cultures has been discovered.[25] A key challenge is how to assess whether traditional values are consistent with the rights of the child. A dynamic model needs to be developed so that change can be embraced by the communities at present resisting what they perceive as being the western disregard for the significance of ritual.

The approach to such reconciliation has so far has been generally unsatisfactory, a mixture of an *ad hoc* list and a broad principled approach without any indicators to take us through the maze.[26] Arguably a solution may be easier to achieve through regional approaches, bearing in mind the caveat that geographical regions are rarely homogenous.

The aforementioned *ad hoc* list can be drawn from treaties, *travaux preparatoires* of treaties and from the work of the Working Group on Traditional Practices affecting the Health of Women and Children.[27]

Traditional practices which have been prohibited include child marriage;[28] betrothal of boys and girls;[29] female circumcision or female genital mutilation;[30] and preferential feeding.[31] However, an *ad hoc* list without any consistent underlying principles is unsatisfactory.

Three underlying principles can be developed from express treaty provisions. Traditional values which develop into traditional practices become contrary to international law if they are prejudicial to the health of the child and/or are discriminatory to the child on the basis of gender or any other status. A traditional practice also has to be evaluated according to whether it violates any other rights or principles in the Convention on the Rights of the Child.

The Universal Child?

The Convention on the Rights of the Child offers greater opportunities than most human rights instruments for balancing traditional values and international rights because it was not primarily the product of the industrialised west. The Convention therefore promotes an ethos both of cultural plurality and universalism. However, there is an inherent paradox buried in the Convention. The Convention does not want to promote a single fixed universal image of childhood. Yet it does want to promote universal opportunities for children.

Children all over the globe are the objects of prior understanding which structure perceptions concerning them, even though this may vary from culture to culture. As Moscovici observes, representations feed attitudes which project a representational field with a figurative nucleus which is strongly resistant to change.[32] One such traditional value still dominant in many states and so reflected in their interpretation of international law, is the high value placed on child protection at the expense of developing a cultural awareness of child participation. The traditional culture of not listening to children is not limited by geography. According to Qvortrup, the question of objectivity is '... more acute ... because children ... have to leave the interpretation of their own lives to another age group, whose interests are potentially at odds with those of themselves. This is a sociology of knowledge problem, which so far is almost unexplored.'[33] It is also a question of power. Adults have to be willing to relinquish some of their own power before a new culture, that of seriously listening to children, can develop.

The Consenting Child, Traditional Images and Values

Arguably one of the most contentious areas of international children's rights is the issue of consent. The right of children to consent or withhold their consent to issues concerning them has not traditionally been encompassed in the image of childhood. Indeed consent and, in particular the age of consent in some communities, is part of that which distinguishes childhood from adulthood. The right to consent is a civil right derived in international law from at least two rights; the right to respect for privacy[34] and the right to freedom of expression. These are to be to be interpreted within the framework of the Convention's principles: the evolving capacity of the child; the best interests of the child; and the principle of non-discrimination, specifically non-discrimination on the basis of age-related consent[35] and of gender.[36]

There is very little specific binding international law on the issue of the child's consent and what does exist is scattered and ironically not found in many human rights treaties which seek to raise standards,[37] but in private international law treaties resolving conflicts of law. Hence the Hague Convention on Intercountry Adoption 1993[38] provides that children shall freely consent to adoption. Similarly under article 13 of the Hague Convention on Civil Aspects of Child Abduction 1980[39] courts may refuse to return a child if the child refuses to consent and 'has attained an age and degree of maturity'.

There is, however, little guidance at an international level of how children's consent can be solicited and weighed. The broad principle is found in article 12 of the Convention on the Rights of the Child. This obliges States Parties to 'assure to the child who is capable of forming his or her views the right to express those views freely in all matters affecting the child, the view of the child being given due weight in accordance with the age and maturity of the child'. Although this is a useful starting point setting out a three-pronged test: capacity to form views; weight given to the child's opinion according to the child's age; and weight given to the child's opinion according to the child's maturity, there is little evidence from the States Parties reports to the Committee on the Rights of the Child that states have begun to develop a coherent child-oriented approach to freedom of expression strategy.[40] This may not be surprising given that the tests of age and maturity contain both an objective criterion - age - and a subjective opinion - maturity.

Decision-making from the time that the Convention on the Rights of the Child entered into force[41] ought to be influenced by the child's wishes. It is, however, traditional to a number of cultures that children are perceived as being less rational, less secure about their identity and less autonomous than adults.[42] This was an argument frequently utilised against extending the suffrage to women. However just as feminist scholars have criticised the law for being apparently neutral but in reality essentially gendered, embracing masculine values,[43] so the law may be appear to be neutral but in reality embracing predominately the language and the thought processes of adults. The hallmark of law is reason and maturity and therefore children are seen as 'not standard' and because children are regarded as apart from the norm,[44] child-centred proceedings are rare. There is normally only a tampering at the edges with adult proceedings. So for example how is it ascertained that a child freely consents to being adopted? According to the Hague Convention on the Protection of Children and Co-operation in Respect of Intercountry Adoption the child's consent must be freely given, after counselling and 'not be induced by payment or compensation of any kind'. However, with the exception of the prohibition on payment, courts are left to their own devices as to how to weigh the child's consent, even the extent to which they are obliged to create an encouraging environment in which the child feels safe to express opinions.

The language of the right to freedom of expression, although regarded as being neutral, in reality may mask an adult orientation. The way choices are reached is still dictated by a history of adult choice. In most judicial situations children are expected to adopt adult patterns of reasoning, and if they do so they are considered sufficiently mature. It is on the whole the adult and the adult's powers and capacities which are taken as the norm, despite under 18's being a majority in a number of states. This traditional pre-Convention approach centres historically on the potential listener and not on the child.

The Convention on the Rights of the Child, with its dozen references[45] to the child's right to freedom of expression, attempts to change this culture. The Convention challenges the exclusive focus on the child's psychological and biological vulnerability, as such a traditional perspective places insufficient weight on how children's lack of power contributes to that vulnerability. Implicit in article 12 is the assumption that although adults have a duty to protect children from ill-treatment, children are protected not only by giving the state, i.e., adults, greater powers of intervention, but also by giving children power to consent to and challenge decisions which affect their lives. The logic of the Convention on the Rights of the Child is that children's lack of power contributes to their traditionally perceived vulnerability. An example of where insufficient attention was paid to this line of reasoning is *Nielsen v Denmark* before the European Court of Human Rights.[46]

Despite the many States Parties to the Convention on the Rights of the Child, there is still the dominance of child-savers and child protection, attaching insufficient weight to child participation. The cultural traditions surrounding parenthood are not necessarily geographical. There are many in Europe who would agree with the provisions in the American Declaration of the Rights and Duties of Man 1948 that it is 'the duty of children to honour their parents always'[47] and echoed in the African Charter on the Rights and Welfare of the Child that it is the duty of the child 'to respect his parents and elders at all times'.[48] The entitlement of the child to consent or part consent[49] to decisions could appear to run counter to the child's duties.[50] However, duties of 'honour' and 'respect' are different from blind obedience.

Appearing as a leitmotif in many of the newer constitutions in Central and Eastern European states, there persists the traditional view that children's rights are best indirectly protected through equating motherhood and childhood and protecting the mother. The Constitution of the Russian Federation is silent on children's rights *per se* but links motherhood and childhood, 'Motherhood and childhood, and the family are under protection of the state'.[51] Similar approaches are found in the Constitutions of Ukraine[52] and Belarus.[53] This traditional position is seen in extremes with Poland.

Poland has attached a curious declaration in relation to articles 12 to 16 of the Convention on the Rights of the Child, which focus on the more classical civil rights surrounding consent.[54] Poland considers that these rights, 'shall be exercised with respect for parental authority, in accordance with Polish customs and traditions regarding the place of the child within and outside the family'.[55] So far this reservation, unlike others,[56] has not attracted any state objections. The reservation is consistent with the approach of the Polish Constitution which concentrates on parental duties rather than children's rights.[57] The Polish constitution provides that it is the duty of parents 'to bring up children to become law-abiding'.[58] This is more akin to the traditional indirect relationship of the state and the child which the UN Convention on the Rights of the Child has sought to challenge, because in the past such a perspective has helped undermine the potential of the child as an independent social actor capable of exercising his or her right to consent.

Many states, such as England and Wales, are unclear even as to whether children are entitled to consent to actions affecting their own autonomy. There have been flickers of light but no consistency. Hence in *Gillick v West Norfolk and Wisbech Area Health Authority* the House of Lords accepted that 'parental rights yield to the child's right to make his own decisions when he reaches a sufficient understanding and intelligence to be capable of making up his own mind on the matter requiring a decision'.[59] But the judgment has on occasion been restricted on its facts[60] and regrettably has not been incorporated into statute as a general principle governing all family decisions. The Children Act 1989 in contrast to other states' legislation, has no general presumption that children have a right to participate in decision-making. This presumption only comes into play where the child is in situation of conflict, such as with child residence orders. Without such a general principle how do children learn skills, and importantly, the confidence to articulate their views and how do adults learn to listen, if listening to children is not considered a necessary part of daily discourse? Even post-*Gillick* the 1994 campaign to immunise school children against measles and rubella made every effort to obtain the written consent of parents but little attempt was focused on the right of the children to be given information on their right to consent in line with the *Gillick* ratio. Other states such as Scotland and Norway have moved further along the road. Section 6 of the Children (Scotland) Act 1995 provides that

> A person shall in reaching any major decision which involves his fulfilling a parental responsibility ... or his exercising a parental right ... have regard so far as is practical to the views (if he wishes to express them) of the child concerned, taking account of the child's age and maturity ... without prejudice to the generality of this subsection a child 12 years of age or more shall be of sufficient age and maturity to form a view.[61]

Norwegian legislation appears to have influenced legislators in Scotland. The Norwegian Children's Act 1981 provides that 'When the child has attained the age of 12 he shall be allowed to state his opinion before decisions are made on personal matters on his behalf, including with which of his parents he wishes to live. Considerable weight shall be given to the child's wishes.' Although this is a significant improvement on the English situation, there is a case for arguing that the establishment of a minimum age limit for such decisions is incompatible with the Convention on the Rights of the Child, as it raises a presumption of immaturity, which children may find difficult to shift.[62] In relation to religious decision-making, for example, the Convention prefers the evolving capacities of the child rather than age-based distinctions.[63]

There is a second, equally strong, argument against age-based presumptions of immaturity - that they may lead to arbitrariness - as is evidenced between the neighbouring jurisdictions of England and Scotland. In Scotland those aged 16 can marry without parental consent; in England and Wales children aged 16 can marry but only with parental consent.

Finland's Child Custody and Rights of Access Act 1983 makes no such presumptions. Before a child custodian makes a decision he or she 'shall where possible discuss the matter with the child taking into account the child's age and maturity and the nature of the matter ... and give due consideration ...' Although there is no evidence that this more egalitarian and democratic approach to childhood in Scandinavian states places children at greater risk, the States Parties reports under the Convention of the Rights of the Child indicate that such approaches are in the minority. Indeed from the majority of State Party reports, the capacity to consent appears still to be generally regarded as 'the legal benchmark of the adult of full status'.[64] Rodham's suggestion, which predates both her first ladyship and the Convention on the Rights of the Child,[65] argues in favour of a presumption that children, as with adults, are capable of exercising rights and responsibilities unless it is proven otherwise. Hence it would be presumed that children can consent and withhold their consent unless it is proven otherwise. This does not solve but usefully shifts the emphasis of Oscar Wilde's observation that 'experience is the name everyone gives to their mistakes',[66] a bon mot which is rarely applied to children. Rodham's approach is also consistent with principles evolved under the European Convention on Human Rights jurisprudence of proportionality and pressing social need.[67] In general terms these provide that if a right is to be restricted in a democratic society, it can only be restricted in a way which is proportionate to the goal to be achieved and only if there is a pressing social need for the restriction. These principles do not appear to have been applied consistently in relation to issues of consent for children, possibly because the European Convention on Human Rights omits any express reference to the best interests of the child.[68]

This lack of consistency is not a reason to propose the drafting of another new children's treaty but the impact of a child centred philosophy has not been taken on board even within one continent, Europe. A golden opportunity has recently been lost with the adoption of the latest children's treaty, the European Convention on the Exercise of Children's Rights 1995.[69]

A fundamental precondition to informed consent is a right of access to information upon which to base an opinion. Focus should have been directed to how information is made accessible for children of all ages. Instead, in accordance with article 3(a) of the new Convention, a child is only granted the right to 'receive all relevant information' which at first sight would appear to risk placing an unnecessary limitation on the child's right to 'receive and impart information' as occurs under article 10 of the European Convention on Human Rights. Who decides on the relevance, what are the criteria and so forth? In any event the insertion of the qualifier 'relevant' would appear to be redundant in the light of article 15 of the new Convention[70] as all the member states of the Council of Europe are party to or have given an undertaking to become party to the European Convention on Human Rights. The fact that so soon after the almost universal ratification of the Convention on the Rights of the Child such an approach could have been approved, which undermines the philosophy of the Convention on the Rights of the Child, ought to give cause for alarm. The new European Convention on the Exercise of Children's Rights would have been the most appropriate place to explore innovative approaches to the whole issue of children's consent, as the issue of consent is at the heart of such proceedings. However, perhaps because European states are beginning to realise the potentially enormous scope of the UN Convention on the Rights of the Child in relation to child participation in decisions, a narrower and less innovative instrument was preferred. There is a serious risk of the swing of the pendulum and a return to the traditional value of not listening to children.

Conclusion

The lack of a comprehensive approach to children's consent is a reminder of how far we have to travel, even after the near universal adoption of the Convention of the Rights of the Child, for children to be recognised as citizens. Legislators and policy makers need to be persuaded of the need for child-oriented approaches to consent and freedom of expression generally.

The right to freedom of expression implies freedom for expression. Children are more capable of reasoned judgment if they are given the social support and social context to make that judgment. If children do not feel they have the power to make a choice their rational facilities may be underused. Researchers need to develop innovative and embracing approaches to the child's capacity in order to maintain the dynamism which is at the heart of articles 12 and 13 of the UN Convention on the Rights of the Child. So for example, children may have an opinion on the decision facing them but not necessarily on the whole spectrum of decisions. The subdivision of such decisions in such a way that even very young children could participate would be consistent with article 12.

At present children are similar to the *metiokas* of ancient Greece, the alien residents who had some but not all of the attributes of citizenship. Modern theories of democracy are rooted in consent and choice is one of the markers distinguishing us from other animals.[71] Unless we adopt a more egalitarian approach to consent and create a new culture, consent will remain the traditional patronage of the powerful.

As Gunning acknowledges '[i]t is not that there are "universals" out there waiting to be discovered. But through dialogue, shared values can become universal and be safeguarded... A dialogue with a tone that respects cultural diversity is essential.'[72] Now that international law is slowly being absorbed, albeit at different levels and speeds, into national psyches and evolving as part of a developing culture, cultural plurality ought to be viewed as an enriching opportunity and not as an obstacle.

Ultimately we have to decide - was Einstein right? Is everything relative? Cultural relativism implies a recognition that the viewpoint of those inside communities are as valid as those outside. An extreme stance of cultural relativism, as opposed to cultural sensitivity, is just as dangerous as blindly imposing western perceptions of children's rights but proclaiming them as universal.

Notes

[1]   *Tyrer v. United Kingdom* Series A No. 26 Judgment of the European Court of Human Rights 25 April 1978. The Court made it clear that the relevant standard was the standard adopted by contemporary European states and not that which prevailed when the Convention was adopted. The Convention is 'a living instrument, which as the Commission rightly stressed, must be interpreted in light of present day conditions', para. 31. Cf. Mahoney 11 (1990) *Human Rights Law Journal* 57 at 70.

[2]   See for example, Kausikan, 'Asia's Different Standard' (1993) 92 *Foreign Policy*, 24.

[3]   See the contribution of developing states to the formation of the international instruments on children in Van Bueren (1995) *The International Law on the Rights of the Child* 6-16.

[4]   187 States Parties as of 1 July 1996; UN Doc CRC/C/56.

5   As the numerous reservations demonstrate. For texts of the reservations see UN Doc CRC/C/2/Rev 4 1995; for an analysis of the reservations see Bissett-Johnson, 'What did the States Really Agree To? Qualifications of Signatories to the United Nations Convention on the Rights of the Child', 2 *International Journal of Children's Rights* 399.

6   Van Bueren, op. cit. at 53-56.

7   Art 2(7).

8   Para, 5, Section 1. Reproduced in (1993) 14 *Human Rights Law Journal* 352.

9   The British member of the International Court of Justice.

10 Higgins, *Problems and Process: International Law and How We Use It* (1994) at 96.

11 See the discussion in Van Bueren, 'The Challenges for the International Protection of Family Members Rights as the 21st Century Approaches', in (1996) Lowe and Douglas eds. *Families Across Frontiers*.

12 Herodotus, *Persian Wars* Book 3, Chapter 38.

13 'A Traditional Practice that Threatens Health - Female Circumcision' 40 *World Health Organisation Chronicle* 1986, 31.

14 An-Naim, 'Human Rights in the Muslim World, (1990) 3 *Harvard Human Rights J*, 13.

15 There is also reference to a specific religious institution, the *Kafalah* of Islamic Law, in art. 20(3).

16 Art. 24(3).

17 Art. 21(1) The African charter on the Rights and Welfare of the Child has been signed by 17 states and ratified by three - Burkina Faso, Mauritius and Seychelles, 1 July 1992.

18 The author is not defending the practice, merely pointing out the complexities involved; see further Lee, 'Female Genital Mutilation - Medical Aspects and the Rights of the Children' (1994) 2 *International Journal of Children's Rights* 35 and Van Bueren, 'Child Sexual Abuse and Exploitation; A Suggested Human Rights Approach' (1994) 2 *International Journal of Children's Rights* 45.

19 See the example from Bangladesh cited by Ennew, *Childwatch International, Indicators for Children's Rights - A Resource File,* prepared for UNICEF, 1996: (i) Child is translated by a word in Bangla that refers to human beings under two years of age (ii) Rights is translated by a word in Bangla that refers to needs rather than the Western legal notion of rights 'so Children's Rights in Bangla can become babies' needs'.

20 See Pannikar, 'Is the Notion of Human Rights A Western Concept?' (1982) 120 *Diogenes* 75; Renteln, *International Human Rights: Universalism versus Relativism*, 1990.

21 An-Naim, op. cit. See also Howard, 'Cultural Absolutism and the Nostalgia for Community' (1993) 15 *Human Rights Quarterly* 315; Freeman also

prefers An-Naim's approach, see 'The Morality of Cultural Pluralism' (1995) 3 *International Journal of Children's Rights* 1.

22 I am grateful to Monia Hejaiej, Professor of Comparative Literature, University of Tunis for this point.

23 See further the discussion in Van Bueren, *The International Law on the Rights of the Child* op. cit. at 151-169.

24 Cover, 'Obligation: A Jewish Jurisprudence of the Social Order' (1987) 5 *J of Law and Relig.* 65.

25 American Anthropological Association Statement of Human Rights (1947) 49 *American Anthropologist* 539.

26 In relation to the need for indicators and the methodology, see Ennew and Miljeteig, 'Indicators for Children's Rights: Progress Report on a Project' in (1997) 5 *International Journal of Children's Rights* (forthcoming); in relation to indicators for the sexual exploitation of children see Ennew, Gopal, Heeran and Montgomery 'Children and Prostitution, How Can We Measure and Monitor the Commercial Sexual Exploitation of Children?' Prepared for the Congress of Commercial Sexual Exploitation of Children, Stockholm 1996.

27 See for example UN Doc E/CN.4/1986/42.

28 See for example art. 21 (2) African Charter on the Rights and Welfare of the Child.

29 Only prohibited for states parties to the African Charter on the Rights and Welfare of the Child once it enters into force.

30 Art. 24 (3) Convention on the Rights of the Child.

31 Ecuador has stated that the preferential treatment of male children is common practice in both rural areas and marginalised urban areas, see at Van Bueren, *The International Law on the Rights of the Child* at 309.

32 Moscovici, 'On Social Representations' in Forgas ed (1981) *Social Cognition: Perspectives on Everyday Understanding* 181.

33 Qvortrup et al, (1994) *Childhood Matters. Social Theory, Practice and Politics* 6.

34 The right to privacy is relevant because in certain circumstances the unauthorised touching of a human body violates the right to privacy and may amount to an assault. The question is, therefore, at what point in a child's life is he or she regarded as having the legal capacity under international law to consent to medical treatment. See further Van Bueren, *The International Law on the Rights of the Child*, 310-313.

35 See further below.

36 Art. 2(1).

37 See also World Health Organisation and Council for International Organisations of Medical Sciences *Guidelines for Biomedical Research involving Human Subjects*. See particularly Guideline 8.

38 Reproduced in Van Bueren, *International Documents on Children*, 2nd ed (in print).

39   Reproduced in Van Bueren (1993) *International Documents on Children* at 167.
40   See further below.
41   On September 1990.
42   Dickenson and Jones, 'The Philosophy and Development Psychology of Children's Informed Consent' (1995) 2 *Philosophy, Psychiatry and Psychology* 287.
43   See generally Naffine (1990) *Law and the Sexes: Exploration in Feminist Jurisprudence*; Sachs and Hoff-Wilson (1978) *Sexism and the Law*.
44   O'Donovan makes this point in relation to women; see 'With Sense, Consent or Just a Con? Legal Subjects in the Discourse of Autonomy' in Naffine and Owens (eds) *Sexing the Subject of Law* (1997) pp 47-64.
45   Arts. 2(1), 2(2), 9(2), 9(4), 12(1), 12(2), 13(1), (13) (2), 17, 24(e), 30, and art. 31.
46   11 EHRR 175. See the criticism of *Nielson v. Denmark* in Van Bueren, *The International Law on the Rights of the Child* 1995 at 73-75.
47   Art. 30.
48   Art 31(a).
49   See below.
50   However weak the basis for such duties in contemporary international law.
51   Art. 38(1) Constitution of the Russian Federation.
52   Art. 33 Constitution of Ukraine.
53   Art. 32 Constitution of Belarus.
54   UN Doc CRC/C/2/ Rev 4.
55   Ibid.
56   See Van Bueren *The International Law on the Rights of the Child* at 396.
57   Art 79(2) Constitution of Poland 1992.
58   Art. 79(2).
59   [1986] AC 112. Per Lord Scarman at 186. Lord Fraser argued that there was a 'dwindling right', at 172.
60   See for example, *Re R (a minor)* [1992] Fam, 11.
61   The Age of Legal Capacity (Scotland) Act 1991 provides that the consent of children 12 and over is required for adoption and at 12 they can make a will.
62   See, for example, the comments of Stevens J. dissenting in part in *Planned Parenthood v. Danforth* 428, US, 52 104-5 (1976), 'chronological age' is utilised 'to protect minors from the consequences of decisions they are not yet prepared to make ... it is perfectly obvious that such a yardstick is imprecise and perhaps even unjust in particular cases'.
63   See art. 14 Convention on the Rights of the Child.
64   O'Donovan op. cit. at 9.
65   Rodham, 'Children under the Law', (1974) 9 *Harvard Educational Review* 22.
66   Wilde *Lady Windermere's Fan*, Act 111.

67   See for example, *Sunday Times v. United Kingdom*, European Court of Human Rights, Series A No 39 (1979).

68   Van Bueren, 'Protecting Children's Rights in Europe', (1996) *European Human Rights Review* 171.

69   The Convention opened for signature in January 1996. The goal of the Convention is 'in the best interests of children, to promote their rights, to grant them procedural rights and to facilitate the exercise of these rights by ensuring that children are, themselves or through other persons or bodies, informed and allowed to participate in the proceedings affecting them before a judicial authority'. Article 1(2) enshrines a facet of the wider article 12(2) of the UN Convention on the Rights of the Child. The new Convention is limited to civil family proceedings affecting children. However, it is also concerned with the duties of the judicial authority and of the representatives. In contrast with the UN Convention, the new European Convention does establish a clear net of application to all those under 18.

70   '[t]his Convention shall not restrict the application of any other international instrument which deals with specific issues arising in the context of the protection of children and families and to which a Party to this convention, is or becomes a Party'.

71   O'Donovan op. cit.

72   'Arrogant Perception, World Travelling and Multicultural Feminism: The Case of Female Genital Surgeries' (1991-2) 23 *Columbia Human Rights. L. Rev.* 189 at 238.

3   Children's Rights, Cultural Diversity and Private International Law

Introduction

The United Nations Convention on the Rights of the Child,[1] in its Preamble, presents a challenge to States - how to guarantee the universality of the fundamental rights which attach to every child irrespective of the child's origins, while at the same time recognising the importance for 'the protection and harmonious development of the child' of the diverse traditions and cultural values of each people.[2] Recognition of cultural diversity and respect for human rights sometimes entail contradiction and require difficult choices. However, this potential for conflict should not be exaggerated. More often than not the tension between tradition and rights can be creative, leading us certainly to reassess the validity and value of certain traditions, but also to avoid the absolutism and orthodoxy which sometimes characterises human rights discourse. Traditional practices can sometimes reveal more than one way to vindicate a right. This paper, while not blind to the dangers to children inherent in some traditional practices, is more concerned with the need to respect cultural diversity.

Children in the modern world cross frontiers and move, or are removed, with increasing frequency from their cultural and traditional roots. The typical situations are well known - refugee children, runaways, intercountry adoptees, abducted children, children who are the subjects of international custody disputes, or simply children within mobile families. The legal protection of vulnerable children in these different situations requires us to consider, *inter alia,* how to give appropriate respect to the traditions and cultural values of the communities from which they originate. The rules of Private International Law constitute an important element within this legal environment, and it is this area of the law which forms the subject matter of this paper.

The matters discussed focus on two recent Conventions drawn up by the Hague Conference on Private International Law, first the 1993 *Convention on Protection of Children and Co-operation in Respect of Intercountry Adoption*[3] (hereafter described as the 1993 Convention), and second the 1996 *Convention on Jurisdiction, Applicable Law, Recognition, Enforcement and Co-operation in Respect of Parental Responsibility and Measures for the Protection of Children*[4] (hereafter described as the 1996 Convention).

Adoption and *Kafala*

It is well known that the institution of adoption is not permitted under Islamic law. On the other hand, *Kafala*, a form of long term fostering is possible to provide for the welfare of a child in need of care outside the natural family. The essential difference between *Kafala* and adoption is that the latter does not have the effect of integrating the child into the new family. The child remains in name a member of the birth family, and there are no inheritance rights in respect of the new family. However, *Kafala* may if necessary involve delegation of guardianship in respect of the person and property of the child, and in an intercountry situation it may result in a change in the child's nationality.[5]

During the discussions which preceded the adoption of the Preliminary Draft of the 1993 Convention on Intercountry Adoption, the subjects of *Kafala* and the non-acceptance of adoption under Islamic law were raised by the expert of Egypt, Mr W. Hanafi. The matter had been discussed previously, but Mr Hanafi felt sufficiently concerned to make a formal statement.[6] He felt that it was unfortunate that the Draft Convention did not recognise forms of alternative care other than adoption, including in particular the one recognised by Islamic Law. He was also concerned that the Draft Convention could create a situation in which 'Muslim Egyptians residing in a Contracting State [might] be involved by the provisions of the Convention'.

The source of this second concern was Article 2, which remains basically unchanged in the 1993 Convention. It provides that the Convention is to apply where a child habitually resident in one Contracting State (the State of origin) is moved, after or for the purposes of adoption, to the State where the adopters have their habitual residence (the receiving State). Thus, it is possible under the Convention for a Muslim child of Egyptian nationality to be made the subject of a Convention adoption provided that the child is habitually resident at the relevant time in a Contracting State which permits this to occur. The argument seems to be that adoption of the child in these circumstances would constitute a failure to give due regard to the child's national law, and his or her cultural and religious background and interests, and that this would breach, *inter alia,* the United Nations *Declaration on Social and Legal Principles relating to the Protection and Welfare of Children, with Special Reference to Foster Placement and Adoption Nationally and Internationally.*[7]

One reply is that the law of the State of the child's habitual residence, while accepting adoption generally, might regard adoption as an inappropriate option for the child in circumstances such as those outlined. But this would not necessarily be so. There is, by way of analogy, a case in which an English court granted an adoption in respect of a child who was not domiciled in England in the knowledge that the adoption would not have been possible under the law of the child's domicile.[8] There have also been occasions on which adoptions have taken place in Northern Ireland in respect of children domiciled in the Republic of Ireland precisely because adoption was not possible in the Republic.[9] The possible non-recognition of the adoption in the child's domicile is not a bar to the adoption.[10] The matter is generally decided on the best interests criterion, taking into account the possible impact on the child of non-recognition.

The Egyptian delegate was correct in assuming that the circumstances he feared could arise. Whether this is or is not acceptable raises questions of principle. The 1993 Convention does not specify the religion or the nationality of the child as being in any way determinant of the child's eligibility to be adopted. The matter of adoptability is left for determination, under Article 4(a) to the competent authorities of the State of origin, which may or may not be the State of the child's nationality. The clear intention was not to give a veto to the child's national authorities nor to allow a child's religion to predetermine adoptability.

The weight to be given to matters such as nationality or religion was to be left for determination by the authorities of the State of the child's habitual residence. Where that State is a party to the Convention on the Rights of the Child it will in any case be bound by Article 20, paragraph 3, which requires that a State, when considering appropriate forms of alternative care for a child, should pay due regard to 'the desirability of continuity in the child's upbringing and to the child's ethnic, religious, cultural and linguistic background'. The approach of the 1993 Convention is not, therefore, to ignore ethnic, religious or cultural considerations in intercountry adoption, but rather to entrust the authorities of the child's habitual residence with the responsibility of deciding what weight should be attached to those matters in an individual case.

There remains the question of whether the principle contained in the above-mentioned Article 20, paragraph 3, of the Convention on the Rights of the Child should have been embodied in the 1993 Convention. This matter will be taken up later.[11]

The Omission of *Kafala* from the 1993 Convention

The omission of *Kafala* from the Convention raises different issues. Article 2, paragraph 2, states that the Convention covers only adoptions which create a permanent parent-child relationship. The explanation in the *Explanatory Report* [12] is as follows:

> The second paragraph of Article 2 clarifies that the Convention covers all kinds of adoptions that bring about the creation of a permanent parent-child relationship, no matter whether the pre-existing legal relationship between the child and his or her mother or father is ended completely (full adoption) or only partially (simple or limited adoption). But the Convention does not cover 'adoptions' which are only adoptions in name but do not establish a permanent parent-child relationship.

The reason for the inclusion within the Convention of simple adoptions was the wish to ensure that the substantive principles and procedural safeguards of the Convention should extend to as wide a range of adoptions as possible. The shortcomings and abuses which have been a feature of some intercountry adoption arrangements in the past have not been confined to full adoption. To have left out simple adoptions would have created a massive gap in the Convention's protective cover.

Given these underlying arguments, the case for the inclusion of *Kafala* within the Convention had merits. Even though *Kafala* is not the same as adoption, it is another form of alternative long-term care for a child, and, where the arrangements are 'intercountry' involving the transfer of the child to a new jurisdiction, the application of many of the Convention principles and safeguards may well be appropriate. To put the matter simply, long-term intercountry fostering arrangements, including those arranged by *Kafala*, may require the same kind of regulation as that provided for in the 1993 Convention.

There is, therefore, some justification in the view that the 1993 Convention has failed to give adequate recognition to cultural and legal diversity in the forms by which long-term alternative child care is arranged, that it is based on a model (full or simple adoption) which is not universal, and in particular that it excludes the Islamic tradition for reasons which are not clearly based on the best interests of the child.

The reasons for the approach taken in the 1993 Convention are understandable. Concerns of delegates at the Hague Conference centred largely on the experience of intercountry adoption outside the Islamic world, and no evidence was presented relating to either the extent of intercountry *Kafala* or any specific problems or abuses associated with it. There was no indication of a serious problem requiring international action, as there certainly was with intercountry adoption. In this respect the Hague Conference was taking its lead from Article 21(c) of the Convention on the Rights of the Child which encourages the conclusion of bilateral or multilateral arrangements or agreements in the context specifically of adoption. There was also some concern among delegates about the problems of definition which might arise were the Convention to be extended to long-term fostering arrangements, with the concomitant danger that, if the Convention went too far, it might result in placing excessive procedural or even bureaucratic restraints on relatively simple child-care arrangements.

In the more recent 1996 Hague Convention on the Protection of Children, a very deliberate decision was taken to ensure that *Kafala* would be included among the measures of protection covered by the Convention. Article 3(e) refers to 'the placement of the child in a foster family or in institutional care, or the provision of care by *Kafala* or an analogous institution'. However, the 1996 Convention is very different in its objectives from the 1993 Convention. Its emphasis is on the more traditional concerns of Hague Conventions - jurisdiction, applicable law, and recognition and enforcement. While co-operative arrangements between States do form an important element in the 1996 Convention, they do not play the same central role as in the 1993 Convention. It was therefore not possible, by including *Kafala* in the 1996 Convention, to subject it to the same regime that applies under the 1993 Convention to intercountry adoption.

The absence of an appropriate regulatory structure for intercountry *Kafala* is highlighted by Article 33 of the 1996 Convention which attempts to fill part of the vacuum. This requires that prior consultations should take place between authorities in the concerned contracting States where the placement of a child abroad for the purposes of, *inter alia,* fostering or *Kafala* is being contemplated. It also requires consent to the placement by the authorities of what is in effect the receiving State. One of the States sponsoring Article 33, the Netherlands, offered as an explicit justification of this provision the problems that already exist for certain receiving States in the absence of internationally agreed means of regulating the transfer of children between States under *Kafala* arrangements. The exclusion of *Kafala* from the 1993 Convention is thus already giving rise to practical difficulties which are only partially addressed by Article 33 of the 1996 Convention. I believe that in time consideration may need to be given to extending the scope of the 1993 Convention to *Kafala*, and indeed to all forms of long-term alternative care which involve inter-State transfer of the child.

Full and Simple Adoptions

Traditional approaches to adoption differ from country to country, and one of the most pronounced distinctions is that between simple and full adoption. Full adoption involves the integration of the child into the new family and a complete severance of ties with the biological family. Simple adoption, while recognising the child's new relationship with the adoptive parents (i.e., the parental authority or responsibility vesting in the adoptive parents), does not entirely end the legal relationship between the child and the biological family. The nature of the continuing ties with the biological family will differ in different systems. The child may, for example, maintain some inheritance or support rights, or the biological parents may retain some vestigial rights in respect of the child in the event of the adoption breaking down. Simple adoptions are often revocable in certain limited circumstances, for example when the child reaches majority and so wishes or all parties consent.[13] Simple adoptions are most common within the legal systems of South America where they operate usually as an alternative to full adoption (for example, Argentina, Bolivia, Brazil, Chile, Colombia, Paraguay). Simple adoption also operates in a number of Asian and African countries, and is available as an alternative in certain European countries such as France and Belgium.

Where simple adoption is exclusively practised there are sometimes strong reasons of culture or tradition. It has been pointed out, for example, that for persons from Papua New Guinea, Oceania and Aboriginal communities in New Zealand and Australia:

the idea that adoption means that a child was lost forever was considered intolerable, not only for the immediate family but for the wider kinship network, as the adoption of the child diminishes the family group and is a loss for the wider society.[14]

It has already been pointed out that the 1993 Convention extends to both full and simple adoptions. There has been an assumption in some Western countries that, given the distances involved in many intercountry arrangements, and the impracticality in most cases of maintaining links between the child and the family of origin, adoption (and in the view of some States, full adoption) is the best method of securing the interests of the child. However, attitudes are changing and the world is becoming smaller. Within domestic adoption in several countries there has been reappraisal of the clean break approach to adoption and a willingness, where this is in the interests of the child, to move towards more open arrangements involving continuing contact between the child and birth parents.[15] Within intercountry adoption, the inclusion of simple adoption within the scope of the 1993 Convention is itself a recognition of the need for a certain flexibility in considering what arrangements are best suited to the needs of certain children, having regard in particular to their ethnic, religious or cultural backgrounds.

The insistence by some receiving States on a particular legal model of adoption, in the intercountry context, is noteworthy. In England and Wales, for example, there appears to be a strong preference for full over simple adoption. In a recent Consultative Document on adoption,[16] there is a proposal that, where the UK is the receiving State, a simple adoption made under the 1993 Convention in the child's state of origin will be converted automatically to a full adoption in the UK, provided that the birth parents have consented in the knowledge that such conversion will occur.[17] What would occur if that consent were not forthcoming is not made clear. Presumably the Central Authority would refuse permission for the adoption to proceed, as it is entitled to do under Article 17. If that is the case, then in effect the UK would, as a receiving State, be refusing to become involved in simple adoption.

There is also a proposal that simple adoptions entitled to recognition under the Convention should, where the UK is not the receiving State, be given the same effect in England and Wales as full adoptions, subject to a right in the birth parents to apply for a contact order.[18] The reasoning is that this would put the internationally adopted child on the same footing as any other adopted child and would confer a clear and permanent status under the law of the United Kingdom. Quite apart from the concern, which is recognised in the Consultative Document, that this would not protect the rights of birth parents as the Convention intended, there is an element of parochialism in the proposal - an underlying assumption that the form of adoption accepted in the United Kingdom is the best model to promote the interests of the child, even where the receiving and sending countries have both accepted simple adoption. Considerations of equal treatment as between nationally and internationally adopted children, as well as clarity of status, are undoubtedly important. But if children are in fact adopted overseas and in different cultural contexts, respect for their rights may on the contrary demand recognition of a differential status. There is the danger of employing the principle of equality to justify a cultural or legal orthodoxy. This having been said, it should be noted that there may be other considerations in the background, in particular the immigration implications of recognising continuing legal links between the adopted person and his or her family of origin.

Choice of Law in Child Protection

The choice of law process in proceedings involving the status or care of children is, in most common law systems, heavily biased towards forum law. It must be asked whether the practical advantages of this approach are ever purchased at the price of ignoring a child's cultural background.

In Dicey and Morris' *The Conflict of Laws*, for example, the following statement appears:

> According to English rules of the conflict of laws, the parental rights of a father or mother domiciled abroad over his or her minor child, whether born of a monogamous or polygamous marriage, are governed by English law, whenever an English court has jurisdiction to determine these questions between such parties. This is so even if the minor is residing outside England and is a foreign national.[19]

It may be thought that this emphasis on forum law is unobjectionable because most courts will, in any case, regard the welfare of the child as a primary, if not the first and paramount, consideration - an internationally accepted principle.[20] Yet, may there not be some, perhaps exceptional, cases in which the cultural context of the child will suggest that his or her interests may best be met by the application of foreign law? For example, the child may be a member of an immigrant family of the Moslem faith, soon to return to an Islamic country of origin. Might there be a case for the forum to consider the legal regime under which the child is soon to live, and to avoid making an order which may soon be altered when the family returns? The argument that the court must not be limited in its application of the welfare principle may be met by the following response. The manner in which the welfare of the child is protected must necessarily to some extent be conditioned by cultural context, and any reasonable interpretation of the welfare principle will give some weight to the issues of continuity, nationality, culture and ethnicity. The court could not, in any case, be obliged to make an order which it would regard as positively harmful to the child. It is therefore true that all these matters could be taken into consideration under the welfare principle, without the need to alter the choice of law principles. However, a suitable modification of the choice of law principles would perhaps highlight these special considerations in international cases. This, indeed, is one of the reasons why, in the 1996 Convention, the general principle of application of forum law has been modified as follows in Article 15, paragraph 2:

> However, in so far as the protection of the person or the property of the child requires, [authorities in exercising jurisdiction] may exceptionally apply or take into consideration the law of another State with which the situation has a substantial connection.

The Attribution of Parental Responsibility

Similar considerations arise in relation to Article 16 of the 1996 Convention which sets out choice of law principles governing the attribution and extinction of parental responsibility[21] where this occurs by operation of law, by agreement or a unilateral act, without the intervention of a judicial or administrative authority. The basic rule, in Paragraphs 1 and 2 of that Article, is that the attribution or extinction of parental responsibility in such circumstances is governed by the law of the child's habitual residence at the relevant time.[22] For example, the question of whether, at the time of a child's birth, parental responsibility vests in one or both parents by operation of law is determined by the law of the child's habitual residence. Similarly, the question whether an unmarried father may acquire parental responsibility by an agreement with the mother is determined by the law of the child's habitual residence at the time when the agreement takes effect.

This basic rule did not give rise to serious controversy during the Special Commission discussions. It flows from one of the fundamental premises of the Convention, namely that the most realistic connecting factor in determing both jurisdiction and governing law in matters of child protection should be the child's habitual residence, rather than domicile or nationality.

This principle will necessarily involve in some cases the parent/child relationship being made subject to a legal system which may be remote from the religious, ethnic or cultural traditions of the family. Indeed it has been claimed as an advantage of domicile or nationality, with all their technical deficiencies, that they do at least offer some prospect of a link between personal status and cultural origins.[23] However, in an increasingly mobile world concepts such as domicile and nationality often produce artificial results. The habitual residence principle is at least based on factual connections, and it is after all the State of the child's habitual residence which will usually have the most direct interest in, and responsibility for, the protection of the child.

If it is accepted that habitual residence is the appropriate link in determining whether parental responsibility exists or has been extinguished for the purpose of Article 12, difficult problems nevertheless remain in cases where the habitual residence of the child subsequently changes.

Example (a)
A child is born to parents habitually resident in State X. According to the law of State X the parents by operation of law are vested with joint parental responsibility. Some years later, the family moves to State Y. Under the domestic law of State Y parents do not automatically enjoy joint responsibility. (This may be because they are unmarried; or perhaps, for traditional or religious reasons, responsibility vests in only one married parent.) Does the change in habitual residence necessarily affect the position as regards parental responsibility?

Example (b)
A child is born to married parents habitually resident in State A, whose laws vest parental responsibility solely in the father. Some years later the family moves to State B, under whose domestic law married parents have joint responsibility by operation of law. Does the principle of joint responsibility now apply?

One possible solution is to adopt a principle of mutability, according to which the rules governing the attribution of parental responsibility by operation of law change as the child's residence changes. This has the advantages of simplicity and certainty. The authorities of the child's present habitual residence know their own rules best, and it may be a cause of some practical difficulties if they need to determine, before deciding which parent has responsibility (for the purposes, for example, of obtaining consent to medical treatment for the child), where the child's previous residence was, and whether one or both parents had responsibility under its law. On the other hand, considerations of continuity and respect for the child's previous social and cultural context, suggest that a parental responsibility once established by operation of law should not be forfeit as a result only of a change in the child's residence.

In the end a compromise was struck at the Hague under which a parental responsibility already acquired by operation of law in a previous habitual residence remains effective, though additional persons may acquire parental responsibility by operation of law in the new habitual residence. Paragraphs 3 and 4 of Article 16 state:

> 3 Parental responsibility which exists under the law of the State of the child's habitual residence subsists after a change of that habitual residence to another State.

> 4 If the child's habitual residence changes, the attribution of parental responsibility by operation of law to a person who does not already have such responsibility is governed by the law of the State of the new habitual residence.

As a consequence, in case *(a)* above the parents would retain joint responsibility despite the change in habitual residence. In case *(b)* the principle of joint responsibility would operate as from the change of habitual residence. Thus respect is accorded to what may be the traditional rules of the child's former residence in so far as they confer responsibility, but they may in effect be supplemented by a more liberal regime in the child's new habitual residence.

All of this is also subject to the general principle, contained in Article 17, that the actual exercise of parental responsibility is governed by the law of the State of the child's current habitual residence. A vital distinction is drawn between the *attribution* and the *exercise* of parental responsibility. So, while the identification of persons having parental responsibility may to some extent be influenced by the child's country of origin, what constitutes appropriate parenting, and the circumstances in which the State may intervene to limit the exercise of parental responsibility, remain governed by the laws of the child's new residence.[24]

Uniform Laws and Fundamental Principles

Hague Conventions do not in general attempt to resolve conflict between the laws of different systems by establishing uniform domestic laws. They concentrate rather on achieving uniformity in the principles governing jurisdiction, choice of law and the recognition and enforcement of judgments. This tradition has many justifications. Not least is the recognition and respect which it gives to the diversity of different systems of domestic law. The 1993 Convention is something of an exception in that it does prescribe certain basic rules of substance and procedure which are to be applied to all intercountry adoptions made under the Convention. But these are basic principles which can be accommodated without radical restructuring in very different domestic adoption systems.[25] It was emphasised time and time again during debates in the Special Commission that the Convention is not designed to produce a uniform international adoption law. Indeed the Convention even takes a flexible approach to choice of law and jurisdictional issues, matters on which there remain very significant differences of approach in different systems.[26]

   During the debates in Commission on the 1996 Convention there was strong resistance to the inclusion of even the broadest of principles outside the familiar Private International Law rules. Suggestions that certain principles drawn from the Convention on the Rights of the Child should be included in the body of the 1996 Convention were rejected as inappropriate in a Private International Law Convention.[27] Moreover, it was argued, States that become parties to the 1996 Convention will almost invariably be parties also to the Convention on the Rights of the Child, in which case they are bound already by its provisions.

   In this writer's view the approach taken may be questioned for a variety of reasons, one of which is especially relevant in the context of this paper. One of the general principles which might usefully have been embodied in the 1996 Convention, based on the Preamble to the Convention on the Rights of the Child, may be formulated as follows:

In determining and exercising jurisdiction under the Contention, the competent authorities of Contracting States shall take into account the importance for the protection and harmonious development of the child of giving due regard to the traditions and cultural background of the child.

This principle would be of importance at several key points within the Convention. First, it may become relevant when an authority of the child's habitual residence is considering whether to cede jurisdiction to the authorities of another State (such as the State of which the child is a national) under Article 8 or Article 9. Indeed a provision of this kind would have provided some further reassurance for those who remain concerned about the near demise of nationality within the Convention. Second, it may be relevant when an authority is considering whether to adopt the exceptional course of applying a law other than that of the forum under Article 15.2.[28] Third, the principle may well be relevant in determining what particular measures are in a child's interests, particularly if that child originates from a culture which is different from that of the forum.

If the general principle of applying forum law is to avoid becoming an instrument of parochialism or cultural indifference, it needs to be balanced by a substantive requirement to take some account of the child's origins, culture and traditions. It may well be that in many countries this is already the case, and one hopes that the Convention will in fact be applied in this spirit. It would have helped if the principle had been made explicit.

Conclusions

International Conventions concerning the protection of children must respect legal and cultural diversity. This makes their acceptance and ratification more likely; it is a necessary prerequisite for international co-operation, which has become a notable feature of recent Hague Conventions; but, most important, it is a vital element in upholding certain rights and interests of the child. The balance between respect for diversity and the insistence on certain universal standards needs to be maintained. This has in broad terms been achieved in the two recent Hague Conventions concerning the protection of children.

This paper has indicated some points at which greater emphasis might be placed on issues of legal and cultural diversity. In both the formulation and implementation of Private International Law Conventions concerning child protection, great care needs to be taken to accommodate the diverse models and institutions which in different countries serve similar needs, especially where they reflect different cultural traditions, provided always that they are consistent with the child's fundamental rights. It is also suggested that national authorities, when exercising discretion in matters of jurisdiction or choice of law, and when applying the best interests standard in international cases, should be made more aware of the importance of taking into account the cultural and legal traditions associated with the child's country of origin.

Notes

[1]   Adopted by the General Assembly of the United Nations on 20 November 1989.

[2]   Compare paragraph 3 of the Preamble with paragraph 12.

[3]   Of 29 May 1993. The Convention entered into force on 1 May 1995. By 2 July 1997 the Convention had been ratified by 16 States, acceded to by one state, and signed by another 14.

[4]   Of 19 October 1996.

[5]   See the Koran and see Pearl, Chapter 5 below. *Kafala* is mentioned in Article 20 of the Convention on the Rights of the Child as an alternative form of child care. See also J.H.A. van Loon, *International Co-operation and Protection of Children with Regard to Intercountry Adoption, Hague Receuil des Cours,* Vol 244 (1993-VI), 209-211.

[6]   Recorded in Preliminary Document No 7 of Sept 1992 for the attention of the seventeenth Session, 156.

[7]   General Assembly Resolution 41/85 of 3 December 1986, referred to in the Preamble of the 1993 Convention.

[8]   See *Re B (S) (An Infant)* [1968] Ch. 204, where it was held that the English Court had jurisdiction to make an adoption order in respect of a child who was domiciled in Spain (where the father was domiciled) 'notwithstanding that by the law of the infant's domicile the court there could not make an order or could only make one having different consequences' Per Goff J. at 210.

[9]   Prior to the Adoption Act in 1968 in the Republic of Ireland a non-orphaned legitimate child was not eligible for adoption. It is known (though not documented) that some children having this status were adopted in Northern Ireland.

[10]   See Cheshire and North, *Private International Law*, 12th Edition at 762.

[11]   See discussion below under 'Uniform laws and fundamental principles'.

12   By G Parra-Aranguren, Hague Conference on Private International Law, May 1994, at para. 94.

13   This is the case, for example, under Paraguayan Adoption Law, which also permits full adoption.

14   M. O'Collins, 'The influence of Western Adoption Laws on Customary Adoptions in the Third World' in P.H. Bean (ed) *Adoption, Essays in Social Policy, Law and Sociology*, London 1984, 288 at 299, quoted in J.H.A. van Loon, loc cit, at 208.

15   See W. Duncan, 'Regulating Intercountry Adoption - an International Perspective' Chapter 3 in A. Bainham, D. Pearl and R. Pickford (eds), *Frontiers of Family Law* (2nd edition), at pp. 43-45.

16   See Department of Health and Welsh Office, *Adoption - A Service for Children. Adoption Bill - A Consultative Document*, London, March 1996, paras 4.31 to 4.34.

17   Ibid at para 4.32. Article 27 of the 1993 Convention makes provision for such conversion.

18   Ibid at para 4.33.

19   Dicey and Morris, *Conflict of Laws* (11th ed) Vol II, at 787. In relation to the last line, the following footnote appears '*Re P... (G.E.) (An Infant)* [1965] Ch. 568 (C.A.) Cf *Re Ullee* (1886) 54 L.T. 286 (C.A.), where no distinction was drawn between those children who were and those who were not within the jurisdiction'.

20   Convention on the Rights of the Child, Article 3, Paragraph 1.

21   Article 1, Paragraph 2, defines 'parental responsibility' as including 'parental authority, or any analogous responsibility or authority in relation to the person or property of the child'.

22   Article 16:
1 The attribution or extinction of parental responsibility by operation of law, without the intervention of a judicial or administrative authority, is governed by the law of the State of the habitual residence of the child.
2 The attribution or extinction of parental responsibility by an agreement or a unilateral act, without the intervention of a judicial or administrative authority, is governed by the law of the State of the child's habitual residence at the time when the agreement or unilateral act takes effect.

23   The 1961 Convention on the Protection of Minors provided for the recognition of a relationship of authority arising automatically under the law of the State of the infant's nationality.

24   The authorities of the child's current habitual residence also have jurisdiction to terminate parental responsibility in accordance with Article 18 of the 1996 Convention.

25   See W. Duncan, 'The Hague Convention on the Protection of Children and Co-operation in respects of Intercountry Adoption 1993. Some Issues of Special Relevance to Sending Countries', in E.D. Jaffe (ed), *Intercountry*

Adoptions: Laws and Perspectives of Sending Countries, M. Nijhoff 1995, 217.

26   See W. Duncan, 'Conflict and Co-operation. The Approach to Conflicts of Law in the 1993 Hague Convention on Intercountry Adoption' in N. Lowe and G. Douglas (eds), *Families Across Frontiers*, M. Nijhoff 1996, 577.

27   There was even resistance to the inclusion of such principles in the Preamble. It was decided that a specific reference to the 'best interests' principle, coupled with a general reference to the Convention on the Rights of the Child, was sufficient.

28   See above, under 'Choice of Law in Child Protection' at p. 38.

4   The Interpretation of the Concept 'The Best Interest of the Child' in Israel

YEHIEL S. KAPLAN*

Introduction

Rabbinical and civil courts in Israel have parallel jurisdiction in certain matters concerning Jewish children.[1] Section 9 of the Rabbinical Courts Jurisdiction (Marriage and Divorce) Law, 5713-1953, states that in certain matters of personal status of Jews, such as guardianship, 'a Rabbinical court shall have jurisdiction after all parties concerned have expressed their consent thereto'. Section 3 of the same law sets out an alternative way to grant jurisdiction to a rabbinical court in matters concerning children: 'where a suit of divorce between Jews has been filed in a Rabbinical court, whether by the wife or by the husband, a Rabbinical court shall have exclusive jurisdiction in any matter connected with such suit, including maintenance for the wife and for the children of the couple'. The Israeli Supreme Court has interpreted this section as follows: custody matters are connected by their character and nature to the divorce litigation,[2] and therefore need not be linked explicitly to a suit of divorce.[3] Other matters, including certain matters concerning the fate of children, such as their education,[4] are not linked by their character and nature to the divorce litigation, and therefore they have to be linked explicitly and the linkage should be sincere.[5]

When one tribunal, the rabbinical or the civil court, has jurisdiction in matters concerning children, the other tribunal is not allowed to rule in litigation regarding the same case. The same tribunal has jurisdiction in present litigation and in future litigation[6] regarding the same matter.

Rabbinical courts usually apply their law, namely Jewish law. Civil courts apply the principles of Israeli civil law.[7] There are also differences between these two court systems, resulting from a different interpretation of the same rules,[8] such as the rule regarding the best interest of the child.

Section 15 of Basic Law: Judicature states:

> (c)   The Supreme Court shall sit also as a High Court of Justice. When so sitting, it shall hear matters in which it deems it necessary to grant relief for the sake of justice and which are not within the jurisdiction of another court (*beit mishpat* or *beit din*).
> (d)   Without prejudice to the generality of the provisions of subsection (c), the Supreme Court sitting as a High Court of Justice shall be competent .....
> (4)   To order religious courts (*batei din*) to hear a particular matter within their jurisdiction or to refrain from hearing or continue hearing a particular matter not within their jurisdiction, provided that the court shall not entertain an application under this paragraph if the applicant did not raise the question of jurisdiction at the earliest opportunity; and if he had no measurable opportunity to raise the question of jurisdiction until a decision had been given by a religious court (*beit din*), the court may squash a proceeding taken or a decision given by a religious court (*beit din*) without authority.

The rule in section 15 of Basic Law: Judicature allows for judicial supervision by the Israeli Supreme Court regarding acts and decisions of religious courts. Occasionally, the Supreme Court has ruled that decisions of Jewish religious courts - the rabbinical courts - are void since they did not implement a rule or doctrine which they should have implemented according to Israeli legislation.[9]

General Rule

Sometimes children in Israel cannot take full responsibility for their lives or make autonomous decisions in important matters for themselves. They have to be protected and so decisions regarding their fate are made for them by others, especially their parents, and also judges, social workers, psychologists and guardians. In taking such decisions these people are guided by the principle of the best interest of the child. This principle requires that their decisions will enhance the physical and material needs of the child, such as providing the child with reasonable clothing and food, suitable accommodation, devoted and proper care, etc., and especially the child's cultural, spiritual and emotional needs, such as the right educational, cultural, and social environment, love, affection, emotional warmth, security and trust, encouragement and support, and a feeling that he is desirable to his parents and the surrounding society, which will enable him to fulfil his desires, will and potential.[10]

Israeli legislation directs various religious courts, including Jewish religious courts - the rabbinical courts - and Israeli civil courts, to implement the principle of the best interest of the child.

Section 3 of the Women's Equal Rights Law, 5711-1951, states:

> a)　　Both parents are the natural guardians of their children; when one parent dies, the survivor shall be the natural guardian.
> b)　　The provisions of subsection (a) shall not derogate from the power of a competent court or tribunal to deal with matters of guardianship over the persons or property of children with the interest of the children as the sole consideration.[11]

Section 17 of the Capacity and Guardianship Law, 5722-1962, states that the duties of parents towards their minor children are to 'act in the best interests of the minor in such manner as devoted parents would act in the circumstances'. They should implement the principles of this section when they reach an agreement concerning guardianship, custody, right of contact etc., of each parent.

Sections 24 and 25 of the Capacity and Guardianship Law, 5722-1962, (hereinafter: 'Capacity Law') state:

> Where the parents of the minor live separately - whether the marriage has been annulled or dissolved or still exists - they may agree between them as to which of them shall exercise the guardianship of the minor, wholly or in part, who shall have custody of the minor and what shall be the rights of the other parent with regard to having contact with him. Such an agreement shall be subject to the approval of the Court, and upon such approval shall, for all purposes, other than for the purpose of an appeal, have the effect of a judgment of the Court.
> Where the parents have not reached an agreement as provided in section 24, or where they have reached an agreement but it has not been carried out, the Court may determine the matters referred to in section 24 as may appear to it to be in the best interests of the minor providing that children up to the age of six shall be with their mother unless there are special reasons for directing otherwise.

Section 1(b) of the Adoption of Children Law, 5741-1981, states: 'an adoption order and any other decision under this Law shall be made if the court is satisfied that they are in the interest of the adoptee'.[12]

The Israeli Attorney-General, or his representative, can act on behalf of a minor in court when he believes he should do so in the best interest of the child.[13]

Israel has signed and ratified the United Nations Convention on the Rights of the Child, which states in Article 3(1):

> In all actions concerning children, whether undertaken by public or private social welfare institutions, courts of law, administrative authorities or legislative bodies, the best interests of the child shall be a primary consideration.[14]

Rabbinical courts - which in their rulings apply the principles of Jewish law - hold that 'the best interest of the child' is an important principle in Jewish law concerning the relationship between parents and children.[15] However, the interpretation of the principle of the best interest of the child by rabbinical courts is different from that of the civil courts. The gap between the doctrines and values of Jewish and Israeli law in this field is sometimes evident when both court systems apply the specific doctrines regarding the child's welfare. These are discussed below.

Custody of Children

Child's Age

Rabbinical Courts   There are legal presumptions in Jewish law regarding the custody of children. These reflect the views of Jewish Sages regarding the best interest of the child. A nursing child needs the care of his mother and should not be separated from her if he or she has come to know her. Therefore, the presumption is that this child, when he knows his mother, should be in her custody.[16] However, these legal presumptions are not absolute. If it is proved that in a specific case the best interest of the child requires that custody be granted to the father, for instance when the mother is physically or mentally ill and cannot take care of the child and meet his emotional needs, then custody will be granted to the father.[17]

The same rule applies regarding a male or female child until the end of his or her sixth year of life, for most Jewish law Sages believe that until the child is six years old he needs his mother, especially emotionally.[18] Therefore, when the mother is fit to meet her child's needs the right of custody of a child up to the age of six will be granted to her.[19] Above the age of six a son should be in the custody of his father, who is obliged to teach him the principles of Jewish law and a profession.[20] The father should teach him the religious principles of Jewish Law,[21] as well as a profession and what a man should know in order to fulfil his social role in life. A daughter older than six should be in the custody of her mother,[22] who will teach her what a woman should know in order to fulfil successfully her female social role in the future.[23] Some scholars believe that it is not proper for a daughter to be in the custody of her father since the rules of sexual modesty demand that a daughter should be living with her mother.[24] However, the rules regarding children both younger and older than the age of six have to be evaluated in each case.[25] Sometimes it is in the best interest of a daughter or son younger than six, or of a daughter older than six, to be in the custody of their father and of a son above this age to be in the custody of his mother.[26]

Civil Courts   The gap between the rabbinical and civil courts concerning custody rules that take into consideration the child's age is not wide. Civil courts apply the rule in section 25 of the Capacity Law concerning children up to the age of six. This rule, which was enacted as a result of the influence of the parallel rule in Jewish law,[27] favours the mother in custody disputes concerning young children, up to the age of six. As regards older children, the legislator directs the court to apply the general rule of the best interest of the child. Israeli legislation does not favour the mother or the father of children at this age. However, the consequences of the preference for the mother of young children are that children raised by their mother until the age of six will probably remain in her custody at an older age due to the principle of continuity, which requires that there should be no changes and no instability in the child's life. When there are several children, the court will not wish to separate the older children from their younger siblings, who are under seven years old, and probably one parent will be granted custody of all the children.[28] According to the custody assumptions of Jewish law the mother should be the custodian of daughters at this age; similarly according to the interpretation of justices in the Israeli Supreme Court, the mother should be preferred in custody disputes concerning daughters older than six. Their rationale is the same as that of Jewish law scholars: the mother understands her daughter more than the father, and is more suited to educate her.[29]

Spiritual Benefit

(a) Education

Rabbinical Courts Rabbinical courts hold that the child's spiritual welfare is an important factor in evaluating his best interest. The child has a right to receive the spiritual and vocational education that will best prepare him for his spiritual and professional tasks as an adult.

When a spouse requests that the child be in his or her custody in order to give him a religious education, and the other spouse wishes to give the child a secular education, the rabbinical courts tend to grant custody and the right to decide educational matters to the parent who will provide the child with a religious education, since they believe that spiritual-religious benefit is important.[30] They are also obliged by Jewish law to prevent the violation of principles of Jewish law by other Jews.[31]

Religious education is more important than the aforementioned rules of custody in Jewish law. Thus, a rabbinical court has ruled that in certain circumstances a father can request that his son who is older than six, and should be educated by his father, be taken from his mother in order that he be educated in an institution that will afford him a religious education.[32] When a rabbinical court understood that the father would give his child, who was younger than six, a religious education, while the mother would not, or the mother would give the son, who was older than six, a religious education, while the father would not, the court ruled that custody should be granted to the parent who would provide religious education, despite a specific custody rule that the other parent should be the custodian.[33]

Civil Courts The Israeli Supreme Court holds that the secular interpretation of the best interest of the child, which guides social workers and psychologists, in their professional opinions, should be the basis for decisions concerning the best interest of the child in civil and rabbinical courts.[34]

The Israeli civil courts do not view the principle 'best interest of the child' according to the legal interpretation of a religious sect. Justice Goitein held that the Israeli Parliament - the Knesset - had guided the judges in the religious courts to ignore the theoretical doctrines of religious sects concerning the best interest of the child.[35] Justice Haim Cohn wrote in the *American European Beth El Mission* case:

> In the eyes of religious officials ... the concern for the soul of the child is no less important than the concern for his physical health and his healthy development ... the criterion for interpretation of Israeli legislation is not to be found in one kind of religious outlook, or another, but has to be based upon a general secular perspective ... and from this point of view there is no significance attached to religious concerns for the soul of the child.[36] (translation)

The civil judge believes that the religious perspective is irrelevant in the interpretation of the concept 'best interest of the child'.[37] It is relevant only when it coincides with the professional evaluation of 'best interest of the child', on the part of social workers or psychologists. If, for instance, a child was educated in a religious school and his family had encouraged him to live according to the religious rules of Jewish law, it is possible that a psychologist would recommend that no change occur in the future in order to avoid an emotional conflict due to differences between old and new education and habits. A court which wants to maintain stability in the child's life will rule that religious education be continued, and custody will be granted to the parent who observes the religious rules of Jewish law. However, the opposite is also true. If in the past the child's education and lifestyle were not religious, the court would rule that in order to maintain stability in the life of the child there should be no change in the status quo.

In a case where the children had been educated in the past at a religious school and the custodian (their mother), who led a religious lifestyle and educated them to observe Jewish religious commandments, kidnapped them to Israel, the court accepted the professional views of a social worker and a psychologist that the children should remain with their mother since this was in their best interest. One consideration was that if the children returned to the US, to a father who was not religious and would not educate them at a religious school, this change in their lifestyle and education could cause emotional harm.[38] In another case the court ruled that the religious education of a child of a secular mother and a religious father should be maintained, in the best interest of the child, since the child's experience at the school was positive and it was important to maintain a good relationship between the child and the father.[39]

(b) Parent's moral behaviour

Rabbinical Courts   The priority given to a child's religious-spiritual welfare is also evident when rabbinical courts rule in a custody suit brought by a parent, usually a mother, who is cohabiting with another person outside marriage.

Jewish law scholars and rabbinical courts hold that if a parent sets a bad moral example it could have a bad effect on the child. When, according to the usual custody rules the rabbinical courts would normally grant custody to a parent; but according to the religious perspective of the *dayanim*, his/her moral behaviour is improper, custody may be granted to the other parent.[40] In one case a rabbinical court explained that since the child would be exposed to a bad moral example set by a mother who did not observe the traditional rules regarding modesty and morality that have prevailed among the Jewish people for many generations, she might not be granted the right to be the child's custodian.[41] Sometimes, however, a rabbinical court will grant custody to such a mother/father when it believes that this is in the best interest of the child.[42]

Civil Courts On the other hand, in Israeli civil courts this kind of improper 'moral' behaviour[43] of a parent is not accorded the same weight.[44] However, they believe that it is legitimate for rabbinical courts to take into consideration, among other factors, the effect of cohabitation of a parent with a person who is not a parent. This, however, should be only one of the considerations. They should also grant custody to the more suitable parent after receiving data, testimony, or written opinions of professionals on the best interest of the child.[45]

(c) Residence in Israel

Rabbinical Courts The religious-spiritual welfare of the child is enhanced in a proper environment. As the rabbinical courts assume that the best place for raising and educating a Jewish child is Israel, they prefer to grant custody to that parent who will raise and educate the child in Israel.[46] However, sometimes they grant custody to a parent who will live outside Israel when they believe that this is in the best interest of the child.[47]

Civil Courts On the other hand, prior to 1991 (see below), in Israeli civil courts, residence in Israel was preferable only when it coincided with the psychological theory that continuity of the existing custody arrangement and stability is desirable for the child. When the child had been raised and educated in Israel and a major change in his life would be hard for him, a civil court would probably have ruled that he should remain in Israel in his best interest. Education of a Jewish child in Israel and preventing his separation from this country are a desirable national purpose which should be implemented when possible, but a civil court would not have forced a minor to grow up in Israel when the secular interpretation of the concept best interest of the child led to the conclusion that he should be raised abroad. A contrary decision would cause injustice and would not enhance any national purpose.[48]

These were the rules which were applied when Israeli courts implemented the principle of best interest of the child in habeas corpus proceedings regarding abducted children.[49] However, in 1991 Israeli internal legislation adopted the rules of the Hague Convention on international child abduction, including Article 13, which guides the courts to refuse to return an abducted child, only, *inter alia*, when 'there is grave risk that his or her return (to the country he was abducted from) would expose the child to physical or psychological harm, or will otherwise place the child in an intolerable situation'.[50]

(d) Maintaining the religion of parents or parent

Rabbinical Courts A Jewish religious court will want to maintain the religion of a Jewish child. When both parents, or the mother, are Jewish, it will rule that the child should be raised and educated in a Jewish home in his best interest.[51]

Civil Courts Civil courts will also rule that when both parents are Jewish the child should be raised and educated in a Jewish home in his best interest, in order to prevent emotional harm as a result of conflict between the child and his family and environment.[52] When the parents do not agree about the child's religion, the civil court will prefer the religion which is in the child's best interest.[53]

Prevention of Emotional Harm

There are certain common custody rules applied by the rabbinical and civil courts which are intended to prevent emotional harm. They are based on theories of developmental psychology.

(a) Child's will, desires and preferences taken into consideration

Israeli and Jewish law take into consideration the child's desires and preferences concerning his custody and the parents' visitation rights. When civil courts make a custody decision they tend not to force a child to be in the custody of a parent against his will, considering that this is contrary to his best interest.[54]

Israeli legislation does not specify a particular age of maturity of a child at which he is deemed able to understand all the relevant considerations in custody cases. In each individual case, the courts determine whether the child is mature and can understand all the pros and cons, so that giving weight to his view would be justified. The general trend of the courts is not to rule against the wishes of a child, where possible, after he reaches the age of 10-11. They take into consideration not only the child's age but also individual subjective factors, such as the extent of the child's determination and his mental development, which enables him to understand, distinguish and judge in a proper manner.[55]

This principle is also implemented in the rulings of Jewish law scholars and rabbinical courts in Israel. They give the child's desires and preferences concerning his custody due weight according to his age and development. When they are convinced that a mature and well developed child has expressed his own real will, and did not act as a result of manipulation by another person, they prefer not to act against the child's will in his best interest.[56]

However, if the civil[57] or religious[58] courts are convinced that acceptance of the child's wishes will not be in his best interest they will not accede to them.

(b) Continuity

Changes and instability in the child's life are emotionally harmful. Therefore, continuity of custody with the same custodian is an important consideration in the civil courts.[59]

Continuity is not a factor mentioned in ancient Jewish law sources regarding custody. However, rabbinical courts are guided by professional opinions of experts, especially social workers, concerning the best interest of the child. These professionals attach importance to continuity of custody with the same custodian.[60]

Paternity

Rabbinical Courts

According to Jewish law a child born as a result of sexual relations between parents who are in the category of *isurey arayot* (forbidden relations) - such as relations between mother and son, brother and sister, other first-degree relatives, and a married woman with a man who is not her husband - is considered a *mamzer*. The personal status of a *mamzer* is highly problematic, since he cannot marry most Jews.[61] The laws regarding a *mamzer* are a result of the religious outlook that holds that the offence of *isurey arayot* is one of the most grave offences since it is opposed to the values of sanctity of the Jewish family. On the other hand, when parents sin why should their children suffer?[62] Therefore, for many generations rabbinical courts were extremely cautious and only on rare occasions did they rule that a child was a *mamzer*. They used the rules of evidence as a means to obviate the need to declare that a child was a *mamzer*.[63]

Modern science maintains that a person's blood comes from the father and the mother.[64] But an old Jewish text states that a child's blood is derived from his mother.[65] There are Jewish law scholars who interpret this text literally and do not base their decisions on tests founded on scientific doctrines contrary to the scientific beliefs of the Jewish Sages.[66] Therefore, some rabbis and rabbinical courts hold that scientific tests are not relevant in paternity cases.[67] Other rabbis and rabbinical courts hold that the results of scientific tests are relevant.[68] Sometimes, when the mother is not married, the *dayanim* in rabbinical courts hold that the refusal of a party to a paternity case to submit to a scientific test that could produce results regarding paternity may be used as evidence against him. They believe that they can rule that this party has to undertake scientific tests since there is a legal and religious duty in Jewish law to present before the court all the relevant evidence.[69] However, when the results of these scientific tests could lead to an outcome that was not in the best interest of the child, such as the conclusion that the child is a *mamzer*, rabbis and rabbinical courts would probably rule that these scientific tests should not be used.[70]

Civil Courts

In the past there were Justices in the Israeli Supreme Court who held that in certain circumstances the civil court system should accept evidence that would not be valid in rabbinical courts in paternity cases.

In the *Ploni* case, the applicant claimed that he was the father of a child who had been born four years before and raised by a married couple as their child. The mother denied his claims regarding her relationship with him. The mother and her husband claimed that the applicant's motivation was evil: an attempt to destroy their life and the life of their child. The judge in the district court ruled that the laboratory was not to perform the scientific tests. The applicant was seeking to lead the court to the conclusion that the child was a *mamzer*, and the court should not assist him.[71]

The applicant's appeal to the Israeli Supreme Court was unsuccessful. Justice Olsham held that the application was contrary to public interest and morality. Justice Landau held that this request was a great iniquity, since its aim was extremely harmful to the child and couple, and therefore was not moral or legal, and it was an abuse of rights. On the other hand, Justices Sussman and Berenson held that the appeal should be dismissed because of the special circumstances of the case. The applicant had not explained why he wanted the court to declare that he was the father. He had waited four years, and only after the child had been raised during this time by the couple did he request a declaratory judgment, which would be very harmful for the child, legally and socially. The principle they applied was different from the religious principle of the rabbinical courts. They held that if the applicant had presented them with a legitimate reason for his legal request, such as the determination of inheritance rights, the court would have had to decide what was more important: the legitimate interest of the applicant or the best interest of the child. In such a case in the rabbinical courts, when the result could be that the child would be regarded as a *mamzer*, the application that could lead to this result would be dismissed.[72]

In the *Sharon* paternity case, a religious judge, Elon, held that the civil courts should not rule that scientific tests regarding paternity be performed when their result might be that the child would be regarded as a *mamzer*.[73] On the other hand, Justice Ben-Ito has argued that the rule that in certain cases courts will not accept evidence that could lead to an undesirable conclusion, should not exist, since it discriminates against certain litigants. She added that the results of scientific tests regarding paternity are not necessarily contrary to the best interest of the child, since the Rabbinate and the rabbinical courts apply their own rules regarding paternity. A civil court could rule that a person was the child's father; on the other hand the religious authority approached for approval of the child's marriage to a person who cannot marry a *mamzer* could rule that these scientific tests were not sufficient evidence, and therefore the child is not to be regarded as a *mamzer*.[74] In the *Sharon* case the views of Justices Elon and Ben-Ito were *obiter dicta* since Ms Sharon was not married.

Undesirable Consequences of Different Interpretations

Confrontation Between Rabbinical and Civil Courts

Especially when rabbinical courts apply rules concerning spiritual benefit, they interpret the concept of the best interest of the child according to their religious values. Do they thereby fulfil the requirement of the Israeli legislator that rabbinical courts should implement the principle of the best interest of the child?[75] In the past, scholars and Justice Elon held that rabbinical courts could interpret this principle according to their values and beliefs.[76] However, the Israeli Supreme Court has ruled that rabbinical courts are not entirely free in their interpretation. In the *Mor* case[77] the Israeli Supreme Court ruled that they may not base their interpretation only on religious values but must also consider all the relevant data regarding the best interest of the child, such as data about the ability of each parent to fulfil the child's physical and emotional needs.[78]

In the *Biares* custody case the only factors the rabbinical courts considered were that the children were living with their mother and a man to whom she was not married, and that their father was willing to place them in an institution where they would receive a religious education. The Israeli Supreme Court ruled that the rabbinical court should have obtained opinions from experts as to the best interest of the child. It should have taken the initiative and not waited until one of the parties asked for such an opinion. Therefore the Supreme Court ruled that the rabbinical court's decision in this case was not valid. However, if the rabbinical court had considered all the relevant factors regarding the best interest of the child, and its final decision had been that one of the considerations was the fact that the mother was setting a poor example by living with a man who was not her husband, the Supreme Court would have ruled that the rabbinical court's decision was valid.[79]

In the *Bloygrond* case Justice Cheshin read between the lines of the decision of the rabbinical court that the court preferred the father since he was more religious, and therefore would give his son a better religious education. He also held that the rabbinical court had misinterpreted the professional evaluation of social workers regarding the best interest of the child. The rabbinical court of appeal - the 'High' Rabbinical Court - was not willing to accept the request of the representative of the Attorney-General to appoint a specialist psychologist who would present his professional recommendation concerning custody.

Justice Cheshin considered ruling that the decision of the rabbinical court was void. However, in this case there was no clear clash between the religious and secular interpretation of the best interest of the child. Since he was not sure that granting custody to the father was contrary to the best interest of this child he ruled that the decision of the rabbinical court was valid.[80]

If Justice Cheshin's viewpoint prevails in the future it will enable Israeli justices to override sophisticated decisions of the *dayanim* in rabbinical courts who might add to their custody decisions, which attach major importance to spiritual benefit, a statement that they also considered all factors regarding the best interest of the child.[81] Justice Cheshin believes that the court should read between the lines of such decisions of the rabbinical courts in order to determine the real motive of the *dayanim*.

Bridging the gap between the interpretation of rabbinical and civil courts is desirable in order to prevent confrontation between rabbinical courts and their supervising authority, the Israeli Supreme Court. However the aforementioned cases lead to the conclusion that the gap concerning the religious-spiritual best interest of the child is wide and probably unbridgeable.

The decision of the Justices in the Israeli Supreme Court in the *Bavli* case has widened this gap. These Justices ruled that *dayanim* in rabbinical courts should implement doctrines of Israeli law in 'civil' matters.[82] This decision creates a dilemma for the *dayanim* since they claim that the implementation of these doctrines is contrary to their beliefs and values.

Jurisdiction Race

The different interpretations of the rule concerning the best interest of the child in civil and rabbinical courts in Israel is one of the factors that leads to what is called the jurisdiction race.[83] Sometimes the lawyer advises his client speedily to present the divorce suit to that court which would interpret the concept of best interest of the child in a manner most favourable to him. Sometimes people who are not certain that they wish to divorce are hurried into divorce litigation by their lawyers, who warn them that their spouse may present a divorce suit to the court system that will apply the more favourable rules or interpretation for him or her.

These undesirable results of the jurisdiction race should be minimised. Preventing unnecessary divorces resulting from the jurisdiction race certainly best serves the interest of the children involved. In addition, parties to a divorce dispute feel that it is just and fair when legal rules and their interpretation are the same, or at least similar, in parallel court systems. An arbitrary choice of a tribunal by a party could lead to bitterness in the other party.

Bridging the Gap: Practical Methods

Rabbinical Courts

Jewish custody law developed in a few stages as follows: older sources of Jewish law, from the Tanaic and Amoraic period, sometimes mention rules concerning custody. However, the Sages in this period did not state that specific custody rules should not be implemented when they are not in the best interest of the child.[84] The basic principle in Tanaic and Amoraic Jewish sources concerning parental authority was that the father had authority regarding his minor children.[85]

In the medieval period some important Jewish law scholars explained that assumptions concerning custody of children at different ages were not absolute. They ruled that when a parent who, according to these assumptions, should be the custodian, would not raise the child in a suitable manner, custody should be granted to a parent or relative who otherwise, according to these assumptions, should not be the custodian.[86]

In modern Jewish law some *dayanim* in rabbinical courts and Jewish law scholars have held that the best interest of the child is the sole or main consideration in custody cases. They held that since this general rule is the basis for the evaluation of proper custody arrangements, the assumptions regarding custody in old Jewish texts do not always[87] (or according to a similar interpretation of Jewish Law scholars[88] or Rabbinical Courts[89] usually), place in an inferior position a parent who according to these assumptions, should not be the custodian. Some of these Jewish scholars have explained that the supremacy of the concept of best interest of the child results from the general doctrine in Jewish law regarding parental authority. These scholars held that in Jewish law parents have *obligations* towards their children and no *rights* as parents.[90]

However, other *dayanim* in rabbinical courts and twentieth-century Jewish law scholars grant less weight to the general principle of the best interest of the child and more weight to Jewish custody assumptions.[91]

This new interpretation of Jewish law, which ascribes major importance to the principle of the best interest of the child, enables scholars and *dayanim* in rabbinical courts to rule in a similar manner to the civil courts in custody cases, especially when Jewish law assumptions regarding custody could lead to confrontation between rabbinical courts and their supervising authority, the Israeli Supreme Court. This interpretation enabled Justice Elon to argue that the legal scholars should not

> distinguish ... between the policy of Jewish law and the rule of the Israeli legislator in section 25 of the Capacity and Guardianship Law, 5722-1962. It seems to me that there is no essential difference between these two legal systems. I am inclined to claim that there is also no real difference [between these systems] concerning the onus of proof. In both legal systems the major rule requires that the court will investigate, on its own initiative, in every case, what is the best interest of the child, and it should not rely upon a legal assumption (regarding custody) without further investigation (translation).[92]

This new interpretation is a desirable development, and should be applied as far as possible in rabbinical courts in order to bridge the gap between the secular and religious interpretations of this principle.

The gap between the interpretation of rabbinical and civil courts is also partially bridged by the practical method of collecting and evaluating data in rabbinical courts in custody cases. The Chief Rabbinate of Israel has directed all *dayanim* in rabbinical courts in Israel to require the assistance of social workers, and sometimes psychologists, who evaluate all the relevant data and present their professional recommendations in custody cases. The *dayanim* request a professional opinion from social workers on the child's welfare in custody cases where the parents have not reached an agreement as to which of them will have custody of the minor.[93] In practice, the secular perspective of these experts concerning the best interest of the child is important in rabbinical courts.[94]

Civil Courts

Some justices in the Israeli Supreme Court and the Israeli legislator bridge the possible gap between the secular and religious interpretation of the concept best interest of the child by an interpretation that prefers, in the case of girls, a custodian - the mother - who is the preferable custodian according to the custody assumptions of Jewish law. The Supreme Court has also bridged the possible gap concerning paternity.

Custody   The Israeli legislator assumes in section 25 of the Capacity Law that usually the mother should be the custodian of a child who is under seven years old in his best interest. For children at this age it adopts a doctrine of Jewish custody law.[95]

The father of a child up to the age of six in Israel is in an inferior position. He has to present proof and convince the court that there are 'special reasons for directing otherwise', that should lead the judge to the conclusion that in the circumstances of the case departure from the assumption in section 25 is justified.[96]

When the child is older than six the Israeli legislator does not direct the court to prefer the mother or father in custody cases. However, Justices in the Israeli Supreme Court have held that the mother is the preferable custodian of daughters at this age. Justice Elon held that the mother should be the custodian of a daughter before and after the age of six since she is more suitable: her qualifications to understand her and educate her are better than those of the father.[97] Justice Sheinbaum held - in the *Naor* case - that the mother should be the custodian of the daughter when the mother and father are good parents, equally qualified to be custodians, since a mother could fulfil her daughter's emotional needs - for affection, love, understanding - more than a father. He held that this contribution of the mother enables her daughter to develop in a proper manner.[98]

These legal doctrines are contrary to the principle of equality of male and female in Israeli constitutional law.[99]

There are also practical undesirable consequences of this preference of the female. The mother is in an advantageous position in her negotiation with the father regarding the provisions of their divorce agreement. She can receive benefits from the father in return for her consent to grant him certain custody or visitation rights. Sometimes the father consents to giving the mother financial benefits such as more property, maintenance, etc., in return for her consent to grant him the aforementioned rights.[100] The mother can also limit the implementation of the visitation rights of the father when she is the custodian. She can utilise this advantage in her bargaining with her husband/former husband. This advantage of the female is balanced by other factors in the Israeli legal system which favour the male.[101] A very important factor is Jewish divorce law, which is the law applicable to Jews in Israel.[102] It grants the Jewish male a superior status. His major advantage is that he can refuse to grant the divorce writ - the *get*. The female can also refuse to accept the *get*. However, according to Jewish law, when the male refuses to grant the *get*, his wife may not marry another man, but the male can receive a permit to marry another woman after his wife's refusal to accept the *get*.[103] There is perhaps an 'equal' balance between unequal principles. This is not desirable. The goal should be legal rules which enhance equality between male and female. Equality should be achieved without discrimination.

When assumptions regarding custody favour the mother, who is considered the preferable custodian, supposedly in the best interest of the child, there are emotional consequences that do not enhance the child's welfare. Paradoxically, custody assumptions, which should prevent unnecessary emotional damage as a result of custody battles, can at times cause more emotional damage. The best interest of a parent cannot be separated from the best interest of his child. A bitter parent cannot fulfil all the emotional needs of his child, such as love, warmth, understanding, etc. When a father is considered a good parent, equally qualified to raise his child, but he loses the right to be the custodian because the custody assumptions favour the mother,[104] he feels the verdict is not just. The agony emanating from the separation from his children is in most cases accompanied by an economic duty, which is sometimes a substantial monetary burden, to maintain his children. Professor Shifman has pointed out that the mother can also be an emotional victim of the application of these custody assumptions. Society expresses in legal doctrines its expectations that usually the mother should be the custodian, especially of young children and daughters. When she is not made their custodian she is hurt since she feels that the court and society have judged that she is a 'bad' mother.[105]

At the end of the twentieth century the assumption that the mother can devote more time to the child should be re-examined. Many women in Israel go out to work and during their working hours they cannot devote time to their children. Many fathers live with a new spouse. Sometimes, they and their spouse can devote more time to these children.

Psychological theories have also changed. Psychologists hold that children are able to attach themselves emotionally to several individuals.[106] Therefore the assumption that separation of a young child from the mother is graver than separation from the father is sometimes doubtful.

Israel should follow western countries which have abolished custody rules favouring the mother.[107] Perhaps it has not done so in order not to widen the gap between civil and rabbinical courts, which apply

Jewish custody assumptions that favour the mother concerning young children and daughters. However, important twentieth century Jewish law scholars and rabbinical courts hold that the sole or main consideration in custody cases is the best interest of daughters and sons of all ages. This point of view should be the legal rule in section 25 of the Capacity Law and the doctrine of Justices in the Supreme Court concerning custody of daughters and sons.

Paternity In *The Attorney General* case, concerning a married woman, the Israeli Supreme Court adopted an approach which is similar to that of the rabbinical courts regarding the results of scientific tests when the mother is married. The civil court system in Israel accepts the results of scientific tests regarding paternity when the mother is unmarried. The civil courts in Israel are aware of the fact that the status of a *mamzer* is very problematic for the child. They fear that certain results could cause the child embarrassment owing to gossip and hold that they could influence the decisions of the rabbinical courts when they determine the paternity of the child. Therefore the Supreme Court held that defending the child from the severe consequences of being regarded a *mamzer* is more important than an investigation that leads to the true answer.[108]

The aforementioned point of view of Justices Berenson, Sussman and Ben-Ito, concerning the policy of secular courts in paternity cases,[109] was not adopted. The ruling of the Supreme Court in *The Attorney General* case bridges the possible gap between the secular and religious interpretation of the concept best interest of the child regarding paternity.

Was this decision of the Supreme Court necessary? For the purposes of marriage and divorce of Jews in Israel a rabbinical court and the Rabbinate in Israel will not determine paternity according to the findings of a civil court. Only the rules of Jewish law will be applied.[110] If a person is not considered a *mamzer* according to Jewish law the marriage limitations concerning a *mamzer* will not be applied. The possible connection between the paternity ruling of a civil court and the ruling of a rabbinical court in the same matter is doubtful. A gap between civil and rabbinical courts concerning paternity is not necessarily contrary to the best interest of the child. Financial rights, such as maintenance and inheritance from the real father, might be more important for the child than prevention of embarrassment and gossip. Perhaps the child or his guardian or representative should have the right to choose whether performance of paternity tests is in his best interest.

Conclusion

Different interpretations of the concept of the best interest of the child exist in the rabbinical and civil courts in Israel. Civil courts define the best interest of the child according to criteria of professionals in the social sciences, namely social workers and psychologists. Rabbinical courts define the best interest of the child according to their interpretation of the child's welfare and attribute major importance to the child's spiritual benefit. Some twentieth century Jewish law scholars and *dayanim* in rabbinical courts hold that the general principle of the best interest of the child is the sole or main consideration regarding children in Jewish law. This modern interpretation of Jewish law - and the assistance of professionals: social workers and psychologists - bridges part of the gap between the secular and the religious interpretations of the concept of the best interest of the child. There will always remain a gap between the secular and Jewish-religious interpretation of this concept concerning the spiritual benefit of the child. This is a very important consideration in rabbinical courts, while Justices of the Israeli Supreme Court hold 'that there is no significance in religious concerns for the soul of the child'. The new interpretation of Jewish law, which ascribes major importance to the principle of the best interest of the child, is a desirable development and should be applied as far as possible in rabbinical courts in order to bridge the gap between the secular and religious interpretations of this principle.

Notes

*   I wish to thank Dr D. Frimer, who referred me to several important sources.

[1]   See P. Shifman, *Family Law in Israel, II* (Jerusalem, 1989), 27; 241-242; 251 (hereinafter: Shifman, *Family Law, II*); A. Rosen-Zvi, *Israeli Family Law, The Sacred and the Secular* (Tel Aviv, 1990), 27 (hereinafter: Rosen-Zvi, *Israeli Family Law*); B. Schereschewsky, *Family Law in Israel* (Fourth edition, Jerusalem 5753-1993), 241-242, 251; 397, note 1a. (hereinafter: Schereschewsky, *Family Law*).

[2]   See *Goldman v. Goldman* (1959) 13 P.D. 1085, 1091.

[3]   See *Winter v. Beeri* (1961) 15 P.D. 1457, 1466-1467 (hereinafter: *Winter*); *Deutch v. Deutch* (1975) 29 (II) P.D. 525, 529; *Mor v. The Rabbinical Court, Haifa* (1983) 37 (III) P.D. 94, 100 (hereinafter: *Mor*); *Dotan v. Dotan* (1984) 38 (V) P.D. 1, 4; *Shalev v. Shalev* (1984) 38 (II) P.D. 67,75; (hereinafter: *Shalev*).

4 See *Florsheim v. The Rabbinical Court, Haifa* (1968) 22 (II) P.D. 723, 727-728; *Shalev*, 75. However, the husband and wife can agree to grant jurisdiction to a rabbinical court: *Nagar v. Nagar* (1984) 38 (I) P.D. 365, 375, 385 (hereinafter: *Nagar*). Professor Shifman and other scholars have criticised the artificial and problematic distinction between custody and education. See: S. Meron, 'Education as a Factor in Decisions of Rabbinical Courts in Custody Cases' (translation). *Torah Shebeal Peh*, 23 (5742-1981), 101 (hereinafter: Meron, 'Education As'); P. Shifman, 'Child Welfare in the Rabbinical Court', *Mishpatim*, 5 (1974) 423, note 7 (hereinafter: Shifman, 'Child Welfare'); Rosen-Zvi, *Israeli Family Law*, 57, note 42.

5 This linkage enables a party to divorce litigation to link to the divorce suit the matter of education. See Shifman, *Family Law, II*, 242; Rosen-Zvi, *Israeli Family Law*, 57.

6 See P. Shifman, *Family Law in Israel, I* (Jerusalem, 1984), 45-48 (hereinafter: Shifman, *Family Law, I*); Rosen-Zvi, *Israeli Family Law*, 33-34, 65 note 65, 378 note 58.

7 See Shifman, *Family Law, I*, 25-26; Shifman, *Family Law, II*, 241-253; Rosen-Zvi, *Israeli Family Law*, 66-76, 93-99.

8 See Shifman, *Family Law, I*, 25-26; Shifman, *Family Law, II*, 242-243; 249-253; Rosen-Zvi, *Israeli Family Law*, 72-76, 91; Schereschewsky, *Family Law*, 400-404.

9 See *Sidis v. The High Rabbinical Court* (1958) 12 P.D.1528, 1539; *Levi v. The Rabbinical Court, Tel Aviv* (1959) 13 P.D. 1182, 1189-1192; *Bachar v. The Rabbinical Court, Rechovot* (1973) 27 (I) P.D., 568, 572-575; *Plonit v. The Rabbinical Court, Beer Sheva* (1975) 29 (II) 433, 437-442; *Prizand v. The Rabbinical Court, Jerusalem* (1978) 32 (II) P.D. 485-490; *Gothalf v. The Rabbinical Court, Tel Aviv* (1981) 35 (III) P.D. 561, 566-568; *Amrani v. The High Rabbinical Court* (1983) 37 (II) P.D. 1, 10; *Mor*, 107; *Nagar*, 383, 411; *Biares v. The Rabbinical Court, Haifa* (1984) 38 (I) P.D. 673, 683 (hereinafter: *Biares*); *Shani v. Shani* (1985) 39 (II) P.D. 444-448 (hereinafter: *Shani*); Shifman, 'Child Welfare', 429-430; Shifman, *Family Law, II*, 243-253; Rosen-Zvi, *Israeli Family Law*, 61-63; 117-118; 198-199.

10 The Israeli legislator has not defined the concept 'best interest of the child'. Statements of justices in the Israel Supreme Court are the basis of the definition of this concept in legal research. See: A.H. Shaki, 'Main Characteristics of the Law of Child Custody in Israel, With Emphasis on the Application of the "Child's Best Interest" Doctrine', *Tel Aviv University Law Review*, 10 (1984), 5, 15 (hereinafter: Shaki, 'Main Characteristics'). See also: *A.B. v. C.D.* (1957) 11 P.D. 261, 267-268; *Yansen-Zohar v. Zohar* (1981) 35(I) P.D. 1, 19, 26-27 (hereinafter: *Yansen-Zohar*). Frequently in custody cases the optimal best interest of the child is not an achievable aim. Since the parents are getting divorced the child will

not be raised in a warm, united family. In these circumstances the best interest of the child is determined after the examination of priorities. The court will prefer the lesser of two evils: see *Wolf v. Wolf* (1961) 15 P.D. 760, 764 (hereinafter: *Wolf*); *Bulstein v. Bulstein* (1978) 32 (I) P.D. 378, 380-381 (hereinafter: *Bulstein*); *Tzukerman v. Tzukerman* (1980) 34 (IV) P.D. 689, 693-694 (hereinafter: *Tzukerman*).

[11] Religious and civil courts are expected to implement section 3 of the Women's Equal Rights Law. This obligation of religious courts stems from the rule in section 7 of Women's Equal Rights Law, 5711-1951, which directs religious courts to implement all sections of the aforementioned law. See: *Berie v. The Qadi of the Muslim Court in Acre* (1955) 9 P.D. 1193, 1196-1199 (hereinafter: *Berie*); *Biares*, 683. Justices in the Israel Supreme Court held that the best interest of the child is the sole or main consideration in custody cases in civil and religious courts. See: *Steiner v. The Attorney General* (1955) 9 P.D. 241, 251 (hereinafter: *Steiner*); *Deri v. The Head of the Execution by Court Officer, Jerusalem* (1955) 9 P.D. 1938, 1943 (hereinafter: *Deri*); *El-Zafdi v. Binyamin* (1963) 17 P.D. 1419, 1425; *Lorentz v. The Head of the Execution by Court Officer, Haifa* (1963) 17 P.D. 1709, 1716, 1717; *Landerer v. Landerer* (1971) 25 (II) P.D. 258, 269; *Plonit v. Almoni* (1972) 26 (I) P.D. 85, 100; *Seliech v. Arshid* (1981) 35 (I) P.D. 100, 106; *Biares*, 683; *Yechezkeeli v. Yechezkeeli* (1989) 43(II) P.D. 467, 468 (hereinafter: *Yechezkeeli*).

[12] 'The court' is a civil or rabbinical court. Section 16 of Adoption of Children Law, 5741-1981, enables rabbinical courts to rule regarding adoption of children in a manner which is not contrary to the principles of Jewish law. The authority of rabbinical courts in adoption matters stems from the rule in section 27 of this law, which authorises rabbinical courts to rule regarding adoption matters in certain conditions. Regarding authority of rabbinical courts in adoption matters see: N. Maimon, *Adoption of Children, Legal Principles* (Tel Aviv, 1994), 448-453; A. Ben-Dror, *Adoption and Surrogacy in Israel* (Tel Aviv, 1994), 49.

[13] Section 8 of Welfare (Procedure in Matters of Minors, Sick Persons and Absent Persons) Law, 5715-1955, states: 'The Attorney General or his representative may, if in his opinion the interests of any minor, mentally sick person or absent person, so require, institute any proceeding in a court and appear and plead in any trial in which a matter of a minor, a mentally sick person or an absent person is dealt with'.

[14] *Kitvei-Amana (Treaty Series)*, 1038, Volume 31, 221, 224. Signed by Israel on 20.11.89, ratified by Israel on 4.8.91 and valid in Israel as an international Convention from 2.11.91.

[15] See Shifman, 'Child Welfare', 421-438; E. Shochetman, 'The Essence of the Principles Governing the Custody of Children in Jewish Law', *Shenaton Ha-Mishpat Ha-Ivri*, 5 (1978); 285-320 (hereinafter: Shochetman, 'The Essence'); R. Warburg, 'Child Custody: A Comparative

Analysis', *Israel Law Review*, 14 (1979), 480-500 (hereinafter: Warburg, 'Child Custody'); E. Shochetman, 'Rabbinic Court Judgments Entered by a Panel Lacking a Quorum or Based on Incorrect Legal Analysis Concerning the Welfare of the Child - Are They a Basis for Intervention by the High Court of Justice?', *Mishpatim*, 15 (1985), 312-316 (hereinafter: Shochetman, 'Rabbinic Court'); I.Z. Gilat, 'Is 'The Benefit of the Child' a major criterion according to Jewish Law in a Parental Conflict on Custody of the Child?', *Bar-Ilan Law Studies*, 8 (1990), 297-349 (hereinafter: Gilat, 'Is The Benefit'); Y.Z. Gilat, 'The Role of Religio-Halachic Factors in Custody and Rearing Disputes', *Diné Israel*, 16 (1991-1992), 133-166 (hereinafter: Gilat, 'The Role').

[16]   See *Tosefta, Ketuboth*, 5, 5; *Nida*, 2, 5; *Jerusalem Talmud, Ketuboth*, 5, 6 (30, 1[36b]); *Babylonian Talmud, Ketuboth*, 59b; *Mishneh Torah, Ishut*, 21, 16; *Sefer Haturim, Even Haezer*, 82; *Shulchan Aruch, Even Haezer*, 82, 5. See also *Responsa of Rashba (Rabbi Shlomo ben Aderet)*, 7, 492; Shochetman, 'The Essence', 291.

[17]   See Shochetman, 'The Essence', 291. The rabbinical court will not approve agreements between parents or the ruling of a lower court regarding custody when they are contrary to the best interest of the child. See PDR 2: 298, 300; 11: 172-173. See also Shochetman, 'Rabbinic Court', 314, note 107. The policy of civil courts is similar. See *Klein v. Klein* (1971) 25 (I) P.D. 501, 503.

[18]   See *Babylonian Talmud, Ketuboth*, 65b, and *commentary of Rabbi Shlomo Yitzhaki (Rashi)* there, on 'Yotzeh beeruv imo'; and *commentary of Rabbi Yeshayahu di Trani, Tosefot Rid*, there, on 'Yotzeh Beeruv Imo'; *shita mekubetzet, Ketuboth*, 65a , on 'Lav Mishum'.

[19]   See *Mishneh Torah, Ishut*, 21, 17; *Sefer Haturim, Even Haezer*, 82; *Shulchan Aruch, Even Haezer*, 82, 7. See also PDR 7:10;   11:368-396. However, Rabad of Posquieres, in his criticism to Mishneh Torah, held that the mother should not be the custodian of sons up to the age of six since the father should educate his son when he is younger and older than six years old.   Some Jewish law scholars share this point of view. See *Responsa of Rabbi Asher ben Yechiel*, 82 (2); *Responsa of Rabbi Shimeon ben Tzemach Duran*, 1, 40, *Responsa of Rabbi Meir (Maharam) di Buton*, 24; *Osef Piskei Din Shel Harabanut Harashit Leretz Yisrael*, I, 8, 11 (hereinafter: *Osef*, I); *Responsa Minchat Yitzhak*, 7, 113; *Responsa Tzitz Eliezer*, 15, 50.

[20]   Professor Shochetman has explained that this rule is not an explicit Talmudic rule. The legal doctrines in *Babylonian Talmud, Ketuboth*, 65b; 102b; *Bava Batra*, 21a, can lead to the conclusion that this rule exists.   See Shochetman, 'The Essence', 297. Concerning the relationship between custody rules and the obligation of the father to educate his children, see *Otzar Hageonim, Ketuboth, Responsa*, 435; *Responsa of Rabbi Asher ben Yechiel* 82 (2); *Responsa of Rabbi Moshe Mitrani (Mabit)* I, 165; PDR 1:55, 60; 2: 298, 301; 7: 10, 34; *Responsa Yaskil Avdi*, 2, *Even Haezer*, 9;

6, *Even Haezer*, 34; *Responsa Tzitz Eliezer*, 15, 50, 51. Rabbinical courts hold that this rule is applicable to every Jewish father. See PDR 13: 3, 12. Rabbi Meron explained that the *dayanim* hold that the child should be raised by a parent who will grant his child the best education, in his best interest. See Meron, 'Education As', 98. Professor Shifman argues that implemention of the custody assumption concerning a father of a son who is older than six is problematic. Since today the education of religious women has changed, when the parents are religious, both are able to contribute to the religious education of their son and therefore the preference for the father is not justified. When neither parent is religious, since neither takes part in the process of religious education of their children, a custody rule based on an assumption which grants too much weight to the role of the father in the Jewish education of the sons is not relevant. He explains that rabbinical courts apply the same rule regarding every Jewish father since they hold that discrimination between a religious and secular father could be controversial. See Shifman, *Family Law, II*, 248-249. However, there are new trends in rabbinical courts which take into consideration the new role of the mother and the school system in the education of sons. See PDR 7:10, 17, 34; 13:335-336; Meron, 'Education as', 100-101; Shochetman, 'The Essence', 302. See also *Responsa Teshuvot Vehanhagot*, 783, of the ultra-Orthodox rabbi, Moshe Shterenbuch.

[21]   Maimonides held that the father can force a son older than six to be in his custody in an indirect way. He can stop the maintenance payments for a son who is not willing to be in his custody after the age of six. See *Mishneh Torah, Ishut*, 21, 17; PDR 2: 298, 301-303; *Responsa Yaskil Avdi*, 6, *Even Haezer*, 34. However, this rule is controversial and rabbinical courts hold that it is not applicable when the mother should be the custodian in the best interest of the child. See PDR 1: 61-62; Meron, 'Education As', 95, 97-98; Shochetman, 'The Essence', 298. Education of the child is one of the relevant factors which the court should take into consideration when it evaluates what is his best interest. See Meron, 'Education As', 98-100. The father also cannot force a daughter, who should be in the custody of her mother in her best interest, to visit him, by stopping maintenance payments. See *Responsa Yaskil Avdi*, 6, *Even Haezer*, 31.

[22]   See *Babylonian Talmud, Ketuboth*, 102b-103a; *Mishneh Torah, Ishut*, 21, 17; *Sefer Haturim, Even Haezer*, 82; *Shulchan Aruch, Even Haezer*, 82, 7.

[23]   Rabbi Joseph Iben Migash explained that usually the mother is the preferable custodian of her daughter in her best interest. She takes care of her more than the father, teaches her and guides her concerning what the daughter should learn and know in order to fulfil her feminine role in life. See *Responsa of Ri Migash*, 71. See a similar theory concerning the rationale of this rule: *Responsa of Rashba (Rabbi Shlomo Ben Aderet)*,

attributed to Nahmanides, 38; *Responsa of Rabbi Asher ben Yechiel*, 82(2); *Responsa of Rabbi Meir (Maharam) di Buton*, 24.

24 See *Responsa of Maimonides*, 367; *Responsa of Rabbi Shmuel di Medina, Choshen Mishpat*, 308; *Mishpatey Uziel, Even Haezer*, 83, 6; Shochetman, 'The Essence', 304.

25 See the *Responsa of Rabbi Joseph Iben Migash*, note 23. Rabbi Joseph Iben Migash took into consideration the circumstances: the father used to leave his home for other countries and he did not believe he would remain in the future in his place of residence. See also the Responsa of Rabbi Meir Halevi Abulafia: *Responsa of Remah*, 289. Rabbi Shlomo Ben Aderet explained that the mother is considered the best custodian of her daughter since she can enhance her best interest more than the father. However, he added that the court, which is 'the father of orphans', should investigate the matter and grant the right of custody to the parent who will enhance the best interest of the child. See *Responsa of Rashba (Rabbi Shlomo Ben Aderet), attributed to Nachmanides*, 38. Rabbi Moshe Isserlis held that the following rule is the basic principle in the *Responsa of Maharam Padua*, 53: The mother is the preferable custodian of her daughter only when granting her the right to be the custodian is in the best interest of her child. See *Hagahot Harama, Even Haezer*, 82, 7.

26 See *Responsa of Rabbi David Ben Zimra (Radbaz)*, I, 123; *Responsa of Rabbi Moshe Mitrani (Mabit)*, II, 62; *Responsa of Rabbi Shmuel di Medina (Maharashdam), Even Haezer*, 123; *Steiner*, 251-252; *Deri*, 1943-1944; PDR 1: 55, 59-60; 65, 75-76; 145-147; 11: 366-370; 13: 335-337. *Osef*, I, 8, 11; 28, 32, *Osef Piskei Din Shel Harabanut Harashit Leeretz Yisrael*, II, 7, 8 (hereinafter: *Osef*, II); *Responsa Yaskil Avdi*, 6, *Even Haezer*, 30; 32; Rabbi Herzog, *Pesakim Uktavim, Even Haezer*, 7, 91; *Responsa Minchat Yitzhak*, 7, 113; *Responsa Tzitz Eliezer*, 15, 51; Shochetman, 'The Essence', 307-309; *Nir v. Nir* (1981) 35 (I) P.D. 518, 523 (hereinafter: *Nir*).

27 See note 95.

28 See D. Shnit, '"The Tender Years Doctrine" in Solving Child's Custody Disputes', *Tel Aviv University Law Review*, 19 (1995), 185, 187-188. (hereinafter. Shnit, 'The Tender').

29 See notes 97-98.

30 See PDR 4: 66; 13: 335, 336-338; *Osef*, I, 8, 12; 28, 31-32; *Responsa Yaskil Avdi*, 6, *Even Haezer*, 32; 33; 39; 75; *Responsa Minchat Yitzhak*, 7, 113. See also D. Shnit, *The Law, The Individual and the Social Services* (Jerusalem, 1988), 194 (hereinafter: Shnit, *The Law*); Gilat, 'Is The Benefit', 300; Gilat, 'The Role', 144-166; and the circumstances of the decisions of the rabbinical courts which were mentioned in *Mor*, 97-98; *Nagar*, 376-378; *Biares*, 679; *Shani*, 445; *Bloygrond v. The High Rabbinical Court in Jerusalem* (1992) 46 (III) P.D. 423, 443 (hereinafter:

Bloygrond). However, Shochetman holds that the main consideration is not the spiritual benefit of the child. See Shochetman, 'The Essence', 316-319.

[31]   A verse in the Bible states: 'And they shall stumble one brother over the other' (*Leviticus*, 26, 37). The Jewish Sages explain that the verse states that one Jew will stumble through the sins of the other, and consequently all Jews are held responsible for one another. Jews who had the power to restrain their fellow-men from sins but did not will be punished. See A.H. Weiss (ed), *Sifra, Bechukotay* (Vienna, 5622-1962) 7,5 (112 B); *Babylonian Talmud, Sanhedrin*, 27b; *Shebuoth*, 39a; Responsa of Rabbi Joseph Tov Elem: I.A. Agus (ed), *Responsa of the Tosaphists* (New York, 1954), 1. The *dayanim* in rabbinical courts hold that they are obligated not to grant custody to a parent who will educate his child to violate the commandments of Jewish religious law. According to Jewish law if the parent does not do so he commits a religious sin. See Gilat, 'Is the Benefit', 300; Gilat, 'The Role', 148, 157-166.

[32]   See PDR 4: 66, 73-74. In another case, a rabbinical court ruled in a manner which was contrary to the principle of continuity, when professional experts had not presented their recommendations. It rejected the mother's request that moderate religious *Mamlachti Dati* education should continue and accepted the father's request that his son should be educated in the ultra-Orthodox *Chabad* school system. See *Amir v The Rabbinical Court, Haifa*, (1996) 50 (3) PD 321, 327.

[33]   See Shochetman, 'The Essence', 294, note 44; *Osef*, I, 28, 31-32; PDR 13: 335, 337.

[34]   See Shaki, 'Main Characteristics', 14-15; Shnit, *The Law*, 222-225; *Biares*, 684.

[35]   See *Berie*, 1198; *Biares*, 683-685.

[36]   *The American European Beth El Mission v. Minister of Welfare* (1967) 21(II) P.D. 335-336 (hereinafter: *The American*). See also *Steiner*, 250.

[37]   In the *Nagar* case a religious and secular court ruled on the proper education of the children of a religious father and a secular mother. Their rulings reflect the general trend. A civil court held that they should be educated in a secular school, since this was in their best interest, and a rabbinical court held, in the same circumstances, that they should be educated in a religious school. A judge in the civil district court held that the rabbinical court did not fulfil its duty to implement the principle of the best interest of the child. See *Nagar*, 377-379, 381.

[38]   See *Ploni v. Plonit* (1981) 35(IV) P.D. 658, 666. See also a similar consideration in *Plonit v. Almoni* (1972) 26 (I) P.D. 96-97. However see also *Bulstein*, 378.

[39]   Secular evaluation of the facts, by a professional expert, led the judge to the conclusion that religious education, which would be conducive to maintaining a good relationship with the father, was in the best interest of this child. See: *Yechezkeeli*, 467-473.

40   See *Responsa of Rabbi David Ben Zimra (Radbaz)*, I, 263; 360; *Responsa of Rabbi Shmuel di Medina (Maharashdam)*, *Even Haezer*, 123; PDR 4: 332, 333, 335-336; *Osef*, II, 23, 24-25; *Responsa Yaskil Avdi*, 6, *Even Haezer*, 36; Rabbi Herzog, *Pesakin Uktavim*, *Even Haezer*, 7,91; *Responsa Tzitz Eliezer*, 15, 50; Shochetman, 'The Essence', 309, note 102. *Gabai v. Gabai*, P.M., 19, 231, 235; *Biares*, 679.

41   See PDR 4: 332, 333, 335-336. Shifman has criticised this policy of a rabbinical court: see Shifman, 'Child Welfare', 430, note 25. Shifman, *Family Law, II*, 250-251, note 34. However, Shochetman justifies this policy; see Shochetman, 'The Essence', 309, note 102.

42   When a mother was living with a man who was not her husband, but her child had lived with her for many years, so separation from her would be very hard for him, and the father could not take care of his child in a proper manner, and was not sure that the child was his son and had requested that the rabbinical court should investigate the identity of the child's father, the rabbinical court granted custody to the mother. The court explained: 'How can we grant the father the rights of the care, education and custody of the child when he has these kinds of thoughts regarding the child. How could we expect him to treat the child well when he claims that the child is not his?!' (translation). PDR 1:55, 63. See also PDR 1: 145, 157-158; Warburg, 'Child Custody', 498, note 89.

43   The 'fault' of a spouse is one of the factors that civil courts take into consideration when they decide upon the fate of children. In particular, in cases in which both parents are equal according to all other criteria for determining what is the best interest of the child, this 'fault' may be a cause for taking a child from the custodian or not granting custody to a parent. 'Fault' could be improper behaviour of a parent towards the child, or towards the spouse, which led directly or indirectly to the dissolution of the family. There is 'fault' in the behaviour of a parent who destroys the image of his or her spouse in the eyes of the child, since such behaviour endangers the mental health of the child. See Shaki, 'Main Characteristics', 21. However, 'fault' in the behaviour of a parent towards his or her spouse, and even criminal behaviour towards a spouse, is not a decisive cause for taking away custody from a parent. See *Roi v. Roi* (1962) 16 (II), P.D. 1390. The civil court does not punish a parent for bad behaviour or reward him for good behaviour when it decides on custody. 'Fault' is a factor which is taken into consideration when the court has to evaluate whether the character of a parent justifies granting him or her the right to raise the child. It is one factor which, together with other considerations, leads the court to a general conclusion concerning the best interest of the child.

44   In the *Ploni* case the Israel Supreme Court preferred to grant custody to the father, who fulfilled his parental obligation to his children in a satisfactory manner, in their best interests. The mother left her husband suddenly and took the children to her new residence, her lover's home, without the

consent of her husband. The court held that she should not be the custodian since she set a bad educational example for her children and she might mislead them regarding their father's character and behaviour towards her. See *Ploni v. Almoni* (1963) 17 P.D. 2213, 2200-2221. Justice Kister held that in certain circumstances cohabitation of the mother with a person who is not the father is not in the best interest of the child. See *Plonit v. Almoni* (1972) 26 (I) P.D. 85, 97. When, according to secular standards, there was no fault in the behaviour of the mother - cohabitation with a man who was not the father of her children - her behaviour did not lead the Israeli Supreme Court to the conclusion that the father should be the custodian. After seven years of separation from her husband she was not expected to live alone. See *Pat v. Pat* (1991) 45(II) P.D. 297, 299.

45   The Israeli Supreme Court is willing to accept that rabbinical courts apply different standards concerning cohabitation in custody disputes. However, it is not willing to accept an interpretation of the best interest of the child which is based *only* upon this consideration. The rabbinical court should consider all the relevant considerations: economic, emotional, moral, etc. Cohabitation of the mother with a man who is not married to her is one of the legitimate factors that a rabbinical court may consider. See *Biares*, 683-684.

46   See PDR 1:103. See also PDR 1:175-176; 13: 335, 337; *Responsa of Rabbi Shmuel di Medina (Maharashdam), Even Haezer*, 123. When children who were raised and educated in Israel were kidnapped by a parent to another country a rabbinical court held that they should be returned to Israel - their 'natural environment' - in their best interest. See PDR 11:366, 367-369.

47   See: PDR 1:103 107; 7: 3, 8; PDR 13: 335, 337; Warburg, 'Child Custody', 494. See also *Responsa of Rabbi Meir (Maharam) di Buton*, 24.

48   See *Tzukerman*, 695. See also the point of view of Professor Shifman concerning desirable law: Shifman, *Family Law, II*, 227. In the past, different Justices expressed different views concerning enhancement of a child's welfare as a result of his residence in Israel. In the *Amado* case Justice Cheshin held that when a court decides the fate of a Jewish child it should consider the special situation of the Jewish nation in the world. A Jewish child who lives in Israel is saved from assimilation. See *Amado v. Director of Immigrant Camp in Pardes Channah and others* (1950) 4 P.D. 4, 22-23. In the *Hershkovitz* case Justice Goitein held that the best interest of a Jewish child is to be raised in Israel. See *Hershkovitz v. Haifa District Attorney* (1959) 13 P.D. 502. In the *Wolf* case, Justice Cohn wrote that the special importance of residence of a Jewish child in Israel is a well-known fact that does not have to be proven when a court decides regarding the best interest of the child. See *Wolf*, 764. Justice Kister held that a Jewish child should be raised in his nation and culture. See *Tzabar v. Tzabar* (1968) 22(I) P.D. 162, 167. (hereinafter: *Tzabar*); See also Justice Kister in *Plonit*

v. *Almoni* (1972) 26 (II) P.D. 94, and Justice Elon in *Nagar*, 408. However, in the *Martinson* case, the children were Christian and born in Sweden, but the right to be the custodian was not granted to the Christian Swedish mother since there were contrary considerations which outweighed the consideration of raising a child in his nation and culture. See *Martinson v. Bozo* (1986) 40(III) P.D. 498, 503. Statements of Justices in the Supreme Court in the past led Dr Ben-Or to conclude that judges in civil courts in Israel grant special importance to residence of a Jewish child in Israel when they determine what is the best interest of the child. See Ben-Or, 'In the Best Interest of the Child', *Hapraklit*, 29 (1974/75), 608, 614-616 (hereinafter: Ben-Or, 'In The Best'). See also Shifman, *Family Law, II*, 227, note 28. However, Justice Olshan held that these national considerations should not be the sole basis for the decision of the court when it determines what is the best interest of the child: see *Steiner*, 246. In the *Wolf* case, Justice Vitkon held that the national consideration itself is not legitimate. The court should consider it when it coincides with doctrines of developmental psychology. When a child is emotionally loyal and attached to Israel the court will take his feelings into consideration in the best interest of the child. See *Wolf*, 767. He assumed that an Israeli child would be emotionally attached to Israel, and wrote in the *Roi* case that Israel was the natural place of residence of an Israeli child. See *Roi* 1391. See also *Wolf*, 765, 766.

[49] Justice Elon held that the national consideration is relevant when a Jewish child is abducted to Israel. See *Yansen-Zohar*, 25. However, in the *Bulstein* case, children of a Jew, an Israeli national, were returned to Argentina, to their Christian mother, an Argentine national, in their best interest. See *Bulstein*, 378-383. The Israeli civil courts which ruled in habeas corpus proceedings did not want to reward the abducter. They wanted to deter future abductors. They also felt obligated to respect and implement custody rulings of foreign courts. This trend was strengthened in 1991, after the Israeli legislature incorporated the principles of the International Hague Convention into domestic law. Consequently, the need to return an abducted child to his former country is a decisive factor which is more important than the national consideration.

[50] *Kitvei-Amana (Treaty series)*, 1026, p. 43.

[51] See note 53.

[52] See *The American*, 325; *Yansen-Zohar*, 25. When the parents were Christian the court ruled they should raise the child in his best interest. See *Consalos v. Turgeman* (1991) 45 (II) P.D. 626, 650, 653. However, there are limitations. When the child is eighteen years old, he can decide his religion. After he is ten years old he also has to give consent to a change of his religion and there are other limitations. See Capacity Law, Section 13a. See also, concerning adoption, section 5 of Adoption of

Children Law, 5741-1981: 'The adopter shall be of the same religion as the adoptee'.

[53]   When children have a double religious identity, such as children of a Jewish mother and a Muslim father, who are Jews according to Judaism and Muslims according to Islam, the court has to decide concerning their religious identity. A Jewish religious court will declare that they are Jews, and a Muslim religious court will declare that they are Muslims. See *Mizrachi v. The Muslim Court, Nazareth* (1976) 30 (III) P.D. 377, 379 (hereinafter: *Mizrachi*); *Barak v. The Muslim Court, Jaffa* (1987) 41 (II) P.D. 745, 750. (hereinafter: *Barak*). An Israeli civil court will prefer to declare that a child's religion is the religion which is in the best interest of the child. See *El-Zafdi v. Binyamin* (1963) 17 P.D. 1419, 1425-1426, 1429, 1431; *Mizrachi*, 380; *Barak*, 752;   Ben-Or, 'In the Best', 616-619. When each parent wanted the child to receive an education which coincided with his/her religious convictions the Justices in the Israeli Supreme Court were guided by the rule of the legislator in section 25 of the Capacity Law, which directs the court to implement the principle of the best interest of the child. See: *Plonit, Minor, and others v. Ploni* (1995) 49 (I) P.D. 221, 241, 249, 261, 267, 270, 273, 274, 277.

[54]   Israeli legislation concerning custody does not state explicitly that the court should take into consideration the child's wishes although in other matters concerning children, such as adoption, the Israeli legislator rules explicitly that the court should take it into consideration.   See section 30 of the Capacity Law; section 7 of Adoption of Children Law, 5741-1981; section 8 of Youth Care and Supervision Law, 5720-1960, etc. The obligation to take into consideration the wishes of the child, at a suitable age, stems from the interpretation of civil courts of the obligation, in section 25 of the Capacity Law, to enhance the best interest of the child. The court will not want to sadden the child and cause unnecessary emotional stress and harm. Therefore, it will tend not to rule in a manner which is contrary to the child's feelings and wishes. See *Yelin v. Yelin* (1971) 25(I) P.D. 172, 173 (hereinafter: *Yelin*), A.H. Shaki, 'Rethinking Parental "Right" of custody', *Tel Aviv University Law Review*, 9 (1983), 79. (hereinafter: Shaki, 'Rethinking Parental'); Y. Ronen, Shituf Hayeled Bikviat Mishmorto, Tel Aviv (1997), 121-131.

[55]   See Justices Olshan, Silberg and Witkon in *Levi v. The Head of the Execution by Court Officer, Jerusalem* (1952) 6 P.D. 1264, 1265; Justice Cheshin in *Bar v. Bar* (1955) 9 P.D. 1367, 1370-1371; Justices Sussman and Cheshin in *Paltiel v. Paltiel* (1959) 13 P.D. 599, 604-605, 606-607; Justices Kister and Cahan in *Plonit v. Almoni* (1972) 26(I) P.D. 85, 99, 102-103; Justice Cohn in *Yaholomi v. Yahalomi* (1973) 27 (II) 434, 441-444; Justices Cohn and Witkon in *Wolf*, 765, 767; Justice Kister in *Tzabar*, 166-167; Justice Ben-Ito in *Tzukerman*, 694; Justice Netanyahu in *Mazor v. Mazor* (1984) 38 (III) P.D. 37; Justice Beiski in *Plonit v. Almoni* (1989)

43(I) P.D. 661, 666-667; Shaki, 'Rethinking Parental', 79; Shaki, 'Main Characteristics', 33.

56 There are different views concerning the right of a father to force a son older than six to be in his custody, in order to educate him, when the son does not want to be in his custody. See note 21. However, when the son reaches the age of maturity - 13, it is clear that custody will not be granted to the father against the child's will. See PDR 1: 55, 59-61. Rabbi Meir of Padua wrote that when an eleven year old daughter expresses her own will concerning custody the court should fulfil her wish. See *Responsa of Maharam Padua*, 53. See also *Responsa of Rabbi Moshe Mitrani (Mabit)* II, 62; *Responsa Yaskil Avdi*, 6, *Even Haezer*, 39; Shochetman, 'The Essence', 312, note 118; Shaki, 'Rethinking Parental', 78. The general rule in rabbinical courts is that when a child is mature and can decide which custody arrangement is better for him his will should be taken into consideration. See PDR 2: 298, 303. *Osef*, II, 7, 8; Rabbi Herzog, *Pesakim Uktavim*, *Even Haezer*, 7, 91; Schereschewsky, *Family Law*, 407.

57 When a child is not emotionally mature his subjective perspective does not enable him to understand basic elements, such as which custody arrangement will ensure his long term happiness and provide him with more love. Sometimes a child expresses his will because one of his parents pressured him, or explained to him, directly or indirectly, that if he expresses a certain desire concerning his custody, he will please this parent or receive a benefit from him. A child cannot always comprehend and evaluate all the complex short- and long-term considerations that have a bearing upon his decision regarding the preferable custody arrangement. Therefore civil courts take into consideration the child's desires when his will is not contrary to his best interest. See *Yelin*, 173; *Tzabar*, 166; *Plonit v. Almoni* (1989) 43(I) P.D. 661, 667-671. When a child strongly rejects a custody ruling, it will not be enforced, directly or indirectly, by depriving him of his right to maintenence. See *Hess v. Hess* (1967) 21(II) P.D. 738, 740; *Maskil Leetan v. Maskil Leetan* (1969) 23(I) P.D. 309, 323; *Plonit v. Almoni* (1989) 43(I) P.D. 661, 667-671.

58 See PDR 1: 55, 61-62; *Responsa Yaskil Avdi*, 6, *Even Haezer*, 32; 39.

59 See *The Attorney General v. Plonit* (1984), 38(I) P.D. 461, 474-475. The specific circumstances of each case are also taken into consideration. See *Plonim v. Palmoni* (1985) 39(II) P.D. 1, 11.

60 Rabbinical courts ask for a written opinion of professional experts regarding the best interest of the child, or evaluate all the data concerning the best interest of the child and reach their own conclusion. See PDR 11: 153, 156, 157, 161, 171; Shochetman, 'The Essence', 319-320; Shnit, *The Law*, 224. They implement the policy of the Chief Rabbinate of Israel which directed the rabbinical courts in Israel to rule in light of the opinions of professional experts in custody cases. See *Winter*, 1457, 1479 (*Ezer Mishpat*, Responsa 28, p. 342). The *dayan* Goldschmidt explained in the

Winter case that the legal basis of this procedure in custody disputes is the legal obligation of a religious Jewish court to find out what is the best interest of the child since the court is 'the father of orphans'. See also concerning continuity in the *Responsa* literature: Rabbi Herzog, *Pesakim Uktavim, Even Haezer*, 7, 91.

61 See B. Schereschewsky, *'Mamzer'*, *Encyclopaedia Judaica*, 11 (Jerusalem, 1971), 840; *Principles of Jewish Law* (Jerusalem, 1975), 435-436. Schereschewsky, *Family Law*, 51, 354-355; M. Elon, *Jewish Law - History, Sources, Principles* (Philadelphia-Jerusalem, 5754-1994), 827, note 178.

62 See *Bible, Deuteronomy*, 24, 16; 2 *Kings*, 14, 6; *Jeremiah*, 31, 29; *Ezekiel*, 18, 2. *Chronicles*, 25, 4. However, see also *Jeremiah*, 32, 18.

63 See *Chelkat Mechokek*, 9, on *Hagahat Harema, Even Haezer*, 2, 5; *Babylonian Talmud, Kiddushin*, 71a; *Mishneh Torah, Melachim*, 12, 3; *Tosefta, Yevamot*, 12, 8; *Tosefta Kifshuta, Yevamot*, p. 129; *Babylonian Talmud, Sota*, 27a; *Hulin*, 11b; *Jerusalem Talmud, Sota*, 17, 1; *Mishneh Torah, Isurey Biah*, 15, 20; *Sefer Haturim, Even Haezer*, 4; *Shulchan Aruch, Even Haezer*, 4, 15. *Babylonian Talmud, Yevamot*, 80b; *Commentary of Rabbi Shlomo Yitzhaki (Rashi)*, there, on 'Veachsherey'; *Mishneh Torah, Isurey Biah*, 15, 19; *Hagahat Harema, Even Hazer* 4, 14; *Responsa Yaskil Avdi*, 5, 13; Schereschewsky, *Family Law*, 360-362;. Rabbi S. Goren, *Judgment Concerning the Brother and Sister* (translation) (Jerusalem, 1973-5733), 31.

64 See E. Kaplan, C. Brautbar and D. Nelken, 'HLA: Ascertaining Paternity by Means of Genetics', *Tel-Aviv University Law Review*, 7 (1979), 46-74.

65 See *Babylonian Talmud, Niddah*, 31a; *Sefer Haagudah, Shabat*, Chapter 19 (Rabbi Eliezer Demilah), 164, and other sources which are mentioned in the following articles: D. Frimer, 'The Establishment of Paternity Through Blood-Testing in Israeli Law and Jewish Law', *Shenaton Ha-Mishpat Ha-Ivri*, 5 (1978) 225-229 (hereinafter: Frimer, 'The Establishment'); D. Frimer, 'The Establishment of Paternity Through Blood-Testing [A, B, O system] in Israeli Law and Jewish Law' (translation), *Asia*, 5 (5746-1986), 185-209 (hereinafter: Frimer, 'The Establishment, II'); S. Dichovesky, 'Negative Results Concerning Paternity as a Result of HLA Test' (translation), *Asia*, 5 (5746-1986), 163-178; D. Frimer, 'Establishing Paternity by Means of Blood Type Testing in Jewish Law and Israeli Legislation', *Proceedings of the Association of Orthodox Jewish Scientists*, 8-9 (5747-1987), 158-160 (hereinafter: Frimer, 'Establishing Paternity').

66 See note 65.

67 See PDR 2: 122-124; *Responsa Mishpatei Uziel*, 2, 40, 1, 18; *Responsa Tzitz Eliezer*, 13, 104; *Responsa Meshaneh Halachot*, 4, 163-165; and note 65.

68 See Frimer, 'The Establishment', 228-230; Frimer, 'The Establishment, II', 194-197; Frimer, 'Establishing Paternity', 160-163.

[69]   See D.I. Frimer, 'Medical Examinations by Order of the Court and the Right to Privacy: The Common Law and Jewish Law Experiences', *Israel Law Review*, 17 (1982), 100-102; D. Frimer, 'Court Order to Undertake Medical Tests and the Right to Privacy' (translation), *Takdim*, 3-4 (5752-1992), 237-240, especially 240, note 38.

[70]   Rabbinical courts tend not to order paternity tests when the results could be harmful. In the case *241/5748* (unpublished) the *dayanim* Ovadya Yosef, Yosef Kapach and Eliezer Shapira ruled in the case of a married mother. They explained that the results of scientific tests were not considered as sufficient evidence since 'We should not rely upon current (scientific) findings, which might prove to be false in the future, and we should not impose upon the daughter the defect of a "*mamzer*".... Scientific tests are not sufficient in order to rule with certainty (that the child is a *mamzer*) ... more evidence is necessary' (translation). When the statistical probability that the husband was the father was very low and the mother claimed she became pregnant as a result of artificial insemination, and therefore requested that the visitation clause in her agreement with her former husband should not be enforced, and the former husband requested that scientific tests to determine paternity should not be performed, his request was accepted in the best interest of the child. A psychologist and social worker held that the visits of the former husband were in the best interest of the child and therefore the court accepted the request of the former husband. See *Shurat Hadin*, I, 47, 48, 51.

[71]   See *Ploni v. Almoni and Almonit*, (1959) 13 P.D. 903. (hereinafter: *Ploni v. Almoni and Almonit*). Rules of evidence of rabbinical courts are not applied in civil courts. See *Kutik v. Wolfson* (1951) 5 P.D. 1341, 1344-1345. Professor Rosen-Zvi explained that the civil court was willing to let religious law evidence rules prevail in paternity cases since these rules are in the best interest of the child. See Rosen-Zvi: *Israeli Family Law*, 96. This rule is relevant only when the result of the scientific test may be that the child will be considered a *mamzer*, i.e., especially when the mother is Jewish and married. See *Ploni v. Almoni and Almonit*, 903; *Sharon v. Levi* (1981) 35 (I) P.D. 736 (hereinafter: *Sharon*); *The Attorney General v. Plonit* (1994) 48(I) P.D. 711 (Hereinafter: *The Attorney General*). When a married mother was Christian the child would not be considered a *mamzer* according to Jewish law and this rule was not relevant. However, the court held it should consider all the other relevant consequences of this scientific test and it should decide whether to perform the scientific test after it weighs all the pros and cons. The dominant consideration is the best interest of the child. See *Almoni v. Ploni* (1995) 49 (II) P.D 58-61.

[72]   See PDR 1: 147.

[73]   See *Sharon*, 736. See also the critique by Professor Shifman, *Family Law, II*, 51.

[74]   See *Sharon*, 761.

75   Professor Shifman holds that it is not clear whether the rule of section 79 of the Capacity Law should apply to religious courts. See: Shifman, 'Child Welfare', 422-425; Shifman, *Family Law, II*, 242; *Nagar*, 395. However, the Israeli Supreme Court was in no doubt. It ruled that section 79 directs religious courts to implement all sections of the aforementioned law, including sections 17, 24, 25. See *Natzer v. The Rabbinical High Court of Appeals* (1972) 26 (II) P.D. 403, 407; *Sobol v. Goldman* (1979) 33 (I) P.D. 799, 793; *Mor*, 98; *Nagar*, 383; *Biares*, 683; *Bloygrond*, 439; Shifman, *Family Law, II*, 243, note 13.

76   See Shifman, 'Child Welfare', 425-430. Shifman, *Family Law, II*, 243, note 13; Rosen-Zvi, *Israeli Family Law*, 91, notes 28-29; *Nagar*, 408-409. Shifman argues that usually rabbinical courts can implement Jewish custody assumptions. There is no clear contrast with the requirement of the Israeli legislator in section 25 of the Capacity Law since Jewish Law custody assumptions are not strictly binding rules. They are not implemented when in a specific case the court is convinced that the best interest of the child requires that they not be implemented. See Shifman, *Family Law, II*, 250-251.

77   The *dayanim* wrote that they determined custody according to the best interest of the child. However, Justice Ben-Porat ruled that their decision was void since they did not mention any relevant facts which could enable the court to determine what was in the best interest of the child - such as the parents' personality, their economic status, the professional opinion of social workers regarding their qualifications as parents, etc. She was under the impression that the only relevant factor was that the father would grant the children a religious education which the court regarded as a 'spiritual and moral education', while the mother would grant them a secular education. See *Mor*, 94, 98, 107; see also Shnit, *The Law*, 194-195.

78   When a rabbinical court preferred the parent who requested that the child be educated in a religious school and did not evaluate the relevant secular considerations concerning the best interest of the child, the Israeli Supreme Court ruled again that the decision of the rabbinical court was void. See *Shani*, 447.

79   See *Biares*, 683-686. See also the criticism of Shochetman: Shochetman, 'Rabbinic Court', 312-316.

80   See *Bloygrond*, 431-440.

81   See Shifman, *Family Law, II*, 253. See also, concerning a similar possibility in a Muslim court, *Berie*, 1199.

82   See *Bavli v. The High Rabbinical Court* (1994) 48 (II) 221, 236-252.

83   Concerning the jurisdiction race see Rosen-Zvi, *Israeli Family Law*, 49-50, 54.

84   See: *Babylonian Talmud, Ketuboth*, 46b. See also: J. Neubauer, *The History of Marriage Laws in Bible and Talmud* (Jerusalem, 1994), 28-29; 114; (hereinafter: Neubauer, *The History*), M.A. Rabello, '*Patria Potestas*

in Roman and Jewish Law', *Diné Israel*, 5 (1974), 142-143, (hereinafter: Rabello, *'Patria Potestas'*); Scherschewsky, *Family Law*, 40.

85   See: A. Gulak, *Yesodey Hamishpat Haivri*, (Foundations of Jewish Law), C (Tel Aviv, 1966), 66-68, (hereinafter: Gulak, *Yesoday*); Neubauer, *The History*, 114-118; Rabello, *'Patria Potestas'*, 85-149. However, see the interpretation of Dr Gilat: Y.Z. Gilat, 'Do the Financial Rights of the Father over His Children Stem From His Guardianship Role? Jewish Law Perspective', *Bar Ilan Law Studies*, 12 (1995), 119, 157-161. There are also certain rights of the mother regarding her children. See V. Aptowitzer, 'Spuren des Matriarchats im Juedischen Schrifttum', *Hebrew Union College Annual*, 4 (1927), 207-249; 5 (1928), 261-297. See also *Mishnah, Gitin*, 5, 7; *Babylonian Talmud, Gitin*, 55a; B. Scherschewsky, 'Apotropos', *Encyclopaedia Judaica*, 3 (Jerusalem 1971), 218-222 = *Principles of Jewish Law* (Jerusalem, 1975), 441-445; A. Kirschenbaum, 'Orphan', *Encyclopaedia Judaica*, 12 (Jerusalem, 1971), 1478-1479 = *Principles of Jewish Law*, (Jerusalem, 1975), 438-440.

86   See note 25.

87   The *dayan* Goldschmidt held that the best interest of the child is *always* the sole consideration in rabbinical courts. See *Winter*, 1485; PDR 1: 145, 157; See also PDR 3: 353, 358; 11: 366, 368-369; *Steiner*, 252; *Deri*, 1943-1944; Schochetman, 'Rabbinic Court', 314, note 107.

88   Rabbi Eliezer Yehuda Waldenberg held that it is the *main* consideration. He explained that when a Jewish court holds that the father should be the custodian of a child under six or the mother should be the custodian of a son who is older than six, or the father should be the custodian of a daughter who is more than six years old, in the best interest of the aforementioned children, the rabbinical court should grant the right of custody to the parent who will enhance the best interest of the child. He held that custody assumptions of Jewish law are implemented in practice only when the application of the principle 'best interest of the child' leads to the conclusion that the mother and father are equal and they can both enhance the best interest of the child. Only in these circumstances should a rabbinical court grant the right to be the custodian according to Jewish law custody assumptions, and it should implement these assumptions since they are based upon life experience of the Jewish Sages concerning the best interest of the child. See *Responsa Tzitz Eliezer*, 17 (Jerusalem, 5750-1990), 50.

89   The Chief Rabbis Herzog and Uziel and Rabbi Shabtai ruled that two daughters should remain in the custody of their father in their best interest. These *dayanim*, in the High Rabbinical Court of Appeals, explained in their decision that the rule that the mother should be the custodian of daughters is not intended to give preference to the mother in custody cases concerning daughters. The rule is an attempt to determine what is the best interest of the child. The mother and father are equal in custody disputes.

The main and decisive factor in custody of children is the best interest of the children. Therefore when special circumstances justify deviation from custody rules the court will grant custody to the suitable custodian in the best interest of the child. See *Osef*, II, 7, 8. Rabbi Herzog also wrote that the best interest of the child is the 'main consideration'. See Rabbi Herzog, *Pesakim Uktavim, Even Haezer*, 7, 99; Some *dayanim* in rabbinical courts also hold that the 'best interest of the child' is the main consideration in custody cases. See PDR 13: 335, 338.

90   See PDR 1: 145, 157; PDR 3: 353, 358; *Winter*, 1485. Scherschewsky, *Family Law*, 401, explained that the rights of parents regarding their children in Jewish Law are external - to fulfil their obligation to raise and educate their children. There are no internal rights of parents concerning their obligation to children. In the internal sphere they have only obligations. The *dayan* Kapach held in the *Nagar* case that parents have rights and obligations concerning their children according to Jewish law. See *Nagar*, 412. Concerning the rights of parents in Jewish Law see also *Responsa of Rabbi Shmuel di Medina, (Maharashdam), Even Haezer*, 123, PDR 13: 335, 338. There is also no clear connection between the obligations of parents and custody. Parents do not have to be custodians of their children. They can fulfil their obligations when they are non-custodians. The mother does not have to raise her children after the end of the nursing period. See *Shulchan Aruch, Even Haezer*, 82, 2; *Mishneh Torah, Ishut*, 21, 18; *Responsa Yaskil Avdi*, 6, *Even Haezer*, 38. The father is also not obligated to keep his children in his custody. See *Deri*, 1943.

91   See end of *Chelkat Mechokek*, 10, on *Even Haezer*, 82, 7; PDR 2: 298-303; 4: 66, 74; *Plonit v. The State of Israel* (1976) 30 (III) P.D. 561, 565; *Natzer*, 406; Scherschewsky, *Family Law*, 403, note 9; Shifman, 'Child Custody', 426-427; Shifman, *Family Law, II*, 244-247.

92   *Nir*, 523-524.

93   See note 60.

94   Lawyers tend to believe that Jewish law custody assumptions are important in rabbinical courts. The findings of Hedva Porat-Martin concerning the views of lawyers in Israel at 1983, were: 'While theoretically both rabbinical and district courts consider the "interest of the child" to be the prevailing principle behind their decisions in custody cases, in actual fact their interpretation of this principle can sometimes be very different. The *dayanim* consider the mother to be the natural and preferred guardian of her children as long as they are young and require her close attention and love. As the children grow older and their need for education is stronger, the father is considered to be more fitting for this role, especially when Jewish religious education for boys is considered. The generally prevailing concept among the *dayanim* is that daughters should be raised by their mothers so they can learn the womanly virtues - modesty, honesty, and devotion to family life - so prized by traditional Judaism. On the other

hand, boys of school age and older lads benefit from close association with their fathers, who are more adept as religious educators. Thus, among the main considerations lawyers take into account when choosing a forum for their client in matters of personal status are the sex of their client, and the age and sex of the children. A lawyer representing a woman in a custody case will generally prefer to file the suit in a district court, since civil judges tend to allow children of a divorced or separated couple to remain with the mother. When the husband is the client and the children involved are boys, lawyers will prefer to file the case with a rabbinical court where, because of religious considerations, i.e., Jewish education, the father is preferred as the guardian of the children.' - H. Porat-Martin, 'Representation and Its Role In Concurrent Jurisdiction', *Diné Israel*, 10-11 (1981-1983), 35-36. However, since the secular perspective of the experts is important in rabbinical courts the lawyers probably are mistaken when spiritual benefit is not a relevant factor.

[95] See Shifman, 'Child Welfare', 421; Shifman, *Family Law, II*, 244; *Yansen-Zohar*, 37; N. Rakover, *Jewish Law in the Debates of the Knesset* (Jerusalem, 1992), 400, note 6; Gilat, 'The Role', 137; Shnit, 'The Tender', 185, 186.

[96] In the *Roi* case Justice Berinson held that deviation from the rule in section 25 of the Capacity Law is possible only when the father presents strong proof that this deviation is in the best interest of the child. See *Roi*, 1393. In the *Aberbuch* and *Fadida* cases Justice Ben-Porat held that 'special reasons for directing otherwise' are a sincere and serious dispute concerning custody - See *Aberbuch v. Aberbuch* (1985) 39(I) P.D., 65 (hereinafter: *Aberbuch*) - and the child's need to be raised and educated by his mother and father and not separated from the area of residence of one of them - See *Fadida v. Fadida* (1985) 39(III) P.D. 584-585 (hereinafter: *Fadida*). Justice Goldberg held that one reason is also the need of a young child not to be separated from an older sibling, who should be in the custody of his father in his best interest. See *Martinson v. Bozo* (1986) 40(III) P.D. 498, 504. These rulings of these Justices cast some doubt on the claim of Prof. Shnit - which is based upon earlier statements and policy of Justices Cohn and Sheinbaum in the *Zemora* (*Zemora v. Zemora* (1977) 31 (II) P.D. 352-353) and *Naor* (*Naor*, note 98) cases - that it is not enough for the father to prove that he is the more suitable parent for the children and should be their custodian in their best interest. Concerning young children the father has to prove that due to the personality and behaviour of the mother the children can suffer damage and they will not develop properly if they are in her custody. See Shnit, *The Law*, 202-204.

[97] See *Nir*, 523.

[98] See *Naor v. Naor* (1982) 36(II) P.D. 384; quoted in *Plonit v. Almoni* (1989) 43(I) P.D. 667, 670. Concerning preference for the mother in custody cases see also *Roi* 1393; *Aberbuch*, 65; *Fadida*, 65. Professor

Shifman, *Family Law, II*, 232,233 points out that the unequal consequences of the doctrine in section 25, concerning a child over six years old, are more severe at second glance. When some of the children are older than six and some are younger, the court will rule that the mother will be the custodian of all the children in order to prevent separation of siblings from each other. When the mother is the custodian of children who are under six years old she will probably maintain her right of custody after the younger children reach that age. The assumption that continuity of custody with the same custodian is in the best interest of the child acts in her favour. It will be hard to convince the court that the circumstances justify granting custody to the father.

[99]   See concerning equality between male and female; *Labour Party Representatives in Tel Aviv Municipality v. Tel Aviv Municipality* (1988) 42(II) P.D. 145; *Shakdiel v. The Minister of Religious Affairs* (1988) 42(II) P.D. 221, 240-242, 274-277; *Nevo v. National Labour Court in Jerusalem* (1990) 44(IV) P.D. 749-771; *Women's Lobby in Israel v. State of Israel* (1994) 48(V) P.D. 501-542; *El Al v. Danilovitz* (1994) 48(V) P.D. 749-784; *Miller v. The Minister of Defence* (1995) 49(IV) P.D. 94; Rosen-Zvi, *Israeli Family Law*, 137-138; A. Rubinstein, *The Constitutional Law in Israel* (Fourth Edition, Jerusalem-Tel Aviv, 1991), 325-334; F. Raday, C. Shalev, M. Liban-Kooby (eds), *Women's Status in Israeli Law and Society* (Jerusalem-Tel Aviv, 1995), 19-63.

[100]   See Rosen-Zvi, *Israeli Family Law*, 164-165.

[101]   See Rosen-Zvi, *Israeli Family Law*, 157-158.

[102]   See section 2 of Rabbinical Courts' Jurisdiction (Marriage and Divorce) Law, 5713-1953.

[103]   See Rosen-Zvi, *Israeli Family Law*, 138-141, 186; Shnit 'The Tender', 188; Scherschewsky, *Family Law*, 278-279, 293, note 7; 331-337.

[104]   See the circumstances of the *Naor* case: *Naor*, 385. See also *Plonit v. Almoni* (1989) 43 (I) P.D. 664, 670.

[105]   See Shifman, *Family Law, II*, 229.

[106]   In the past a dominant theory was the theory of the psychological parent, who develops a mutual relationship with the child. See J. Goldstein, A. Freud, A.J. Solnit, *Beyond the Best Interest of the Child* (New York, 1973). These scholars held that it is difficult for children to maintain a positive relationship with two parents who are in a situation of conflict. Therefore, the children should develop a psychological relationship with one parent and pay the price of loss of the relationship with the other parent. However, recent research has proven that a child can develop a positive relationship with more than one psychological parent. The decisive factor is warm and stable care by parents, who enhance the material and emotional needs of the child. See Shnit, 'The Tender', 192-193; Shifman, *Family Law, II*, 225.

[107]   See Shnit, 'The Tender', 186, 189.

[108]   See *The Attorney General*, 711.

[109]   See *Plonit v. Almoni and Almonit*, 915; *Sharon*, 759-761.

[110]   See P. Shifman, 'Determination of Paternity as a Matter of Personal Status', *Mishpatim*, 4 (1972-1973), 664, 665-666; P. Shifman, 'Paternity of Children Born by Artificial Insemination', *Mishpatim*, 10 (1980), 63, 82; *Sharon*, 761; *The Attorney General*, 739. See on the other hand the explanation of Justice Elon in *The Attorney General* at 739-740, that results of scientific tests can lead to the conclusion that the child is a *mamzer*.

5   A Note on Children's Rights in Islamic Law

HIS HONOUR JUDGE DAVID PEARL

Introduction

It is often suggested that the language of rights, which will not be explored in detail in this paper, fits uncomfortably in any discussion of the position of the child in Islamic law. Thus, any attempt to develop a universal approach to children's rights is doomed to failure, and theorists and practitioners alike would best be advised to stick to their own patch. Others, alarmed perhaps by the negative and perhaps even damaging result which would be achieved if this view were to prevail, argue strongly that we should at least try to develop universal norms; and point to the United Nations Convention on the Rights of the Child as a good beginning.

Abdullahi An-Na'im, an Egyptian scholar, has raised the question as to how normative universality can be achieved on the rights of the child in general, or the best interests principle in particular.[1]

If one looks at the Convention, one sees that a number of specific as well as general reservations have been made by Muslim states. For example, *Algeria* made reservations to Art 14(1) which lays down that States shall respect the right of the child to freedom of thought, conscience and religion. Algeria has declared that that paragraph shall be interpreted in compliance with the basic foundations of the Algerian legal system and in particular that a child's education is to take place in accordance with the religion of the father as laid down by the Family Code of 1984. *Bangladesh* and *Jordan* have entered a similar reservation to this Article. So far as general reservations are concerned, provision is made by, for example, Djibouti, Indonesia, Iran, Kuwait and Pakistan, that they shall be bound only by those provisions of the Convention which are in conformity with Islam and the Shariah. More particularly, *Iran* on signature declared:

> In signing this Convention, the Islamic republic of Iran is making reservation to the Articles and provisions which may be contrary to the

Islamic shariah, and reserves the right to make such particular declaration, upon its ratification.

On ratification, it 'reserves the right not to apply any provisions or Articles of the Convention that are incompatible with Islamic laws and the internal legislation in effect'. Finally, *Egypt* expressed its reservation with respect to all the clauses and provisions relating to adoption, in particular to Articles 20 and 21.

It is therefore of some interest to see whether any concept of universality can be attained in the light of such far sweeping reservations. Are the well known principles of the Convention incompatible with the generally understood substantive laws of the Shariah as it applies to the law of children?

One fundamental issue, identified amongst others by Geraldine Van Bueren,[2] shows that whereas the Convention emphasises equality of parenting as a norm, Islamic law has developed a series of norms whereby the responsibility for the early life of a child is that of the mother and the later life that of the father. The ages where physical custody, or *hadana,* of the mother is transferred to guardianship, or *wilaya,* of the father will vary from school to school, but the principle remains the same in all Islamic schools. Is this division of responsibility compatible with the internationally recognised norms? Van Bueren points to the practical difficulty underlying this question because, as she says, it is difficult to see how international child abduction can be countered if it is regarded as the religious legal responsibility of the mother to look after the younger child and the exclusive religious legal responsibility of the father for the older child. This, in effect, exposes universality principles in a stark form.

There is a clear tension, in the sense defined by An-Na'im, between commitment to indigenous perspectives and self-reliance on the one hand, and the realities of under-development and dependency of the Islamic world on Western intellectual and technical resources and expertise, on the other. An-Na'im himself, in my view adopting a pragmatic approach, redefines 'best interests' in the Arab, and I would say wider Islamic perspective, as 'basic needs of the child'.[3] Using this approach, he argues strongly for an emphasis on procedures and processes to ensure what he calls 'dynamic diversity of perspectives'.

Parents and Children under Islamic Law

It is necessary to set out if only in briefest outline the substantive law of parent and child in the Islamic tradition. For the moment I draw no distinction, except where I expressly mention it, between a male and a female child.

A child has no legal capacity in Islamic law, based in effect on the Islamic principle of *'akl* (reason). Thus, without reason there can be no act which carries with it a legal consequence. The child acquires capacity, and thus ceases in effect to be so described, when he reaches the age which Islamic law presumes him to have acquired *'akl*. This is different in the various schools, but it would appear that a so-called 'empirical test', as described by the Israeli scholar, Meron,[4] has been adopted; namely the 'maturity of mind' (*rushd*) in the context of certain transactions[5] which enables the child a limited capacity.

Thus Islamic law, as a general proposition, creates a system of steps. Below a certain age, in Hanafi law 7, the child is totally incapable. Above that age, when of 'perfect understanding' he can participate in legal acts, but these acts are the subject of interdiction by the guardian or *wali*, if this is 'in the interests of the minor'. After a certain age, interdiction is no longer possible. In contrast, the guardian, usually of course the father, has complete power over his ward in the sense both of his property and his person. The most extreme perhaps is the power to contract his minor ward in marriage, although on attaining puberty the child has a right to annul the marriage. The inter-relationship between capacity and power is put graphically by the mediaeval Muslim scholar, al-Misri in his chapters on prayer:

> when a child with discrimination (meaning he can eat, drink and clean himself unassisted) is seven years of age, he is ordered to perform the prayer; and when ten, he is beaten for neglecting it.[6]

It has been suggested by Nasir[7] that a child's first right is to establish parentage. This provides the child with rights of maintenance, of expectation of custody and guardianship relating to maintenance, shelter, religious education and health provision, and of fixed inheritance provision. Nasir, adopting similar language to that of An-Na'im, states that 'it shall be the duty of the parent to ensure that such needs are satisfied with the interest of the child deemed paramount to any other consideration'.[8]

It is important to state that the concept of illegitimacy is rare in Islamic law. It can arise only when a child is born of parents who *cannot* be married to each other. Examples of such prohibitions would be where the father is a non-Muslim or within the 'prohibited degrees of relationship' with the mother. Otherwise, once paternity has been established, by the doctrine of *ikrah* or acknowledgment, there is a presumption in law that the mother and father are married to each other.

Adoption, a matter on which many Muslim states[9] have made reservations to Article 21 of the Convention, is generally speaking not acceptable to any section of Islamic law, although variants of adoption techniques have been introduced. There is a specific verse in the Qu'ran[10] which would appear to prohibit adoption. 'Nor hath He made those whom ye claim to be your sons your sons.' The Islamic variant (*kafala*) enables a child to be brought up in another family but without inheritance rights.

The father is under a legal obligation to maintain the child, as part of his responsibility as *wali*. If the father dies, then according to the Sunni Hanafi school, responsibility falls on the mother, at least to some extent. In Maliki law, this does not happen, and the mother has no responsibility even if the father is dead, the financial responsibility remaining with the male agnatic relatives. Section 974 of the *Mejelle* reserves guardianship to the father alone and in his absence to other agnatic male relatives, following the Hanafi law in this area. So far as *hadana* is concerned, or physical custody of the child, the mother has sole responsibility, and in her absence this devolves to female relatives on the mother's side.

Perceptions

The perception in the Western world of Islamic law is of a system of law based on a divinely inspired set of principles stemming from a different age, which provides limited rights to children in general and to girls in particular. It is perceived that marriages can be arranged without the consent or even involvement of the child, and solemnised at an early age. The child has no say at all in his educational preference or in his religious upbringing. Discipline is a matter for the person with guardianship who will be the father, or in his absence a male agnatic relative. The mother has only limited responsibility for the child during the early years, and even then it is possible for her to lose even this limited responsibility in certain situations. It is even possible that her conduct as a wife will be viewed as relevant to her ceasing to have continuing contact with her child. The mother is herself dependent on her husband for her own support and residential requirement. In classical Islamic law, with a possibility of polygyny available to the husband, the mother and her children will have to share the support of the husband with other wives and children, albeit that they have to be treated 'equally' at least in theory. Inheritance rights are fixed, but the female child is entitled to only half that available on inheritance to the entitlement of the male child.

Islamic writers and others would view this description of rights of the child in Islamic law with some circumspection. Indeed, Geraldine Van Bueren has said that the very concept 'that children possess rights has a far older tradition in Islamic law than in international law, where the notion did not emerge until the twentieth century'.[11] That of course may well be, although it is worth bearing in mind that other writers such as Goonesekere[12] have suggested that the concept of paternal power enabled adult interests to prevail over the health and developmental needs of children. But it is also true that many of the provisions of the Convention have not had reservations attached to them by Islamic states, and some Islamic states have of course refrained from introducing any reservations at all.

There is, as is suggested, ample scope for dialogue, especially because modern Muslim scholars would mostly agree that many of the legal principles in this area of child law are developments of *Ijma* or consensus of the scholars (in particular using the notion of *ijtihad* or independent search) rather than being categorically based in Quranic verses or Hadith literature being attributable directly to the Prophet or his immediate followers. Thus divine law it may be; but open jurisprudentially to development in a way that other areas of the law, such as inheritance rights for example, are not.

It is clear that some Pakistan and Bangladesh cases in particular illustrate that courts, when applying the Islamic law, have departed from the strict rules if, in a particular case, such a strict application would involve a decision against the interests of the minor, although the stress is always laid 'from a Muslim point of view'.[13] Some countries in the Muslim world have introduced laws in this area, such as Tunisia in relation to adoption. There have been some reforms in the inheritance field, especially providing rights to orphaned grandchildren and equalising the inheritance rights of males and females. Child marriages have been tackled by a variety of strategies, and polygyny also (which obviously affects children's rights) has also been contained by making it incumbent on a person wishing to take a second wife to seek permission, usually from a court. There have also been a number of specifically Islamic declarations on rights of children; and reference is made to the Charter on the Rights of the Arab Child, and the Cairo Declaration on Human Rights in Islam.

But the court decisions dealing with the few cases which go to litigation; the limited reforms in a few Muslim countries; the rather vague terminology of the few Charters and Conventions: do these factors affect in any meaningful way the clear fact, that for the vast bulk of children living in families in the Muslim world, as perceived through Western eyes, their rights are limited, if existent at all? The answer I must give, from my review of the literature in the field is 'no'. The major question which then follows of course is whether this matters. Rights, as contained in the Convention, are not universal at the present time. The Convention is understandably preoccupied with the issues of the Western world, and an attempt to reconcile culture and human rights singularly fails.

Onora O'Neill[14] talks despairingly of the Declarations and Charters constantly urging 'those who are powerless to claim their rights and so to take the first step away from dependence'. She has little to say in favour of the language of rights in this area. From a different perspective, I support, amongst others, the views of Freeman who disagrees with O'Neill. He says '[a] child deprived of the sort of rights envisaged in the UN Convention will grow up very differently from one accorded them'.[15] Or at least I agree with Freeman in the generality of his comment as it affects the children I know and grew up with. He does not address the universality issue; and in this context it is my view that it would be better to adopt the approach of An-Na'im.

An-Na'im proposes 'the establishment of procedures and processes to ensure not only dynamic diversity of perspectives ... but also opportunities for subsequent contestation, revision and change of such action'.[16] Thus procedural universality is an achievable goal; substantive universality is not, and should not even be attempted. In effect I agree with John Eckelaar[17] when he says:

> The presumption is that the best response to whatever issue has arisen may lie within the child, even though the child may need direction to an accommodation with the social world surrounding it, rather than in a manipulation of that social world to which the child is left to respond.

We ignore the social world surrounding the child at our peril. [18]

Notes

1 'Cultural Transformation and Normative Consensus' in Alston, P. (ed) *The Best Interests of the Child* Clarendon Press, Oxford (1994) at p. 62.

2 *The Best Interests of the Child - International Co-Operation on Child Abduction*, Programme on the International Rights of the Child, QMWC, London (1993).

3 See above n 1.

4 Meron, Y. 'Parents and Children under Moslem Law' Vol X *Jewish Law Annual* 213.

5 Sections 986, 969 and 973 of the *Mejelle*.

6 Ahmad Ibn Naqib al-Misri, *The Reliance of the Traveller* in Arabic, with facing English text, Commentary and Appendices edited and translated by Noah Ha Mim Keller, Modern Printing Press, Dubai 1991 at p. 109.

7 Nasir, J.J. *The Islamic Law of Personal Status*, Graham and Trotman, London (1986).

8 Op. cit. at p. 140.

9 E.g., Kuwait and Egypt.

10 Sura XXXIII, 4-5.

11 Above n 2 at p. 51.

12 Goonesekere, S. 'The Best Interests of the Child: A South Asian Perspective' in Alston (ed) above n 1 at p. 117.

13 An old case is *Mohammed Bashir v. Ghulam Fatima* 1953 PLD Lahore 73. See generally Pearl, D. *Textbook on Muslim Family Law*, Croom Helm, London (2nd ed: 1987).

14 'Children's Rights and Children's Lives' in Alston, P. et al (eds) *Children, Rights and the Law* Clarendon Press, Oxford (1992) at p. 24.

15 Freeman, M.D.A. 'Taking Children's Rights More Seriously' in Alston et al above n 14 at p. 59.

16 Op. cit. at p. 80.

17 'The Interests of the Child and the Child's Wishes: The Role of Dynamic Self-Determinism' in Alston (ed) above n 1 at p. 58.

18 For commentaries which have heeded this message, see King, M. 'Children's Rights as Communication' (1994) *Modern Law Review* 385; Freeman, M.D.A. and Veerman, P. *The Ideologies of Children's Rights* Martinus Nijhoff, Dordrecht (1992); King, M. (ed) *God's Law versus State Law* Grey Seal, London (1995); Hamilton, C. *Family Law and Religion* Sweet & Maxwell, London (1995).

6 'Honour Thy Father and Thy Mother': Children's Rights and Children's Duties

ANDREW BAINHAM

Introduction

Honour thy Father and thy Mother: that thy days may be long upon the land which the Lord thy God giveth thee.[1]

If we were to look for a 'traditional value' which best describes the historical relationship between children and parents we could do worse than start with the familiar fifth commandment. But just what does respect for parents entail in the late twentieth century? As far as English law is concerned the recent tendency has been to deny that parents have 'rights' as such and to reconceptualise their position solely in terms of 'responsibility'.[2] The emphasis is on their 'duties' and there has been a distinct downgrading of any proprietorial claims over children which they might be inclined to assert. This trend has been accompanied by much greater interest in the whole subject of children's rights[3] evidenced in particular by the extremely widespread ratification of the United Nations Convention on the Rights of the Child.[4] This view of children as the bearers of rights raises the question of how much respect is due to parents - this time from the children themselves. Put succinctly, in these days of liberation and self-determination[5] how far do children have *duties*, both in relation to their parents and in relation to wider society?

I seek to explore these issues under two broad headings which distinguish respectively between the duties which *children themselves* may owe to their parents and the respect which *other decision-makers* may owe to them in the discharge of their parental functions. First, I address specifically the question of children's duties, arguably neglected both in English law and in academic commentaries. I seek to demonstrate, with the aid of a few examples, the need for more explicit recognition of the duty aspect of the child's legal position. I then return to the more familiar theme

93

of the proper weight to be attached to the parental position where important decisions affecting children are taken. The question here, in essence, is whether the traditional value of respect for parents can be properly accommodated while promoting the new value of respect for children as persons possessing rights. Here I return to some tentative arguments which I first presented in Oxford in 1993[6] and I seek to develop these further.

Children's Duties

So then, from the child's perspective, what does it mean to 'honour father and mother'? It sounds as if we ought to be able to find somewhere a neat little list[7] of legal duties owed by children to their parents. But I can confidently predict (since I have tried it) that if we were to ask most academic family lawyers in England what legal duties children have we would be met with blank expressions at worst and unconvincing waffle at best. The truth of the matter is that is extremely difficult to find *any* express acknowledgment in the law that children owe their parents *any* duties.

The closest that the common law came to doing so was probably the adaptation of the master's right to sue for loss of his servant's services. This was extended by analogy to enable a parent to sue for the loss of his child's services so that, from the mid-seventeenth century, it became an actionable tort to do any act which deprived a parent of his child's services.[8] There is no doubt that this action was grounded in an independent parental claim and that the parent had to prove that the child in question did owe, and did perform, some service for him - even if this amounted to no more than making tea![9] The requirement was real and meant that no action could lie for injury to a child too young to render any services, such as the hapless two year old run down by the defendant's carriage in *Hall v Hollander*.[10] In due course the action fell into disuse and was eventually abolished.[11] Since then the Court of Appeal in *F. v. Wirral MBC*[12] has ruled that there is no tort of interference with parental rights (now parental responsibility). There is thus no longer any independent parental cause of action arising from any duty owed by the child to the parent. In the modern law, such legal obligations as children may have, invariably seem to arise by implication. Thus, children are criminally liable with qualifications from the age of ten[13] and without qualifications from the age of fourteen and are in principle (again with qualifications) liable for their own tortious actions.[14] From this we can say that they have a legal duty to refrain from committing criminal or tortious acts to the extent of their evolving capacities as children. More *positive* duties, and duties imposed directly on children *qua* children are difficult to find. Again, if they exist at all, they exist by implication.

There is no better example than education. One would think that the very existence of a compulsory education system would involve a duty on children to attend school.[15] Yet this is not the case. The statutory duty is not the child's but the *parents'*. The duty, under legislation dating from 1944,[16] is to ensure that every child (between the ages of 5 and 16) receives an efficient full-time education suitable to his age, ability and aptitude either by regular attendance at school 'or otherwise'.[17] Truancy is a major problem in England, yet the enforcement mechanisms relating to school attendance are invoked against the *parents* and not against the child.[18] I would not argue that either the parents' statutory duty or the enforcement measures which can be taken against them should be removed. But I think there is a case for incorporating in the education legislation an express duty on the part of the child to attend school. The absence of such a duty implies (I think wrongly) that children are under the complete control of their parents up to the age of 16. The reality is surely that many truants, especially those at the older end of the spectrum, are beyond the control of their parents and ought to be taking some responsibility for their own actions. Indeed, it has even been suggested by one commentator[19] that some children under compulsory school-leaving age might have enough maturity and intellectual capacity to exercise a choice to leave school. There are difficulties with this view which I will not explore further here,[20] but it does rather focus attention on the increased autonomy some people are inclined to give to adolescents. The central point is that if children are to enjoy more independence in the educational sphere and elsewhere thought needs to be given to creating a framework of responsibility within which this greater freedom of action is to be exercised.

This leads me to my general thesis about children's duties which applies, by analogy to children, the so-called 'exchange view' of parenthood.[21] According to this theory, parents have rights *because* they have responsibilities and they have responsibilities *because* they have rights. A similar reasoning can be applied to children. In crude terms, the younger the child the less legal capacity that child is likely to possess and the less justification there is for imposing duties or responsibilities on that child. But with gathering independence, as the child gets older, should come increased responsibility. The child should acquire this responsibility precisely because he or she is given more decision-making capacity. In short, what is true for parents is also true for children. Children too have responsibilities *because* they have rights and the law should recognise this. If this is a reasonable model, how might it work? I have already suggested that one duty which might be put on a statutory footing is the duty to attend school. I will now take a couple more areas which relate more directly to the parent-child relationship.

My first example is one with which students of criminal law will be familiar - the 'shallow pool' scenario. Under English criminal law there is no duty of easy rescue so that a bystander who watches a child drown in a shallow pool without going to the child's assistance commits no criminal offence however easy it might have been to intervene and however morally reprehensible not to do so. The position is different for a parent. The parent, *by virtue of his relationship with the child,* has a duty to act and will be liable for the murder or manslaughter of the child depending on his mental state. Others, such as relatives or childminders, can similarly be held criminally responsible not because of their relationship with the child *per se* but on the basis that they have assumed the *de facto* care of the child. This reasoning also applies where the care of an adult has been assumed.[22] Well, adults can also drown, albeit less easily, in shallow pools. What about the following hypothetical example. Suppose that Child C (a healthy and able-bodied teenager) has always disliked his father F. One day F, in a drunken stupor, falls into the shallow end of the family swimming pool. C, who is on hand and could easily assist, instead watches F drown. We will assume that there is no question of C having assumed the actual care of F. The question is whether C, *by reason only of the relationship of child to parent* is, or ought to be, criminally responsible for his failure to act. The answer is that he is probably not liable since the general principle of the responsibility of parents for children has not been applied in a reciprocal way. But perhaps this is another area of the law in which legal duties of children could be acknowledged.

My second example relates to what we in the United Kingdom now call 'contact' and others still call 'access'. We have heard a great deal about the new conceptualisation of contact as a right of the child.[23] There has also been a certain amount of debate about whether it ever was, or still is, a right of the parent.[24] It has also long been regarded as a parental duty in the indirect sense that the residential/custodial parent has been expected to co-operate over contact arrangements between the non-residential/non-custodial parent and the child. The courts have repeatedly asserted that they will not allow beneficial contact to be obstructed just because it is opposed by the parent with care, although in practice enforcement has been problematic.[25] More recently, we have seen the first signs of children themselves trying to force an 'absent' parent to maintain contact with them on the basis that it is their right and that the recalcitrant parent is under a corresponding duty.[26] But we have heard very little, if anything, about the *duty* of the child. I would argue that we are talking here about the *mutual* society of parent and child and would propose that the child claiming a right to contact should be under a corresponding duty - with rights come responsibilities. It might be objected that, in some instances, contact will not be in the child's best interests and that it would be quite wrong to put pressure on the child to see a parent in these circumstances. True enough, but the very principle of contact (whether described as the right of the child or the right of the parent or both) is qualified and limited by the welfare principle.[27] Thus, neither the child's right, nor the parent's right is absolute. With this limitation in mind, why not place children under a prima facie duty to maintain contact with their parents? The older and more independent the child, the greater may be the scope for such a duty. Perhaps the time has come to recognise the importance to parent and child of maintaining contact with each other by the clear enunciation in legislation of reciprocal rights and duties. With very high rates of divorce and separation there is widespread concern about the loss of parents, especially fathers, which many children experience. But this cuts both ways - might not 'honouring father' in the post-divorce context mean making an effort to stay in touch with father?

These are just some areas in which we might want to think more seriously about the duties of children and young people. Many more instances could doubtless be conjectured. And we ought also to note that there is no *general* duty in English law to honour parents corresponding with that in the Decalogue or with the provision in the Israeli legislation referred to in Professor Falk's contribution below.[28]

Children's Rights and Respect for Parents

The recent promotion of children's rights by the international community is taking place within the context of respect for parents and family life. The United Nations Convention on the Rights of the Child recognises in the Preamble the need for protection of the family 'as the fundamental group of society and the natural environment for the growth and well-being of all its members and particularly children'. It goes on to state 'that the child, for the full and harmonious development of his or her personality, should grow up in a family environment in an atmosphere of happiness, love and understanding'. When we turn to the body of the Convention we find several substantive provisions which directly acknowledge the duty to show proper respect to parents. Thus, Article 3(2)[29] requires states parties in ensuring the care and protection of the child to take into account the rights and duties of, *inter alia*, the parents. Article 5[30] requires them to 'respect the responsibilities, rights and duties of parents to provide, in a manner consistent with the evolving capacities of the child, appropriate direction and guidance....' Article 14(2)[31] is in similar vein and Article 29,[32] dealing generally with education, requires that the education of the child be directed to, *inter alia*, 'the development of respect for the child's parents ...' This latter provision is mirrored to some extent in the European Convention on Human Rights and Fundamental Freedoms which, in stating the general right to education, requires states parties to 'respect the right of parents to ensure such education and teaching in conformity with their own religious and philosophical convictions'.[33]

Such international statements encapsulate the dilemma which has had to be faced domestically, in England and elsewhere, for many years and increasingly over the last decade or so - just how much weight has to be attached to the parents' position when giving effect to children's rights? And, where the interests of parents and children appear to conflict, what basis can be found for preferring the interests of one rather than the other? A trite answer to these questions might be that of course we prioritise children. Is this not the thrust of the international commitment to children in the UN convention and do we not, domestically and internationally, have a 'welfare principle' which makes this plain? The best interests of the child are either 'paramount' or at least the 'primary' consideration.[34] In my view such a response would be an immature and unsophisticated approach to the complexity of human relationships and to the interpretation of the laws which regulate them. In my Oxford paper[35] I put forward some tentative suggestions about how the law might attempt to strike the right balance. The paper was largely concerned with decision-making involving adolescents and with conflicts of interest between parents and children at divorce. Both of these subjects have received the extensive scrutiny of academics and I do not propose to rework them again here.[36] Rather. I will summarise briefly my earlier argument and then attempt to refine it with the aid of two recent and controversial decisions in England. These deal, respectively, with the alleged sexual abuse of children and with disputed paternity.

In my earlier paper[37] I argued that it is a fundamental mistake to assume that we can ever come up with a legal formula which could lead to a universal priority being given to the interests of children over parents or vice-versa. I suggested that it was rather a question of putting the specific issue into context and weighing the competing interests in that context. In order to do this I argued that it would be necessary to devise a criterion for evaluating and ranking the respective claims. In essence I thought that it all came down to measuring *what is at stake* for the child and the parents. This would require one interest to be designated as the superior or 'primary' interest and the other as the subordinate or 'secondary' interest. Preference ought then to be given to upholding the primary interest which might be the child's but, equally, might be the parents'. The more fundamental the interest, and the more serious the potential consequences of failing to uphold it, the more likely it would be that it would be regarded as the primary interest. I concluded my paper with some examples of how this might play out in practice. Without reiterating my reasoning, I suggested that in lifesaving cases there were sound reasons for designating the child's interests as primary and the religious objections of parents to surgery as secondary. Conversely, I felt that where the issue was whether divorce should be made available there were good reasons for regarding the parents' interests as primary and the child's as secondary. I also considered the issue of taking a child abroad against that child's wishes and thought that this was a marginal or borderline case.

I am now inclined to think that this balancing or weighing process may need to accommodate an additional component. A third factor or interest may need to be thrown into the equation which might be described as the 'collective family interest'. In short, children are not just individuals, with individual interests. They are also members of a family unit and have an interest which forms part of the collective interests of that unit. The same point can obviously be made in relation to parents. They too are individuals with independent interests but are also part of the family community. While, therefore, it may be a necessary condition for upholding children's rights that children be accepted as individual persons with claims and interests which are independent of, and can conflict with, those of their parents[38] this is not the complete picture. There may also be a collective interest of the family (of which they are part) which needs to be taken into account. And it is conceivable that, in some instances, the combined interests of the parents and the family taken as a whole may outweigh the interests of a particular child. There is perhaps a flavour of this thinking in *Re C (A minor)*.[39] In that case a 14 year old girl had sought the leave of the court to apply for a residence order and a specific issue order under the Children Act 1989[40] to enable her to live with a friend's family and to take a holiday in Bulgaria with them. In refusing leave for the 'holiday' application and adjourning the residence application, Johnson J. was plainly influenced by the interests of the family as a whole and by the feeling that these were issues which ought to be resolved internally with the wider interests of the family in mind.[41] So perhaps this was one case in which the family's interest was given priority over the child's prima facie claim to bring the dispute to court. Although the judge did not explicitly reason it this way it is possible that he took the view that what was at stake for the girl individually was less than what was at stake for the family as a whole.[42]

It is this broader family interest, existing as a distinct entity separate from the rights and interests of individual family members, to which Leora Bilsky may in part be referring in her contribution to this volume.[43] There is force in her argument that too great a concentration on individual rights can result in a dilution of the interests of communal units such as the family. And, in a rather different context, I am reminded of the current Danish debate about the 'family principle' versus the 'individual principle'.[44] This is concerned with whether, in order to secure the equal treatment of families inside and outside marriage, social legislation should assess the constituent members of the family as separate individuals (the individual principle) or as part of a family unit (the family principle). While these issues are far removed from the subject of the present discussion, the Danish example again draws attention to the existence of a community interest in the family which is at least distinguishable from the interests of its individual members. If indeed it exists, how might this distinctive family interest be incorporated in the earlier analysis and might it lead to different conclusions? I will try to approach this by looking at two significant decisions of the English courts.

The first is the decision of the House of Lords in *Re H (minors) (Sexual Abuse: Standard of proof).*[45] This case was concerned with the correct standard of proof required before a child could be said to be likely to suffer significant harm and, hence, be made the subject of a care or supervision order.[46] A girl of 15 alleged that she had been repeatedly sexually abused by her mother's cohabitant. The man was charged with rape but was acquitted. The state acting through the local authority was concerned enough about three younger girls in the same household that it wanted to make them the subject of care orders. The problem was that it had not been proved that the alleged abuser had in fact abused the eldest girl. It was her word against his, and the jury in the criminal trial, it must be assumed, were not prepared to believe her. The judge in the care proceedings was suspicious however that she had been abused and thought there was a real possibility that she was telling the truth. But he felt unable to make the care order in relation to the younger children because he could not be sure to the 'requisite high standard of proof' that the criteria for the order were satisfied.

By a narrow majority of 3-2[47] the House of Lords dismissed the appeal from the Court of Appeal which had upheld the judge's decision. The arguments and the reasoning in the Lords were highly technical. In essence, the majority decided that the standard of proof was the ordinary civil standard of balance of probabilities but that suspicion alone was not enough to satisfy this. It was necessary to adduce evidence which was simply not present in this case. Here the only relevant evidence was the unproven allegations of the eldest girl. It was however acknowledged that there could be cases where the totality of the evidence could produce a combination of 'profoundly worrying features' which together might be sufficient to establish the necessary risk to the child. The minority[48] in contrast took the view that the allegations of the eldest girl, which triggered the suspicions, were still evidence which could be relied upon in making a prognosis of risk. It was not, they thought, absolutely necessary to substantiate the truth of the allegations before the court was empowered to act to protect the other children.

Our concern here is not so much with the technical evidential arguments (crucial though these were to the determination of the appeal) but with the respective merits of the majority and minority judgments when analysed in the context of the competing interests of the various parties. On the one hand we have the interests of the mother not to have her children compulsorily removed from her by the state without good reason. On the other hand we have the interests of the three young girls not to be subjected to the risk of suspected abuse. The majority reasoning relies on considerations of 'due process' and a strict application of the ordinary rules of evidence. It may be argued that this inclines more towards respect for parents than it does towards children's rights. The minority view takes a more liberal or relaxed attitude to evidential matters where the suspicion of abuse is tangible and real. This would appear in contrast to emphasise children's rights rather than respect for parents.

Which approach then, is more justifiable on policy grounds? To answer this question we must try to identify the 'primary' interest and the 'secondary' interest and to do this we must examine what is at stake for the parent and the children. Let us postulate the worst thing that could happen if the court makes the wrong decision. This might arise (1) Where the court makes a care order but *in fact* the parent (or in this case parent's cohabitant) was not guilty of abuse and therefore in reality there was no risk to the children or (2) If the court fails to make the order, the children are left at home and in fact are abused. In the first scenario the mother will have suffered unwarranted state intrusion into the privacy of her home and family life and a violation of her civil liberties. In the second scenario the children will have suffered invasion of their bodily integrity and will probably have been the victims of criminal offences. They will have suffered physical and psychological injury of lesser or greater permanence and severity. We need to ask whether anyone who is serious about the protection of children's rights could really argue that the primary interest here is the parent's. And if the primary interest is that of the children this is good reason for preferring the minority decision.

But what about considerations of the wider family interest? Could this make a difference to the analysis? Instead of just looking at the result from the apparently polarised positions of the parent and the children we might need to throw in to the calculation the desirability of preserving the family unit and holding it together if at all possible.[49] The argument might be that there are benefits in keeping all the children together, avoiding institutional care etc. and that some weight should be given to this. I doubt that in this care context giving due credit to the family interest would make a great deal of difference. The essential point is that a care order does not necessitate removal of the children from the family home and this is true, *a fortiori*, of a supervision order where such removal cannot be authorised.[50] The family interest ought not therefore to be significantly influential in the initial determination of whether the criteria for a care order are satisfied, but might legitimately have more influence when, at the later stage, the court has to decide whether to make a care order, supervision order or no order at all.[51]

The second case is the Court of Appeal's decision in *Re H (Paternity: Blood Test)*.[52] This concerned the much litigated question of when a court should direct blood tests[53] to establish paternity of a child where the mother and her husband oppose it and tests are being requested by another man claiming to be the father. It was an unusual situation since the husband had undergone a vasectomy some years previously and it was established that the mother had had an ongoing affair with the other man during the period when she conceived. But she became reunited with her husband and the couple were raising the resulting child as a child of the marriage. The mother claimed that her husband had not checked the success of the vasectomy and that some sexual relations had taken place between them during the relevant period. Accordingly, supported by her husband, she refused to allow the child to be tested. Again here there were technical arguments (about the court's power to direct blood tests) which I will not rehearse.[54] Suffice it to say that the Court of Appeal held that the court could direct blood tests for the child and that it was not against the child's best interests for it to do so.

The conclusion reached by the court is significant and somewhat against the drift of previous decisions. These had generally been to refuse tests which might have the effect of displacing the presumption of legitimacy - at least in those cases where a married woman continued to live in a functioning family with her husband.[55] Generally the thinking seems to have been that greater weight should be attached to the child's need for stability than to establishing the biological truth. In *Re H* the Court of Appeal, and Ward LJ in particular, struck out in a different direction relying on Article 7 of the United Nations Convention which asserts the child's right as far as possible 'to know and be cared for by his or her parents'.[56] The court emphasised the importance to the child of honesty and the duty of the mother not to 'live a lie'. It was also not convinced that if the biological parentage of the mother's lover were established, this would necessarily detract from the social or psychological parentage of her husband who was de facto raising the child.

Where does the 'primary' interest lie in a case like this? How ought such a dispute to be resolved as a matter of policy? We have the interest of the mother (together with that of her husband) in continuing to regard and raise the child as their own, free from external interference. The stability of the family environment, perhaps the stability of the marriage, could be threatened by the outside challenge. Arguably, this is a particularly good example of a situation in which the collective family interest ought to be weighed in the balance. We are considering not merely the child's stability, nor merely the stability of the mother's marriage, but perhaps the very stability and continued existence of the family unit. Yet, there are powerful countervailing considerations. There is the additional complication of the interests of the mother's lover who might indeed be the biological father with a significant interest (right?) in establishing his parentage and, thereafter, having some sort of continuing role in the child's life.[57] Then there is the child's own interest in knowledge of origins and an ongoing relationship with the potentially biological father although this would need to be set against the child's interest in stability and continuity of care by the social parent, whether or not that parent should also turn out to be the natural parent.

So the balancing exercise in cases like this is liable to be complex and I am not at all surprised that there are plenty of English decisions which go either way on the question of ordering tests.[58] The courts have clearly not found this an easy issue. *Re H* does however suggest that we may be about to enter a period in which greater importance may be attached to biological truth and relatively less to considerations of family stability. The Court of Appeal's ruling seems to be based in part on the view that a definite stance has been taken under international law. The child has a right to know as far as possible and, with the arrival of DNA testing, it is usually now very possible to get at the truth definitively. The right of the child in Article 7 'to be cared for by his or her parents' surely refers to *natural* and not to social or psychological parents. Similar support for the position of natural parents can be found in the European Convention on Human Rights and in the jurisprudence of the European Court in its interpretation of Article 8 which protects 'family life'.[59] In other words, whatever may be the academic arguments about social versus biological parenthood and the competing value of each,[60] international commitments arguably require domestic laws to give greater weight to the latter. And perhaps, to return to the principal theme of this paper, the rather obvious point should be made that the child can scarcely 'honour' his parents unless he knows who his parents are. Whether, and to what extent, a child ought to honour social, non-biological parents is a fascinating question but, perhaps fortunately, one that is beyond the scope of the present discussion!

Conclusion

This paper has been concerned with the 'traditional value' of respect for parents from its biblical foundations to its application in modern society. The central issue is the extent to which parents' interests can be appropriately accommodated in the new era of children's rights.

In the first part of the paper I argue the case for a clearer articulation in legislation of children's duties. Duty or responsibility is the concomitant of possessing rights, especially those 'autonomy' rights which reflect the progressive emancipation of older children. I speculate on some particular duties which might reasonably be imposed on children. Some of these, such as the duty to maintain contact with a parent, relate directly to the parent-child relationship while others, such as the duty to attend school, impact on the child's relationship with outsiders. However, even here the duty indirectly relates to the child's relationship with his parents since parents are held accountable, to a degree, for the child's actions outside the home. This is self-evidently so regarding school attendance.[61] In this sense, this second kind of duty on the child may also be said to reflect respect for parents.

Is there perhaps an argument against imposing any duties on children? If there is it might run something like this. Society owes to children the best that it can offer and this requires that children be accorded respect as persons and legal subjects capable of bearing rights. But it does not follow from this that society should be demanding something in return. Children are more vulnerable and deserving of greater protection than adults and should not therefore be held legally responsible for their actions in the way that adults are. In fact it is interesting to note that the highly protectionist United Nations Convention, in granting all manner of rights to children, at no point says anything about their responsibilities. I think the argument is untenable, first, because if we want to recognise children as persons we should not patronise them and, secondly, because children's rights are increasingly associated in the popular consciousness not with protection but with empowerment.[62]

In the second part of the paper I look at the wider question of respect for parents, not by children themselves, but under the general law. I note that this is an obligation imposed on states by international conventions. Where the interests of parents and children coincide there is no problem. Here it is possible to uphold the rights of children while simultaneously showing due respect to the parents' position. But where there is an apparent conflict of interest the law will have to determine where the priorities should lie. I suggest that this requires the law to rank the competing interests by weighing what is at stake for the child and the parents. There is probably no escape from value judgments in the final analysis and I readily concede, as I did in my earlier paper, that the conclusions reached to specific problems will reflect the value judgments of the decision-maker and will not be shared by everyone. Whether, for example, truth is a commodity to be valued more highly than stability is a matter upon which reasonable people (and reasonable judges) may legitimately disagree. But if we wish both to honour parents and to vindicate the rights of children it is these core values, whether traditional or modern, which need to be opened up to debate.

Notes

1.   *The Bible,* Authorised version, *Exodus* 20, verse 12.

2.   'Parental responsibility' is defined by section 3(1) of the Children Act 1989 to include 'all the rights, duties, powers, responsibilities and authority which by law a parent of a child has in relation to the child and his property'.

3.   This has been shown particularly in England by an interest in the rights of adolescents to take their own decisions or at least to have their views taken into account. This movement was given considerable impetus by the decision of the House of Lords in *Gillick v. West Norfolk and Wisbech Area Health Authority* [1986] 1 AC 112 and by a number of provisions in the Children Act 1989.

4.   Adopted in November 1989.

5.   I discuss the self-determination aspect of children's rights in 'Growing up in Britain: Adolescence in the Post-*Gillick* Era' in Eekelaar, J. and Sarcevic, P. (eds) (1993) *Parenthood in Modern Society* Martinus Nijhoff, Dordrecht, pp. 501-518.

6.   A Bainham, 'Non-intervention and Judicial Paternalism' in Birks, P. (ed) (1994) *The Frontiers of Liability* Oxford University Press, Oxford, pp. 161-174.

7.   In fact English law has never favoured 'neat little lists' and there has never been a statute which sets out in one place a list of parents' rights or duties.

8.   For a detailed discussion see Bromley, P.M. *Bromley's Family Law* 6th ed (1981) Butterworths pp. 329-332.

9.   Ibid. at 330 referring to the remarks of Abbott CJ in *Carr v Clarke* (1818) 2 Chit 260, 261.

10.   (1825) 4 B & C 660.

11.   By the Administration of Justice Act 1982 s 2(b).

12.   [1991] Fam 69.

13.   It must be shown that the child in question possessed a 'mischievous discretion'. An attempt to abolish the *doli incapax* presumption was overturned by the House of Lords in *C v. DPP* [1996] 1 AC 1, but the newly-elected Labour government proposed to abolish it by statute in 1997: see further, Douglas at Chap. 15 below.

14.   The qualification is that for an action based on negligence the child is only expected to take the degree of care which it would be reasonable to expect a child of his age to take: *Yachuk v. Oliver Blais Co Ltd* [1949] AC 396. Parents will not generally be liable for the torts of their children but may be liable if they have authorised the child's actions or been themselves negligent in failing to prevent the child from causing injury to a third party.

15.   For a general discussion of the statutory framework, see Harris, N. (1993) *Law and Education: Regulation, Consumerism and the Education System* Sweet & Maxwell, London, pp. 208-212.

16 Education Act 1944 s 36.
17 It is technically possible for a parent to discharge the statutory duty by educating the child 'otherwise' than by attendance at school. But it has always been difficult to satisfy the statutory requirements in this way, the more so since the introduction in England and Wales of a National Curriculum. See Harris, above n 15 at p. 209.
18 Parents may be prosecuted and fined. Since the Children Act 1989 it is possible for the court to make an 'education supervision order' (under s 36). Under this, the person appointed to 'advise, assist or befriend' the child may, *inter alia*, give directions to the parent and the child with a view to recommencing schooling. But, interestingly, the parents' failure to comply with such directions may constitute an offence whereas the child's failure may not (Schedule 3, paras 18 and 19).
19 Grenville, M.P. 'Compulsory School Attendance and the child's wishes' (1988) *Journal of Social Welfare Law* 4.
20 Perhaps the principal argument is that the child's development into a rationally autonomous adult requires compulsory school attendance although the age at which this should cease is obviously a matter of debate.
21 See Bartlett, K.T. 'Re-Expressing Parenthood' (1988) 98 *Yale Law Journal* 293.
22 See *R v. Stone and Dobinson* [1977] 2 All ER 341 where the Court of Appeal upheld the convictions for manslaughter of the deceased's brother and his cohabitant. They had allowed the deceased to lodge with them (thereby assuming responsibility for her care) but failed to call adequate medical attention for her when she became ill. She died of toxaemia from infected bed sores and prolonged immobilisation.
23 Described as such originally by Wrangham J. in *M. v M. (Child: Access)* [1973] 2 All ER 81, the contact order in s 8(1) of the Children Act 1989 is 'child-centred' in form, 'requiring the person with whom a child lives, or is to live, to allow the child to visit or stay with the person named in the order, or for that person and the child otherwise to have contact with each other'. Article 9(3) of the UN Convention on the Rights of the Child also explicitly recognises the child's right to contact providing that states parties must 'respect the right of the child who is separated from one or both parents to maintain personal relations and direct contact with both parents on a regular basis, except if it is contrary to the child's best interests'.
24 It would certainly appear to be recognised as such under the interpretation of Article 8 of the European Convention on Human Rights. See particularly *Hokkanen v. Finland* (1994) Publ. Eur. Ct. H.R., Series A No. 229 A.
25 For a useful discussion see Barton, C. and Douglas, G. (1995) *Law and Parenthood,* Butterworths pp. 182 - 185.
26 See, for example, the report of the *Lucas* case, *The Times,* 16 April 1993.
27 This principle was made clear in English domestic law (also in the light of the European Convention) by the House of Lords in *Re K.D. (A minor)*

(Access: Principles) [1988] A.C. 806. It is also expressly acknowledged in the wording of Article 9(3) of the United Nations Convention (note 23, above).

28   At Chap. 7. Section 16 of the Capacity and Guardianship Law 1962: 'The minor shall, by way of honouring father and mother, obey his parents in any matter within the scope of their guardianship'. Examples of statutory duties owed by children to parents can be found in other jurisdictions. In Indonesia children have an obligation to respect their parents and, when they are grown up, to support and take care of them if necessary. See Wila Chandrawila Supriadi, 'Indonesian Marriage Law' in Bainham, A. (ed) (1997) *The International Survey of Family Law 1995,* Martinus Nijhoff, The Hague, London. In Croatia the new law on family relations adds responsibilities of children towards their parents to children's rights. These responsibilities include the duty to respect, help and be considerate in the interests of family solidarity. See Alincic, M. and Hrabar, D. 'Croatia: Family legislation in the Period of Creating a New Legal Order' in the same volume.

29   The full text is: 'States parties undertake to ensure the child such protection and care as is necessary for his or her well-being, taking into account the rights and duties of his or her parents, legal guardians or other individuals legally responsible for him or her, and, to this end, shall take all appropriate legislative and administrative measures'.

30   The full text is: 'States parties shall respect the responsibilities, rights and duties of parents or, where applicable, the members of the extended family or community as provided for by the local system, legal guardians or other persons legally responsible for the child, to provide, in a manner consistent with the evolving capacities of the child, appropriate direction and guidance in the exercise by the child of the rights recognised in the present Convention'.

31   'States parties, shall respect the rights and duties of the parents and, when applicable, legal guardians, to provide directions to the child in the exercise of his or her right in a manner consistent with the evolving capacities of the child.' The right referred to here is the right to freedom of thought, conscience and religion (Article 14(1)).

32   Article 29(1).

33   Protocol 1, Article 2 of 20 March 1952.

34   'Paramount' in s 1(1) (Children Act 1989) but, interestingly, by way of contrast only 'a primary consideration' in Article 3(1) of the UN Convention which provides: 'In all actions concerning children, whether undertaken by public or private social welfare institutions, courts of law, administrative authorities or legislative bodies, the best interests of the child shall be a primary consideration'. An important distinction is that while the Children Act provision applies only to the decisions of courts, the

UN Convention provision catches a much wider range of public and private institutions.

35 See above n 6.

36 I discuss the first area ibid. at pp. 161-169 and the second at pp. 169-172.

37 Ibid. at pp. 173-174.

38 The recognition that parents' interests can conflict with those of their children was an essential pre-condition of the establishment of children's rights - a point forcefully made by John Eekelaar in 'The Emergence of Children's Rights' (1986) 6 *Oxford Journal of Legal Studies* 161. See also Michael King at Chap. 1 above.

39 *Re C. (A minor) (Leave to Seek Section 8 Orders)* [1994] 1 F.L.R. 26.

40 Under s 8(1) Children Act 1989 a residence order (which broadly approximates to the old custody order but with important differences) is an order 'setting the arrangements to be made as to the person with whom a child is to live'. A specific issue order is 'an order giving directions for the purpose of determining a specific question which has arisen, or which may arise, in connection with any aspect of parental responsibility for a child'.

41 Thus, he was not in favour of the making of a residence order at the time of the application since he felt that it could enshrine in a court order a state of affairs that should be resolved by discussion between the young woman and her parents.

42 In his view parliament had not intended that every disagreement between a child and her parents should be up for litigation. Parliament, he thought, had intended the jurisdiction to grant leave to children to be reserved for matters of importance and exercised cautiously. In particular the issue of the Bulgarian holiday was not sufficiently important.

43 See Chap. 9 below.

44 See Neilsen, L. 'Denmark: The Family Principle and the Individual Principle - And recent Legislative News' in Andrew Bainham (ed) (1997) *The International Survey of Family Law 1995,* Martinus Nijhoff, The Hague, London.

45 [1996] 2 WLR 8.

46 The criteria are in s 31(2) Children Act 1989 which provides: 'A court may only make a care order or supervision order if it is satisfied (a) that the child concerned is suffering, or is likely to suffer, significant harm and (b) that the harm, or likelihood of harm, is attributable to (i) the care given to the child, or likely to be given to him if the order were not made, not being what it would be reasonable to expect a parent to give to him; or (ii) the child's being beyond parental control.'

47 The majority speech was given by Lord Nicholls.

48 Lords Lloyd and Browne-Wilkinson.

49 I concede that this balancing calculation is yet more complicated by the consideration that the child arguably has an independent interest in staying in the family.

50   The criteria for both orders are identical. Above n 46.

51   Under s 1(5) of the Children Act 1989 the Court is required to apply the so-called 'non-intervention principle' and must not make any order 'unless it considers that doing so would be better for the child than making no order at all'.

52   [1996] 2 FLR 65.

53   Section 20 of the Family Law Reform Act 1969 empowers the Court to direct blood tests. The court may not order an unwilling party to undergo a test but may under s 23 draw adverse inferences from refusals. See O'Donovan at Chap. 12 below.

54   I comment on these in 'Vasectomies, Lovers and Disputed Offspring: Honesty is the Best Policy (Sometimes)' (1996) *Cambridge Law Journal* at pp. 444-446.

55   See particularly *Re F. (A minor) (Blood Tests: Parental Rights)* [1993] Fam. 314.

56   The full text is: 'The child shall be registered immediately after birth and shall have the right from birth to a name, the right to acquire a nationality, and, as far as possible, the right to know and be cared for by his or her parents'.

57   It is clear from the wording of Article 7, above, that the child's right is not limited to knowledge of parentage but extends to being 'cared for by his or her parents'.

58   See O'Donovan at Chap. 12 below, and Barton and Douglas op. cit. note 25 at pp. 57-63.

59   For a general analysis of Article 8 and the decisions of the Court interpreting it see Janis, M. Kay, R. and Bradley, A. (1995) *European Human Rights Law: Text and Materials*. Clarendon Press, Oxford at pp. 229-260.

60   See generally Barton and Douglas op. cit. for the competing arguments.

61   And, as noted above, parents may be liable to some extent for their children's crimes and tortious acts although it is a matter of heated debate how far they should be.

62   In fact, at least one critical commentary on the UN Convention thinks that it is over-protectionist and insufficiently acknowledges the empowerment claims of children. See Le Blanc LJ (1995) *The Convention on the Rights of the Child,* University of Nebraska Press, Lincoln and London.

7 Rights and Autonomy - or the Best Interests of the Child?

ZE'EV W. FALK

There is a certain irony in the fact that at this 'post-modern' time rejecting all other ideologies, the ideology of 'children's rights' and 'children's autonomy' has gained a lot of authority. As Michael Freeman formulated it:

> The liberationist movement challenged those who claimed the status of children should be advanced exclusively by conferring on children increased protection. The emphasis shifted from protection to autonomy, from nurturance to self-determination, from welfare to justice.[1]

The reason for preferring children's rights and autonomy to their best interests lies, probably, in the experience that parental rights were often misused and in the uncertainty as to what really constituted 'the best interest of the child'. Hence, instead of a paternalist decision according to the doctrine of *parens patriae*, the court is now expected to decide between the child's view and the view of those who purport to care for and protect him. Although in practice this may be quite similar to the criterion of 'the best interests', there seems to be less certainty on the part of the court to choose what is good for the child.

This uncertainty seems to be connected with the 'post-modern' trend in philosophy, as represented by Ludwig Wittgenstein (1889-1951),[2] Karl Raimund Popper (1902-1994)[3] and Emmanuel Levinas (1906-1995).[4] As a result of universal doubt it was realised that the child's welfare may well be 'trumped' in certain situations (which are not spelt out) by 'cultural values and traditions'.[5]

But 'autonomy', as is well known, was defined by Immanuel Kant as 'a property of the wills of all adult human beings in so far as they are viewed as ideal moral legislators, prescribing general principles to themselves rationally, free from causal determinism, and not motivated by sensuous desires'.[6]

It is a capacity and disposition to make choices in a rational manner; and this means choosing in the absence of certain particular attitudes and inner obstacles, such as blind acceptance of tradition and authority, neurotic compulsions, and the like.

The paradigm of a person who is non-autonomous in this sense includes the child who accepts authority without question, the adolescent who rebels against authority with as little understanding, the traditionalist who will not consider new ways of doing things, the compulsive gambler, who cannot stop gambling even though he wants to, and the masochist and the sadist who impulsively hurt themselves or others without any idea why.[7]

According to Kant, a child cannot therefore be autonomous, though many adults are equally non-autonomous.

Until the emergence of the new ideology of 'children's autonomy' and 'children's rights', the guiding concept was 'the best interests of the child'.[8] However,

the child becomes increasingly able to provide for his own needs and his rights are assured by how the parents increasingly take into account the child's preferences as he develops. At the same time, the ordinary devoted parent does not 'abandon' the child to his rights by burdening him with the responsibility for decisions that he is not yet capable of making soundly ... Children need the insulating, protecting, decision-making authority of nurturing parents who do not abandon them to their rights.[9]

Indeed, parents, guardians and welfare authorities should ask for the child's opinion before making a decision on his behalf, but this need not be an indication for the existence of the child's rights beyond the child's best interests.

Meanwhile, the United Nations Convention on the Rights of the Child (UNCRC), adopted by the General Assembly on 20 November, 1989, and having entered into force on 2 September, 1990,[10] has given international recognition to the new ideology of 'children's rights' and a basis for the termination of what were formerly known as 'parental rights'.[11]

Article 12 of the UNCRC requires states to 'assure to the child who is capable of forming his or her own views the right to express those views freely on all matters affecting the child, the views of the child being given due consideration in accordance with the age and maturity of the child'. Nevertheless, Article 3 of the UNCRC still refers to 'the best interest of the child', which may therefore be invoked against a child's claim of rights or autonomy, if by the exercise of such a right or autonomy the child would be harming himself.

However, in a recent decision of the Israeli Supreme Court,[12] delivered on 22 February, 1995, a mother's claim for exposure of her child to her religious views and practices was weighed against the father's opposition and the child's best interests or the child's right of religious freedom. Shamgar P., dismissing her appeal, held, in an *obiter dictum*, that the child's 'rights' or 'autonomy' was the more inclusive concept. It covered the 'child's best interest', which now had become part of the child's rights or autonomy. Recognition of a child's rights is *ipso facto* guaranty of his or her best interest. The child is an autonomous creature whose rights and interests are independent of those of his parents. In the President's opinion, the concept of the child's rights is preferable to that of the child's best interest, first because it better expresses the child's status in the family quarrel, and secondly - because of its greater neutrality.

Strasberg-Cohen J., on the other hand, agreeing to the dismissal of the appeal, preferred the concept of 'best interests' to that of 'child's rights'. In her opinion, the more inclusive concept remains the 'child's best interests', while the 'child's rights' could be taken into consideration in the determination of the former principle. Or and Zamir JJ. concurred with this view, while Mazza J. sided with the President's reasoning.

In my view, Justice Strasberg-Cohen's interpretation seems to be closer to the spirit of the law. The guiding concept should remain the child's best interest, though the child's human rights should not be overlooked. Take, for instance, s. 13A of the Capacity and Guardianship Law, 1962, as enacted in 1965, which is based on the former principle:

> (a) The religion of a minor shall not be changed, unless both his parents have given their written consent ...
> (b) If the minor has completed his tenth year, his religion shall not be changed, unless, in addition to the consent of his parents ... he, too, has given his prior written consent.

At least this section limits the child's right of self-determination in favour of a principle derived from the doctrine of either the 'child's best interests' or the interest of his or her religion. In the absence of parental consent the change of religion, though demanded by the child, is not permitted. Sections 16, 17 and 25, moreover, clearly limit the child's autonomy:

> 16. The minor shall, by way of honouring father and mother, obey his parents in any matter within the scope of their guardianship
>
> 17. In the exercise of their guardianship, the parents shall act in the best interest of the minor in such manner as devoted parents would act in the circumstances.
>
> 25. Where the parents have not reached an agreement ... , the Court may determine the matters ... as may appear to it to be in the best interest of the minor; Provided that children up to the age of six shall be with their mother unless there are special reasons for directing otherwise.

True, sections 7 and 8 of the Children Adoption Law, 1981, refer not only to the child's best interest but also to the child's rights to a hearing:

> 7. When the adoptee is nine years of age or over, or where he is under nine years of age but is able to understand the matter, a court shall not make an adoption order unless it is satisfied that the adoptee wishes to be adopted by the adopter ...
>
> 8. (a) A court may make an adoption order only if it is satisfied that the parents of the adoptee consent to his being adopted ...
>
> (c) The consent of a parent who is a minor does not require the consent of his representative.

These provisions, however, follow from the special circumstances of the adoption, after the natural family, obviously, does not function in the child's best interests. They do not indicate that the 'child's best interests' should be replaced by 'the child's rights' or 'the child's autonomy'.

In the case referred to above, President Shamgar adopted an approach supported in some British and American cases and by some writers, where the child's rights is given preference over the child's best interests. In the writer's view, he should rather have followed s. 1 of the Legal Foundations Law, 1980:

> 1. If the court meets with a legal problem to be decided, and does not find an answer either in a statute, precedent or by way of analogy, he should decide it according to the principles of freedom, justice, equity and peace in the tradition of Israel.

While this provision is applicable in any case where a lacuna is found in the law, in the case under consideration this solution was clearly indicated. As already mentioned, s. 16 of the Capacity and Guardianship Law, 1962, refers to the child's duty of honouring his parents, which, being a reference to the Decalogue, clearly demands an interpretation according to the tradition of Israel.

Hence the problem whether the child's best interest or his autonomy should prevail should have been resolved according to the principle of freedom in the tradition of Israel.

Freedom, according to this tradition, means the right of a child to be taken care of by his parents, or by a guardian, as long as he cannot yet be held responsible. In this sense, freedom means not to have to make decisions beyond one's capacity. It also means having a right to receive a good education, sometimes in spite of his own will. Such an education should include the ability to use reason and withstand impulses, to prepare for the future as a responsible bearer of the tradition of Israel.

According to this tradition, 'paternalism' is of the essence of parental duties, especially to teach the child Torah.[13]

> Parents cannot avoid forming their children's characters ... Upbringings can only be evaluated by recognising other desired adult traits apart from the single one of self-determination ... First, we should want someone to be able to make and act upon choices of the morally good. This will not be secured merely by developing a child's faculty of choosing. It also requires the inculcation of a sense of what is good and bad, and consistent exposure to good rather than bad ways of living.[14]

The present trend towards a preference for children's rights and autonomy over children's best interests clashes also with the efforts on the national and international level for the protection of children even against their own will.[15]

Although the title of the UN Convention on the Rights of the Child seems to suggest preference for the rights approach rather than for that of best interests, the latter approach is still of great importance both in international documents and in state legislations.

There is at least one field where the best interests of the child and his rights are curtailed by other considerations, such as the best interests of the state or of international society. Take for instance the Hague Convention on the Civil Aspects of International Child Abduction of 1980, which places the principles of international jurisdiction above that of children's rights, perhaps even above their best interests.

In another recent decision of the Israeli Supreme Court[16] delivered on 14 August, 1995, a child aged eight was ordered to be returned to his father in the United States from where his mother had wrongfully brought him to Israel. The Israeli court of first instance had held that the best interests of the child were opposed to him being returned to the US. Nothing was said about the child's view and the child's rights, but, having been with his mother in Israel for more than three years, he probably preferred not to leave either of them.

Nevertheless, Dorner J. (Levin and Kedmi JJ. concurring) held the Convention had abolished the jurisdiction of the Israeli court to decide on the child's best interests. A child snatched out of the jurisdiction must be brought back into this jurisdiction, so that the court having jurisdiction before the illegal removal should decide upon his best interests.

In the words of Adair Dyer, quoted with approval in the judgment,

> The Hague Convention intrudes upon the jurisdiction of the courts in the country to which the child has been taken, even if that is the country of the child's nationality, and insists that the child be returned ... so that the courts of another country may exercise jurisdiction over the merits of custody. The execution of this obligation requires discipline on the part of the courts and a willingness to let the best interests of the child be framed not merely within the context of the judge's own culture, but also in a three-dimensional, multicultural setting, including the child's interest in not being abruptly jump-started from one culture to another.

In other words, although lip service is being paid to the principle of the child's best interests, the Israeli Supreme Court, as a result of the Hague Convention, has changed its prior view that immigration to, and living in, Israel is usually the best interests of a Jewish child.[17] This abdication of jurisdiction is due to the court's preference for the best interests of the State of Israel, and of its international relations at the expense of the child's best interests and probably also at the expense of the child's rights and autonomy.

Notes

[1]   Michael D.A. Freeman, in M.D.A. Freeman and P. Veerman (eds.): *The Ideologies of Children's Rights*, Dordrecht 1992, 3; P.E. Veerman: *The Rights of the Child and the Changing Image of Childhood*, 1992. On the new attitude see also: J.M. Eekelaar: 'What are Parental Rights?' 89 *L.Q.R.* 210; J.M. Eekelaar: 'The Emergence of Children's Rights', 6 *Oxf J Leg St* 161; B.M. Dickens: 'The Functions and Limits of Parental Rights', 97 *L.Q.R.* 462; H.D. Krause: *Child Law*, 1992.

2   In his concept 'Language Games' developed in the 'Blue Book' and his later writings. An introduction to his thought is Joachim Schulte: *Wittgenstein; Eine Einfuehrung*, Stuttgart, Reclam 1989.

3   Especially in his rejection of all kinds of 'essentialism' and totalitarian ideology.

4   Especially in his teaching on the responsibility for the other person. For a selection of his writings cf. Sean Hand: *The Levinas Reader*, Oxford, Blackwell, 1989.

5   Freeman, loc. cit., 5.

6   Thomas E. Hill Jr: *Autonomy and Self-Respect*, Cambridge UP 1991, 29, 44.

7   Ibid. 31.

8   Cf. Joseph Goldstein, Anna Freud, Albert J. Solnit: *Beyond the Best Interests of the Child*, New York, Free Press, 1973; id.: *Before the Best Interests of the Child*, New York, Free Press, 1979.

9   Al J. Solnit: *Children's Rights and Needs in the Light of New Research*, Jerusalem, Hebrew University School of Education, pp. 7,19.

10   Ratified by the State of Israel on 4 August, 1991, and published in the Official Gazette, 31 *Kitvey Amanah*, 1038.

11   Which in their turn had replaced the 'Patria Potestas'.

12   C.A. 2266/93, *Ploni (Minor) et al. v. Ploni*, 49 (1) PDI 221-277 (1995).

13   *Deut.* 6:7; 11:19; *Prov.* 22:6; *Mishnah Qiddushin* 1:7; *Tosefta Qiddushin* 1:11; *BT Qiddushin* 29a.

14   David Archard: *Children; Rights and Childhood*, London, Routledge, 1993, 56.

15   See, e.g., the statements made by the American Coalition on Smoking and Health, and the reports issued by international agencies on these issues.

16   C.A. 5532/93, *Gunsburg v. Greenwald*, 49 (3) 282-302.

17   H.C. 125/49, *Amadu v. Director of Pardess Hanna Immigrants' Camp*, 4 PDI 4; C.A. 503/60, *Wolf v. Wolf*, 15 PDI 760.

8 Multiculturalism, Parental Choice and Traditional Values: A Comment on Religious Education in Israel

STEPHEN GOLDSTEIN

Introduction

The system of religious schools in Israel is inextricably linked with the more general aspects of the multicultural nature of Israeli society and, in particular, the primary role of religion and attitudes towards religion in that society. These in turn are connected with Israel being a Zionist Jewish State with a sizeable non Jewish minority as well as the traditional status of religious-ethnic-national groups in the Middle East. Discussion of these complex issues would necessarily take us well beyond the confines of this short paper. Thus we will merely note them herein.[1]

As stated by Prof. Izhak Englard:

> The mainstream of modern political Zionism, which led to the establishment of the State of Israel in 1948, was ... guided by ... [the] idea of a national-secular Jewish state.... A first central conception of the Jewish State's nature and function thus emerges: Beyond the ordinary tasks of a modern democratic state Israel's specific mission is to constitute the national state of the Jews and to preserve and further Jewish national culture. Religion is relevant but merely as part of the national heritage. We shall call this approach - with all its manifold contrasting political sub-currents from right to left - the *secular Zionist view*.[2]

For our purpose, it is important to emphasise that although Prof. Englard denotes this mainstream of modern political Zionism 'secular', he acknowledges that this secular Zionism does recognise the Jewish religion as part of the Jewish national heritage that its mission is to preserve and promote.

Moreover, in terms of the Jewish national heritage, secular Zionism recognises, as it must, that it is impossible to distinguish definitively between the religious and the secular parts of Jewish culture. As is generally true of ancient peoples, historically the Jewish people, as a people, has possessed a national religion, with Jewish peoplehood and the Jewish religion being coextensive. The dilemma of the secular Zionists, therefore, is how to promote and further that culture while not believing in the religious premises on which it historically has been based.

Turning now to the religious segment of the Jewish population, it should be noted that the vast majority of Israeli Jews who describe themselves as religious are followers of various streams of Orthodox Judaism. There are in Israel relatively few followers of other current streams of religious Judaism, such as Conservative or Reform. For orthodox believers, Jewish tradition is seen as exclusively a religious one, based on divine revelation as interpreted by authorised rabbinical tradition. A very small and extreme part of this orthodoxy completely denies the legitimacy of political Zionism and the Jewish State. Another, and much larger part, had historically been opposed to political Zionism, but following the establishment of the State reconciled itself to the State's existence and participates, to an ever increasing extent, in its political structure. The largest part of this orthodoxy, however, is made up of religious Zionists who have always had a most positive attitude towards political Zionism and the Jewish State. Yet religious Zionists are distinguished from their secular counterparts in that for the former, 'contrary to secular concepts, the Jewish state is viewed as an instrument to achieve beyond the satisfaction of human needs the transcendent objectives of the Jewish religion'.[3]

We should note at this point that, in the same way as several movements, based on different political, economic and social philosophies, made up secular Zionism, the followers of the different views of religious Orthodoxy, described above, formed themselves into political movements well before the establishment of the State of Israel. With the establishment of the State, these political movements, both secular and religious, became political parties, creating a structure of secular and religious parties that, with some modification, continues until today.

This separatist nature of the Israeli political and social structure based on religious views was further reinforced by the retention in the State of a characteristic feature of the organisation of the Ottoman Empire: the

Millet system, pursuant to which organisational autonomy and legal jurisdiction in matters of personal status were granted to recognised Muslim, Christian and Jewish religious communities.

Under the Ottoman Millet system, the laws of personal status - including marriage, divorce, support of wives and children and custody of children incidental to divorce - were not within the general competence of the civil courts; rather they were under the jurisdiction of the Muslim, Christian and Jewish Communities who applied the personal, i.e., religious-communal law of the individuals. This system was retained in substance by the British mandatory authorities, and, in essence, continues today in the State of Israel. It is important to emphasise, however, that, while under the Ottoman Empire these communal groups were nominally determined by religion (i.e., Muslim, Christian, Jewish), they were not just religious communities but rather religious-ethnic-national groups. In the Middle East religious groupings are not just a matter of what church, mosque or synagogue one attends. Instead they are intimately connected with ethnicity and, indeed, nationality.

This ethnic-national aspect of the Millet groupings explains the fact that until the founding of the State of Israel there was little or no opposition from secular Zionists to the control of matters such as marriage and divorce of Jews by Jewish religious law and rabbinical courts. The authority of Jewish law and rabbinical courts was seen even by secular Zionists as an affirmative manifestation of Jewish autonomy *vis-à-vis* their non-Jewish rulers.

However, when the entire State became Jewish, i.e., the State of Israel was founded, control of personal status by Jewish law and rabbinical courts lost its ethnic-national status for secular Zionists and became solely religious. As such it came to be viewed by many secular Zionists as part of unacceptable religious coercion. On the other hand, in the view of many religious Zionists the control of personal status of Jews by religious law and religious courts is a most important and most affirmative manifestation of the State's desirable identification with the Jewish religion. Thus the continuation of the Millet system in the State of Israel, instead of uniting Jews, as it did in the pre-State days, has become a major battleground between secular and religious Jews as to the role of the Jewish religion within the Jewish State.[4]

As to the non-Jewish minority in Israel, however, the Millet system continues to play its traditional role. For Israeli Arabs, both Muslims and Christians, the continuation of the Millet system in the Jewish State is viewed as it was by Jews prior to the State, i.e., as an important manifestation of their autonomy: religiously, ethnically, and, indeed, nationally.

The Educational Structure

General

The primary organising principle of the Israeli educational structure is religion. That is, schools in Israel are distinguished, one from another, in great part by their religious nature.

This fact is the result of three factors. First, the extremely heterogeneous nature of religious belief and the attitudes towards religion in Israeli society as described above - both within the Jewish majority and between this majority and the non-Jewish minorities - results in the fact that each particular group desires to control the religious education of the children of its adherents. Second, as we have described above, in Israel societal groupings, including political movements and political parties, often have been organised traditionally around religion or attitudes towards religion. Lastly, both Orthodox religious Judaism and Islam view religion not as a compartmentalised set of beliefs and actions, but rather as a total way of life which determines all that a person does in all aspects of his existence. Thus, religious education cannot consist merely of specific religious courses taught as part of an overall curriculum the other aspects of which are religiously neutral, but rather must consist of the maintaining of a total religious environment in a given school or system of schools.

The result is that, in addition to the basic divide described below between Jewish and Arab sub-systems, Israeli education is divided further into a number of relatively autonomous systems and sub-systems which are organised primarily along religious lines with the guiding principle being parental choice as to the system in which the child will be educated.

State Schools: The Jewish and Arab Sub-Systems

The Israeli system of State schools is divided into two main sub-systems: one for the Jewish majority of the population and another for the Arab sector. The two systems are distinguished by the language of instruction - in the Arab sub-system the language of instruction is Arabic with Hebrew taught only as a second language - as well as by other aspects of the curriculum and way of life. In the Arab sub-system there is no clear division between regular (secular) State schools and religious State schools as exists in the Jewish sector. However, within the Arab sub-system the schools tend to adapt their curriculum and way of life to the religious makeup of the student population: Muslim, Christian, Druse; and in this context to emphasise general Arab culture along with the specific culture of the relevant religious group.

In addition, schools in which the student body is composed of other, smaller minority groups, such as Samaritans and Circassians (non-Arab Muslims), also adapt their curriculum and way of life in accord with the relevant religion, as well as the relevant ethnic and linguistic culture.

The existence and operation of this separate minority group State school system represents an attempt to achieve the purpose of the Declaration of the Establishment of the State of Israel of May 14, 1948, which provides, *inter alia*, that the State of Israel 'will guarantee freedom of religion, conscience, language, education and culture'.

In both the historic and contemporary context of the Middle East, accomplishment of these aims as to non-Jewish minorities is generally considered to require separate educational systems so as to enable such minorities to preserve and further their religious, ethnic, cultural and linguistic identities which would be swallowed up by the Jewish majority in a unified educational system. The advantages of this system in terms of preserving multiculturalism are obvious. However, such a system of 'separate but equal' education also has serious adverse consequences which we will discuss in Section III.[5]

State Schools in the Jewish Sub-System

The primary purpose of the State Education Law, 1953, was to abolish the 'streams' in the Jewish elementary educational structure. Prior to this law elementary education in the Jewish sector had been divided into four primary systems or streams, none of which was operated by the State, and all of which were connected with political movements. They were the Workers' stream (socialist, secular Zionist); the General stream (non-socialist, secular Zionist); the Mizrachi stream (orthodox religious Zionist); and the Agudat Yisrael stream (ultra-orthodox religious non-Zionist). In addition, there were other elementary schools, much smaller in number, run primarily by ultra-ultra-orthodox religious anti-Zionist groups.

The high schools at this time were relatively few in number, selective in their admissions and somewhat less connected to political movements than the elementary schools.

Despite the declared purpose of the Law to abolish these elementary school streams and to create in their stead State elementary education, the remnants of the streams remain in two main forms. The Agudat Yisrael stream became, in essence, a system of 'independent' schools which are not part of the State system, but are 'recognised' schools which receive most of their funding from State sources; the Mizrachi stream became the sub-system of State religious schools.

We will discuss in greater depth the State support given to non-State, but 'recognised', schools in the following section. We will concentrate in this section on the division within the State system between State schools and State religious schools.

The State Education Law provides in Section 1:

> 'State education' means education provided by the State ... without attachment to a party or communal body or any other organisation *outside the Government, and under the supervision of the Minister [of Education] ...; 'religious state education' means State education, with the distinction that its institutions are religious as to their way of life, curriculum, teachers and inspectors; ...* (emphasis added)

The autonomous and religious nature of the State religious education subsystem is further strengthened by the Law's creation of a Council for Religious State Education with whom the Minister (who at the time of the enactment of the Law and for most of the period thereafter has not been religious) must consult prior to the exercise of his authority in regard to the State religious sub-system and whose agreement is required for the prescribing of a curriculum for this subsystem. In addition, administratively there is a special division, which operates quite independently, within the Ministry of Education, for State religious education.

Finally, and most importantly, pursuant to section 18 of the Law, 'the Council for Religious State Education may, on religious grounds only, disqualify a person for appointment or further service as a principal, inspector or teacher at a religious State-educational institution'. This provision clearly authorises and contemplates control by State religious school authorities over the 'private' religious activities and observances of teachers and other professional employees in that system. This supervision is based on two important foundations. First, as we have repeatedly emphasised, religious education is viewed not merely as a matter of curricular subjects but as a system that inculcates religious belief and observance through the creation of an entire environment that is appropriate for that purpose.

Second, and no less important, is the view that a teacher is not merely a transmitter of material but is an educator who educates his pupils to religious belief and observance not only by his words but also by his actions, not only in class but also outside of class. In this view the teacher serves as a constant role model, as an object of emulation for his pupils in each and every one of his activities. In short, under this view, in terms of his religious behaviour and observance, a teacher has no 'private' life.[6]

The Law provides a parent with a choice between State (secular) education and State religious education when the child is registered in the State educational system. Furthermore, there are specific provisions in the Law and accompanying regulations which create mechanisms which are designed to prevent the application of pressure on a parent as to this choice.

The free choice of parents in this regard is further emphasised by the regulations concerning transfer of students between schools. Pursuant to these regulations, a local education authority, may, under certain circumstances, transfer a child against the will of the parents. However, it is specifically provided therein that 'a local education authority shall not transfer a student from a State educational institution to a State religious educational institution, or vice versa, except with the consent of his parents'.[7]

'Private' Schools

As noted above, State funding of education in Israel is not confined to State schools, but includes private schools, both elementary and secondary. As with State education the primary defining character of private education is religion. This situation is again a function of the recognition of the desire both for autonomy as to religious education and for the creation of exclusive and total religious educational environments.

In discussing private schools in the Israeli system it is necessary to distinguish between elementary and secondary education. We will begin with the former. As noted above, at the time of the adoption of the State Education Law, 1953, the ultra-orthodox Agudat Yisrael stream did not become a part of State education, but rather remained *'independent'* and officially outside the State system as a private system. The schools in this system received the status of 'recognised' educational institutions and as such may and do receive State financial support, which in practice is substantially equivalent to that received by the official State schools.

The division for State religious education in the Ministry of Education serves also as the arm of the Ministry for the supervision of this private school system. Yet the Agudat Yisrael stream is distinguished from the State religious schools in two very important respects. First it is part of a political movement, Agudat Yisrael, which is non-Zionist, or at least less Zionist, than the religious Zionist movement that controls State religious education. It is also more fundamentalist religiously and may, therefore, be described as religiously ultra-orthodox as distinguished from the merely orthodox orientation of the State religious schools. These differences find expression in all aspects of its religious totality: life style, curriculum and teachers, as well as, of course, its student body.

While the Agudat Yisrael system represents the largest number of 'recognised' private elementary schools, it should also be mentioned that there are other 'recognised' religious private schools in the Jewish sector, which are more closely akin in their religious orientation to the State religious schools, but have been organised privately, partly for religious reasons, but primarily for other, educational reasons. Within the last few years there has also been created a rather extensive new network of ultra-orthodox private 'recognised' schools affiliated to the 'Shas' political party.

In the Arab sector, there are a number of Church-related schools that are 'recognised' educational institutions.

Finally, it should be mentioned that in the Jewish sector there are ultra-ultra-orthodox groups, which may, indeed, be anti-Zionist, which are permitted to operate their own schools in accordance with their tenets. In these schools secular education is very minimal. They operate outside the system of 'recognised' private schools and thus do not receive financial support from the Ministry of Education.[8] However, the attendance of children in these schools does satisfy the requirements of Israel's compulsory education law.

As emphasised above, the State Education Law, 1953, was adopted to create official state-administered education at the elementary school level (from kindergarten up to 8th grade), which at that time was the only education which was compulsory and free. Secondary education was then much less developed. Even today, when secondary education is much more developed and is compulsory until the 10th grade and free until its culmination, i.e., 12th grade, the secondary schools administered by governmental authorities form a much smaller percentage of the total than do the elementary schools. Moreover, the governmental secondary schools that do exist are generally maintained by local governmental authorities rather than centrally by the Ministry of Education.

In short, State education, as we discussed it above, does not exist officially beyond the 8th grade level. However, historically, the State has provided extensive support to secondary education, even beyond the grade level to which students were entitled to free public education. When, in 1978, the legislature extended the right to free education at public expense through the 12th grade, it still did not incorporate the secondary schools in the State education system. Rather it provided for a system by which the state pays the tuition for students to attend local government or private schools. For this purpose the latter must be 'recognised' respecting the student ages of 13-15, but for the ages 16-18 need not even be recognised.

In essence, therefore, the state supports a wide range of private secondary education, which, indeed, is even wider than the range of private education supported at the elementary level. A significant percentage of these secondary schools are owned and administered by local governmental agencies; however, an equally significant percentage are owned and administered 'privately', often as networks owned and operated by independent non-profit organisations.

In the Jewish sector, while not officially part of the State education system, the secondary schools belonging to local governmental authorities generally tend to be divided along lines that continue the educational patterns in terms of religiosity that exist in the State elementary schools and in the State religious elementary schools as discussed above. Within the secondary 'secular' trend, the private schools also may be viewed as continuations of the State (secular) education system in general and in terms of their attitude towards religion in particular. There are, however, significant variations among them in this regard. Within the secondary religious trend, there are private secondary schools, termed *yeshiva* secondary schools, *or yeshivot*, which are ideological continuations of the State religious system, as well as ultra-orthodox *yeshivot* which serve as a continuation of the Agudat Yisrael recognised elementary school system. Here again, however, there are many variations among these institutions and exact correlations between the elementary school trends and specific secondary school institutions are, at times, difficult. Finally, there are ultra-ultra orthodox *yeshivot* that may be viewed as educational continuations of the elementary education operated by these ultra-ultra orthodox groups.

In the Arab sector, the secondary schools operated by the local governmental authorities tend to adapt their curriculum and general environment to the religious composition of their student body, as is true of

State elementary education. In this sector there are also private secondary schools, which are primarily church-related.

As stated above, all these private secondary schools are entitled to and, indeed, receive substantial financial assistance from the State.

Evaluation

General

We have thus far described an educational system that, at least in terms of religion, may be viewed as a model of multiculturalism and parental choice. Moreover, since religion is such an important aspect of cultural and, indeed, political norms in Israel, religious preferences serve as surrogates also for those norms. Thus the view that the Israeli system is an 'ideal' of multiculturalism is even further enhanced.

The Israeli system may well approach one such ideal of multiculturalism: an ideal based on separatism. As such, it presents a good vehicle for evaluating the advantages and disadvantages - or at least the problems - of such separatism. The advantages in terms of respecting parental choice and recognising and preserving multiculturalism and traditional values provided by this separatism are quite clear and speak for themselves. Less obvious are the problems created by this separatism. Thus, in the remainder of this section we will focus on these problems.[9]

Macro-multiculturalism - Micro-uniculturalism

First there is the fact of the separateness itself in a young State that still has a great need to create a common civil society. In terms of education, Israel has opted strongly for multiculturalism and parental choice at the expense of national integration. This is true both within the Jewish majority and between that majority and the Arab minority. While this choice may have been a correct one, and, indeed, may have been the only possible one in the Israeli situation for the reasons described above, it obviously has costs in terms of the desirable unity of the population. Moreover, it also has significant costs in terms of the aim of multiculturalism itself. For the Israeli system is only multicultural in one specific meaning of that term: but in another it is very unicultural. On the macro-systemic level it is multicultural, the system being composed of very diverse sub-systems and individual schools based primarily on religious preferences. Yet each sub-system (or individual school) is itself unicultural in terms of its religious beliefs, which beliefs also generally coincide quite strongly with other cultural and political norms and ideologies. This is invariably true as to the general educational atmosphere and curriculum, and is also generally true as to the teachers and student body. Thus while the system viewed on the macro-level is open, diverse and multicultural, on the micro-level of the individual student in a given sub-system or individual school it is quite the opposite, i.e., closed, uniform and unicultural. Moreover, as we have emphasised above, this closed, uniform, and unicultural educational experience of the individual child is not limited to the express factor that divides the schools, i.e., religion. Rather, since in Israel religious preferences generally coincide with other cultural norms and political ideologies, the individual child may be educated in a closed, uniform and unicultural system also as to these norms and ideologies.

While this closed nature of the separatist sub-systems is also true to some degree even in the State (secular) schools, it is most evident in the State religious schools and the private religious school systems. This is so since the State religious schools are effectively run by the religious-Zionist political party, the National Religious Party, and the two main private religious school sub-systems are owned, maintained and run by ultra-orthodox political parties.

Thus, while the Israeli educational system is very conducive to achieving one aim of multiculturalism, i.e., promoting the transference to the young of the culture and traditional values of societal subgroups, it does so at the very significant cost of not promoting the appreciation of diversity and the tolerance of other cultures and social-political ideologies. This is particularly true where the subcultural norms relate to religious views which are based on particularistic beliefs of revealed absolute truths. While this situation may be alleviated somewhat by consciousness of the problem and the taking of special initiatives in regard to it, the basic problem, we believe, is systemic. Endemic to separatist education, particularly that based on religion, is the reinforcement of the specific, particularistic subgroup culture and norms at the expense of the appreciation of diversity and the tolerance of other cultures and norms.

Financing: 'Separate but Equal'?

The second major problem of the Israeli system involves financing. As we have emphasised above, in addition to the financing of different streams of 'public' (State) education, the State also finances 'private' education. This system obviously enhances cultural-religious autonomy as well as parental choice. However, it also raises problems. The financing of private education is not mandated by law, but rather the relevant statutes leave to the discretion of the Ministry of Education both the existence and the extent of such financing. Moreover, in practice the criteria for determining such financing have not been published officially. This situation leads to a great deal of political infighting both among the private schools and between them and the State systems, as well as charges and countercharges as to discrimination against, or in favour of, private educational streams as against State education. There are also such charges within the State system as between the State (secular) and State religious schools. Finally, it is generally agreed that the Arab schools are less well financed than those in the Jewish sector.

Some of these differences can be attributed to objective factors such as geography, e.g., rural as against urban schools, as well as differences in the share of local government in the financing of the schools. Other differentials are also not endemic to the system and could be solved by political will. On the other hand, there are some differentials which are the result of the system itself. While the State can and does specify minimal student attendance figures as to schools that it will support financially, beyond those figures separate schools based on religion will inevitably vary in terms of the number of their students because of variations in the groups involved and their geographic dispersion. Should the extent of State support, therefore, be based invariably on a per student basis or should it recognise that smaller schools generally cost more per student in order to achieve the same or similar results? The problem of the number of students per class or per school may further be accentuated by religious principles that require the separation of sexes even in primary education. Again, what effect should this have on State funding? Also, should a religious school, State or private, receive greater funding per child than a State (secular) school on the grounds that it needs to teach more hours in order to cover both a general and religious curriculum?

Another problem relates to the essence of State funding of private schools. Since these schools are, indeed, private they can also charge tuition fees. Moreover, they may also be able to raise money from private benefactors or be part of movements which contribute to their support. All this together with State support may result in their being able to provide more services and facilities to their students than do the State schools.

This situation may provide the private religious schools with a competitive advantage over, for example, the State religious schools. The former may use their extra funding for such student-attracting services as free or heavily subsidised hot lunches or longer school days, the latter being very significant in a society in which generally both parents work outside the home. While competition between State religious and private religious schools may, in general, be quite desirable, is it so if the private schools have a funding advantage? Should then the ability of private schools to raise their own funds be taken into account when the level of State funding is determined? Does the situation change if the ability of the private religious schools to provide such things as hot lunches or longer school days derives from the fact that their employees, who are members of their particular religious movement, are willing to work for lower salaries than those prevailing in the State schools?

Before closing this discussion, we should note that in Israel the problem of private funding being added to public funding of private schools is alleviated somewhat, but only somewhat, by the fact that in the State schools parents, if they so choose, may provide, at their expense, school 'enrichment' programmes for their children. This system, however, while alleviating somewhat the competitive advantage of private schools, creates its own problem: differentiation among State schools based on parental ability and willingness to supplement the State school funding. Further discussion of this issue, however, would go beyond the scope of this paper.

Conclusion

The primary organising principle of the Israeli educational structure is religion. That is to say, schools in Israel are distinguished, one from another, in great part by their religious nature.

This fact is the result of three factors. First, the extremely heterogeneous nature of religious beliefs and attitudes towards religion, both within the Jewish majority and between this majority and the non-Jewish minorities, results in the fact that each particular group desires to control the religious education of the children of its adherents. Second is the fact that many societal groupings in Israel, including political movements and parties, have been organised traditionally around religion and attitudes towards religion. This fact both strengthens the centrality of religion as an organising principle in Israeli social and political life and often results in religion serving as a surrogate for other cultural and, indeed, political norms and values. Lastly, both Orthodox religious Judaism and Islam view religion not as a compartmentalised set of beliefs and actions, but rather as a total way of life which determines all that a person does in all aspects of his existence. Thus religious education cannot consist merely of specific religious courses taught as part of an overall curriculum the other aspects of which are religiously neutral, but rather must consist of the maintaining of a total religious environment in a given school or system of schools.

The result is that Israeli education is divided into a number of relatively autonomous systems and substance, almost all of which receive State funding, which are organised primarily on religion-related lines with the guiding principle being parental choice as to the system in which a given child will be educated.

As such, Israeli education may properly be viewed as a model of multicultural education based on separatism and parental choice. The advantages of such a system in a highly pluralistic society which is interested in helping societal subgroups to preserve their distinctive heritages and traditional values are quite obvious. The system also advances the liberal objective of respecting and, indeed, encouraging, parental choice as to the type of value system they want for the education of their children.

On the other hand, this system - based as it is on separatism - creates significant problems and has clear costs. Some of these problems are not systemic and may be solved with the proper political will. This is particularly true as to the politicised funding of the schools, as discussed in the preceding Section. On the other hand, while not systemic, perhaps it is not purely coincidental that a separatist system of education based primarily on religion is politicised as to its funding. The Americans have warned us against the 'entanglements' involved in State support of religion.[10]

Similarly, the underfunding of Arab education is not a necessary, systemic effect of separatism. On the other hand, is it purely a coincidental effect? May not there be a probable, if not inevitable, connection between separatism and the underfunding of that separate part that serves a politically weak minority group? Does 'separate' tend probably, if not inevitably, to be 'unequal'?

Other problems are clearly systemic. Separatism itself creates very significant problems in creating a common civil society. Moreover, separatism creates very severe problems of closed systems on the micro-level that do not educate to the appreciation of differences and tolerance of the 'unlike other'. This situation is aggravated even further when the closed system involved is based on religiously held absolute truths.

In our view these problems are endemic to a separatist multicultural system, particularly one based on religion, and thus can never be completely eliminated from such a system. At a minimal level, at least, they have to be accepted as a necessary cost of such a system. Of course, the intensity of these problems can be alleviated by awareness of their existence and by the resulting intensive efforts to educate all students, in all streams and schools, to the appreciation of difference and tolerance of the other. Israel's educational systems have thus far failed to meet this challenge adequately. There is a great need for much more extensive efforts in all streams and schools, but especially in the State religious schools and the ultra-orthodox religious educational streams, to educate all students both as to the rights and obligations of all citizens in a common civil society and to the appreciation of diversity and the tolerance of other cultural norms, views and ideologies.

Yet even were this to be accomplished, we must recognise that at some point there will be a direct clash between such education for tolerance and the particularistic norms - especially when they are founded on religious beliefs based on absolute truths - which a given group wants to inculcate in its youth; this being the basic reason for the separatism. Hence, the endemic nature of the problem which, therefore, can be alleviated but not eliminated.

Notes

[1] For further discussion of these and other issues discussed in this paper, see S. Goldstein, 'The Teaching of Religion in Government Funded Schools in Israel' (1992) 26 *Israel Law Review* 36. See also, S. Goldstein, 'Israel: A Secular or Religious State?' (1991) 36 *St. Louis Univ. L. J.* 145.

[2] Emphasis in the original; I. Englard, 'Law and Religion in Israel' (1987) 35 *Am. J. Comp. L.* 185, at 187. Throughout this Introduction we will be relying heavily on the analysis of Prof. Englard in this excellent article.

[3] Ibid. at 188.

[4] For further discussion of these issues, see S. Goldstein, 'Israel: A Secular or Religious State?' supra n. 1.

[5] It should be noted, however, that despite the existence of this Arab system *de facto,* there is almost no *de jure* recognition of the division of State education into Jewish and Arab sub-systems in the relevant legislation concerning State education. In light of this fact, it would appear that under Israeli law no student could be denied admission to either sub-system on the grounds that because of his religion or nationality he belongs in the

other. In practice, while we know of no Jewish students who learn in Arab schools, there are, indeed, some Arab students in Jewish schools.

[6]   For further discussion of the law and practice of control of the non-school related activities of teachers and other professional employees in the State religious system, see S. Goldstein, 'The Teaching of Religion in Government Funded Schools in Israel', *supra* n. 1, at 55-60.

[7]   Unlike the situation as to teachers, State religious education is not defined in the Law as being 'religious' in terms of its students; see section 1 quoted above in the text. Thus, in our view a child cannot be denied admission to a State religious school on the grounds that he or his family are not religious. And, indeed, in some schools there is a significant minority of students who do not come from Orthodox religious homes. We also believe that, for similar reasons, the religious school authorities have no legal authority to control the non-school related behaviour of their students or their families. Of course, State religious education is defined as religious in terms of the 'way of life' of the schools. This provision clearly gives the school authorities control of the religious behaviour of their pupils in their school-related activities. Also, since it is impossible to insulate completely the religious nature of a school from the religious nature of its student body, the preservation of a given school's religious way of life may justify restricting the number of non-religious students in that school. For further discussion of these issues, see *id.,* at 45-48.

[8]   See, however, Sebba and Shiffer at Chap 10 below.

[9]   The following discussion in this section is a revised version of material that has been published in S. Goldstein, 'Religiously Affiliated and Secular School Systems: Israel', in *Pluralism and Education* (P.M. Roeder, I. Richter and H.P. Fussel, eds.) Univ. of Calif. Press, Berkeley, 1995, pp.243-278.

[10]   See, e.g., *Lemon v. Kurtzman*, 403 U.S. 602 (1971).

9 Child-Parent-State: The Absence of Community in the Courts' Approach to Education

LEORA BILSKY

Introduction

The family context has long been a source of perplexity for liberal theories. How can a theory committed to individual freedom and choice make sense of an institution built upon mutual obligation and love? The traditional solution was to hold a distinction between two separate realms of life: the private and the public. According to this view shielding the individual against the coercion of state power calls for a recognition of the family as a private sphere beyond the reach of state intervention. By granting privacy rights to the family we help create a protected sphere in which individuals enjoy the freedom to exercise their autonomy. In other words, the family should serve as a private sanctuary of individual freedom, safe from intervention by government. Such was the traditional story told to us by liberal theory. The fallacy in this story was brought to light by feminists who unravelled the violence and coercion some members of the family (i.e., women and children) had to endure under the veil of family privacy.[1] They exposed a potential conflict between the need to insulate family relations from the power of government and a commitment to safeguard the autonomy of the individual members of the family. Feminist writers argued that within a sphere cordoned off as 'private' and removed from state intervention, family members, including children, remain individuals who may have or who may lack rights to appeal to the state. The challenge that we face today is to find a way to reconcile the doctrine of family privacy with the basic aspiration of a liberal state to enhance the autonomy of its individual members.[2]

I would like to explore these questions by reflecting on the area of education. More specifically, I would like to raise some questions regarding the common assumption that parents should have a right to choose their children's religious education according to their own beliefs and values.[3] Protected by the doctrine of family privacy, the educational decisions of parents are usually shielded from governmental scrutiny. This protection is meant to strengthen the autonomy of the individual in accordance with the basic liberal value of freedom of choice. The question remains, however, whose freedom and whose autonomy does this doctrine actually protect? What happens, for example, when parents are divided about the proper education of their children? Whose freedom does a privacy right protect in this case? What happens when parents agree about their child's education but their choice conflicts with basic values of the larger society regarding the well-being of children? How should we reconcile the universalist-liberal values of autonomy and equality with the particularist values of religious communities? And finally what happens when the parents' educational choice conflicts with the manifested will of the child? In short, how should the law settle disputes concerning the education of children?

Recently the Supreme Court of Israel has attempted to clarify the analytical perplexities that arise in decisions concerning the religious education of children provided by their parents. The court, under the leadership of Chief Justice Meir Shamgar, considered a new framework for deciding these matters. The case under consideration involved a custody conflict between parents who disagreed as to whether to expose their children to the beliefs and values of the Jehovah's Witnesses sect.[4] These beliefs were held by the mother at the time of the trial. Chief Justice Shamgar, in a long and well-reasoned opinion, introduced a new approach to resolve the controversy. Shamgar suggested that a *children's rights* model that he elaborated can resolve many of the analytical, ideological, and practical difficulties arising in disputes about the religious education of children.[5] This new approach, however, was received with reluctance by the other members of the court. Their reluctance can be explained as stemming from the radical transformation that such an approach might bring about to a very sensitive and delicate area of law.[6] In order to evaluate the changes that a 'children's rights' approach entails in conflicts about the religious education of children, I begin my investigation with two earlier court decisions by Israeli courts. Thereafter, I turn to explore the changes that a rights approach can bring about in the balance of powers among children, parents, state, and the religious community. In particular, I inquire how we can *accommodate/reconcile* the role of the religious community in the education of children with a commitment to basic liberal values.

The Two-Tier Model

The first case I would like to discuss is a district court opinion 661/83 *Ploni v. Plonit* (1983) delivered by Judge Zeiler (hereafter, the '*Deri* Case').[7] Here, the parents were engaged in a custody struggle over their youngest child Deri. The mother challenged the custody rights of the father over the son, mainly because of the religious education that the father provided. The father belonged to a small religious sect (Jews for Jesus), a group that leads an insular life from the outside world in a small settlement in the desert. The mother, a former member of this religious group, asked the court to grant her the physical custody over her son and the right to educate him according to her present secular beliefs, in Jerusalem, where she lived at the time of the trial.

In order to decide the controversy Judge Zeiler began by elaborating an analytical map to guide his ruling. This map was meant to reconcile two basic liberal values, the autonomy of the family and the freedom of the individual. Judge Zeiler offered a two-tier model to delineate the line between parents' control over their children's education, and legitimate state interference in parents' decisions. According to this model, in the ordinary situation, where the family unit is functioning and parents agree about the education of their children, the state should respect the family's autonomy and refrain from intervention (unless there is a clear indication of harm to the health or life of the child). In other situations, where there is a complete breakdown in family relations and an agreement between the parents about their children's education cannot be found, the state has the right to intervene through its court system. Interventions in such cases can be reconciled with the fundamentals of liberal theory, since the family unit has already dissolved, and as a result there is no longer a need to protect its privacy. Moreover, by bringing the controversy to court, the parents indicate their consent to state intervention. According to liberal theory, however, not every decision by the court will be upheld, only one that remains neutral as between the values and beliefs of the parents. The traditional solution in Israeli law was to apply the 'best interests of the child' test as a neutral yardstick to adjudicate the competing claims of the parents. This test was understood as protecting the interests of the child while paying due respect to the parents' beliefs and values. Applying this test to the case at hand, Judge Zeiler decided that neither the father nor the mother should be granted custody rights over their child Deri. Instead, the child would be sent to a state institution or to a foster family. I will return to this part of the decision later on.

The First Tier

Let us examine more closely the two-tier model that guides Judge Zeiler's decision. Is it really capable of accommodating basic liberal values? I would like to suggest that a closer look of the two-tier model reveals its shortcomings at both stages of its application. Take for example cases falling under the first tier where the state is required to defer to parents who agree about their children's religious education. Is there no situation short of criminal misconduct (child abuse and neglect) that should warrant the state's intervention? Are we not neglecting the child's present and future autonomy by giving absolute precedence to the parents' choice?

A serious commitment to an individual's autonomy requires that the child will enjoy the physical as well as the cognitive and cultural conditions that will enable him to exercise meaningful autonomy in the future.[8] However, according to the two-tier model, the court is allowed to intervene only in extreme situations of demonstrable physical or emotional harm to the child. Consider the example that the court offered to demonstrate the extent of the court's deference to parents' choices. A father who is a medical doctor decides to go and help starving people in Africa. The father takes his child with him to be raised in an isolated place. Judge Zeiler maintains that as long as the mother agrees to this arrangement, the state should not intervene.

How can we reconcile this hypothetical example with a liberal commitment to the autonomy and freedom of the individual child? What can justify privileging the rights of one class of individuals (parents) over another (children)? One answer would be to view the child as lacking, in the present time, the full capacity to exercise her freedoms, and to see the parents as social agents who are responsible for acting on the child's behalf (trusteeship theory).[9] This answer, however, does not give a good enough reason why the state should refrain from interfering when the parents' educational decision today has the tendency to undermine the future autonomy of the child. Nor does it give a good reason why we should ignore the autonomous choices of the child when the parents agree to the contrary.[10] Judge Zeiler could remain silent about these troubling questions, however, because the *Deri* case presented him with an easier situation in which the parents disagree among themselves, and 'invite' the state to intervene. The court's opinion regarding the hypothetical case remains a *dictum* and our questions remain unanswered on this matter.

In order to answer these troubling questions we shall introduce our third case, which was decided long before the Deri case. In this case, the concerns we raised materialised into a grim reality for the Reuben children. The case of *Attorney General v. Reuben*[11] (hereafter, the '*Reuben* Case') tells the story of an Israeli Jewish couple who, after a failed attempt to arrange for their children's adoption, decided to send their children to be educated in a Christian Mission. The state petitioned the court to intervene and to appoint an attorney *ad litem* on the children's behalf. If we were to apply the two-tier model to this case, it would have dictated non-intervention, since the parents were in full agreement as to their children's religious education (i.e., first tier). One recognised exception to the rule of non-intervention is when parents neglect their minimal legal duties towards their children, and Judge Kister examined this issue.[12] However, the judge was not satisfied with the whole framework of the two-tier model, apparently because he thought that it did not probe the issues deeply enough. Judge Kister explained that in his view parents' freedom of religion was not a sufficient reason to grant the parents absolute control over their children's education. This was so because protecting an absolute right of parents' freedom of religion involves, *inter alia*, the well-being of their children. This danger exposes the limits of the two tier model in the area of parent-child relations. A conception of family autonomy serving as a boundary against state intervention cannot accommodate the complexity of the problem, because in family matters granting rights against the state to one individual always has an impact on the internal balance of power among the other members of the family. Judge Kister suggested, therefore, balancing the parents' interests and rights against the children's interests and rights - including the right of a Jewish child to receive a Jewish education.[13]

Judge Kister's approach deviates from the two-tier model in three central respects. First, the judge was unwilling to give an absolute priority to the parents' rights without first balancing them against the needs, interests and rights of the child. Secondly, he did not limit his enquiry to the child's physical and emotional well-being but was also concerned with providing the child with a consistent moral and religious environment. Thirdly, Kister's approach is informed by a deep understanding of the role of community in the development of the child's identity, a consideration which makes him sensitive to the potential clash between communities in relation to the education of children.

To sum up, the rule against intervention in cases falling under the first tier fails to respond to the full complexity of situations like the *Reuben* controversy, because it requires that the state keep out of the controversy when parents agree among themselves, even though their decisions impede the present or future autonomy of the child.

The second tier

The difficulties with the two-tier model are not restricted to cases decided under the first tier. Situations involving the second tier, when parents disagree about the education of their children and the state intervenes, raise their own difficulties. Here the main issue that the court confronts is how to guarantee the *neutrality* of state intervention. Israeli courts developed the 'best interest' test in order to decide these conflicts in a neutral and professional way. Doubts arise, however, as to the capability of this test to guarantee the court's neutrality. For example, it is a well known fact that when familial conflicts are brought under the jurisdiction of Rabbinical courts in Israel, the child's best interest is interpreted according to Jewish law.[14] An ideological bias in the application of the 'best interest' test can be detected in secular court decisions as well. For example, there is a growing body of research documenting the gender bias in custody decisions in the US court system.[15] In cases of this type we can detect value judgments underlying the professional language of 'best interests'. To what extent are these value judgments shaped by the values of the communities to which the parties and the judges belong?

The court's decision in the *Deri* case can demonstrate that the district court was not immune from the particularist values of its community in determining Deri's best interest. The court, you may recall, was asked to evaluate the potential harm to Deri, the child, from receiving the religious education of his father and his religious community. Deri's father had to answer charges concerning the impact of his religious education on the child's best interests, especially the potential harm from the lack of exposure of the child to outside stimulation. It can be argued that similar charges can always be raised against those who choose a pioneer way of life. Applying the best interest test to such cases is suspected of an ideological bias because it tends to burden unequally those who choose a pioneer way of life and those who conform to the standard way of living. Responding to the charge of ideological bias, the court tried to defend the neutrality of its decision by distinguishing adults from children, and by introducing the incapacity doctrine. Judge Zeiler explained that choosing to endure the physical and spiritual difficulties in pursuing a pioneer way of life should be recognised as the prerogative of an adult (an autonomous person) and the court will refrain from interfering. However, when such a decision involves children who are not yet fully autonomous, the court is justified in protecting them from the irresponsible decisions of their parents. Put another way, the future autonomy and well-being of the child require that the court restrain the parents from burdening their children with their idiosyncratic ideals which result in hardship and lack of outside stimulation for their children. The court's purpose is to protect the future autonomy of the child by exposing him at the present time to the variety of life styles and beliefs within a heterogeneous society like the Israeli one. Only through such an exposure will the child be prepared to make an informed decision when reaching adulthood. Notice, however, that such scrutiny of a pioneer way of life, notwithstanding its professional aura, is difficult for an Israeli court to uphold. It stands in conflict with a long line of decisions that defended the rights of Israeli parents to decide their children's education even when these decisions subjected their children to a pioneer way of living.[16]

In order to tackle this difficulty the court introduced yet another distinction between a well established movement like Zionism, and esoteric and marginal groups such as 'Jews for Jesus'. The court explained that

> [Golda Meir] set out to fulfil an ideal that was upheld by representatives from all quarters of the Jewish people, a movement that received the blessing of the United Nations.

In contrast, Deri's father

> belongs to a new religious belief that has no historical roots among the Jewish people; it is a pioneer movement that has very few believers among the Jewish people and within Israel. There are merely twenty people or so in this settlement.

Paradoxically, according to this distinction, a pioneer way of life would receive the blessing of the court only when it had stopped being a pioneers' movement. The court justified its distinction by tying it to the best interest of the child, i.e., measuring objectively the amount of exposure to outside stimulation that the child receives. Thus, judicial bias in favour of the dominant ideology of Zionism is camouflaged by professional language about children's best interests.

Another example of the ideological underpinning of the best interest test is revealed through the examination of the conditions of 'difference and idiosyncrasy' imposed on Deri by the father's education at home. The court explained that Deri was likely to feel alienated and different from the larger society of children at school who dressed differently from him and did not share his religious beliefs. Taken to its extreme, this type of reasoning, if applied, for example, to children of orthodox Jews in the Diaspora, would have justified intolerance by the larger community towards differences in clothing, language, or beliefs that the parents' education might impose on the child.[17] Indeed, the court admitted that an experience of alienation and difference is not unfamiliar to Jewish children living in the Diaspora, but distinguished between living in the Diaspora and in Israel: Here in Israel, as opposed to the Diaspora, a Jewish child who lives among his own people should not be made to feel so very different from his peers.[18]

Finally, the court considered the anarchist outlook of the father's conduct, and the practices of his community. This community sets its own norms of behaviour and leads a life independent from the larger norms of society. Although members of this community commit no criminal offences, they ignore the laws of the land in areas that conflict with their religious beliefs. For example, they marry Jews and non-Jews, ignore conventional medical standards and in general lead a life of total lack of respect for the laws of the country.[19] This atmosphere of lawlessness, the court reasoned, is sure to harm the proper education of the child.

These three examples demonstrate how the court's interpretation of the child's 'best interest' tends to favour dominant Israeli culture (secular Zionism). It has little protection to offer to an insular community that claims a right to educate its children according to its own beliefs (and lacks political power). Notice that the cultural conflict between the religious community and Israeli society at large (and the court as its agent), a conflict that is typical in this type of case, tends to disappear under the guise of professional talk about the 'best interest' of the child. Under the guise of professional talk, the court never confronts the communal tensions surrounding its decision and, therefore, this aspect of the decision remains immune from critical evaluation.

Children's Rights

Concerns about the neutrality of the best interests test, similar to the ones I have mentioned, convinced Justice Shamgar in the Jehovah's Witnesses case to consider an alternative approach to resolve such disputes. Justice Shamgar acknowledged the possibility that an ideological bias was likely to appear in the application of the best interests test to disputes about the religious education of children. Indeed, this consideration was one of the main reasons for Shamgar's suggestion to replace the best interests test with a new approach which he called 'children's rights'. This approach, he claimed, can better guard against an ideological bias in courts' decisions because it requires that the claims of the parties to the dispute be linked to recognised rights. Under the children's rights approach the court considers the child's rights independently of the parents' rights, and in this way the objectivity of the decision is enhanced. We shall examine this claim by examining the place of particularist values of different communities under the new rights approach.

From a traditional liberal perspective the advantages of the children's rights approach seem clear. First, it claims to give an independent voice to the child in matters of family life that concern his or her well-being, thus strengthening the court's commitment to individual autonomy. Secondly, it purports to set clearer boundaries to state intervention by limiting the court's ability to introduce ideological considerations under the guise of the 'best interests' test.[20] In particular, it requires that the state's agents demonstrate firmer grounds such as legal rights to justify intervention.[21] In this way, Shamgar explains, a rights' approach can provide better safeguards against undue intrusion by state officials in family matters. It also claims to ameliorate some of the drawbacks that we identified in the 'best interests' approach. In particular, granting legal rights to each member of the family ensures that the court will strike a more informed balance among the interests of all the concerned parties to the dispute (at least, all the parties whose interests are protected as legal 'rights').[22]

Leaving aside the question to what extent the court achieved its goals[23], I would like to consider a rather neglected aspect of the children's rights approach: its effect on the balance of power between child, parent and state. At the outset of the paper I suggested that the two-tier model can be viewed as an attempt to strike a delicate balance between individual autonomy and family privacy. I would like to examine now what happens to this balance under the rights approach. Justice Shamgar claims that the balance does not change significantly under a children's rights approach since it accepts the two-tier model as the larger framework. This statement is a bit misleading since replacing a 'best interests' test with a 'children's rights' approach signals the beginning of the framework's collapse. Indeed, Justice Shamgar admits at one point that the adoption of a children's rights approach would tend to justify a greater intervention in family matters by the state. It could, therefore, undermine in some respects the 'privacy' accorded to the family unit under the two-tier model. Apart from this erosion in family autonomy, which can be justified from a children's rights perspective, I would like to suggest that the new approach has repercussions for the court's ability to take into account the positive role of the religious community in the development of the child's identity.

The Child and the Religious Community

The analytical clarity that the model of rights produces is bought at a cost. The model has the tendency to downplay the communal aspects inherent in decisions about children's education. The model of children's rights as interpreted by the court is a model of individual rights, i.e., it is atomistic in nature. Communal units that are affected by the decision, such as the family, the religious community, cultural and ethnic groups, etc., cannot find a legal form to articulate their concerns. This has obvious effects on the protection of the interests of the cultural and religious community in the education of its children. I would like to evaluate the effects of a change to rights discourse from the child's viewpoint. My point is that in so far as the community has a role to play in shaping the child's identity and enabling his or her future autonomous choices, a rights approach that fails to consider this aspect might prove deficient. In other words, a rights approach that has no tools to articulate the role of the community in the identity-formation of the child and in the development of capacities for autonomous choice, cannot confront the ideological considerations within the court's decisions in this area.

From liberty to identity

A recent article that discusses the issue of community rights within a liberal framework argues that liberal theories do not pay enough attention to issues of cultural identity in their discussion of human rights.[24] This observation is true of the children's rights discourse as well. The court's discussion focuses on the protection of the liberties of the individual child and has difficulty discussing the interest of the individual child in the protection of her identity culture. This deficiency is particularly apparent in controversies about the education of children since such controversies raise mixed issues of identity and liberty.[25] We can point out the lack of attention to the identity-culture of the child in the decisions we have discussed so far. In the *Deri* case, for example, the court's decision to grant custody to the mother was followed by a change in the identity culture of the child (from 'Jews for Jesus' to secular Judaism). Likewise, for the *Reuben* couple the court's decision involved a choice between two religious-cultural identities - Jewish and Christian. Finally, Justice Shamgar's decision in *Plonim* protected the children's identity as Jews by forbidding their mother to continue to expose them to the Jehovah's Witnesses culture.[26] When dealing with children who are in the process of becoming autonomous persons, the centrality of the community in the formation of the child's identity is apparent.[27] However, since rights are traditionally understood as protections of the liberties of the individual by setting boundaries between individuals (and between the individual and the state), they fail to address the child's interest in an identity culture as a pre-condition for practising liberties. The rights discourse does not provide answers to the difficult question of how to secure a meaningful interaction between the child and other members of her community(ies) to address the child's interest in an identity culture.

A liberal state is committed to enhancing the autonomy of the individual. When we consider the issue of individual autonomy, taking adults as our example, we tend to focus on the *liberty* of the individual against undue intrusion by the state (and other individuals) as helping the individual protect his or her identity culture of choice. However, when we shift our attention from adults to children we tend to approach questions of autonomy by deciding a controversy between communities about a choice of the child's *identity* culture. For a child the future promises autonomy and freedom of choice, but the present is often characterised by restrictions and hierarchical relationships, at home, in school, and elsewhere. The child's interest in autonomy, therefore, requires that we probe the issue of identity formation directly and examine the role of communities in developing and nurturing the identity culture of the child. Indeed, the efforts of parents, siblings, teachers and other significant adults in the child's life are directed to shaping the child's identity in a way that will enable him or her to practise meaningful choices in the future. Hence, conceptualising autonomy solely in terms of liberty does not resonate well with the needs and experiences of children.

The two points of view about autonomy (that of an adult and that of a child) are related to the different life experiences that shape them. The adult's viewpoint points in the direction of enhanced protection of liberty interests (identity following on the way). The child's viewpoint emphasises identity interests (autonomy following on the way). By moving between these standpoints, we can gain a more complete understanding of autonomy as a condition that depends on a mixture of the two ingredients (liberty and identity).[28] Moreover, entertaining both viewpoints simultaneously helps us notice that a static framework (either the two-tier model, or a rigid interpretation of rights as boundaries) can hinder our understanding of the temporal dimension of children's education.[29]

Considering the question of autonomy with the child in mind, we are reminded that identity is always a communal enterprise that involves more than a free-willing individual. The identity of the individual is always shaped in relation to a larger set of communal identities. In turn, a viable collective identity, be it religious or secular, needs a community for its creation and preservation. In as much as the future autonomy of the child is dependent upon the successful formation of his or her identity, it remains indebted to the community (or communities) that provides the child with the necessary cultural materials. But communities are not created overnight. They are dependent upon the continuing commitment of their members to pass the tradition on to the younger generation.[30] Sometimes in the name of this tradition communities demand that we limit the freedoms of some individual members of the community, in particular children, in order to preserve the community's identity. In such cases courts have to make a difficult decision whether to allow the survival interest of the community to enter the equation.[31] But even in disputes that fall short of these extreme situations, focusing on questions of identity is likely to expose a clash among communities about the education of the young, a clash that tends to disappear under the traditional framework of rights. When this clash involves agents of the state (in the name of basic liberal values) and a religious community, it is often about the treatment of weaker members of the community, and about the claims of the religious community to exclusivity.

From identity to equality: The clash between communities

Robert Cover, in his seminal article 'Nomos and Narrative', reminds us of the communal aspects that are involved in legal disputes about education. Cover argues that often controversies about the education of the young are also conflicts about the collective identities of social groups. He explores this tension in American society, saying,

> Precisely because the school is the point of entry to the paideic and the locus of its creation, the school must be the target of any redemptive constitutionalism ... Through education, the social bonds form that give rise to autonomy, to the jurisgenerative process .... The judge must resolve the competing claims of the redemptive constitutionalism of an excluded race, on one hand, and of insularity, the protection of association, on the other.[32]

Cover uncovers the clash between two communities and two collective narratives in America: the constitutional narrative of larger American society about racial equality and the narrative of the insular religious community of fundamental Christians about racial exclusivity. According to Cover, the abstract language of rights and freedoms of individuals fails to give due respect to the struggle over communal identity implicit in these educational controversies.

Israeli courts face a similar dilemma in cases concerning violence against women and children in which a 'cultural defence' is raised.[33] One famous case dealt with the use of violence against children by an Arab nun in a Greco-Catholic orphanage.[34] In this case (hereafter, *Dalal Rasi*) an Arab Nun was blamed for biting and maiming several of her female students. The attorney for the defence raised a 'cultural defence' argument, i.e., the need to respect practices of the minority community even if these practices contradict the values of larger Israeli society. The Supreme Court decided to reject the 'cultural defence' argument and convicted the nun of battery. The reasons given by the three Justices for their decision are illuminating. They are indicative of the way in which the conflict between communities in Israel shape the Justices' interpretations. Justice Cheshin construed the controversy as one between a modern enlightened community (Israeli) and a traditionalist backward community (Arab-Christian). He relied on legal materials from the common law that dealt with the cultural conflict between the British colonialists and the native Muslim culture regarding 'family honour'. Justice Cheshin suggested replacing the word

'British' with the word 'Israeli' and proceeding to apply the English precedents to the case at hand.[35] His conviction of the nun carried with it the additional effect of presenting the conflict between the Israeli and Arab communities as one between a higher culture and a lower one. Justice Asaf (a Jewish Rabbi) also saw the controversy as a conflict between two communities. However, for him the real clash was between the Orthodox Jewish community (one with a long and respectable tradition) and all 'other' communities in Israel (identified negatively as those that have not received the 'secret wisdom' of the Jewish tradition). According to Justice Asaf the court should turn to 'our' tradition (i.e., Jewish *Halacha*) in order to decide the case. In the *Halacha* Asaf discovered a 'secret wisdom' according to which the harms of hitting a child exceed the benefits.[36] Justice Landau's opinion strikes a different note. Although he agreed with his brethren that the teacher should be convicted according to the Israeli penal law, he refused to interpret the dispute in terms of 'us' against 'them'. Landau J. chose, instead, to base his conviction on testimonies of witnesses for the defence who testified that the teacher's behaviour was unacceptable according to the norms of her own culture. Thus, by refusing to reify the tradition of the 'other' to 'our' traditions, and by noticing different voices in the Arab-Christian community, Justice Landau managed to justify the state's intervention without extracting the additional cost of painting the Arab-Christian community as inferior.[37]

An approach that tries to reduce conflicts about education to their very basic units (rights of individuals) obscures the fact that the liberal state does not function in the area of education as a neutral body. As the *Dalal Rasi* case demonstrates, the state acts as a collective, interested in transmitting its own values (such as values of equality and autonomy) to the younger generation.[38] Similarly, a religious group which claims a right over education does it as a way of preserving the group's distinct culture, tradition, and social practices. A rights approach as interpreted by the court tends to obscure these elements and to shield them from critical evaluation. A crucial point in Justice Shamgar's judgment warrants our attention in this respect. Justice Shamgar classified the controversy in the Jehovah's Witnesses case under the legal rubric of 'parent-child relations' and not under the rubric of 'freedom of religion.'[39] This formulation helped neutralise the cultural clash that the case displayed between two communities (secular Israeli society, and Jehovah's Witnesses). In other words, the court's rhetoric tended to privatise (or domesticate) the conflict.

The children's rights approach, as interpreted by Justice Shamgar, does not avoid the ideological conflict among communities that we identified in the 'best interest' approach. It only drives the conflict underground. It allows the judge to introduce value judgments and wrap them up in the universalist language of rights. For example, by adopting a certain interpretation of children's rights as the right to remain within the religion of one's birth, Shamgar's decision favours established religious communities and discriminates against new ones.[40] Applying this interpretation to the case at hand happens to match the interests of the larger Jewish community, since the children were born Jews and only later did their mother join the Jehovah's Witnesses. If the court were to apply this approach to the *Deri* case it would have granted custody to the father and his community ('Jews for Jesus'), because both parents shared these beliefs at the time of Deri's birth. I have doubts, though, whether the *Deri* court would have adhered strictly to this test, given the fact that Judge Zeiler preferred to send Deri to a state institution, where the child would be raised as a Jew, rather than allow him to continue his religious education with his father. [41] Note that Judge Zeiler presented his decision as a neutral one since he claimed to refrain from choosing between the parents. However, if we consider the conflict from the stand-point of the communities involved in this case, we realise that Zeiler's decision (sending the child to a Jewish educational institution) is biased in favour of the Jewish community to which the mother belonged at the time of the trial. Note that the *Reuben* court, rejecting the two-tier model, was willing to engage in a more candid approach to resolving such clashes between communities. Note also that Judge Kister was willing to examine the conflict between the Jewish and Christian communities directly by balancing their respective claims with regard to the education of the *Reuben* children. [42] This type of balancing, as our exploration of the new rights' approach reveals, is unlikely to occur under a legal framework that leaves no space for the consideration of the interests of communities.

The Role of Community from a Child-Centred Perspective

Introducing children to our theories of rights can offer a more dynamic understanding of autonomy, as a capacity that is shaped over time. It also helps articulate the child's interest in her identity-culture. Finally, it exposes the communal aspects that are involved in many of the legal controversies about children's education. The traditional concept of rights as static and atomistic is inadequate to deal with the dynamic and communal aspects of children's education. My criticism, however, should not be read as suggesting that we abandon the model of rights altogether.

Instead, it should encourage us to be creative in finding ways to combine the value of protecting the community with a commitment to the basic liberal values. It calls for a greater attention to the interpretation we give to rights in the area of children's education. Indeed suggestions in this direction have been previously offered by two scholars, Martha Minow and Jennifer Nedelsky, who developed a relational framework for rights.[43] The gist of their argument is that the dependency of children on adults (which shifts over time to a dependency of old people on their children) makes the traditional conception of rights as boundaries between individuals inadequate.[44] Rights should not be understood simply as walls between individuals because they have an important role to play in facilitating human relations within a community.[45]

In contemporary writing one can identify two opposing views about the value of the community to the individual. Communitarian writers such as Michael Sandel and Alasdair MacIntyre praise the value of the community to the individual and criticise liberal theories for adopting an atomistic conception of the individual that ignores this role.[46] Feminist and critical writers, on the other hand, expose the role of community in oppressing the weakest members in the community, often women and children.[47] Even though the two schools perceive themselves as diametrically opposite, I would like to suggest that their teachings can be integrated with our approach to children's education. Both approaches criticise the private/public divide by pointing to their intermingling in institutions such as the family and the religious community.[48] A closer look at their arguments reveals that the two schools emphasise opposite sides of the same coin and highlight an ingredient that is missing from liberal discussion in courts - the place of the cultural community in litigation about children's education.

Both the value of the community to the individual child and the dangers of oppression by a given community are manifest in controversies about the religious education of children. On the one hand, a child's religious community can provide the cultural resources to reinforce the child's developing identity. It often shields and protects the child from parents' violence and indifference by supervising parents' behaviour, and by acting as a buffer between the parents and the child. On the other hand, due to the special vulnerability of children to adults who have power over them, a religious community can enhance the imbalance by isolating the child from reaching external sources of help, to a degree far more complete than the parents can achieve on their own accord.[49] The unique value of a viable community to the child's development, and the special vulnerability of the child to it, are important starting points for a critical evaluation of the role of the community in children's education.

A critical evaluation should examine what is hidden behind the professional language, such as considerations of 'continuity'[50] and 'reducing cultural conflicts'. Thus, for example, in both the *Deri* and *Plonim* decisions professional talk about the 'conflict of cultures' to which the children were exposed justified putting restrictions on the exposure of the child by one of the parents. In the *Deri* case the court's intervention meant sending Deri away from his father's community, and in *Plonim* it meant forbidding the mother from continuing to expose her children to her religious beliefs. The alternative of exposing the child to two different cultures was depicted as 'unhealthy' to the child. The value judgment in preferring homogeneity over plurality was hidden and the conflict was transformed into a professional decision about the 'health' of the child. This move is apparent in a case where a more candid discussion about the conflict in the district court disappeared in the appellate court's decision. The controversy was about the education of a child aged thirteen, the son of a Muslim father and a Jewish mother.[51] The physical custody of the child was granted to the father because of his better suitability as a parent. Thereafter, the issue of 'cultural contrast' was raised in the district court by the mother who complained about the father's decision to relocate with the child in an Arab village. The father continued to send the child to a Jewish boarding school. The district court decided that the 'best interest' of the child required the reduction of the cultural conflict in the child's life, but the court left the choice between the cultures to the father (to remain in the Arab village and send the child to an Arab school, or to move to a Jewish settlement and continue the child's education in a Jewish school). When the question was appealed to the Supreme Court, the court narrowed down the choice to one, i.e., sending the child to a Jewish school and relocating the family to a Jewish settlement. The court used the professional language about the need to mitigate the 'religious and social contrast' in the child's life. No justification was given for the priority that the court gave to the 'Jewish' alternative, notwithstanding the father's Muslim religion. Introducing the community factor to our discussion can help expose this gap in the Supreme Court's reasoning. Further questions could be raised about the desirability of giving an absolute priority to the need to reduce 'cultural and social clashes' in the child's life. It may well be that from a certain age an exposure of the child to different cultures might strengthen the child's capacities for autonomous choice as well as our commitment as a society to social pluralism.[52]

This point brings us back to the Supreme Court's decision. My criticism of Justice Shamgar's approach is not meant to suggest that we should give priority to the community over the individual in matters of education. On the contrary, I believe that Justice Shamgar identified the particular sources of danger to the child from a religious community and made a strong case for extending the protection of rights to children in this area. My argument is that when granting rights to individual children we should not ignore the interests of children in their identity culture. I have suggested some central issues that a critical approach to children's rights would have to consider but the full model will have to be developed elsewhere. I would like to conclude by reminding ourselves that matters of education are complicated precisely because they require us to balance the respective rights of individuals and groups. Reducing the controversy to a single matrix (of individual liberties) will buy us analytical clarity instead of deeper understanding of the problems.

Notes

[1]   Frances Olsen, 'The Family and the Market: A Study of Ideology and Legal Reform', 96 *Harv.L.R.* 1497 (1983); Catharine A. MacKinnon, *Toward A Feminist Theory of the State* (Harvard University Press, 1989) 184-194.

[2]   For contemporary re-interpretations of liberal theory extending autonomy rights to women and children 'behind the veil of family privacy' see, Bruce A. Ackerman, *Social Justice in the Liberal State*, (Yale University, 1980) pp. 139-167; Will Kymlicka, *Contemporary Political Philosophy, An Introduction* (Oxford University Press, 1990) pp. 247-262.

[3]   The issue was discussed in a series of American court decisions about the proper limits of public education see: *Meyer* v. *Nebraska*, 262 U.S. 390 (1923); *Pierce* v. *Society of Sisters*, 268 U.S. 510 (1925); *Wisconsin* v. *Yoder*, 406 U.S. 205 (1972); *Mozert* v. *Hawkins County Board of Education* 827 F.2nd 1060 (1983). American courts drew the line between legitimate state interference in the education of children and family's autonomy according to the public/private distinction. Parents were allowed control over their children's private education, while the state retained its control over the public school curriculum. In Israel the balance between state and parents is drawn differently. For example, public education of Jewish children is divided into two separate systems, secular and religious, and parents can choose between the two systems. In addition, the government finances a large portion of the budget of private schools belonging to ultra-religious groups. For an evaluation of the Israeli system of education, see Stephen Goldstein's contribution to this volume at Chap.

8 above. My paper does not examine the Israeli system of public education in general but is limited to the narrower issue of the state's intervention in the religious education provided by parents to their children. This issue is often raised in custody disputed between parents. I will focus on three such cases and examine the balance between the competing interests involved.

4   C.A. 2266/93 *Ploni* v. *Ploni*, 49(1) P.D. 221 (1995).

5   The 'children's rights' approach has been used in different contexts to mean different things. Some advocates of children's rights refer by the term to increased *protection* for children; others use rights to advance the *autonomy* of children. For an analysis and classification of the different uses of the term 'children's rights', see Michael S. Wald, 'Children's Rights: A Framework for Analysis' 12 *U. of California*, 255-281 (1979). Wald suggests distinguishing between those approaches that are based on a new conception of children as autonomous human beings, and those approaches that continue to uphold the traditional view of children as dependent. It is unclear what conception of children's rights Justice Shamgar adopts. According to the theoretical part of his opinion, it is rights as autonomy (giving an independent voice for the child in custody disputes). However, when it comes to application, Shamgar does not give much weight to the children's own preferences. Instead, he advocates a narrow rule that forbids any change in the religion of the children until they are mature enough to decide for themselves. This test seems to respond to the more traditional use of rights as enhanced protection to children.

6   It seems that the main disagreement among the Justices was about the priority that should be given to the children's rights model over the 'best interest of the child' test whenever they point in opposite directions (see the separate opinion of Justice Strasberg-Cohen). For a discussion of the differences between the two approaches (children's rights, and best interests analysis) see P. Shifman, *Family Law in Israel* (vol II.) pp. 236-240.

7   P.M. 45(2) 353 (1983).

8   Ackerman, *supra* note 3.

9   See, Richard J. Arneson and Ian Shapiro, 'Democratic Autonomy and Religious Freedom: A Critique of *Wisconsin v. Yoder*', in *Nomos* vol. 38 (Ian Shapiro and Russell Harding eds., 1996) pp. 365, 366. This approach draws a rigid line between childhood and maturity and neglects to take into account the child's developing capacities for autonomous choice over time. The limitations of such an approach can be demonstrated in cases that deal with teenagers such as B.N. 26/92 Tel Aviv Youth Court (Judge Rotlevi) (not published, on file with author) in which a teenage girl left her parents' (religious) household to lead a secular life and enrolled in a secular high-school. The court refrained from returning the teenager back to her parents' home and upheld her freedom of choice. The court explained, however, that its decision is not meant to give preference to one lifestyle over another

because the conflict between the teenager and the parents goes deeper than a disagreement about religious beliefs. In recent years we witness a growing number of Israeli teenagers who leave their secular homes (partly or fully) in order to lead a religious life in a 'yeshiva'. See A. Kesler, 'Standing against the Yeshiva' *Tel Aviv* (3.1.97); Y. Adiram, 'Parents whose son 'hazar be'tshuva' would ask the court to order him back to them' *Yediot aharonot* (10.2.97). In such cases, applying the two-tiers model would require that the court refuse to take into account the child's choice no matter what her age is and defer exclusively to the parents' decision.

10 As Judge Rotlevi from the Tel Aviv Youth Court explains: 'In matters of choosing a way of life and a life style ... we must give greater weight to the child's choice as the child approaches maturity.' B.N. 26/92 *id.* The judge focuses on the *gradual* development of autonomy in the child and the need of the court to respond to this process by refraining from drawing rigid lines.

11 P.M 39 (1963) p. 15.

12 See, Capacity and Guardianship Law (1962) (Laws of Israel, 1962, p. 120) section 17 (the parents' duty to act as devoted parents would have applied under the circumstances.)

13 A similar question was considered by the court under a different legal rubric. C.A 103/67 *The American European Beith El Mission v. Ministry of Welfare*, P.D 21(2) (1967) 325. In this case a Christian institution for the education of children petitioned the court because of the terms of the licence granted to it by the Minister of Welfare. According to the terms of the licence the institution was not to accept any child who did not belong to the Christian religion. The institution challenged the constitutionality of this condition because it interfered with the free exercise of religion by the parents. Justice Witkon, rejecting this contention, explained that the child's welfare (avoiding religious conflicts) should be given priority over the right of the parents to choose their child's religious education. The court was willing to classify matters of education as concerning the parents' freedom of religion only in cases where the parents (and not just the children) first converted to another religion. See also, *Change of Religious Community Ordinance*, 1927. P.G. - No. 201 of the 16th December 1927, p. 908 (English Edition). This explanation does not apply in cases where the conflict results from divisions within the same religion (such as between religious and secular Jews). See for example, B.N 109/86 *supra* note, 10. (after the court denied the parents custody of their children on welfare grounds, the father requested that the children be sent to a religious boarding-school. The court refused to grant the father's request because it did not recognise the parents' lifestyle as religious. Interestingly, the court's interpretation of what constitutes a 'Jewish religious' lifestyle reveals a deep cultural bias against the self understanding of Sephardic Jews (such as the father) who regard going to the synagogue on the Sabbath

and having a Sabbath dinner as constituting a religious lifestyle. The court's interpretation coincides with the 'Ashkenazi' orthodox Jews' interpretation and disregards alternative interpretations of conservative Jews and reform Jews, as well as of Sephardic Jews.

[14]   Shifman, *supra* note 6, at 241-253.

[15]   S. Berns, 'Living Under the Shadow of Rousseau', 10 *U. of Tasmania L.Rev.* 234 (1991)

[16]   This factor is known as the 'nationality consideration' according to which the best interest of a Jewish child is to grow up in Israel. It can be identified in court decisions in custody disputes between parents who do not share a domicile. See for example C.A. 125/49 *Amado* v. *Amado*, PD 4 at p. 5 (Justice Cheshin's dissenting opinion at pp. 22-23) (1949). See also, H.C. 201/57 *Hershkovitz* v. *District Attorney of Haifa*, PD 13 492, 502 (1957). For a general discussion of the revolutionary ideas about children's education in Israeli kibbutzim see, Bruno Bettelheim, *The Children of the Dream* (Avon, 1969).

[17]   A similar question was raised in C.A. 2266/93, *supra* note 4, where Justice Shamgar suggested distinguishing the religious pluralism present in the US (indicated by the level of religious inter-marriages) from Israeli type pluralism. In Israel different religious groups are treated separately (different school systems, different courts, etc.). Therefore, educating the child under more than one religion might label him as different from the more or less homogeneous social environment (pp. 250-251).

[18]   Note another distinction that the court ignored that seems to be crucial in the *Deri* case: the distinction between insulated communities and relatively open communities. An insulated community that provides its children a separate education can protect them from feeling different from children of the larger society. In contrast, a relatively open community that sends its children to public schools and is more tolerant to the values of the larger society, exposes its children to feelings of difference and is more likely to fail the 'best interest' test. This point was demonstrated in American law where the court found that the educational practices of parents in insular communities such as the Amish group could be reconciled with the 'child's best interests' and deserved the court's protection. See, *Yoder*, *supra* note 3. In contrast, American courts found it much harder to deal with Fundamental Christians who agreed to send their children to public school and only asked for permission to exclude them from reading certain materials that contradicted their religious beliefs. See, *Mozert*, *supra* note 3. See, Nomi M. Stolzenberg, ' "He Drew A Circle That Shut Me Out": Assimilation, Indoctrination, and the Paradox of Liberal Education', 106 *Harv.L.Rev.* 581 (1993). In Israel, not only does the government recognise the right of ultra-religious parents to educate their children according to their beliefs, but it also finances a large portion of their private system of education. The difficulties that were faced by Deri's father can be partly

explained by the fact that he exhibited a more tolerant attitude to secular Israeli culture and agreed to send his child to a public school. The irony is that the decision to send Deri to a public school was probably induced by the father's fear that he would be accused of not exposing his child to 'outside stimulation'. In other words, the logic of the best interest test puts the father in a double bind (lose-lose situation): either he sends his child to public school and exposes him to feelings of alienation and difference, or he refuses to do so, and can then be blamed for failing an equally important obligation to prepare the child for living in a modern pluralist society. In either case the father fails the 'best interest' test. The issue was also raised in C.A. 2266/93 *supra* note 4. The mother asked the court merely to 'expose' the children to her religious beliefs (Jehovah's Witnesses) but did not require exclusivity. The mere fact that granting this request would cause the children to be 'different' from the larger society of children justified, according to the court, a refusal to grant this request.

[19] In particular the court was concerned with the sex education provided to Deri's sisters by the father and with the untraditional family structure in the 'town'. (Deri's father cohabited with two women in the same household.)

[20] See p. 250 of the opinion. For a critique of the claim for 'enhanced objectivity' of a rights discourse see, Mark Tushnet, 'An Essay on Rights', 62 *Tex.L.R.* 1363 (1984) (Tushnet argues that a rights' discourse is informed by existing social structures and therefore cannot guarantee objective results, see pp. 1371-1382).

[21] In the court's words: 'The advantage of children's rights is that the concept of the child's best interest is emotional and subjective, based on the court's interpretation of the facts, while children's rights is a normative and constitutional concept based on recognised rights.' (p. 254)

[22] A 'more informed' decision in the sense that when rights are interpreted as giving an independent voice to the child such an approach broadens the scope of the court's examination before deciding the case. This is particularly important in situations where in the past the investigation of the child's interest was cut short because of a demonstrable right by the parent. See for example an earlier decision by Justice Shamgar C.A. 783/81 *Plonim* v. *Palmoni* 39(2) P.D. 1 (1981). Here the Supreme Court decided to remove the child from his grandparents' custody interpreting the parent's rights as 'trumps' that closed any further considerations of the child's 'best interest'. Under a children's rights approach the court might have been more willing to balance the right of the child to the continuation of a meaningful relationship with his grandparents against the right of the parent to establish his custody over the child. For a discussion of the rights of grandparents see, 'Note, Grandparents versus the State: A Constitutional Right to Custody', 13 *Hofstra Law Review*, 375 (1985); 'Comment: The Coming of Age of Grandparent Visitation Rights,' 43 *Am.U.L.Rev.* 563

(1994); For a general theory of rights as 'trumps' see, Ronald Dworkin, *Taking Rights Seriously* (Harvard University Press, 1977).

23   I do not discuss the children's rights model at length in this paper as it is discussed by Professor Falk (Chap. 7 above). I would just like to note, however, that the actual application of the rights approach in this case fell short of its full potential to bring about a radical change in the court's conception of children's autonomy as the basis for granting them independent rights, see *supra* note 5.

24   Haim Gans, 'National Liberalism' (unpublished manuscript, on file with author).

25   For example, a change of focus from liberty to identity would have allowed the court in C.A. 2266/93 to consider the effects of its decision not to allow the mother to discuss her religious beliefs with her children, on the religious identity of the mother as well as on the developing identities of the children.

26   The decision directly influenced the children's forming identity since they were raised from infancy by a mother who exposed them to the Jehovah's Witnesses religion. The court's ruling prohibited any 'exposure' of this kind until the children matured.

27   For general discussions of this matter, see Charles Taylor, *Sources of The Self, The Making of the Modern Identity* (Harvard University Press, 1989); Will Kymlicka, *Liberalism, Community and Culture* (Oxford University Press, 1989).

28   Gans, *supra* note 25.; Amy Gutmann, 'Communitarian Critics of Liberalism', (1985) *Philosophy and Public Affairs*, vol. 53, pp. 308, 316-318 (criticising the dualism that separates identity from liberty).

29   See *supra* note 10, B.N. 26/92 (The judge adopts a flexible test that attaches more weight to the child's choice as the child matures). For an attempt to introduce a temporal dimension to a liberal discourse of rights see, Ackerman, *supra* note 2 at pp.139-167; For a call to abandon a model based on strict lines and apply a more flexible test to determine the retirement age see, Ruth Ben-Israel, 'Retirement Age under the Equality Test: Biological or Functional Retirement' (1997, Hebrew, on file with author).

30   An example from Jewish tradition is the reading of the Hagada, a story describing the Exodus from Egypt, on Passover evening.

31   In the limited space I have here I do not discuss the difficult issue of granting collective rights to communities and how to reconcile them with basic liberal rights of individuals. For an elaboration of this topic see, Will Kymlicka, *supra* note 27.

32   Robert Cover, 'Nomos and Narrative', in *Narrative, Violence and the Law* (Minow, Ryan and Sarat, (eds), University of Michigan Press, 1992) p. 170

33   For a general discussion of cultural relativism in the context of murders induced by 'family honour' see, Dani Rabinovitch, 'The White Woman's

Burden', 7 *Theory and Critique* 5, John Simons, 'Feminism in the Boundary Region', 7 *Theory and Critique* 20.

[34] C.A. 7/53 *Dalal Rasi v. Attorney General of the State of Israel*, 7 P.D. (1953) 790.

[35] Ibid. p. 796. According to article 46 of The Palestine Order in Council, 1922. P.G. - No. 75 of the 1st September 1922, p. 2 (English Edition), the Israeli court was expected to turn to English precedents where there were no Israeli precedents. However, it is clear from the decision that the Justice also identifies with the 'superior' British values of the English precedents and is proud to put Israelis and British together by opposing to the Arab as the 'other'.

[36] Ibid. p.800. Interestingly, the justice's sole reliance on Jewish sources effaced the gender context of the controversy (a nun and her female students) since the Halacha discusses male education (described as an unbroken chain of rabbis-fathers-sons). Jewish girls according to the Halacha do not enjoy an equal right to education. For an elaboration of changes in women's education according to Jewish law see the opinion of Justice Elon, H.C. 257/89, 2410/90 *Hofman v. The Minister of Religious affairs*, P.D 48 (2) 265,

[37] For a critique of simplistic views that regard the Arab community as homogenous and stable see, Manar Hasan 'Growing up Female and Palestinian in Israel', *Calling the Equality Bluff - Women in Israel* (Swirski and Safir, (eds), Pergamon Press: 1991) p. 66.

[38] Stolzenberg, *supra* note 18.

[39] At p. 233.

[40] It gives preference to older and established religions (Judaism, Islam, Christianity, etc.) over less established groups that are labelled 'religious sects'. This result is due to the fact that people tend to join these sects only later in their life. On the high level of abstraction manifested in the opinion ('normative, constitutional rights' discourse') the children who are deemed Jewish (having been born Jews and never converted) have a right to remain Jewish. However, a more concrete examination reveals that the children were all raised as Jehovah Witnesses from infancy.

[41] A case that can demonstrate a difference between a children's rights approach (interpreted as a right to remain within one's religion) and a 'best interest' approach is case no 86/63 *Hasan Al Safdi v. Baruch Benjamin*, P.D. 17, pp. 1419, 1426. In this case the court validated a decision to move a Muslim child to a Jewish institution rather than allowing her to be raised by her Muslim family because of the child's 'best interest' (health conditions). A children's rights model would have required that we leave the child with the family (and improve the sanitary conditions) or place her in a Muslim institution with proper hygienic conditions.

[42] This investigation leads Judge Kister to acknowledge what he considered to be the justified claims of the larger Jewish society in this case. Indeed,

158 *Children's Rights and Traditional Values*

acknowledging the clash between communities in areas of education does not dictate a solution; rather, it calls for judicial integrity in discussing what is really at stake in the decision, and balancing the respective claims. Robert Cover criticises the American court for lack of candour in this area. See *supra* note 32, p. 170: 'The court assumes a position that places nothing at risk and from which the Court makes no interpretative gesture at all, save the quintessential gesture to the jurisdictional canons: the statement that an exercise of political authority was not unconstitutional.'

43 Martha Minow, 'Rights for the Next Generation: A Feminist Approach to Children's Rights' 9 *Harvard Women's Law Journal* (1986) 1; Jennifer Nedelsky, 'Reconceiving Autonomy: Sources, Thoughts and Possibilities,' 1 *Yale Journal of Law and Feminism*, (1989) 7.

44 Nedelsky, ibid., p. 21.

45 Martha Minow, *Making all the Difference: Inclusion, Exclusion, and American Law,* (Ithaca: Cornell University Press, 1990) at pp. 267-311.

46 Alasdair MacIntyre, *After Virtue* (University of Notre Dame Press, 1984); Michael J. Sandel, *Liberalism and the Limits of Justice* (Cambridge University Press, 1982).

47 See for example, Iris M. Young, *Justice and the Politics of Difference* (Princeton University Press, 1990).

48 Arneson, *supra* note 9. For an approach which suggests viewing the family as part of the public sphere, see Anne C. Dailey, 'Constitutional Privacy and the Just Family' 67 *Tulane Law Review*, 955 (1993).

49 For one, the parents usually cannot afford to educate their children all by themselves and, hence, have to allow other social agents to take part in this process. A religious community with its independent educational institutions and cultural activities can isolate the child from external influences to a much larger degree. Indeed, in Israel in recent years we have faced a cultural war conducted through a competition with regard to children's education. Thus, the Sephardic religious party (Shas) has directed much of its public funding to establish a network of kindergartens and schools (El-Ha'maayan) that tries to insulate the children from secular influences of Israeli society. See N. Mendler, *Ha'arez*, 24.1.90 ('The pied piper lives in Ofakim'), 28.6.90 ('Ensnared in the orthodox net'), S. Erlich, *Ma'ariv*, 5.10.90 ('The temptation of the *Shas* day-care centres'); H. Kim (arguing that *Shas* is deliberately trying to discourage the children from receiving general education in order to enhance the party's power and control over them). For the historical roots of the connections between education and political parties in Israel see, Arick Carmon, 'Education in Israel - Issues and Problems', in *Education In An Evolving Society, Schooling in Israel*, 125-186 (Walter Ackerman, Arick Carmon, David Zucker, (eds), 1985) (Hebrew).

50 For the importance of continuity in children's life see J. Goldstein, A.J. Solnit, S. Goldstein and the late A. Freud, *The Best Interests of the Child - The Least Detrimental Alternative* (The Free Press: 1996).

51 C.A. 2991/91 *Plonit* v. *Ploni*, (1992) (not published, on file with the author).

52 Ackerman, *supra*, note 2 at pp. 150-167; Amy Gutman, *Democratic Education* (Princeton University Press, 1987) (Gutman argues that every child should receive an education that enables her to engage in a critical evaluation of different conceptions of the good). A more unsettling question is related to the value of autonomy for the child's welfare. This question can be raised in cases in which adhering to the child's choice of a custodian parent exacts a considerable psychological cost for the child. See for example, H.C. 1842/92 *Bloygrond v. Rabbinical Court* 46(3) P.D. (1992) 423; C.A. 113/89, 740/87 *Mazar v. Kabiliyo*, P.D. 43(1) (1989) 661.

10 Tradition and the Right to Education: The Case of the Ultra-Orthodox Community in Israel

LESLIE SEBBA AND VARDA SHIFFER*

The objective of this paper is to describe and discuss the educational system of the Ultra-Orthodox (*Haredi*) Jewish community in Israel and its relationship with the state, in the context both of the Israeli legal system and the wider liberal-communitarian debate. We will begin with a description of the community and its attitude towards education. We will then examine the legal provisions governing education in Israel in the context of current trends towards constitutionalisation. After a brief analysis of the law prevailing in other jurisdictions and of the provisions of the relevant international documents, we will consider this topic in the wider context of our understanding of the concept of rights, and specifically the right to education and rights of groups. As a corollary to this, we will consider how far it is appropriate that the state should recognise Haredi education for the purposes of compliance with compulsory education laws and, if so, whether it is appropriate that such education be financially supported by the state.

The Ultra-Orthodox Community and its Education System

The term Ultra-Orthodox, which is commonly used in research relating to this section of the Jewish population, in fact represents several rather distinct groups. Nevertheless, for the purposes of this paper, the term will be appropriate, as it reflects the characteristics which these groups have in common, and those which are relevant to our topic.

All the groups which form the Ultra-Orthodox community in Israel share a mission of total commitment to the 'Halacha' - the Jewish Law -

with a distinct inclination to choose the stricter of possible interpretations offered in the literature of laws and rulings, together with a strong affiliation to the tradition of (pre-1945) Jewish life in Eastern-Europe.[1] The learning of the Torah and other Jewish religious scriptures is perceived to be a religious command, and is therefore a focus of community life and activity.

The community lives in ghettos (in the geographic and demographic sense of the word) within several urban centres, mainly (about 50 per cent of the community) concentrated in the city of Bnei Braq (which is in the main urban area in the centre of Israel, adjacent to Tel-Aviv) and in Jerusalem. The ghettos are well defined in geographic and cultural terms. As the community has grown quite substantially over the last 20 years, new ghettos have been established within other urban centres (Zichron Yaacov, Eilat and others). Members of the community are distinguishable by their appearance (e.g., dress and hair style). They maintain a separate educational system and their own social institutions, including elaborate provisions for mutual help, such as fund-raising for the needy and for young women about to be married. No cinemas, theatres, big department stores or even public libraries with secular books exist within the boundaries of these ghettos.

The Ultra-Orthodox community does not readily provide information regarding their overall numbers or the number of children in their educational institutions - or of the curriculum followed in the schools. Nevertheless, some population estimates can be extrapolated from election results, from information on the allocation of the education budget, from reports issuing from the State Comptroller's office and from other secondary sources.

There are three religious parties in the Israeli Knesset (parliament). One is the National Religious party, whose supporters are not Ultra-Orthodox, and do not form part of the community we are discussing; this party received 7.8 per cent of votes in the 1996 elections. The second party – 'Shas' - received 8.5 per cent of votes. Its supporters are not of uniform affiliation, but are strongly identified with the Sephardi or 'oriental' community, mainly of Jews who immigrated from North Africa. It is assumed that the majority of Shas supporters are religious but not very Orthodox and they send their children to the State religious schools (as do most of the supporters of the National Religious Party).[2] Nevertheless, a growing hard-core of Shas supporters together with the leadership of this party forms one group within the Ultra-Orthodox community. They have established their own educational system, similar to that of the other Ultra-

Orthodox groups, and this is the fastest growing educational subsystem in Israel. The third party (Yahadut Hatora) represents a coalition of most of the Ashkenazi Ultra-Orthodox sub-groups - i.e., those of European descent. This party received about 3 per cent of the votes in the last elections. However, some small sections of the Ashkenazi Ultra-Orthodox are unwilling to participate in a 'secular' political process at all.

The Ultra-Orthodox educational system includes institutions for all age groups but maintains a separation, in form as well as in content, between girls and boys from the age of three. From a formal (and legal) point of view it is divided into two main categories. The first is the 'exemption institution'; in 1994, 24,441 children attended 121 such institutions.[3] These institutions were exempt from fulfilling the terms of the educational system,[4] and special terms were designed for them, which exempt them from abiding by the law of compulsory education. These 121 institutions are financially supported by the State, though there may be other, unsupported, institutions with an unknown number of students.

The other category, which includes the majority of Ultra-Orthodox educational institutions, is known as the 'independent system'.[5] The *first* category is only partially supported by the State, and is thus more genuinely 'independent'; the latter, despite its name, enjoys extensive State funds - officially 85 per cent of cost (but in reality probably more, as a result of political-coalition agreements), and private funds. The applicability of state education programmes and supervision to these schools will be considered below.

According to the Statistical Abstract of Israel,[6] in 1995/6 11.4 per cent of Jewish children in elementary schools studied in the 'independent system'.[7] In high schools this percentage dropped to 7.2; however, a considerable, and perhaps the majority of Ultra-Orthodox male students in their teens, study in boarding schools. According to the Statistical Abstract, over 20 per cent of Jewish students in boarding schools, at the high school level, belong to 'other religious' supervision (meaning other than the State religious), which in fact means mainly the Ultra-Orthodox system. The statistical data indicate that many orthodox parents (not Ultra-Orthodox) send their children to the Ultra-Orthodox educational system, especially at the elementary school level. In sum, while the Ultra-Orthodox community in Israel forms about 7-8 per cent of the population, their children form close to 10 per cent of schoolchildren in Israel. In Jerusalem, in the last two years, Ultra-Orthodox children registering in the first grade constituted over 50 per cent of first graders in the city.

In so far as the schools of the Ultra-Orthodox community (in particular the 'independent' or 'recognised' schools) receive public funding, it might be anticipated that their teaching programme would substantially reflect the national curriculum - or at least that a minimal standard of general education would be required. Hard data are in short supply, since it appears that the Ministry of Education refrains from any active role in terms of inspection and supervision. Some of the more formal aspects of the system have been reviewed by the State Comptroller who found that teachers were often unqualified and uncertified.[8] Additional knowledge about the system is available from secondary sources - such as from academic scholars who have observed the community, and from the policy of the community as declared by its representatives. Implicit in the descriptions and policies deriving from these sources is a reality very different from what might have been anticipated.

The 'independent' Ultra-Orthodox educational system has four levels of education for their boys (girls have a separate and different system):

1. 'Talmud-Torah' (TAT) - for children of age 5 -13.
2. Small Yeshiva – for ages 13-16 - usually a boarding school.
3. Big Yeshiva – from 17 until marriage - boarding school.
4. Kollel - learning institutions for married men - usually for 4-5 years after marriage, during which time they receive a modest stipend.

Friedman describes the social and economic circumstances which enabled the Ultra-Orthodox community to become a 'society of learners' after World War II.[9] More funds were forthcoming from Western Jews who saw, in their support of the Ultra-Orthodox community, a way to commemorate their relatives who, together with the majority of Jewish traditional communities, were exterminated by the Nazis. This, combined with the fact that the State of Israel, when established, retained the Ottoman Millet system, which allowed substantive internal autonomy for religious communities (Jews and Non-Jews) in Israel,[10] enhanced the growth and development of the 'society of learners' of the Ultra-Orthodox community.

One of the main objectives of the Ultra-Orthodox community is to preserve its own traditional way of life. The main tool used to attain this ideal is education. As Shilhav and Friedman point out,[11] the Ultra-Orthodox community is characterised by its wish to differentiate itself from the society which surrounds it, and this seclusion finds its main expression in having designated living areas, and in the content of its educational materials. The community feels threatened by the modern world around it, and lives with a deep fear that its young members may abandon it, as they did from the mid 19th century until the Second World War. This constant perception of threat is the main explanation for the fact that general, secular education is almost completely absent from the curriculum of the Ultra-Orthodox educational institutions. '... Holy teachings have the only legitimate cultural content, therefore there is a demand to deny general education from every youngster throughout the whole of the socialisation period, at least until his marriage.'[12] Rabbi Israel Eichler says on the same point:

> it follows that the entire Ultra-Orthodox outlook is based upon the rejection of secularism. Does not the Ultra-Orthodox person have enough spiritual anti-bodies so as to face secularism or a foreign culture which lures him? ... The answer is clear: A mother who would let her son drink petrol instead of milk, arguing that his stomach should be made strong enough to deal with this poison, is a cruel mother. A parent who abandons the soul of his children to knowledge which contains heresy, and to information which includes obscenity, extinguishes his Judaism. Because there is no Judaism without 'Torah' and belief, and 'Torah' and belief would not be taken in by a heart filled with obscenities of 'Goyim' [foreign nations] and by a brain washed with theses of heresy.[13]

In her book *Educated and Ignorant* dealing with education for girls and women in the Ultra-Orthodox community, El-Or[14] discusses the paradox of the centrality of education in the community, and the amount of time and effort invested in it on the one hand, and its content on the other hand. The content, she claims, ensures that the women of the community will not be more educated than their mothers. Continuity of the tradition, with its all-encompassing features, is the purpose of the women's education; thus they become educated in the minutest details of traditional cooking, child-rearing and housekeeping, and ignorant of ways of life in the outside world.

Education in the Ultra-Orthodox community has thus become a most effective tool of social control. The Ultra-Orthodox education prepares the young member of the community to fulfil the ideals of that community; it has a totally doctrinaire orientation.[15] The content of this education blocks the possibility for these youngsters to join the professional and technological world around them. The Ultra-Orthodox youngsters become totally dependent upon the social network of their own community, and are denied the basic conditions which would make it possible for them to make choices (autonomous or not) about their preferred way of life. By presenting only one way of life, by denying the knowledge of other options, and by denying the means to acquire such knowledge, members of the community are deprived of their autonomy.

The Haredi Educational System under Israeli Legislation

Israeli legislation relating to education is somewhat complex. Legislative developments in this area appear to have occurred in an *ad hoc* fashion, with post-independence legislation superimposed upon provisions dating from the British Mandate in Palestine (which in principle remained in force after the establishment of the independent state). The resulting complexity was aggravated by the dual policy of enacting grand universalistic principles for the (then) new, dynamic, socialist (or at least welfare) state, while retaining elements of communalism, multiculturalism, and voluntarism that characterised the Mandatory system. A general account of this system is provided in the article by Goldstein appearing in this volume.[16] Here we shall emphasise the provisions relating to community schools such as those administered by the Haredi community, especially with regard to educational standards and supervision.

The Education Ordinance adopted during the period of the British Mandate referred to six categories of school: 'government' schools, 'public' schools, 'community' schools, 'supported' schools, 'unsupported' schools, and 'private' schools. Within a year of independence, however (in 1949), the Compulsory Education Law was adopted. Parents were required to register their children for either 'official' schools owned by the state or local authority, or 'unofficial' schools, if recognised by the Minister of Education. However, under section 5 of this Law, parents of children attending certain institutions (and the children themselves) could be exempted from their obligations under this Law.

The above Law made little reference to the required *content* of the educational system. This topic was dealt with by the State Education Law of 1953, which divided public (or 'official') education into two main branches - 'state' (secular) and 'state religious'. Independent (or, to use the terminology of the legislation, 'unofficial') schools which were 'recognised' under the Compulsory Education Law could also be subjected to certain conditions and could thereby qualify for state funding under section 11 of the State Education Law (see below). As noted by Goldstein, four main categories of school had thus been created: state secular, state religious, unofficial but recognised, and unofficial exempt - only the latter being fully independent. The Education Ordinance enacted during the Mandatory period remained in force, however, and indeed was reissued in a new Hebrew version in 1978.

The State Education Law, unlike the 1949 law, alluded to the content and functions of education. The aims of 'state education' were formulated in section 2, replete with the ideologies of the reborn state, in the following terms:

> The object of State education is to base elementary education in the State on the values of Jewish culture and the achievements of science, on love of the homeland and loyalty to the State and the Jewish people, on awareness of the memory of the Holocaust and the heroism, on practice in agricultural work and handicraft, on (*chalutsic*) pioneer training, and on striving for a society built on freedom, equality, tolerance, mutual assistance and love of mankind.[17]

Further, under section 4 of the Law, the Minister of Education had to determine the *curriculum* for every official institution; this curriculum was, under the definitions section of the law, intended to achieve the aims specified in section 2, and had to incorporate a 'basic curriculum', designated as being compulsory. These provisions for determining the ideology and regulating the curriculum of the educational system applied in principle only to 'official educational institutions' - i.e., state (including local authority) schools.[18] Thus they were not directly applicable to Haredi schools.

However, as noted, section 11 of the State Education Law empowered the Minister to provide for the regulation of recognised unofficial schools:

> The Minister may determine by regulations arrangements and conditions for declaring unofficial institutions to be recognised educational institutions, for their having a basic curriculum, for their management, for their supervision, and for state support for their budgets, should the Minister decide upon support and to the extent that he should so decide.

While this provision is drafted in discretionary language it seems to imply that financial support from the state was to be conditional upon a degree of regulation.[19] Similarly, the expression 'basic curriculum' appearing here, which the Minister was authorised to determine, seems to refer to the 'basic curriculum' that constitutes the compulsory element in the teaching curriculum which the Minister has to determine for official schools under the same Law[20] - unless it was anticipated that he would provide for a *different* basic curriculum for unofficial schools. Regulations were in fact gazetted shortly after the law was passed, and these Regulations impose upon recognised schools many of the standards applicable to state schools - *including adoption of the basic curriculum.*[21] Haredi schools are formally bound by these regulations unless they fall under the exemption from attending a recognised school under section 5 of the Compulsory Education Law.

The Schools' Supervision Law of 1969 extended the net of supervision considerably further; and in this case the focus of the law was upon *non*-state schools. This law provided for the licensing of new schools - defined in section 1 as 'any educational institution', and applying to educational institutions in which more than 10 pupils were enrolled, and where the staff were not state employees (section 2); it thus applies to all unofficial schools, whether 'recognised' or 'exempt'. Sec. 28(a) of the Law empowered the Minister to issue instructions 'to ensure that the education given in the school will be based upon the principles specified in section 2 of the State Education Law, 1953' - i.e., that it would share the ideologies prescribed for state schools - even though the 1953 Law itself, as noted, did not purport to apply these ideologies to unofficial schools. Section 28(b) specified the items which would be included in the ambit of the supervision provided for by the Law, such as books, educational achievements, etc. Here too, however, as with the Compulsory Education Law, there were provisions for the granting of exemptions from supervision, whether in whole or in part;[22] but the regulations laying down the principles according to which exemptions were to be granted do not appear to be directed at Haredi schools.[23] Thus, while under the State Education Law, 'recognised' schools could be required to adopt the basic curriculum provided for under that Law, under the Schools' Supervision Law *all* unofficial schools, recognised or 'exempt' (except those still operating under the Education Ordinance[24]) may be subjected both to curricular requirements and to the application of the pioneering ideologies of the State Education Law.

The only types of school to which the latter requirements do not apply are older schools operating under the Education Ordinance; these continue to be regulated by this Ordinance, unless the Schools' Supervision Law has been specifically applied to them.[25] The Ordinance provides for regulation of the curriculum only for 'public' and 'supported' schools.[26] It also provides for school inspection, although in the case of an unsupported community school, no changes in the curriculum or in the management of the school can be required as a result of the inspection.[27]

It seems that hitherto the courts have not been afforded much opportunity to interpret the above provisions. However, an indication of the Supreme Court's attitude to unofficial schools may be gleaned from the recently decided *Jabarin* case.[28] In this case the Supreme Court was called upon to consider how far an 'unofficial' Christian school, operating within the framework of the Education Ordinance, was obliged to make allowances for the religious opinions and practices of a pupil affiliated to a different religion. The petitioner in the *Jabarin* case, a Muslim, asserted her right to wear head covering, and to special arrangements with regard to her participation (or non-participation) in certain school sporting activities which were unacceptable to her on religious grounds. Deputy-Pres. Barak (as he then was) held that since the school was an 'unofficial' one, and was bound neither by the objectives of State education under section 2 of the State Education Law, nor by the provisions of the Schools' Supervision Law, the court would defer to the policy set by the school to prefer legitimate educational considerations over the pupil's freedom of religion. Justice Barak indicated that if the school had been an 'official' or state school, the court would have given precedence to the principle of freedom of religion.[29]

In the present context we have to consider to what extent the position of Haredi schools is similar to that of the Christian school in the *Jabarin* case in terms of their autonomy and relative immunity from judicial review. It should be borne in mind, however, that the problem we are considering in the present article is the obverse of that which arose in *Jabarin*. That case considered how far a school should be entitled to *insist upon* educational norms (albeit not in the purely learning context, but rather in relation to its 'extra-curricular' activities) at the risk of infringing a pupil's religious sensibilities. In the context of this paper, on the other hand, we are dealing with the question whether schools may *sacrifice* accepted educational standards for the purpose of maintaining religious (and arguably sectarian) values.

The general picture which emerges from the above review of Israel's education law is that the overall objectives of compulsory schooling based on a shared ideology, a national curriculum - including a compulsory core (varying only between a secular and a religious version) - have been applied explicitly and comprehensively only to the 'official' schools. The norms applying to unofficial schools - including the Haredi ones - are more complex and subject to the exercise of regulatory powers and administrative discretion. However, much of the content and ideology of the state schools seems in principle to be applicable to all of these schools, and the core curriculum in particular seems to be applicable to 'recognised' schools. Yet it seems from the evidence presented in the introductory section of this article that little effort has been made to ensure their implementation.

In some degree it has been Israel's legislative policy in the field of education to make concessions to the religious character of educational institutions. The old Palestinian Education Ordinance made provision for community schools, while the new structure introduced in 1953 for the new State was based primarily upon the secular-religious dichotomy (as well as providing for unofficial schools, 'recognised' and otherwise). Moreover this very dichotomy acknowledged that the issue was not merely the conveying of different bodies of knowledge in the respective systems, but the development of different *lifestyles*.[30] Religious state education under the 1953 law is defined as 'State education, with the distinction that its institutions are religious as to their way of life...', while the 'supplementary programme' (which may comprise 25 per cent of the school curriculum) for a state religious school 'comprises the study of the written and oral way of life, and includes religious observance and a religious atmosphere within the institution'. It may thus perhaps be understandable that in practice additional concessions were made for the accommodation of the Haredi lifestyle - but these go well beyond what the prevailing legal provisions permit.

In considering the relationship between formal education and religious lifestyle, it seems pertinent to refer also to the norms applicable in that area of the law primarily concerned with lifestyle and upbringing, viz. family law.

Education, Religious Upbringing and Family Law

Responsibility for the upbringing of children normally rests with parents who, under section 14 of the Legal Capacity and Guardianship Law, 1962, are designated the 'natural guardians' of the child. This guardianship incorporates 'the duty and the right to take care of the child's needs, including his education, studies, training for work and an occupation, and his work, as well as looking after his property, its management and development; linked to this is a licence to have custody over the child and determine his dwelling place, and the authority to represent him' (section 15). This formula, which differentiates between 'studies' and 'education', is clearly wide enough to incorporate the child's religious upbringing.[31]

However, the custody of a child (as well as the wider concept of guardianship) is not necessarily a unitary concept, but may be divided up between the relevant parties.[32] In a case discussed extensively elsewhere in this volume,[33] in which a separated mother wished to expose her children to the beliefs of her newly-adopted religion, the then President of the Supreme Court, Mr Justice Shamgar, differentiated between the physical and the *spiritual* custody of the child.[34]

In the instant case, President Shamgar restricted the mother's spiritual custody rights and prohibited her from exposing her children to the tenets and practices of the Jehovah's Witnesses, irrespective of whether or not she would be granted physical custody of the children (an issue which at the time of the judgment was pending in the rabbinical court.) He regarded the exposure of the child to another religion as the equivalent of an attempt to convert the child, a decision which should not be taken on the child's behalf. In the other main judgment in this case, Strasberg-Cohen, J., although she expressed reservations with regard to the physical-spiritual dichotomy in this context, agreed both with the outcome and with the principle of the divisibility of custody.

During the course of the above judgment there were references to the effect that the child's religious upbringing was normally exclusively a matter for the parents. However, it was also stated that the court might intervene not only in cases of dispute between the parents, but also *where the effects of the religion to which the child was being exposed were harmful to the welfare of the child.*[35]

The example cited by President Shamgar of circumstances in which a court might intervene because of the harmful effects of a family's religious practices on the welfare of a child was the refusal to seek medical treatment on religious grounds - suggesting an emphasis on the protection from *physical* harm. Elsewhere in this volume, however, Bilsky cites a case where the court intervened to prevent parents sending their children to a Missionary school.[36]

There is thus clearly room for speculation as to which religious practices could be perceived as being harmful to children, and whether and in what circumstances this might be true of Haredi education. (In the next section we will consider how far the Jewish religion receives - or is likely to receive - special protection in this context.) However, in principle it is surely the case that if the courts are ready in certain circumstances to contemplate an intervention into the sanctity of the *home* in order to protect a child from the harm being inflicted in the framework of his/her 'spiritual custody', they should be more ready to intervene in the *educational regime* to which a child is being exposed - i.e., within an educational institution; for the principle of a degree of governmental or other supervision over educational institutions – and probably also private institutions - is widely accepted as being appropriate. If a degree of state intervention is acceptable in matters affecting a minor's upbringing within the family, how much more is this true in the context of the educational system - both in respect of its curricular and its 'spiritual aspects'?

Judicial Review and the Constitutionalisation of the Legal System

Given that there may be doubts as to whether Haredi educational policies are in compliance with prevailing legislation, the question arises as to whether the issues raised may constitute a basis for challenges in the courts. In recent years the Supreme Court of Israel has adopted a generally liberal approach both on the issue of *standing* and *justiciability*. Thus, while a petition to the High Court filed in 1970 on the issue of the granting of exemptions from military service to Yeshiva students failed on the ground of lack of standing, by 1986, with the liberalisation of the court's policy in this respect, standing was no longer an objection to the consideration of the merits of the case.[37] A court would therefore have the power to invalidate a regulation which was enacted or a policy which was operating (even if formally consistent with the provisions of the existing law) if it were in breach of some fundamental principle of administrative law or some other quasi-constitutional principle.

Thus, for example, the principle of equality has been recognised by the Israeli courts as a fundamental principle of law.[38] It follows that a court might intervene if it was found that the Haredi community had been granted preferential treatment *vis-à-vis* non-Haredi institutions, whether in terms of funding or of its exemption from some of the educational requirements imposed upon other groups, unless the policy could be justified on some other ground. Such a ground might be the attribution of a privileged status to the promotion of the Jewish religion (or of some particular expression of this religion).[39]

The relationship of religion and the State in Israel is complex,[40] but it is in any case clear that Judaism is an established religion. Raday argues that the 'preferred status of Judaism' derogates from the rights of non-

Jewish communities, of non-Orthodox sects within Judaism and of the secular community, in breach of the principle of equality.[41]

In the present context we have to consider the likelihood of the courts intervening to restrict Haredi education. While President Shamgar in the Jehovah's Witnesses case claimed that the courts were impartial *vis-à-vis* different religions,[42] Bilsky argues elsewhere in this volume[43] that *marginal* sects are more likely to be perceived as harmful as compared with mainstream religions. From this perspective, it may be hard to classify the Haredim for this purpose as a 'marginal sect', given their relatively large numbers and their affiliation to the majority religion of the country.

As to the weight placed by the courts on religious interests, England found that the courts differentiated between 'rules based on purely religious motives' and 'rules aimed at the protection of particular collective or personal interests' - only the latter consideration constituting a legitimate basis for the issuing of delegated legislation.[44] Thus 'hurt feelings', such as may be caused by witnessing breaches of the religious law, will not be taken into account by the court. However, this distinction seems to become somewhat blurred in Shelach's observation, reported by England, of a 'recent general tendency of courts to give more weight to the aspirations of a homogeneous population in maintaining a religious lifestyle'.[45] Raday refers to the possibility that the courts might refuse to recognise Haredi interests (for the purposes of a claim based upon the right to equal treatment) in so far as this community were to be perceived as adopting discriminatory policies, or to be furthering objectives which were in conflict with national interests.[46]

Specifically, she posits that 'for the purpose of educational funding, for instance, there might be equality grounds for drawing a distinction between such a group and funded groups on the basis of the objects of State education'.[47] This suggests that the failure to comply with the minimum requirements of the 'basic curriculum', or even the failure to pursue the declared ideology of the state education system, might justify the deprivation of state funds from these schools - unless these were outweighed by the desire to 'give ... weight to the aspirations of a homogeneous population in maintaining a religious lifestyle'. (See above.)

The power of the courts to review the laws, policies and practices in this area may well have been enhanced by the enactment in recent years of two Basic Laws - the Basic Law: Human Dignity and Liberty, and the Basic Law: Freedom of Occupation. These laws are perceived in some quarters - notably by the President of Israel's Supreme Court, Professor Aharon Barak, as having added a new dimension (frequently termed a 'revolution') to the constitutionality of Israel's legal system. They expressly require that all branches of government respect the rights guaranteed therein, and are thus seen to have increased the power of the courts to review (and where appropriate, nullify) parliamentary legislation.[48] This development may be coupled with the Supreme Court's policy - again, especially of President Barak - of 'judicial activism'.

In addition to this structural transformation, one of the Basic Laws in particular - the Basic Law: Human Dignity and Liberty - also offers considerable possibilities for the expansion of the *substantive* grounds for testing the validity of laws and public policies, of potential relevance to the topic under discussion here.

One of the main objectives of the last-mentioned Law, as its name implies, is the protection of human *dignity*. This objective appears not only in the title of the law and in the general 'aims' section (section 1A), but also in its operative provisions (sections 2 and 4). The concept of dignity is of course vague and is open to varying and subjective interpretations. President Barak regards human dignity as a wide concept, embracing the main rights associated with the autonomy of the person, viz., political rights such as freedom of expression, freedom of assembly, etc.[49]

While education as such would not fall within a list of autonomy rights - and Barak specifically excluded social rights therefrom[50] - the absence of any freedom to choose an alternative belief or life-style following a Haredi education manifestly amounts to a deprivation of personal autonomy. Alternatively, if the child be regarded as non-autonomous by virtue of his or her age, the situation created amounts to the potential for, or even the high probability of, the *future* deprivation of personal autonomy.[51] In the words of Mazza, J., in *Golan v. Prisons Service*, in the context of the freedom of expression: 'What is Human Dignity without the basic liberty granted to a person to hear the words of others, and to make his own words heard, *to develop his personality, to crystallise his view of the world* and to fulfil himself?'[52] The Haredi education system does not seem consistent with this description of human dignity.

The title of the Basic Law also refers to *liberty*. Although section 5 of the law, which deals specifically with this right, has as its marginal title 'personal liberty', suggesting that a broad concept is indicated, the wording of the section emphasises the *physical* side of liberty.[53] On the other hand a related concept - the notion that all humans are *born into freedom* - forms a part of the initial, declaratory section of the law. While this is not therefore framed as an operative norm, it should be taken into consideration when interpreting the concept of 'personal liberty' - as well as that of 'human dignity'. This approach would at the very least strengthen the argument that the weight of the Basic Law should operate against the deprivation of autonomy.

The Basic Law: Human Dignity and Liberty, however, also contains a 'saving clause'. Section 10 of the law preserves pre-existing law, even if it is in breach of the provisions of the Basic Law. Further, section 8 provides that the rights protected by the law may be derogated from if four conditions are fulfilled - (a) the derogation is incorporated in a statute, or expressly authorised by a statute; (b) it is consistent with the values of the State of Israel; (c) it is intended for a suitable objective; and (d) it does not go further than is required (i.e., for the purpose of securing that objective).

The second condition specified here has given rise to extensive analysis and much polemical writing. It is seen as referring to section 1A of the Law, which specifies as its aim the protection of freedom and dignity 'in order to entrench in the Basic Law the values of the State of Israel *as a Jewish democratic state*' (emphasis added). The phrase 'Jewish democratic state', which seems to hold the key to the proper interpretation of the Basic Law, has itself spawned an enormous literature. In a non-legal context, the view has been adopted by at least one writer that the epithet 'Jewish' qualifies the type of democracy being referred to. According to Schweid,[54] whose views will further be considered below, the phrase connotes a communitarian form of democracy in tune with the ancient values of the Jewish people, rather than the liberal concept of democracy which has prevailed in modern times.[55] Another view holds that there is much in common between universalist humanitarian values and the Jewish tradition which are interrelated historically - thus reducing the need to identify specifically Jewish values.[56]

More commonly, however, the two elements - Jewishness and democracy - are seen as discrete concepts which must somehow be reconciled. The mode of such reconciliation has been the subject of much of the literature referred to, the polemical character of which is particularly intense on the part of those writers who take the view that one of these concepts has to be subjugated to the other.[57] These polemics should be seen against the background of the differing views held since the establishment of the state as to how far its legal system should incorporate - or be based upon - the *Halacha*,[58] a debate which has been rejuvenated by the enactment of the Basic Laws.

On the other hand the debates also have to take into account the implications of section 1 of the Basic Law. This provision (added in 1994) declares that human rights in Israel are based on recognition of the value of the person, the sanctity of life and the freedom of the person, and are to be respected according to the principles embodied in the Declaration of Independence. The Declaration of Independence has a generally universalist orientation, promising 'total equality of social and political rights for all its citizens, without distinction on the basis of religion, race and gender...'; although this document, too, incorporates some Jewish and biblical references.[59] It should be noted that until this relatively recent amendment, the Declaration of Independence was not an integral part of Israel's legal system, but was regarded only as an ideological declaration. Thus only now has it become critical for jurists to resolve these issues in operative terms.

The significance of the three substantive conditions with which Israeli laws or policies must comply if in conflict with human dignity or freedom (or any other right specified in the Basic Law: Human Dignity and Liberty) have been widely discussed in the literature. Their application to almost any issue tends to raise highly loaded ideological questions, and in this respect the present context is certainly no exception. Promotion of or tolerance for the Haredi educational system might be regarded as consistent with the 'values of the State of Israel as a Jewish democratic state' either on the view that the State should be *encouraging* the adoption of Halachic norms (for this is surely one of the main objectives of Haredi education), or on the view that Israel is a pluralistic state and should tolerate *any* community-oriented educational system.

Whether a Haredi education is a 'suitable objective' for the purpose of a derogation from the Basic Law is, again, a question susceptible to the ideological debates referred to above. According to Elon,[60] this condition, like the next following one, must also be read as requiring consistency with the 'values of the Jewish state', and he would apply these values not only to the rights protected under the Basic Law, but also to the *balancing* required between the guarantee of these rights and the conditions for their infringement specified in section 8. It may also be recalled that, in an earlier period, Ben-Gurion supported the continuation of the Haredi lifestyle (i.e., devotion to study) although the scale envisaged was much more limited.[61]

This leads us directly to the condition of *proportionality* - the requirement that any infringement of the guaranteed rights should be 'no more than is required'.[62] Apart from the issue of the number of Haredim who should (on the Ben-Gurion principle) be supported out of public funds,[63] there is the further issue of the extent that it is necessary that their education should negate the fundamentals of a general education normally required in the Israeli schools, including the 'basic curriculum' established under the State Education Law. The problem here is that while on a liberal view some such education should be provided to ensure that the child is equipped with a minimum of knowledge whereby to 'inform' his or her willingness to remain in the Haredi system (and also for the possible adoption of alternatives should he or she so desire), these are precisely the outcomes which this system seeks to avoid.

There is irony in the fact that insofar as the system is successful in achieving its objectives, legal challenges will be unlikely - except possibly by a dissenting parent (where the other parent or guardian was responsible for the decision to send the child to a Haredi school), or by a taxpayer objecting to the financing of such schools (mainly in connection with the 'recognised' schools'). Further the availability of a remedy under the Basic Law: Human Dignity and Liberty is speculative, not only because of the somewhat tenuous link between the topic with which we are dealing and the rights specified in the law,[64] but also because, as noted, laws which were in force prior to the adoption of the Basic Law may not be challenged under its provisions.[65]

On the other hand, the development of so-called constitutional principles and the salience of a 'rights discourse' do not appear to be dependent entirely upon the status and wording of the Basic Laws.[66] In the Jehovah's Witnesses' case President Shamgar referred to the 'child's constitutional right' without referring to the Basic Law.[67] Moreover his judgment in that case may have laid the groundwork for an expansion of the law in areas such as that with which we are here concerned; for he argued that the overriding criterion for adjudicators of children's issues should be children's *rights*, rather than their welfare or 'best interests' - a concept prone, in his view, to subjective interpretation and attaching insufficient weight to the autonomy of the child.[68]

In the instant case President Shamgar held, as noted earlier, that to expose the children to a new religion (the tenets or practices of the Jehovah's Witnesses, the religion espoused by their mother) would be to infringe their right to decide for themselves in the future whether they wished to change their religion.[69] He was thus purporting to protect the children's right to future autonomy. Arguably, the same principle could be applied to the Haredi education system, which, too, inhibits the exercise of free choice in the future as to religious preferences.

Indeed, in practical terms the forces operating against the exercise of free choice are much *stronger* in the Haredi case. The mother in the *Ploni* case did not in fact request that her children be converted to the Jehovah's Witnesses, but merely wished to expose them to some of the beliefs of this sect. Arguably, an exposure to different beliefs, in particular those adopted by parents, might be perceived as being *desirable* in the interests of an informed and free decision in later life.

On the other hand, a number of factors clearly operate against this analogy between the Haredi case and the *Ploni* case. First, in the typical Haredi case there is no difference of opinion between the parents. Secondly, and by extension, some argue for the recognition of *collective* rights on the part of the community, even at the expense of individual rights.[70] Thirdly, the *Ploni* case was dealing with the exposure to a new religion, rather than the maintenance of the status quo, and was thus found to raise the issue of *conversion*.[71] Fourthly, as noted above (and *pace* President Shamgar), the State being legally and institutionally Jewish (albeit 'democratic') renders any restriction on orthodox Jewish education problematical (by comparison with a marginal non-Jewish sect).[72]

As against these difficulties we may recall the principle reiterated on a number of occasions that the infliction of harm upon a child provides a justification for state intervention. Indeed, at one point in his judgment in the *Ploni* case, President Shamgar declared that 'The State will intervene wherever the decisions of the parents and their choices are inconsistent with the rights and interests of the child'.[73] We may also refer to the principle recently affirmed in the leading Supreme Court case of *Bavli* that constitutional principles (in this case a wife's equal right to marital property) override the normative approach of traditional Judaism.[74]

International Norms

In recent years the Israeli government has ratified the main human rights conventions.[75] This may be perceived as another stage in constitutionalisation, in that the state is now bound by a set of superior norms. Following the approach of English law, however, ratification is not sufficient to internalise the conventions and render them binding on the courts; but the courts may nevertheless be expected to apply them where they are not directly contrary to Israeli law.[76]

Among the conventions ratified are the International Covenant on Civil and Political Rights and the International Covenant on Economic,

Social, and Cultural Rights, both of 1966, and the Convention on the Rights of the Child of 1989. These conventions make numerous references to the right to education and freedom of religion.[77] The earlier of these conventions laid greater emphasis on parental rights, in order to ensure the protection of minority cultures,[78] while the Convention on the Rights of the Child guarantees a greater autonomy to the child. Further, although much support may be found in these documents for the need to protect minority schools, there are clear provisions which indicate that all schools should share certain universal objectives in the context of educational values,[79] as well as complying with minimum educational standards.[80]

Thus in spite of a certain ambivalence among the framers of the international norms in this area, it seems clear that their policy of ensuring compliance on the part of the states with the wishes of parents in minority communities was not accompanied by an intention to waive all requirements with regard to the setting of national standards.

Comparative Law

The present analysis has focused upon the status of the Haredi education system from the point of view of the legal norms applicable, directly or indirectly, in Israel. For lack of space other perspectives were omitted, but should not be overlooked. One such perspective is that of comparative law; other legal systems having faced similar issues - and in some cases having dealt with them more directly. The best-known example of this is undoubtedly the US Supreme Court case *Wisconsin v. Yoder*[81] dealing with the right of the Amish community to withdraw their children from school before completing the mandatory 10 years of compulsory schooling under the law of the state in which they resided. Without entering into a detailed discussion of this case, we wish only to note that while the Supreme Court in that case decided in favour of the community, two significant differences between the Amish and the Haredim emerge from the judgment of the Court in that case: (a) the Amish children attended public schools for eight years before being withdrawn, and (b) the Amish community was held not to represent any financial burden on the public.[82]

Similarly, an English case has dealt specifically with the educational programme of a Haredi school. While no substantive conclusions were reached by the court in this case, the High Court indicated that a delicate line needed to be drawn between toleration of community values and the need to preserve future options for the children in the wider society.[83]

In conclusion, it seems clear that the education to which Haredi children are currently exposed is not consistent with the formal norms currently applicable in Israel, whether based upon prevailing educational legislation, the Basic Laws, or the international human rights conventions; nor can unequivocal support for such a system be found in Anglo-American jurisprudence.

Ultimately, however, the courts, if not clearly bound by unambiguous formal norms, will determine the issue (should the issue come before them) in the light of the relevant value systems. The remainder of this paper will be devoted to a consideration of the prevailing views in this area from the perspective of the current theoretical literature.

Individualism, Communitarianism and Multiculturalism

It would seem from the above analysis that the apparent non-compliance with the prevailing education laws may give rise to issues relating to the constitutional protection of the child and the application of universal standards which merit consideration by the courts. Since the prevailing norms adhered to by the courts relating to 'human dignity', the 'values of a Jewish democratic state' and 'children's rights' are open to different interpretations and their application is ultimately determined by ideology, the attitude of the courts may ultimately be determined by the relative weight they wish to give to the protection of community rights and interests as compared with individual rights and the future autonomy of the child. This, in turn, requires a broader analysis of prevailing debates on this issue in the literature of jurisprudence and political philosophy.[84]

Two major doctrines would advocate State support for and protection of Ultra-orthodox (or any community-based) education. The first is the communitarian approach, which for present purposes may be combined with ideas of multi-culturalism,[85] and the second is the classical liberal doctrine of the 'Neutral State'.

Communitarian Approach

Let us start with the communitarian/multi-cultural approach. Israel defined herself in the Declaration of Independence as a Jewish and Democratic state.[86] She has also, quite explicitly, chosen the social democratic, or the welfare version of democracy. As noted above, in recent years an ongoing debate has taken place in Israel about the compatibility of these two concepts - Jewish and democratic. Does Judaism really go together with democracy, and if so, how?

Schweid[87] argues that the authors of the Declaration of Independence had no doubt that Judaism and democracy went hand in hand. They based their concept of democracy on the idea that, the people, in the cultural historical sense of the word, as a group, were the sovereign. For the authors of the Declaration of Independence, as for Schweid himself, it was clear that people, as members of a collective, having their identity moulded as members of a group, have rights which evolve from this position, and which take precedence over individual rights (which, by contrast, stem from a 'neo-liberal model of American Democracy', in which the individual citizen is the sovereign). Likewise, says Schweid:

> Positioning the values of religion, nationalism and society beyond the values of democracy in its narrow meaning, and demanding the right to mould their way of life according to a religious, national-humanistic or social outlook in the socio-public realm as well, does not contradict democracy, rather the opposite: They are legitimate expressions of the wish to live a full life within it [democracy].[88]

Schweid seems to be in agreement with some of the most outspoken communitarian critics of Liberalism. The issue he raises here is the *conception of the person*: Is he or she a totally independent, self-creating autonomous person, as some communitarians argue is the Liberal position, or is he or she a radically socialised person - the embodiment of social values? On the Liberal concept of the person, Sandel writes:

> A self so thoroughly independent as this rules out any conception of the good (or bad) bound up with possession in the constitutive sense. It rules out the possibility of any attachment (or obsession) able to reach beyond our values and sentiments to engage our identity itself. It rules out the possibility of public life in which, for good or ill, the identity as well as the interests of participants could be at stake.[89]

Sandel argues with Rawls about the status of society: Does society constitute the person or does the person, through his autonomous choices, determine the shape of society?[90] Rawls in fact accommodates Sandel's position. First, he distinguishes between citizens' political identity and citizens' non-institutional or moral identity - those non-institutional and moral values citizens would enhance and work for in their non-public life.

> It can happen that in their personal affairs, or in the internal life of associations, citizens may regard their final ends and attachments very differently from the way the political conception supposes. They may have, and often do have at any given time, affections, devotions, and loyalties that they believe they would not, indeed could and should not, stand apart from and evaluate objectively.

Rawls, however, rejects the idea of political community:

> ... Justice as fairness does indeed abandon the ideal of political community if by that ideal is meant a political society united on one (partially or fully) comprehensive religious, philosophical, or moral doctrine.[91]

Margalit and Halberthal[92] introduce another concept to the very same debate – *culture*. Culture is a comprehensive way of life, which can only be implemented in the framework of a group, unlike a 'life style', which expresses the conduct of the individual. The right of a person to his or her own culture is primary and basic, because it is the culture which forms the personality identity; therefore

> The right to culture is not ... a special case of the right to freedom of expression in the liberal society [as Kymlicka argues]. On the contrary, freedom of expression is a special case whose principal justification is the right to culture.

Kymlicka's point is that liberalism

> ... recognises the way that communal and cultural aspects of social life provide the possibility for, and locus of, the pursuit of human values. But it also insists that these values, like most important values, ultimately depend on the way that each individual understands and evaluates them.[93]

Walzer too, seems to agree that the emphasis on the importance of community does not conflict with liberalism:

> Contemporary liberals are not committed to the presocial self, but only
> to a self capable of reflecting critically on the values that have governed
> its socialisation. [94]

What is clear about the position both of Kymlicka and of Walzer is the
supremacy they both attach to the ability to reflect critically and review
one's own values and way of life. It is this very point to which Margalit
and Halberthal object. Culture gives meaning to one's life rather than an
option to choose from, they say. Only Kymlicka and a few of his liberal
friends would wish to review and change their life; most people, in their
view, wish to *preserve* their way of life. This, however, is an empirical
statement, the basis of which is unclear. When members of Ultra-Orthodox
communities in Eastern Europe were exposed to ideas of Modernity,
Enlightenment and Emancipation, major changes within those communities
took place. The new openness brought about changes in the perception of
Judaism, in community life and in the way individuals positioned
themselves *vis-à-vis* the world. It thus seems that personal identity is not as
static as is sometimes assumed; neither is culture nor tradition.[95]

By placing the preservation of culture on a higher level of priority
than the ability to review and criticise one's culture, Margalit and
Halberthal may be lending their support to a community which uses some
degree of coercive measures against its own members. Indeed, they
recognise this possibility. Naming the Ultra-Orthodox and the Arabs in
Israel specifically as two communities with a distinct culture, Margalit and
Halberthal claim that the needs and demands of these two communities
pose a challenge to Israeli democracy.

By associating culture and community with identity formation,
communitarians offer a very forceful argument for group oriented, or
community oriented rights. It nevertheless forces us to choose, in the case
of the Ultra-Orthodox community in Israel, between the right of the
community to flourish (as Margalit and Halberthal advocate) and the
primary rights of the individuals within this community. What justification
could there be for neglecting or ignoring the rights of individuals, members
of a distinct cultural community, in favour of the rights of their
community? Margalit and Halberthal's reply is clear - the very wish of
those members. But what if that wish is a result of 'programming', or of
their education, rather than of a meaningful choice?

Raz offers a different way of looking at the two concepts, which
clarifies the issue. He maintains that, 'given human nature, autonomy can
only be realised within a community which endorses a competitive

pluralistic morality'.[96] '... Autonomy requires the availability of an adequate range of options'. A person 'can be autonomous only if he believes that he has valuable options to choose from'.[97] The choice between a valuable way of life and a valueless life does not make a person autonomous; it is the choice from amongst *a range of good options* which makes a person autonomous.

In other words, autonomy is indeed of extremely high value, but it can only be realised in the framework of a community which is an *open* community - one which presents to its members a variety of good options. So it becomes obvious that a community which deprives its members of the preconditions for autonomy should not be allowed to flourish, whilst a person without a community will in any case be deprived of autonomy. Thus we have a dilemma as to what should be the optimal approach in order to guarantee both a viable community life and the personal autonomy of the individual. This dilemma may have more than one solution, but, whatever it is, we should be prepared to adopt a more dynamic view of culture and tradition than either the leaders of the Ultra-Orthodox community, or even Margalit and Halberthal, are willing to accept.

The Neutral State

Israel chose to incorporate traditional values in its vision of a democratic state. These values found their expression in national holidays, in the national curriculum (obligatory study of the Bible), in the establishment of religious courts for certain family-related issues, and in various other institutions. These reflections of Jewish tradition in the modern Israeli state did not, however, correspond to the special needs of the Ultra-Orthodox community.[98]

Our description above makes it quite obvious that the Ultra-Orthodox community adheres to a comprehensive doctrine (or has a distinct culture) in all realms of life. The community does not adhere to any form of liberal principles. Shilhav and Friedman stress that

> Judaism is not a matter for the individual alone, it is not an intimate matter between the individual and his God, rather it is a public - community matter ... Every member of the community is responsible for the implementation of commandments by all other members of the community.[99]

In other words, according to the interpretation given by the Ultra-Orthodox community to Judaism, the concept of individual rights is alien to Judaism, as is the concept of individual autonomy.[100]

The leaders of the community demand, however, what they define as their fair share of resources needed to carry out their own services. In the realm of education, as was noted before, the State covers the current expenses of the independent educational system, and supports the 'exemption institutions'. Until recently the State did not provide this educational system with classrooms, and children would study in rented houses or rooms, not fit to serve as schools. A few years ago, the municipality of Jerusalem, and later the Ministry of Education, decided to change their policy and to provide the independent system with schools and classrooms. The argument was that it was unfair to discriminate against children. All children of the city, the Mayor of Jerusalem proclaimed, including the children of the Ultra-Orthodox community, should have access to the same amount of resources for education.[101]

Israel's support of the Ultra-Orthodox educational system, and the justification given by the mayor of Jerusalem, could be seen as an example of the State exercising its neutrality in the way liberal neutralists or anti-perfectionists would have approved of. The anti-perfectionist position, shared by Libertarians like Nozick as well as by liberals such as Rawls and Dworkin, supposes that the political framework and political decisions must be neutral, in the sense that they should not favour any particular conception of the good.[102] In other words, the political system is not supposed to make value judgments concerning the particular ends of individuals, or of communities. The political system should provide a framework which allows equal opportunity for all individuals to pursue their ends.

Raz casts serious doubts on the possibility of being strictly neutral. Without going into an in-depth analysis of the four relevant chapters of *The Morality of Freedom*, we shall highlight here a few of his conclusions. It seems that neutrality is concerned with the outcomes or the effects a State's actions have upon people or groups. If so, neutrality cannot depend solely upon the actions or inactions of the State, even if these are carried out in an equal manner,[103] because the outcome of those activities will also depend upon the initial status or condition of each of the recipients. A second argument, says Raz, 'designed to show that neutrality is chimerical, claims that whether or not a person acts neutrally depends on the base line relative to which his behaviour is judged, and that there are always different base lines leading to conflicting judgments and no rational grounds to prefer one to the others'.

The more important question, however, is not whether neutrality is at all possible, but whether it is desirable or morally justifiable.

Towards a More Perfectionist State

Kymlicka, not unlike Rawls, holds to an 'improved' (or a 'corrected', as Walzer would put it) liberal position. He draws a distinction between group-differentiated rights which are aimed at protecting the minority group from the majority, and group-differentiated rights which enable the minority to oppress its own members. The latter, with which the educational system of the Ultra-Orthodox in Israel may most probably be classified, are unacceptable in a liberal society, says Kymlicka. Nevertheless, holding a neutralist (or anti-perfectionist) position, Kymlicka thinks there is very little the majority can actually do:

> In cases where the national minority is illiberal, this means that the majority will be unable to prevent the violation of individual rights within the minority community. Liberals in the majority group have to learn to live with this, just as they must live with illiberal laws in other countries.[104]

Not far away in principle are Margalit and Halberthal,[105] who do not distinguish, as Rawls does, between the political and the personal. In their view people do not wish to revise their conception of the good; rather they wish to preserve it. Furthermore, if their personality identity is formed by their culture, they may not be able to revise or even to review critically their way of life. These are thus not reasons to deviate from the principle of neutrality. Within the principle of neutrality there is only one limitation on the community: 'A cultural minority cannot be granted control over its members' exit'.[106]

As would follow from their arguments, Margalit and Halberthal favour what they call a deviation from the liberal doctrine, namely a clear intervention on the part of the State in favour of *weak* cultures. The State should remain neutral with regard to the dominant culture (which has ample means to take care of itself), but should ensure that weak minority cultures may flourish. This means, *inter alia*, assistance in maintaining their educational system and their autonomous courts ... 'as long as their courts do not impose their norms on other Israeli citizens'.

This position, in line with a non-perfectionist state, ignores the *content*, and refrains from judging the value of the minority 'weak culture' in question. In a way, one could argue that supporting a weak segment of society, in order to provide it with an equal opportunity to flourish, would in no way constitute a deviation from a liberal doctrine. The attitude of Raz, however, is different:

> Moral pluralism asserts the existence of a multitude of incompatible but morally valuable forms of life. It is coupled with an advocacy of autonomy. It naturally combines with the view that individuals should develop freely to find for themselves the form of the good which they wish to pursue in their life. Both combined lead to political conclusions which are in some ways akin to those of Rawls: political action should be concerned with providing individuals with the means by which they can develop, which enable them to choose and attempt to realise their own conception of the good. But there is nothing here which speaks for neutrality. For it is the goal of all political action to enable individuals to pursue valid conception of the good and to discourage evil or empty ones.[107]

Raz is able to justify state perfectionism within the liberal framework. For anyone, including a state, to enable the pursuit of valid conceptions of the good and to discourage evil ones, judgments with regard to values and ideals must be made.

The central importance that we attach to the ability of people to exercise their autonomy and to formulate their own life commits us to a liberal doctrine. Our belief in the embeddedness of people in their community and in the role of culture in forming one's identity commits us, on the other hand, to supporting group-oriented rights, and a fair measure of group autonomy. In the spirit of reconciling these two values, which by now seem to be much more reconcilable than when we started with this project, we would advocate that the State of Israel should exercise its authority with regard to the implementation of its core curriculum within the Ultra-Orthodox educational system, while, at the same time, it should continue to support this system in principle. The judgment we require on the part of the state concerns its basic duty to provide all people with the basic preconditions for autonomy, including exposure to the presentation of other valuable forms of life.

Notes

*   The order of the names is alphabetical. Leslie Sebba takes the main responsibility for the legal analysis, Varda Shiffer for the descriptive background and philosophical discussion. Thanks are due to the Centre for Socio-Legal Studies at Wolfson College, Oxford, and in particular to its Director, Denis Galligan, for providing facilities (and a congenial atmosphere) while writing was in progress, and for arranging a seminar at which our ideas were presented and discussed. Thanks are also due to Leora Bilsky and Yehiel Kaplan for their comments on an earlier draft, Joseph Raz for providing some insights, and Anthony Bradney, Reuven Schwartz and Ephraim Yifhar for assisting with the location of some invaluable sources. None of these, however, bears any responsibility for the final outcome.

1   Shilhav, Y., and Friedman, M., (1985), *Growth and Segregation*, Jerusalem Institute for Israel Studies, Jerusalem (in Hebrew).

2   See S. Goldstein's article at Chap. 8 above.

3   Data for 1994 is the most recent information available. See Ministry of Finance, *The Budget Proposal for the Educational System*, 1996, which became law after having been adopted.

4   See Goldstein, op. cit., and further below.

5   It is administered by an association called the 'Centre for Independent Education'; the legislation, however, refers to these schools as 'recognised' institutions. (See below).

6   *Statistical Abstract of Israel 1996*, Jerusalem, Government Printer.

7   Absolute numbers of children in the Ultra-Orthodox educational system, in 1995 were: 78,033 not including boarding schools - according to the *Statistical Abstract*, and 82,072 in total, according to the Budget proposal for 1996.

8   State Comptroller, *Annual Report No 35*, Jerusalem 1985, 331.

9   Friedman, M., (1991), *The Haredi Community: Sources, Trends and Processes*, Jerusalem Institute for Israel Studies, Jerusalem (in Hebrew).

10   Cf. Goldstein op. cit. (n.2).

11   Op. cit., n. 1.

12   Ibid. at p. 6.

13   Eichler, I., 'Thus the High Court of Justice Saved the Haredi Outlook' *Meimad* No 8, Dec. 1996, pp. 16-19. Rabbi Israel Eichler is a member of the Belz Hassidic group, and is the editor of an Ultra-Orthodox weekly called *In the Haredi Camp*.

14   El-Or, T., (1990), *Educated and Ignorant*, Chamal, Ramat Gan (in Hebrew).

15   Shilhav and Friedman op. cit., n.1.

16   See Chapter 8 above.

17   Translations, where available, are taken from the Laws of the State of Israel series.

18   See s. 4 of the State Education Law, 1953, and the definition of 'official school' in the Compulsory Education Law 1949.

19   Cf. State Comptroller, *Annual Report No 34*, Jerusalem,1984, 265.

20   See s. 1 of the Law; s. 34(3) authorised the Minister to issue Regulations for this purpose.

21   See State Education Regulations (Recognised Institutions), 1953, ss. 1 and 3.

22   See s. 2(5) of the Law. Moreover s. 28(b) provided that the educational elements subject to supervision were to comply with 'the general instructions *customary for that type of school*' (emphasis added).

23   See Schools' Supervision Regulations (Principles for Granting Exemptions), 1970.

24   The question arises whether the Education Ordinance applied to 'exempt' schools. The Legal Advisor to the Ministry of Education, writing before the Schools' Supervision Law was passed, took the view that the Ordinance applied, since 'the law should not be interpreted as assisting in its [own] evasion': Stanner, R. (1966), *The Laws of Education*, Jerusalem, p. 79.

25   See ss. 35 and 36 of the Schools' Supervision Law, 1969. By virtue of these provisions, the 1969 Law was applied mainly to pre-existing high schools and kindergartens; see *Yalkut Hapirsumim* No. 1696 (of 1971, p. 931) and No. 1938 (of 1973, p. 2176), and *Kovetz Hatakanot* No. 3692 (of 1977, p. 1356).

26   See s. 17(6) of the Ordinance; in the case of supported schools, regulation does not apply to religious studies.

27   See s. 6(a) and (b) of the Ordinance. Further, unsupported schools where only religion is taught may be exempted from such inspection.

28   *Jabarin v. Minister of Education et al*, PD 48(5) 199 (1994).

29   Ibid. Goldberg, J. expressed reservations on this latter point. Employing the example of a pupil at a state religious school who refused to cover his head because of his beliefs, he was 'not convinced that, in a conflict between the freedom of expression of the pupil and the educational framework within which he studied, he [the pupil] would win, in spite of the [legal objectives of] education for tolerance and pluralism'.

30   See the discussion in Goldstein's article at Chap. 8 above; see also Goldstein, S. (1992) 'The Teaching of Religion in Government Funded Schools in Israel' 26 *Israel Law Review* pp. 36-64.

31   Interestingly, however, religion is not specified here or elsewhere in this chapter of the Legal Capacity and Guardianship Law, but only in the opening and more general chapter; and the provision here focuses on a change of religion.

32   See ss. 24, 27, 28, and 45 of the Legal Capacity and Guardianship Law, 1962. The problematic nature of such divisions - including the division

between custody and education - is discussed in the sources referred to by Yehiel Kaplan in n. 4 of his article at Chap. 4 above.

[33]   See the articles in this volume by Leora Bilsky (Chap. 9) and Ze'ev Falk (Chap. 7).

[34]   *Ploni v. Ploni* PD 49(1) 221 (1995). The separability of different aspects of the marital relationship have been the subject of continued controversy in the Israeli courts in view of their jurisdictional implications; for while divorce proceedings as such generally fall within the exclusive jurisdiction of the religious court, other aspects of the relationship may fall within the jurisdiction of the civil courts. See, e.g., *Florsheim v. Haifa Rabbinical Court* PD 22(2) 723 (1968), *Amir v. Haifa District Rabbinical Court* Takdin 96(2) 928.

[35]   Ibid., paras. 5 and 12.

[36]   Cf. the criteria for intervention in the case of *'Deri'* cited in the same article.

[37]   See Raday, F., (1996) 'Religion, Multiculturalism and Equality: The Israeli Case', 25 *Israel Yearbook on Human Rights*, pp. 193-241 at 219.

[38]   Cf. Raday, ibid. at 194.

[39]   In the 1986 case referred to above, the Supreme Court refused to intervene in the army's policy of granting exemptions to Haredi students; see Raday, ibid.

[40]   See Englard, I., (1987) 'Law and Religion in Israel', 35 *American J. of Comparative Law*, pp. 185ff.

[41]   In particular, 'women are the ultimate victims of the deference to religious over egalitarian values' (Raday, op. cit. at 226).

[42]   *Ploni v. Ploni* (op. cit. n. 34) para. 13.

[43]   See Bilsky at Chap. 9.

[44]   Englard (op. cit., n. 40) p. 199. Englard's analysis may now have assumed an enhanced practical significance in that he has himself been appointed to the Supreme Court.

[45]   See Englard, ibid., p. 200. Shelach's citation was from 1980. A proposed coalition agreement between the labour and Shas parties in 1994 referred to the granting of legal protection of the way of life of the religious public 'and its sensitivities' (Raday, op. cit., n. 37, p. 240).

[46]   Raday, ibid., p. 200.

[47]   Ibid.

[48]   See *Mizrachi Bank v Migdal* PD 49(4) 221 (1994/5). Previously this power was available only in the context of specifically entrenched provisions.

[49]   Barak, A., 'Dignity of the Person as a Constitutional Right', 41 *Hapraklit* (1994) , pp. 271ff (in Hebrew).

[50]   This view was cited approvingly by Or, J. in *Gilat v. Minister of Education et al.*, Takdin 96(2) 442, 1996.

[51]   Cf. Feinberg, J., (1980) 'The Child's Right to an Open Future', in W. Aiken and H. LaFollette (eds), *Whose Child?: Children's Rights, Parental*

Authority, and State Power, Rowman and Littlefield, Totowa: pp. 124-153, and Bilsky at Chap. 9 in this volume.

52   Takdin 96(3) 704 (1996) (emphasis added).

53   Cf. Feinberg op. cit., and Bilsky Chap. 9 above. Section 5 states as follows: 'There shall be no deprivation or limitation of liberty by means of imprisonment, detention, extradition or any other means.'

54   Schweid, E., (Dec. 1995) 'The Jewish Religion and Israeli Democracy', in *Free Judaism*, No. 7, pp. 24-30 (in Hebrew).

55   Maoz, A., (1995) 'The Values of a Jewish and Democratic State', 19 *Tel-Aviv University Law Review*, p. 547 at 591ff. (in Hebrew), notes the interest in traditional Jewish religious values on the part of contemporary American jurists.

56   Cohn, H., (1993/4)'The Values of a Jewish Democratic State - An Enquiry into the Basic Law: Human Dignity and Freedom', *Hapraklit Jubilee Volume*, pp. 9-52 (in Hebrew).

57   Rozen-Zvi, A., (1995) '"A Jewish Democratic State": Spiritual Parenthood, Alienation and Symbiosis - Can We Square the Circle?', 19 *Tel-Aviv University Law Review*, pp. 479-519 (in Hebrew).

58   Cf. England, op. cit., n. 40, at 203ff.

59   The State of Israel will be open to Jewish immigration and the ingathering of the exiles. It will devote itself to developing the Land for the good of all its inhabitants. It will rest upon foundations of liberty, justice and peace as envisioned by the Prophets of Israel. It will maintain complete equality of social and political rights for all its citizens, without distinction of creed, race or sex. It will guarantee freedom of religion and conscience, of language, education and culture. It will safeguard the Holy Places of all religions. It will be loyal to the principles of the United Nations Charter.

60   Elon, M., (1993) 'Constitution by Legislation: The Values of a Jewish and Democratic State in the Light of the Basic Law: Human Dignity and Personal Freedom,' 17 *Tel-Aviv University Law Review*, pp. 659-688 (in Hebrew).

61   Cf. Raday, op. cit. n. 37, pp. 224-5, esp. n. 129.

62   This is in fact a general principle of administrative law, the importance of which was elaborated by Barak, P., in the recent case of *Atiyah v. Minster of Education* PD 49(5) 1 (1995).

63   The main issue considered by Ben-Gurion and subsequently has been that of the granting of exemption from military service to Haredim engaged in study, rather than the educational aspects considered here which, of course, relate to a younger age-group.

64   Thus, for example, there is no direct reference to the principle of autonomy (seen by Professor Barak as implicit in the concept of human dignity) in the Basic Law - much less to a principle of future autonomy. Even the right to equality is not explicitly mentioned, although it has been read into the law by Or, J., in *Huppert v. Yad Veshem*, PD 48(3) 363 citing some

commentators - and, as noted above, was established by the courts as an independent principle for the purposes of judicial review prior to the enactment of the Basic Law.

[65]   They are, however, to be *interpreted* in the light of the Basic Law: see *Ganimat v. State of Israel* PD 49(4) 589, at p. 654.

[66]   Some jurists, including members of the Supreme Court, have argued that such constitutionalisation is a natural and on-going development. Barak himself regards the new constitutional rights under the Basic Law as following in the wake of previously-established 'basic rights by precedent'.

[67]   *Ploni v. Ploni* (op. cit., n. 34), para. 29; cf the reference to the parent's constitutional right in para. 12.

[68]   See esp. paras. 34ff. Only one of the other four justices subscribed to this view, however. Cheshin, J., argued that 'best interests' was the more inclusive concept since it could incorporate both rights and interests not yet so recognised. Aspects of this controversy are referred to in the chapters by Falk and Bilsky in this volume.

[69]   See ibid., para. 28.

[70]   See below; and see Bilsky's article at Chap. 9.

[71]   But see the preceding paragraph.

[72]   Cf. text accompanying n. 41 above.

[73]   *Ploni,* op. cit. n.34, para .9.

[74]   See *Bavli v. High Rabbinical Court* PD 48(2) 221 (1994). The rabbinical courts were thus precluded from ignoring this principle when ordering the disposition of marital property.

[75]   Cohen, B., (1992) 'The Practice of Israel in Matters Related to International Law', 26 *Israel Law Review*, pp. 559-573.

[76]   Benvenisti, E., (1992) 'The Applicability of Human Rights Conventions to Israel and the Occupied Territories', 26 *Israel Law Review*, pp. 24ff.

[77]   See Van Bueren, G., (1994) *The International Law on the Rights of the Child*, Nijhoff, Dordrecht, chaps. 6, 9.

[78]   See the references to the parents' right to choose their children's schools and to educate their children 'in conformity with their own convictions' - e.g. in Article 13.3 of the International Covenant on Economic, Social, and Cultural Rights 1966.

[79]   Article 29.1 of the Convention on the Rights of the Child states as follows: States Parties agree that the education of the child shall be directed to:
(a) The development of the child's personality, talents and mental and physical abilities to their fullest potential;
(b) The development of respect for human rights and fundamental freedoms, and for the principles enshrined in the Charter of the United Nations;
(c) The development of respect for the child's parents, his or her own cultural identity, language and values, for the national values of the country

in which the child is living, the country from which he or she may originate, and for civilisations different from his or her own;

(d) The preparation of the child for responsible life in a free society, in the spirit of understanding, peace, tolerance, equality of sexes, and friendship among all peoples, ethnic, national and religious groups and persons of indigenous origin;

(e) The development of respect for the natural environment.

80   Thus the same Article in the International Covenant on Economic, Social, and Cultural Rights of 1966 referred to in n. 78 above, which guarantees to parents the right to choose their children's schools, and to ensure their education in conformity with their own convictions, also requires them to 'conform to such minimum educational standards as may be laid down or approved by the State'.

81   406 U.S. 205, 1972.

82   This case is discussed extensively in the literature of American constitutional law; see also Feinberg op. cit., n. 51 and Hamilton, C., (1995) *Family, Law and Religion*, Sweet and Maxwell, London.

83   See *R. v. Secretary of State for Education ex p. Talmud Torah Machzikei Hadass School Trust.* (Q.B.D.), *The Times* 12 April 1985. See on this case Hamilton, ibid. and Bradney, A., (1987) 'Separate Schools, Ethnic Minorities and The Law', 13 *New Community*, pp. 412-420.

84   Yet another debate has been taking place in the human rights literature between the supporters of universal standards and advocates of multiculturalism: see, e.g., Alston, P., (1994) *The Best Interests of the Child - Reconciling Culture and Human Rights*, Clarendon, Oxford.

85   This is not meant to indicate that multiculturalism could not be seen as evolving conveniently also from a classical liberal attitude.

86   See n. 59 above.

87   Op. cit., n. 54 above.

88   Ibid., p. 7.

89   Sandel, M., *Liberalism and the Limits of Justice*, (1982) Cambridge University Press, Cambridge, at 62.

90   See Mulhall, S. and Swift, A., (1996) *Liberals and Communitarians* (2nd ed.), Blackwell Publishers, Oxford.

91   Rawls, J., (1993) *Political Liberalism*, Columbia University Press, New York, p. 201.

92   Margalit, A, and Halberthal, M., (1994), 'Liberalism and the Right to Culture', 61 (3) *Social Research*, pp. 491-510.

93   Kymlicka, W., (1989) *Liberalism, Community and Culture*, Clarendon Paperbacks, Oxford pp. 253ff.

94   Walzer, M., (1990) 'The Communitarian Critique of Liberalism', 18(1) *Political Theory*, p. 21.

95   Gadamer, H-G., (1976) *Philosophical Hermeneutics* (trans: Linge, D.), University of California Press, Berkeley.

[96]   Raz, J., (1986) *The Morality of Freedom*, Clarendon Paperbacks, Oxford, p. 406.

[97]   Ibid. pp. 410 and 412.

[98]   The fact that the Ultra-Orthodox community was recognised as an autonomous unit, and special arrangements were made to allow it to develop its own religious, judicial, social and educational institutions, did not indicate a general recognition on the part of the young state of Israel of group-, or community-related rights. During those first years of the State of Israel, the Arab population of Israel suffered from various restrictions, and could not enjoy any cultural autonomy to speak of. Other Jewish immigrant groups which possessed a distinct cultural heritage were submitted to the 'melting pot' policy, designed to create the 'New Israeli'.

[99]   Shilhav and Friedman, op. cit., n.1, p. 6.

[100]   Interestingly enough, the language of rights is frequently used by representatives of the community in their negotiations with State authorities with regard to the community's entitlement to various services (as if to prove Walzer's point about the inescapability from liberal language even in the context of communitarianism).

[101]   On the issue of how the idea of a fair share to a community relates to liberal theory, see Walzer, (op. cit., n. 94), who says that Liberal theory needs a periodic Communitarian correction, 'but the communitarian correction does require a liberal state of a certain sort...'!

[102]   See Bellamy, R., (1992) *Liberalism and Modern Society*, Polity Press, Cambridge. For a discussion of the range of neutrality, see Raz, op. cit., n. 96, ch. 5.

[103]   Whatever that may be - see Raz, ibid., pp. 120-121.

[104]   Kymlicka, W., (1995) *Multicultural Citizenship*, Clarendon Press, Oxford.

[105]   Op. cit. (n. 92).

[106]   Despite their very lively description of the 'Modesty Guards' and their activities against deviant members of the community, they do not address themselves at all to this issue with regard to the Ultra-Orthodox community.

[107]   Raz (op. cit., n. 96), p. 133.

11 A Child's Right to Privacy or Open Justice?

JAMES MICHAEL

Introduction

The subject of this paper has developed from an earlier paper on 'Open Justice' published as a chapter in *Current Legal Problems*.[1] That paper considered the law and practice on access by the press and public to judicial proceedings, and their freedom to report such proceedings. It was primarily concerned with England and Wales, although it drew upon relevant comparative law from the United States, Sweden, and New Zealand. Although the subject was judicial proceedings in general, much of the discussion was about criminal proceedings in particular, if only because much of the law in England and Wales and other countries is concerned with the effect of access to and reporting of criminal proceedings on the fairness of criminal trials. It concluded with the somewhat heretical suggestion that serious consideration should be given to the proposition that an accused in criminal trials should have the option of a trial in camera, or at least of a ban on publicity, either on all reporting or on identification of the accused, until conviction, or even completely.

All of these restrictions already exist in various circumstances and countries. The suggestion was made, not because I was convinced of its merits, but rather, not quite in the spirit of Swift's *Modest Proposal*, because I wanted to clarify the reasons for declaring and implementing the principle of open justice: that the press and public should be entitled to attend all judicial proceedings and to report on them.

In the same spirit, this paper begins with a proposal that the press and public should be entitled to attend all judicial proceedings involving children, and that reporting of such proceedings should not be restricted. The proposal is made to focus attention on the various reasons and legal authorities for restricting such access and reporting. As with the earlier paper, it is primarily concerned with law and practice in England and Wales, but will refer to other countries from time to time.

There now seems to be a tradition, or at least a consensus, in most countries, that publicity regarding children in legal proceedings should be kept to a minimum. This may seem to be consistent with principles of children's rights. It is likely that most adults involved in legal proceedings would, if given the choice, also prefer that publicity about themselves be kept to a minimum (perhaps with exceptions for some of those successful in civil actions). The publicity required of adults in legal proceedings under the open justice principle is justified by various arguments, some in the interests of those involved, some in the interests of society as a whole. One reason for proposing greater publicity for proceedings involving children, apart from focusing attention on the subject, is to suggest that the long-term interests of children might sometimes be served by greater publicity. Another is that if children are to exercise rights in the judicial process, perhaps they should also be subject to the responsibilities of that process, one of which is publicity.

Before considering the particular justifications for restricting access to and reporting of proceedings involving children, I would like to repeat some observations that have been made elsewhere in considering secrecy and transparency in general. One is that control over information is, if not power itself, at the very least an important aspect of power. Bacon's axiom, *'Scientiae potest est'*,[2] probably is better translated as 'knowledge is power' rather than the more common 'information is power'. One function of the law can be to redress the balance tilted by the natural tendency of those who have power to conceal information about its exercise, and also to obtain as much information as possible about those who are subject to it. This is the function of laws on access to government information (on which an Israeli academic, Itzhak Galnoor, edited one of the first books[3]) and various forms of legal protection of personal privacy.[4]

Another observation is that while the harm done by a particular disclosure, and thus the reason for secrecy, is usually concrete and immediate, the harm done by secrecy is almost always cumulative, and inevitably, less known. In analysing law and practice in England and Wales, it is worth considering the proposition that the real imperatives of the British constitution are not expressed in conventions, but in the aphorisms used by the middle classes (and their nannies) in socialising their children, one of which is 'Least said, soonest mended'. Finally, I would like to recall, and also to bear in mind, an observation by Hans Morgenthau (which I have been unable to trace to its source) that 'Those who exercise power always deceive, and they usually begin by deceiving themselves'.

Kinds of Proceedings Involving Children and Reasons for Secrecy

It is, of course, necessary to attempt an analysis of reasons for restricting access to and reporting of legal proceedings involving children in particular, as distinct from reasons for secrecy in general. One reason is the proposition that proceedings involving children are not judicial at all, and thus are removed by a change of classification from what is supposed to be the general rule of open justice. This obscures the essential characteristics of such proceedings. Important decisions are taken regarding the future treatment of a child, or at the very least with the participation of a child as a witness. Some proceedings in which the child is the subject of decisions about its future are generally classified as 'juvenile justice' while others are classified as wardship or care proceedings. The United States Supreme Court has distinguished between the constitutionality of provisions for closed juvenile hearings and of imposition of penalties on newspapers for publishing identities, holding the penalties to be unconstitutional in *Smith v. Daily Mail*.[5]

Until *Re Gault*,[6] it was thought to be very progressive to deny that juvenile proceedings were criminal in nature at all. The US Supreme Court resiled somewhat from that proposition on the ground that children in non-criminal juvenile justice proceedings were being denied basic rights of fairness that adults would have in procedures that could lead to loss of liberty for longer periods than an adult might face. Such re-classification of subjects is a common technique for avoiding inconvenient rules. For example, torture is never justified as such (in part because it cannot be under international law) but instead is defined as strict interrogation that is not torture.[7] Similarly, sexually explicit speech is re-defined as violence against women to justify its censorship, and commercial speech is re-defined as mere advertising to justify its restriction.

Another reason for restricting public access to and reporting of proceedings in which children provide evidence is the argument that children as witnesses will not provide reliable testimony unless they are shielded from various aspects of publicity to which other witness are subject. This can range from a ban on identifying the witness, to a complete absence of a child witness from the proceedings, with evidence being presented only in the form of a witness statement or a recorded interview. This presents a near-insoluble conflict between the best interests of the child, or perhaps the interests of justice, in that child evidence might not otherwise be available, and the right of an accused person to confront witnesses as a part of the right to a fair trial. In *Unterpertinger v Austria*[8] the European Court of Human Rights ruled that it was a violation of the right to confront witnesses in criminal proceedings to convict a man on the basis of witness statements from his child and wife. The United States Supreme Court has held that the right to confront witnesses was violated by allowing two 13-year-olds to testify from behind screens in *Coy v Iowa,* [9] but that the right was not violated by allowing a six-year-old witness to testify by closed-circuit television.[10] The court also ruled that a state statute requiring *in camera* trials for all rape cases involving minor victims was unconstitutional.[11]

A more general reason for restriction on press and public access to and reporting of proceedings involving children is to protect the child from publicity in general on the assumption that any public attention given to a child is harmful. This is, in effect, a specific application of the general right to privacy, presumed to have more force because a child is more vulnerable than an adult.

International Law Regarding Children in the Legal Process

The Universal Declaration of Human Rights contains no specific provisions about children in the legal process. Article 14 of the International Covenant on Civil and Political Rights guarantees the right to a public hearing, but provides that the press and public may be excluded 'for reasons of morals, public order or national security in a democratic society, or when the interest of the private lives of the parties so requires ....' and makes particular reference to children in providing that judgments in criminal and civil cases are to be made public 'except where the interest of juvenile persons otherwise requires or the proceedings concern matrimonial disputes or the guardianship of children'.

The Declaration on the Rights of the Child provides in Principle 2 that 'The child shall enjoy special protection....' The Convention on the Rights of the Child provides in Article 12 that

> States Parties shall assure to the child who is capable of forming his or her own views the right to express those views freely in all matters affecting the child, the view of the child being given due weight in accordance with the age and maturity of the child.

Article 14(2) further provides that

For this purpose, the child shall in particular be provided the opportunity to be heard in any judicial and administrative proceedings affecting the child, either directly, or through a representative or an appropriate body, in a manner consistent with the procedural rules of national law.

Article 40 provides that a child accused of infractions is entitled to certain procedural rights, although the right to a public hearing is not expressly included, while the child has a right to have 'his or her privacy fully respected at all stages of the proceedings.'

Articles 8(1) and (2) of the Beijing Rules[12] recommend that 'in order to avoid harm being done to juveniles by undue publicity or the process of labelling, their privacy shall be respected at all stages and that information leading to the identification of a juvenile offender should not be published'. The Madrid Principles provide (in Principle 7) that 'Laws may authorise restrictions of the Basic Principle [of open justice] to the extent necessary in a democratic society *for the protection of minors* and of members of other groups in need of special protection'.[13]

The American Convention on Human Rights has no particular provisions regarding children in legal proceedings, while Article 6 of the European Convention on Human Rights and Fundamental Freedoms provides that

In the determination of his civil rights and obligations or of any criminal charge against him, everyone is entitled to a fair and *public* hearing .... Judgment shall be pronounced publicly but the press and public may be excluded from all or part of the trial in the interests of morals, public order or national security in a democratic society, *where the interests of juveniles* or the protection of the private life of the parties so require, or to the extent strictly necessary in the opinion of the court in special circumstances where publicity would prejudice the interests of justice. (emphasis added)

English Law

The leading case asserting the general principle of open justice in England and Wales was *Scott v. Scott*,[14] but even in that case the House of Lords recognised that one of the three exceptions to the rule was exercise of the prerogative jurisdiction over wards. In the years since then the number of exceptions has increased, and the law in England and Wales on this subject is such a jumble that in 1993 the Lord Chancellor's Department produced a working paper[15] which essentially attempted to set out the various existing restrictions, rather than to propose any particular changes in the law and practice. Some, but not all of these restrictions relate to children in one way or another.

Documents deposited with the court in family proceedings may only be inspected or copied by parties to the proceedings unless leave is granted,[16] so the information will only be publicly available if it is presented as evidence in open court with no limitations on reporting. The disclosure of documents in wardship cases was considered in *Re X (Minors)(Wardship: Disclosure of Documents)*.[17] The interests of the child were to be important, but not paramount, and had to be balanced against the public interest in evidence being available for use in other proceedings, as well as the public interest in the administration of wardship proceedings.

In juvenile courts there is an automatic prohibition on identifying young people, whether parties or witnesses.[18] In other legal proceedings section 39(1) of the Children and Young Persons Act 1933 provides that any court may order that no newspaper report or report in a programme service shall reveal the name, address or school of or include any particular calculated to lead to the identification of any child or young person concerned in judicial proceedings.

Criminal Cases Involving Children

Youth Courts

One of the few provisions in English law in which the press is given special privileges is the right of journalists, but not the general public, to attend youth court proceedings, applications concerning supervision orders, and appeals regarding them.[19] Journalists may also report such proceedings, but must not identify the young people, subject to fines. There is a general power for the Youth Court to lift the restrictions on identification in order to avoid injustice to the child. Also, if the child is charged with a violent or sexual offence or an offence which, if committed by an adult, would be punishable by fourteen years' imprisonment or more, and is unlawfully at large, the Director of Public Prosecutions can ask the court to allow reporting of the child's identity for the purpose of apprehension.

Other Courts

Other criminal proceedings involving children in magistrates' courts, the Crown Court, and appeals, have no automatic limit on access of the press and public, or on reporting. But the general provision of section 39(1) of the Children and Young Persons Act 1933 (above) applies. In one case in which an elderly man was charged with acts of indecency with two young girls, however, the judge said that the girls deserved to be identified.[20] Although the Act provides for such orders regarding a child or young person who is a party, witness, or 'in respect of whom the proceedings are taken', they can be made about children alleged to be victims of offences even if they are not to be witnesses. This can mean that the order will prohibit the identification of a defendant if the child victim was a close relative and the effect of identifying the defendant would be to identify the child.[21] In one case involving allegations of sexual abuse of children, the judge ordered that the adult defendants not be identified because it could lead to the identification of child witnesses. The Court of Appeal ruled that this was excessive, and that orders should simply be made in the words of the statute, leaving it to newspapers to decide whether publication of a detail would identify the child, which could lead to the newspaper's prosecution.[22]

　　If a Crown Court judge makes such an order, journalists can appeal against it immediately to the Court of Appeal (Criminal Division),[23] where a local authority who has the child in care may also be heard, as well, it seems, as a guardian *ad litem* appointed to represent a child who is a ward of court.[24] Breaches of such orders can be prosecuted in magistrates' courts. Although the Divisional Court has said that anonymity should be the norm for juveniles appearing as defendants in adult courts,[25] there have been cases in which Crown Court judges have made orders under section 39 prohibiting identification, and then lifted the order after conviction to allow identification. Probably the best-known such case was the trial of two children for the murder of two-year-old James Bulger when they were ten and eleven years of age.[26] After their conviction the trial judge allowed them to be identified. Unfortunately for the purposes of legal certainty, there was no appeal against the order, and so no judicial interpretation of the relevant law, as there was in a somewhat similar case in August 1995.[27] A seventeen-year-old was convicted of indecent assault and wounding, and the trial judge lifted the order prohibiting identification that he had made during the trial, on the grounds of the severity of the crime, the deterrence to the convicted defendant, and the general deterrence to others of the possible disgrace of being publicly identified if convicted of such a crime. The defendant challenged the order unsuccessfully on judicial review, arguing that the publicity would interfere with rehabilitation.

Civil Proceedings Involving Children

> In the Family Division, county courts, and magistrates' courts hearing civil cases concerning children, Lord Halsbury's dictum [in *Scott v. Scott* that 'Every court in the land is open to every subject of the King] is only a faint echo. As a result of a multiplicity of statutory provisions and rules of court, such cases are almost invariably heard in private, and the reporting of their proceedings is effectively prohibited.[28]

It has been clear law ever since *Scott v. Scott* that judicial proceedings involving wardship are not open to the press and public and that reporting of them is prohibited except in very limited terms as to the legal result without disclosure of any information that could identify the child. There is also a line of cases in which the courts have made orders prohibiting communication of information about wards of court beyond reports of wardship hearings. In some of these cases, application has been made for the child to be made a ward of court solely for the purpose of establishing jurisdiction for the court to make an order prohibiting publication of information in some way relating to the child. This has led to cases in which the courts have made orders prohibiting publication of information relating to a child who is not a ward of court in the exercise of the court's inherent jurisdiction as *parens patriae*. Discussing these cases is somewhat difficult because of court restrictions on what can be known or communicated about the cases, even when the application for an injunction is not completely successful (but that is only an example of the inherent difficulty of discussions about secrecy and confidentiality in any particular case).

The case of Mary Bell is a striking illustration of publicity regarding children involved in the legal process in two ways. She was convicted in 1968 at the age of 11 of the manslaughter of two young children and she was identified, as the two boys convicted of killing James Bulger were. Over 25 years later she had a child. The child was made a ward of court at birth, and four months later an injunction was made, prohibiting publication of Mary Bell's present identity and that of her child. The injunction was described as supervisory, in being 'directly about the fact that the authorities were permitting her to be brought up by a mother whom some may have thought to be so evil as not to be entrusted with the care of any young child'.[29]

The Mary Bell case is thus a link between publicity regarding children in criminal legal proceedings and publicity regarding children in wardship and other proceedings. Another case linking criminal and wardship jurisdiction arose out of the charges that Fred and Rosemary West had committed several murders and buried bodies in the garden of their house. He committed suicide in prison while awaiting trial and she was later convicted of murder. The local authority had already obtained care orders for their five children who were still minors in 1992, before the criminal investigations began. In view of the publicity surrounding the case an injunction was made in 1994 and revised in 1995 prohibiting the publication of any information about acts of sexual or physical abuse of any of the children still in care.[30]

One case involved a conflict between civil and criminal courts in restricting information about legal proceedings in the interests of protecting children. In *Re R (Wardship: Restrictions on Publication)*[31] the child had been in the care of the mother and had been taken by the father without the mother's consent to the United States and Israel, from where the father was extradited to the United Kingdom to be tried for kidnapping. He gave an interview to a newspaper describing his case, and the child's guardian *ad litem* obtained an injunction in the Family Court against publication of any information about the child, who was a ward of court. The Court of Appeal (Criminal Division) then ruled that the wardship judge did not have jurisdiction to restrict reporting of a criminal trial, which was the function of the trial judge.

In considering purely civil cases it may be useful to begin with those cases in which children are already wards of court or under judicial supervision in some other way, and then turn to the cases in which courts have asserted an inherent jurisdiction to restrain publicity about children.

In one case a severely mentally handicapped baby was dying, and was made a ward of court to settle questions regarding the medical treatment she should receive. An injunction was made prohibiting the identification of the hospital, the doctors or nurses, and the parents. The reason was not only 'the welfare of [the baby] and her right to confidentiality', but also the court's 'power to protect its own proceedings'.[32]

In *Re M and another (minors)(wardship: freedom of publication)*[33] a local newspaper was allowed to publish a story concerning the removal of two children from their foster parents without proper consultation or notification of the reason for the action, which was taken because of a complaint of sexual abuse against the foster father, although the newspaper was not permitted to publish anything which would have identified the children. One child was already a ward of court, and the other was made a ward of court for the purpose of obtaining an injunction. In *Re W (a minor) (wardship: freedom of publication)*[34] a boy who had been involved in homosexual acts with older men was made a ward of court and placed in the care of a local authority. When he was fostered with two homosexual men a newspaper was allowed to publish the story, but not to identify the boy or the foster parents.

In *Re W (Wardship: Discharge: Publicity)*[35] there was a conflict over publicity between four boys aged 10 to 15, their father, and the Official Solicitor who was their guardian *ad litem* in wardship. The boys were under an order made in wardship to live with their father, who had care and control. With their father's permission they gave a newspaper interview entitled 'Our Fight to Stay With Dad', in which their names were changed and they appeared only in silhouette, expressing their dislike of their mother and their dissatisfaction with their representation by the Official Solicitor, who then applied unsuccessfully for an injunction to restrain the father from giving information or allowing the children to give information concerning wardship proceedings. In *Re H-S (minors: protection of identity)*[36] the Court of Appeal allowed a father who had been given custody of his three children to publish a story of his life as a transsexual, but prohibited the identification of the children or their school.

In some cases the courts have been involved in the upbringing of a child, although not necessarily as a ward of court. A relatively recent case has spelled out the authority of the courts to prohibit publication of information about a child when one of the parents seeks to have the child participate in such publication.[37] The official report of the case gives only limited factual information, because, in the words of Ward L.J.

> It is important to stress that this injunction [prohibiting the soliciting of any information relating to the child] remains in full force. I shall, therefore, say as little as possible about the facts of this case ... Although this judgment may be reported under initials, omitting also the names of the solicitors (except the Official Solicitor, who appears as guardian *ad litem* for the child) I emphasis for the avoidance of doubt that the various judgments and proceedings in the court below are not to be published.[38]

A great deal of information has in fact been published about the identity of the child, her mother, her father, and the clinic where the child was treated, both in some newspapers and in an Early Day Motion in the House of Commons. No legal action was taken against the newspapers or the MP. This account will be restricted to the terms of the court orders.

The parents and the handicapped child had been the objects of publicity and 'on an application made by the mother but in reality made by the parents jointly'[39] the court exercised its inherent jurisdiction to make an injunction restraining the media from revealing the identity of the child or any establishment where she was being educated or treated. The mother then made remarks in a television interview which were considered by the court to be in contempt of court, after which the court ordered her not to communicate, except for ordinary social purposes, any information relating to the child.

The child then received treatment at an institution in another country, and a television company wanted to make a film about the institution to include film of the child and an interview with the mother. The mother's application to permit the production and broadcast of the film was refused as not being in the best interests of the child. Among other points, the first instance judge rejected the argument that because the child was not a ward of court her care and upbringing were not under court supervision, and that 'however sympathetically made or projected the film may be, the overwhelming probability is that [the child] will be adversely affected by it. It is the secondary tabloid media publicity ... which causes me concern.' He also said that 'there is no reason why some other child should not be selected to go through this filming process' and that the court was 'not concerned in any way to protect the father's privacy or that of his family'.[40]

The Court of Appeal upheld the prohibition on the ground that the court had inherent jurisdiction regarding publication directed at an aspect of the upbringing of a child where the publicity would be inimical to the child's welfare under section 1(1) of the Children Act 1989. The court also had jurisdiction to make a 'prohibited steps' order under section 8 of the Children Act 1989 to enforce the parent's duty not to disclose confidential information relating to the child when disclosure would be contrary to the child's best interests, as the welfare of the child would be harmed and not advanced by her participation in the programme.

In another case which attracted wide publicity, a child, through her father, first came before the courts to challenge by judicial review the local health authority's refusal to fund an operation that might save her life. The trial court ordered the operation, but was reversed by the Court of Appeal, after which the operation was funded by a private donor. Throughout, the courts had ordered that the child not be identified. The father then applied for the order to be lifted to allow identification so that the child could appeal for more donations. Giving heed to the child's wishes, the court lifted the order, and the child then appeared in television interviews.[41]

Comparing these last two cases, it may be significant that in the case in which publicity was allowed, the child herself, although aged only ten, was articulate, while the other child, although two years older, was handicapped as a result of brain surgery. Also, in the case in which publicity was allowed, the other parent had not opposed publicity, while the father in the other case was represented in court and argued against publicity.

These cases have all involved children who were already before the courts in one sense or another. There are also cases in which children, through their representatives, invoke the courts' jurisdiction in order to restrain publicity. One such case involved an application by a stepfather to have his 14-year-old stepdaughter made a ward of court for the purpose of applying for an injunction to restrain publication of a book that contained eight pages of description of the child's dead father, who was described as a philanderer. The injunction was granted but reversed by the Court of Appeal on the ground that 'the importance in a free society of the circulation of true information' meant freedom 'not only for the statements of opinion of which we approve, but also for those of which we most heartily disapprove'.[42] Publication of the book thus was allowed, but it should be borne in mind that the child could not be identified from reports of the legal proceedings.

Nearly twenty years later there was a similar case in which there were no pre-existing proceedings, and application for wardship was made by a mother of the five year old daughter solely for the purpose of applying for an injunction to restrain publication of information in a television programme about the father of the daughter, who had been convicted a year before on charges of indecency involving young boys. An order had been made during the trial under section 39 of the Children and Young Persons Act 1933 to prohibit identification of the victims, but that did not apply to bar a film of him (although he was not named in the programme and his former address was not given). An order was made by the Family Division that the programme could be broadcast only if the father's image was obscured, but it was reversed by the Court of Appeal, on the ground that the court did not have jurisdiction because the programme did not concern the child's care and upbringing.[43]

Conclusion

I conclude as I began, with a radical proposal, if only to stimulate, that there should be no exceptions to the general principle of a public right of access to and reporting of legal proceedings on the basis of the best interests of the child. This is, of course, almost the exact opposite of the proposal which I have made regarding open justice in criminal trials, that individuals should have the option of a completely private trial. But I make it to stimulate thought as to exactly why children are to be shielded in legal proceedings in various degrees from scrutiny, and to suggest that special treatment of children may not always be in their true best interests, in the short term or the long term, or sometimes both. It may only seem to be that way to the adults in charge.[44] Traditional values, such as those of publicity for adults and privacy for children in legal proceedings, at the very least require re-examination from time to time, if only to consider whether they have justification beyond habit and custom.

Notes

[1]   'Open Justice: Publicity and the Judicial Process' in Freeman, M.D.A. and Hepple, B.A. (eds) (1993) *Current Legal Problems 1993* vol. 46, Part 2: Collected Papers, pp. 190-203, Oxford University Press.

[2]   *Meditationes Sacrae* (1597).

[3]   *Government Secrecy in Democracies* (1977) Harper & Row, New York.

[4]   At this point in papers on information and power it is now commonplace to describe the system of continual surveillance in Jeremy Bentham's Panopticon model prison, and also Foucault's discussion of it in *Discipline and Punish: The Birth of the Prison* (1977) Allen Lane.

[5]   332 U.S. 97 (1979).

[6]   387 U.S. 1 (1967).

[7]   For example, the Israeli Landau Commission (Report: 1987) regarded as justified the use of 'moderate physical pressure' in the interrogation of Palestinian prisoners; cf the discussion by Nadera Shalhoub-Kevorkian at Chap. 13 below.

[8]   Judgment of 24 November 1986, Series A, Vol. 110.

[9]   487 U.S. 1012 (1988).

[10] *Maryland v. Craig* 497 U.S. 836 (1990).

[11] *Globe Newspaper v. Superior Court*, 457 U.S. 596 (1982).

[12] *The United Nations Standard Minimum Rules for the Administration of Juvenile Justice* (1985).

13   *The Media and the Judiciary* Volume IV (CJIL) Centre for the Independence of Judges and Lawyers Yearbook, December 1995, Appendix 1. (emphasis added)

14   [1913] A.C. 417.

15   Lord Chancellor's Department, *Review of Access to and Reporting of Family Proceedings* (1993).

16   Family Proceedings Rules 1991, rule 10.20 (1) and (3).

17   [1992] Fam 124 CA.

18   Children and Young Persons Act 1933 s. 47.

19   Criminal Justice and Public Order Act 1994, s. 49, replacing Children and Young Persons Act 1933, s. 49.

20   Described in *Punishment, Danger and Stigma: the morality of criminal justice*, Walker N., (1980) Basil Blackwell, Oxford, p. 151.

21   *Ex parte Crook* [1995] 1 WLR 139. But in this case, in which the defendants were charged with the manslaughter of one of their children and cruelty to three others, the Court of Appeal changed the order to allow the identification of the dead child.

22   *R v. Southwark Crown Court ex parte Goodwin* (1991) *The Times* 30 May 1991.

23   Criminal Justice Act 1988, s. 159.

24   In *Re R (Wardship: Restrictions on Publication)* [1994] Fam 255 CA.

25   *R v. Leicester Crown Court ex parte S* (1990) *Independent* 12 December 1991.

26   See Douglas at Chap. 15 below.

27   *R v. Inner London Crown Court ex parte Anthony Barnes* (1995) *The Times* 7 August.

28   'Annual Survey: Media reporting Restrictions', Andrew Nicol QC and Heather Rogers, *Yearbook of Media and Entertainment Law 1995*, (1995) Oxford University Press, p. 294. See in particular the Administration of Justice Act 1960, s. 12 (1).

29   *X County Council v. A* [1984] 1 WLR 1422.

30   *Re West* [1995] 2 FCR 206.

31   [1994] Fam 255 CA.

32   *Re C (a minor) (wardship: medical treatment) (No 2)* [1990] Fam 39 CA.

33   [1990] Fam 211.

34   [1992] WLR 100.

35   [1995] 2 FLR 466, CA.

36   [1994] 3 All ER 390 CA.

37   *Re Z (A Minor)(Identification: Restrictions on Publication)*, [1997] Fam 1 CA.

38   At p. 9F-G.

39   Ibid. at 9E.

40   Ibid. at 11.

41   *R v. Cambridge District Health Authority ex parte B (No. 2)* [1996] 1 FLR 375 CA.

42   *Per* Lord Denning MR in *Re X (a minor) (wardship: restriction on publication)* [1975] Fam 47 at p 58.

43   *R v. Central Television plc* [1994] Fam 192.

44   'Only the public administration of justice will compel judges to ensure that their appraisal of the evidence and the quality of their reasoning reaches the standards of rigour properly demanded by the law in the treatment of adults.' 'Behind Closed Doors: Juvenile Hearings in the Netherlands', Carol Van Nijnatten, *International Journal of Law and the Family* 3 (1989) pp. 177-184.

12 Who is the Father? Access to Information on Genetic Identity

KATHERINE O'DONOVAN

Introduction

Scientific advances in medicine open up possibilities unanticipated in the past. As we enter a new age of biotechnology and genetic engineering, questions arise which present new ethical dilemmas, and which must be answered in law. New scientific developments bring benefits, such as genetic screening for hereditary diseases.[1] New knowledge and information bring challenges to traditional ways of understanding. Reacting to these in legal terms will involve consultation with the public, and a re-examination of the policies and values contained in current legal provisions, and new laws.

This paper is concerned with the effect on family law of new information about genetics. Specifically, where science opens up the possibility of certainty of paternity through DNA testing,[2] are there arguments to justify changes in law or in ethical codes, in response to the new technology? This question is part of a larger question about medical confidentiality, privacy and access to information.[3] In approaching the question, we must first review the position on confidentiality of, and access to, medical information. This question also raises issues about the rights of the individuals involved.

Confidentiality of medical information raises questions of who, what, when, where and why. Analytically these questions can be organised into categories of patients' rights to privacy, patients' rights to information about their own bodies, and medical practice based on ethical and utilitarian arguments. However, as this paper will demonstrate, third party claims to information relating to an individual patient may disrupt these categories, particularly where such claims are couched in the language of rights.

The question of access to information possessed and stored by a person or organisation concerning a particular individual first requires scrutiny of the Data Protection Act 1984, the Access to Health Records Act 1990, the Access to Medical Reports Act 1988, and case law.[4] Access by third parties, even where they have an interest, is curtailed. What of access, by the individual concerned, or by third parties, to information not yet stored electronically, nor in records, nor reports? At issue here is material which could be, but has not yet been, obtained through scientific testing. An example is information stored in the human body. Where an adult obtains information stored in his or her body by electing to submit herself or himself to testing, questions of therapeutic benefit may arise, but access is part of election. But where the information is stored in the body of another person issues of consent and privacy arise. On the one hand genetic information stored in the body of an individual may concern other persons. This point is recognised by the Nuffield Committee Report on Genetic Screening which states that genetic information is family information.[5] On the other hand, privacy rights, as expressed in consent requirements, preclude compulsory testing, even where the interests of others are involved, exceptions being made for public health reasons.[6]

Individual rights and medical practice may be modified where children are involved. In the case of a child, proxy consent by an authorised adult may be accepted as legally valid, depending on the age and understanding of the child.[7] But what if the intervention on the child's body is not justified by therapeutic benefit to the child? At this point the discourses of medical ethics and family law merge. The seeking of genetic information concerning a child through, for example, a blood test, does involve a form of intervention on the child's body. In the discourse of family law, this may be authorised in the child's best interests without reference to therapeutic benefit in medical terms.

The scientific advances, of which DNA testing is an example, have opened up new possibilities of knowledge. How we handle that knowledge is an issue not just for medical scientists, or for lawyers, but for citizens. Diagnostic DNA testing of a child for paternity poses a series of difficult questions about possible changes to law and the introduction of a code of practice for laboratories which offer such a service. Because such diagnosis inevitably involves more than one person, a balancing of interests must be undertaken. And where material susceptible to DNA testing is stored for particular purposes, safeguards to prevent the testing of such material for other purposes need to be considered.[8]

At a time when certainty of paternity was not possible the common law set out a number of presumptions concerning fatherhood. The foundation of these is that the husband of a woman who gives birth is presumed to be the father of her child. This is known as the presumption of paternity: *pater est quam nuptiae demonstrant*. It can be argued that such presumptions are no longer necessary, because science permits certainty; nevertheless, for the moment, English law retains this as a rebuttable presumption. Even where the child is known by both parents to have been born through donor insemination, the Human Fertilisation and Embryology Act 1990 creates the legal fiction that the mother's husband is the father.[9] So both the presumption of paternity, and the Act, permit the separation of legal paternity from genetic paternity. In so far as popular opinion assumes legal and genetic paternity to be unitary, the law creates a fiction. In the case of the presumption of paternity, the effect of the law may be to bestow paternity, without his overt consent, on a man who is not the genetic father.[10] In the case of donor insemination, there is a legal presumption of consent on the part of the mother's husband or partner. The onus is on him to rebut this presumption. However, medical practice is to ensure overt consent.[11]

This paper asks the following questions: where information about paternity is stored in a child's body, under what conditions, if any, should the child be tested to ascertain paternity? What interests can be named as relevant to a discussion of this question. How does the law relating to confidentiality and access to information impinge on this discussion? How does English law measure up to Article 7 of the United Nations Convention on the Rights of the Child which protects the rights of children to 'know' their parents, and to Article 8 which requires states to respect the right of the child to preserve her or his identity?[12] As it is often not possible for children to exercise their rights whilst still children, it is particularly important that domestic legislation is passed or reformed in order to carry out international obligations. This paper focuses on genetic identity, and does not extend to identity, in the sense of belonging to a community and culture, nor to sexual identity. The paper proceeds as follows: part one examines the present law, including international obligations under the UN Convention on the Rights of the Child; part two examines the practice of laboratories which offer a DNA diagnostic service, to ascertain paternity; part three discusses ethical issues, including the welfare of the child; in the final part of the paper identity rights as human rights are considered. The paper must confront the difficulty that examination of a child's body to ascertain information about genetic paternity might be regarded as an invasion of the child's privacy, or it might be regarded as protecting the child's identity rights. The standard 'best interests' or 'welfare' tests, contained in legislation and international conventions, do not provide ready answers to this difficulty.

Present Law

There are two possibilities foreseen by the law for the scientific determination of paternity: voluntary testing and testing directed by a court. Voluntary diagnostic DNA testing is a private matter for parents or putative parents, by agreement. It is self-evident that a child is unlikely to be a volunteer, unless over the age of sixteen or competent in terms of age and understanding, but consenting to such testing on behalf of a child is part of the powers of parental responsibility.[13] Voluntary testing is not seen as problematic in English law. A person with parental responsibility may consent on behalf of the child, and provided the mother and the man, or men, involved agree, testing may go ahead without official intervention. The concept of parental responsibility has its own complexities and is therefore elaborated in the next paragraph.

The legal presumption of paternity applies to the husband of a married woman who gives birth. He is the presumptive legal father, whose name is automatically entered on the birth certificate, and who has parental responsibility by law. The woman who gives birth, whether married or unmarried, also has parental responsibility by law.[14] If the mother is unmarried the name of the father on the birth certificate may provide evidence of paternity. This is called the presumption based on registration. For the father to be registered either the agreement of both parents is required, or a court order naming that particular individual as father.[15] Of children born to unmarried women, research shows that 75 per cent have their births registered in the name of a father.[16] The legal concept of paternity is complex. As already explained, the paternity of the husband of a married woman who gives birth is presumed. However, the man whose name appears on the birth certificate does not have parental responsibility, unless he is married to the legal mother, or jointly registers an agreement with the mother, or acquires parental responsibility by court order.[17] Thus paternity and parental responsibility are not necessarily co-terminous. The birth certificate is evidence of paternity, giving the status of legal father (but not necessarily parental responsibility) to the man named thereon, until and unless evidence to the contrary is presented to, and convinces, a court.[18]

The status of birth certificates as evidentiary documents, leaves space for the rebuttal of evidence by science, as discussed in the next paragraph.

Rebuttal of the legal presumption of paternity, or of the evidence contained on a birth certificate, is possible through scientific testing. This is subject to voluntarily agreed testing or to the control of the courts in contested cases. Where the presumption of paternity is rebutted, or the evidence of the birth certificate not confirmed by testing, the putative father is relieved of the rights and duties of parentage. However, the law may not make it possible to alter an individual's birth certificate, although the man named may no longer have the status and obligations of a legal father.[19] The significant reason for this is the status of birth certificates and the births register in law. The correction of errors on birth certificates is governed by a statutory procedure, and correction does not automatically follow from rebuttal of the presumption of paternity in court proceedings. Furthermore, statutory fatherhood for purposes of child support has no necessary effect elsewhere in the law.[20] Thus, where a support order for her child was successfully obtained by a married woman against a third party after DNA testing, her husband's name remained on the birth certificate, notwithstanding a subsequent divorce and efforts by the former husband to correct the births register.[21] The status of the register as an historical document has been stated in a number of cases.[22] This argument is used to justify refusals to change the register to bring it into conformity with later changes, for example sex-change; but it has also been used to justify a refusal to correct errors of registration of paternity. Even where the statutory procedure for the correction of error is complied with, re-registration does not take place. The correction is placed in the margin of the register. Yet in cases of subsequent legitimation, of subsequent registration of the father of a child born to an unmarried woman, and of adoption, re-registration is permitted by statute.[23] History, it seems, does not necessarily coincide with truth. Although legal technicalities are responsible for this situation, it seems that science, as demonstrated by DNA analysis, may not have anticipated the full legal consequences.

In addition to voluntary testing there may be a legal direction for testing of a child by a court. The Family Law Reform Act 1969, section 20 gives power to the court in the course of civil proceedings to direct scientific tests, with the object of ascertaining the inheritable characteristics of bodily fluids or bodily tissue to determine whether a party to the proceedings is or is not the father or mother of a person whose parentage is in question. The court may give a direction on its own motion, or on application. DNA testing is specifically included as a technique for use in disputed cases. The court has discretion whether or not to direct testing, and must consider whether testing would be contrary to the child's interests.[24] Non-compliance with the court's direction by a person with parental responsibility may give rise to inferences about the child's paternity. According to the Court of Appeal, 'if the truth can be established with certainty, a refusal to produce the certainty justifies some inference that the refusal is made to hide the truth ....'.[25]

The welfare principle - or at least consideration of the child's interests - lies at the heart of the question whether or not a court should direct scientific testing of paternity. However, where voluntary testing is agreed there is silence over welfare. The assumption of the legislation seems to be that the adult with parental responsibility will act in the best interests of the child. Courts also have taken this view.[26] In addition to court ordered and voluntarily agreed testing, there is the possibility of secret testing, without necessary consideration of the child's welfare. The courts have expressed reluctance to allow blood testing to be a 'fishing expedition' to discover whether a wife is adulterous.[27] But secret testing of the child, with or without the consent of person(s) with parental responsibility, has not yet become an issue. One reason for this is that the technology which facilitates such testing has only recently become available. Another reason is secrecy itself.

Comparison with legal measures in other European jurisdictions shows that views about the relationship between the welfare of the child and voluntary DNA testing for paternity differ. French law foresees such a possibility, and prohibits it as not in the best interests of the child. Under the French Civil Code, Art. 16-11, DNA testing, even where all parties consent, cannot be performed without a court order. This is reinforced by the Penal Code, Art. 226-228, which creates an offence of testing without court order, with which laboratories may be charged.[28] Thus the court acts as gate keeper to prevent voluntary testing. It follows that secret testing within France is not a possibility. Swedish law does not permit voluntary testing without official sanction. This is a matter to be determined by the Social Welfare Committee, an administrative body, in accordance with the best interests of the child.[29] Again secret testing is off the Swedish map. Not only are these three jurisdictions governed by the European Convention on Human Rights, which protects the 'right to family and private life', under Article 8, but all three have ratified the United Nations Convention on the Rights of the Child. It is clear that interpretations of the best interests principle, and of identity rights differ. Quite how these articles will be interpreted by international enforcement agencies in practice remains to be seen.[30] It is of interest that three jurisdictions which share a concern with the child's welfare offer such differing interpretations.

Article 7(1) of the UN Convention on the Rights of the Child requires that a child be registered immediately after birth, 'and shall have the right from birth to a name ... and, as far as possible, the right to know and be cared for by his or her parents'.[31] If English law is weighed against the Convention it does seem to be the case, as observed by Barton and Douglas, that

> English law appears to give priority to the parent's right to acknowledge the parental link, rather than the child's right to identity, for apart from the orders requiring him to pay maintenance for the child, all these mechanisms of registration show the father's intention to accept parentage of the child and to be acknowledged as a parent, and will be accepted as such if the matter is disputed in court.[32]

In other words, mechanisms of acknowledgment by the father appear to be structured in such a way as to complicate the establishment of paternity.

There is room for scepticism over a child's right, as far as possible, to know and to be cared for by his or her parents because knowledge of paternity remains largely within maternal control.[33] A number of studies have revealed an apparent discrepancy between recorded fatherhood on the birth certificate and genetic paternity, in that the records are not necessarily accurate.[34] It is important therefore to distinguish between rights of access to recorded information and the veracity of those records.[35] English law appears to give priority to maintenance of a record as a public document, rather than to accuracy. As explained earlier, the procedure for correction of the records of birth is such that a court order naming another man as father is not accepted as sufficient evidence to warrant alteration. Yet if the focus of the law is on the child's identity rights, such correction follows logically. If identity rights are taken seriously there is room for amendment of English law.

Laboratory Practice

The procedures for voluntary diagnostic paternity testing in England appear to be governed by a consensus amongst laboratories. No attempt has been made by government, the medical profession, or other body to impose ethical guidelines, possibly because no moral panic has occurred over DNA testing for paternity. The practice of the laboratories which offer a commercial service is to use the family doctor as intermediary.[36] Leaflets from the laboratories advise parents who have registered and paid the fee, to take the child and photographs of the three parties to the family doctor, who will take blood samples. These samples are then sent to the laboratory for analysis, and the results are communicated directly to the parents.

Interviews with two of the laboratories which offer this service reveal that it is only with reluctance that a departure from the above established practice will be countenanced. Scientific accuracy can only be assured if two parents and the child are tested.[37] However testing based on one adult and a child was conceded as possible; as was testing of bodily samples other than blood. As documented in the Criminal Justice and Public Order Act 1994, DNA testing can be performed on hair roots, saliva and bodily substances other than blood.[38] A scenario in which a father, with parental responsibility, gives consent to the taking of a blood sample from a child and from himself, is not ruled out. It is also possible that hairs with a particle of scalp tissue, taken from a hairbrush, might be sent for analysis. In an age of technology where individuals can buy 'do it yourself' kits for genetic screening for cystic fibrosis, or certain breast cancers, this is hardly surprising.[39] However, the outcome is that secret testing for paternity is possible.

The question whether English law should adopt the approach of French law in insisting on a court direction prior to scientific paternity testing raises a number of issues. As already explained, English law contains a number of assumptions: that voluntary testing may be undertaken through parental agreement; that parents know what is for the welfare of their child; that in contested cases, where parents disagree, the court will order testing provided that this is not judged to be contrary to the child's welfare; that Article 7 of the United Nations Convention on the Rights of the Child establishes that the truth about genetic identity is the right of a child, unless welfare clearly justifies non-investigation; that a parent who refuses compliance with a court direction will have to accept possible legal consequences, notwithstanding that the refusal is based on a belief about the child's welfare; that the legal presumption of paternity can be rebutted by scientific evidence.[40] Welfare enters in specifically only if there is a legal contest. This is in accordance with Article 3 of the UN Convention on the Rights of the Child.[41]

French law, by contrast, assumes that disruption to the legal placement of a child at birth, through scientific testing, must be done only with the sanction of a court. The rebuttal of the legal presumption of paternity in French law is difficult, because the welfare of the child is perceived as being tied to a secure legal placement at birth. Not only do the legal rules operate to make rebuttal of the presumption of paternity difficult, but the doctrine established by the courts reinforces this. In addition there are specific prohibitions on testing without a court order, even where both parents request testing. The effect of French legislation, and interpretation, on laboratory practice is that 'fishing expeditions' to establish the paternity of a child are not possible in France.[42] This is seen as consonant with the best interests principle.

If the English position is seen as in need of reform, a distinction may be drawn between voluntary and secret testing. Only the latter may be considered as a problem. Mechanisms to prevent secret testing do not have to be court centred. An ethical code, agreed by laboratories, whereby the agreement of both parties is always necessary for diagnostic paternity testing would be sufficient to prevent secret testing.

Ethical Considerations

Where medical information concerning an individual is stored electronically or manually, or forms part of a medical report, access to that information by the individual concerned is controlled by the appropriate statute. The statutory regimes in question, which are not identical, impose a paternalistic test of the individual's best interests. This is so even where the individual concerned is an adult. For example, release of information to any patient under the Access to Health Records Act 1990 and the Access to Medical Reports Act 1988 is subject to the discretion of the holder of the information, who is to apply a 'serious harm' test.[43]

As we are concerned in this paper with DNA paternity testing of a child, it is relevant to consider the examples of how the law handles other information stored in a child's body, or in medical records and reports. In the case of consent on behalf of a child by an adult with parental responsibility, the law presumes that the adult acts for the welfare of the child. Yet where information about a child is contained in medical records or reports, that assumption is not made. Such an adult does not necessarily have access to information. The welfare test is applied by a third party, and not by the adult with parental responsibility.

Are there arguments for distinguishing information stored in medical records from information concerning paternity stored in a child's body? It is likely that the major distinction most people will see is between information which may concern only the child herself, and is therefore personal and private, and information which imposes duties and liabilities on a third party. Specifically, the distinction will be formulated as a question of financial responsibility imposed by law on that third party.[44] The basis on which third parties make decisions consonant with welfare about the release of medical information concerning a child is not clear. However a 'need to know' test is often proposed for such situations. Application of such a test to a putative father suggests that, because of financial liability, he has that need. The question of balancing this against the welfare of the child remains. Furthermore, this is an argument that might be used for genetic testing of unco-operative persons, because other members of their family 'need to know' genetic information about family genes.[45]

Information about court interpretation of the welfare standard where an application for paternity testing is contested is available. This suggests that the presence or absence of another man willing to be father is a crucial aspect. Where a third party believes himself to be a child's father, and wishes to displace a man who benefits from the presumption of paternity, or birth certificate evidence, the courts have shown reluctance to allow the challenge. Welfare is interpreted as security and continuity of a child who already has a father.[46] Where the mother wishes to establish the paternity of her child for financial or other reasons, welfare is interpreted in terms of those reasons.[47] Where a quasi-government agency charged with enforcement of child support wishes to attach financial liability to a man as the child's genetic father, it can be predicted that a court will order DNA testing to establish paternity if denied. Scientific issues of genetic identity seem to be of lesser importance than social and material welfare.[48] This could be interpreted as conformity with the primacy of the welfare principle under the UN Convention on the Rights of the Child. Yet the statements in courts about genetic paternity as an issue reveal contested views as to the significance of scientific tests in general and genetic identity in particular. This point can be summarised by contrasting the approaches of the Court of Appeal in two cases: *Re F (a minor)(blood tests: parental rights)*[49] and *Re H (Paternity: Blood Test)*.[50]

In *Re F* the rhetoric of the courts created a dichotomy between welfare and scientific truth, which has reappeared in subsequent cases.[51] *Re F* concerned a man who believed himself to have fathered a child in the course of a sexual liaison. He applied for a parental responsibility order and for contact with the child. The mother opposed these orders, and the child had a presumptive legal father, to whom the mother was married. The court refused to order DNA testing on the basis that the welfare of the child required non-disturbance of the existing family. The case went to the Court of Appeal, which agreed with the trial judge. The reasoning of the appeal court was that, 'the interests of justice will normally require that available evidence be not suppressed and the truth be ascertained wherever possible'.[52] This may or may not coincide with the welfare of the child: 'In many cases the interests of the child are also best served if the truth is ascertained ... but the interests of justice may conflict with the interests of the child'.[53]

Noticeable is the dichotomy which is posed between 'truth and justice' on the one hand and 'the interests of the child' on the other. Truth seems to be equated with scientific testing. Yet, scientific papers on DNA genetic testing are careful to state that the establishment of paternity is a matter of very high statistical probability rather than absolute truth.[54] However, it is fair to say that for legal purposes, particularly those of child support, courts accept and use such statements of probability as establishing a legal truth. The language of certainty is contained in the law reports.[55]

Knowledge of one's genetic paternity has aspects beyond financial support and claims of succession. Of increasing importance, thanks to genetic research, is genetic profiling of families. In *Re F* the Court of Appeal stated that 'knowledge of a person's genetic makeup might be relevant for the possible diagnosis, prevention, mitigation or cure of some medical disorder'. But whilst recognising that there are some risks in ignorance of genes, including that of marriage with a blood relation, the court characterised these as 'infinitesimal' when compared to the harm that disruption of her family unit would cause to the child's interest.[56]

The court showed little awareness of debates about genetic identity, other than for medical or instrumental purposes. The court stated that it will be natural for the child, when she is older, to want to know the truth of her paternity. The judgment robustly confirms the common-sense notions that small children need security, have little or no notion of the blood tie, and that interest in identity arises at adolescence. But this approach raises the issue of whether children can exercise rights during their childhood. Protection of identity under the UN Convention on the Rights of the Child should relate to a child's rights during childhood, and not as the maintenance of an interest which crystallises as a right when the child reaches the age of majority.[57]

Not all commentators agree with the Court of Appeal's reasoning in *Re F.* Jane Fortin is uneasy about the decision on grounds that it may not serve the best interests of the child involved, and because of the rights of the putative father. She sees psychological value to the child 'of knowing the truth about her origins', and points to the lack of coherence in the law and current practice of the courts.[58] Fortin's view is that the issue of genetic identity is analytically distinguishable from issues of who raises, visits, or claims rights over, a child. Yet current procedure and practice appear to link these issues. Jane Fortin makes an important analytical point, which has received some acknowledgement in *Re H*.

Re H concerned a child born to a married woman whose husband was registered as the father. The child was born after the mother had had an affair with another man. There was circumstantial evidence that the lover was the child's father and he applied for orders based on his belief of his parentage, and asked for DNA testing in case of disputed paternity. Directions for testing were given in the High Court and the mother appealed. The Court of Appeal attempted to separate the issue of paternity from the issues of contact and parental responsibility, and stated that the paternity issue must be judged as a free-standing application. The mother's appeal against the direction for testing was dismissed. The inferences drawn by the High Court, if the mother's refusal of consent to testing was maintained following the appeal, are not known. It is likely that such inferences, if any, would take account of the impact on the welfare of the child.[59]

Agreement amongst courts and commentators on the content of the welfare principle is lacking. It is possible, and indeed probable, that those with the best interests of a child at heart will continue to take differing views. Thus the difficulties created by competing rights are augmented by differing interpretations of the best interests of the child. However, in the specific case of determination of paternity, analytical separation of the rights of parentage from a declaration of genetic paternity will clarify issues. The 'certainty' of genetic inheritance offered by science does not inevitably draw legal consequences in its train. In social terms we have a choice about the meaning we wish to give to genes.

Identity Rights as Human Rights

The UN Convention on the Rights of the Child specifically protects identity rights under Articles 7 and 8. However Article 3 gives primacy to the child's best interests and may be used in legal argument as a justification for discretionary decisions on matters such as the determination of genetic identity. Article 8 of the European Convention on Human Rights, which protects private and family life, has been interpreted as covering identity rights. In the jurisprudence of the European Court of Human Rights, rights are not absolute. A balance must be struck between the child's substantive rights and the child's welfare rights. This may be academic. Whilst rights are attributed to children, very often the exercise of such rights becomes possible only after the age of majority. A further balance must be found between the rights of the child and the rights of others.

Balancing of rights is a pragmatic task which courts, faced with conflicts, have to undertake. In the jurisprudence of the European Court of Human Rights this operation is dignified with the concept of proportionality.[60] The idea is of weighing in the balance the impact of decisions between individuals, and on the existing legalities of a jurisdiction. An example is *Gaskin v. UK*,[61] the only case so far in which the European Court of Human Rights specifically referred to a right to know one's identity. *Gaskin* concerned an applicant, brought up in the care of the local state, who applied for access to official documents concerned with his case during his childhood. In particular, he wanted to try to understand what had happened to him, and why he had not been placed for adoption. The judgment in the case reveals a number of different aspects, which can be analysed in terms of identity rights, and in terms of proportionality.

The European Court of Human Rights recognised that the protection of private and family life includes a right of identity in the sense of a right to know one's history. The Commission stated that respect for private life requires

> that everyone should be able to establish details of their identity as
> individual human beings and that in principle they should not be
> obstructed by the authorities from such very basic information without
> specific justification.[62]

However, the Commission distinguished the case of Gaskin applying as an adult and Gaskin applying as a child,[63] stating that had Gaskin applied as a child he would have been refused access to the files requested. In any event, because of the proportionality test, Gaskin's access was denied by the court. Proportionality required that those foster parents and care workers who had written reports on the applicant during his childhood deserved the protection of confidentiality. The case cannot be held up as authority for a child's right to knowledge of genetic identity during childhood. In the sense that all human adults were once children, and may seek in adulthood to enforce rights relating to childhood, the case recognises identity rights as human rights.

Conclusion

This paper investigates DNA paternity testing of children. Although the legal protection of children as vulnerable persons has been accepted as a universal value by the United Nations, the Convention on the Rights of the Child is not self-interpreting. The balancing of substantive rights and welfare has to be worked out, as do the content of welfare and the relationship with the rights of third parties. Science may offer a high degree of certainty in the determination of genetic fingerprints, but can this be matched by the laws human beings make for themselves?

In addition to an inevitable contest over the meanings of welfare and the balancing of rights the paper has demonstrated an avoidable lack of consistency in the law itself. In relation to the same child one man can be a genetic father for purposes of child support, another appears as a genetic father for purposes of a birth certificate. To a certain extent lack of consistency arises from the past. Where certainty of fatherhood was lacking, legal presumptions followed. Full symmetry of rights of fathers and mothers is denied by nature.

Genetic paternity does not necessarily entail legal or social fatherhood. The meaning to be attached to genes is a social choice. It is true that traditionally English law has attached legal consequences to genetic paternity, and has done so recently in relation to financial support. From a child's point of view, it does not necessarily follow that knowledge of genetic identity means a parent/child relationship with a genetic father.

An ethical code for laboratories which offer paternity testing services can be promoted. In accordance with the UN Convention on the Rights of the Child such a code should be centred on the best interests of children. Current thinking suggests that children should not be subjected to DNA testing without the consent of all those adults who have parental responsibility. However, as this paper demonstrates, the possibilities of deception, and of secret testing, cannot be ruled out. It may be that we should re-think our attitudes to paternity testing in order to take account of the virtual certainty that science now offers.[64] In the future it is likely that individuals will have a considerable amount of information about their own genes. It may also be that identity rights in the broad sense will presuppose knowledge of genetic identity. It does not necessarily follow from this that genetic parentage will be conflated with legal parentage. At present these can be legally separated in cases such as adoption or donated gametes. What lawyers do need to recognise is that the now virtual certainty of genetic makeup offered by DNA testing undermines legal rules developed for earlier times. Attempts to regulate in accordance with such rules may be doomed to failure. Science changes attitudes. Law will follow. Rethinking the legal regulation of human relationships is possible.

Notes

1 See Nuffield Council on Bioethics (1993) *Genetic Screening: Ethical Issues.*

2 DNA profiling involves the examination of samples of bodily tissue or fluids to assess the composition of genetic material. As a child's DNA 'fingerprint' is made up of 50 per cent of bands inherited from each parent, the accuracy of diagnosis is considered to be virtually 100 per cent. See D.A. Berry, 'Inferences Using DNA Profiling in Forensic Identification and Paternity Cases', (1991) 6 *Statistical Science* 175. For discussion of DNA paternity testing see, A. Grubb and D. Pearl (1990) *Blood Testing, AIDS and DNA Profiling*; Jordans; A. Bradney, 'Blood Tests, Paternity and the Double Helix', [1986] *Family Law* 378; R. Collins and A. Macleod, 'Denials of Paternity: The Impact of DNA Tests on Court Proceedings', [1991] *Journal of Social Welfare and Family Law* 209.

3 On which see also James Michael at Chap. 11 above.

4 See I. Kennedy and A. Grubb (1994) *Medical Law* 2nd ed Butterworths Chap. 8.

5 Above n. 1, Chap. 5. At 5.7(111), 'In exceptional circumstances, health professionals might be justified in disclosing genetic information to other family members despite an individual's desire for confidentiality.'

6 Under the Public Health (Control of Diseases) Act 1984 compulsory testing may be ordered for the prevention of disease. However, consent requirements in relation to DNA paternity testing have recently been re-emphasised by the Court of Appeal in *Re H (Paternity: Blood Test)* [1996] 2 FLR 65. See A. Bainham at Chap. 6 above for further discussion of this case.

7 *Gillick v. West Norfolk and Wisbech Area Health Authority* [1986] 1 AC 112.

8 This is recognised in medicine and police work, where samples taken for one purpose may not be used for other purposes, such as the determination of paternity.

9 Human Fertilisation and Embryology Act 1990, s. 28.

10   The mother's husband may believe himself to be the father, as he is presumed to be in law. As yet, we do not live in a society where husbands demand genetic proof, but DNA testing for other purposes may eventually become normal. It is possible that the establishment of paternity will become part of this process.

11   See Human Fertilisation and Embryology Authority, *Code of Practice* (1995).

12   Article 7 provides: '(1) The child shall be registered immediately after birth and shall have the right from birth to a name, the right to acquire a nationality and, as far as possible, the right to know and be cared for by his or her parents. (2) States Parties shall ensure the implementation of these rights in accordance with their national law and their obligations under the relevant international instruments in this field, in particular where the child would otherwise be stateless.' Specific reference to this Article as relevant to DNA paternity testing occurred in the judgment of the Court of Appeal in *Re H* above, n. 6. Article 8 provides: '(1) States Parties undertake to respect the right of the child to preserve his or her identity, including nationality, name and family relations as recognised by law without unlawful interference. (2) Where a child is illegally deprived of some or all of the elements of his or her identity, States Parties shall provide appropriate assistance and protection, with a view to speedily re-establishing his or her identity.'

13   Parental responsibility is defined in the Children Act 1989, s. 3. Scientific testing for paternity is governed by the Family Law Reform Act 1969, which uses the earlier language of 'care and control' to describe the adult who may give consent to the testing of a child. In June 1989, under the Blood Tests (Evidence of Paternity) (Amendment) Regulations) 1989, DNA testing was included in the techniques for use in disputed paternity cases which come to court.

14   Children Act 1989, s. 2. Even where the woman who gives birth does so by virtue of receiving a donated egg, and is therefore not the genetic mother, there is an irrebuttable presumption that she is the legal mother: Human Fertilisation and Embryology Act 1990, ss. 27, 29.

15   Births and Deaths Registration Act 1953, s. 10.

16   HMSO, *Social Trends 1995* (1995).

17   Children Act 1989, s. 4.

18   This is a question of evidence. It is possible, however, for a man to be named on the birth certificate as father, but for another man to be declared the father for purposes of child support under the Child Support Act 1991. See J. Eekelaar, 'Parenthood, Social Engineering and Rights' in D. Morgan and G. Douglas (eds) (1994) *Constituting Families*, Franz Steiner Verlag.

19   A declaration of paternity under the Child Support Act 1991 does not alter the birth certificate. The procedure for correction of 'error' is noted below at n. 23.

20 Child Support Act 1991, s. 27(3) (as amended) referring to a declaration of paternity under that Act, provides 'A declaration under this section shall have effect only for the purposes of (a) this Act; and (b) proceedings in which a court is considering whether to make a maintenance order...'.

21 *The Guardian* May 17, 1996. Under the Births and Deaths Registration Act 1953, s. 29(3): '[a]n error of fact or substance in any register may be corrected by the (Registrar) upon production of a statutory declaration setting forth the nature of the error and the true facts of the case'. A court order against a third party, declaring him to be the father, is insufficient.

22 *Cossey v. UK* (1990) 13 EHRR 622; *Re P and G (Transsexuals)* [1996] 2 FLR 90.

23 The Births and Deaths Registration Act 1953, s. 29(3), limits correction of error and insertion of the 'true facts' only in the margin of the register. New entries and new birth certificates are permitted in certain circumstances. Re-registration, and a consequent new birth certificate, can be applied for by legitimated and acknowledged children. Adopted children receive a new birth certificate under the Adoption Act 1976.

24 *S v. S; W v. Official Solicitor* [1972] AC 24.

25 *Re H* above n. 6. The statutory basis of the court's power of direction is the Family Law Reform Act 1969, s. 23(1). In *Re G (A Minor)(Blood Test)* [1994] 1 FLR 495 the High Court directed the testing of a child for paternity although the adult with care and control of the child had refused consent. In *Re A (A Minor)(Paternity: Refusal of Blood Test)* [1994] 2 FLR 463 the Court of Appeal drew the inference of paternity from the putative father's refusal to be tested.

26 *Re T (A Minor)(Blood Tests)* [1993] 1 FLR 901; *Re CB (A Minor)(Blood Tests)* [1994] 2 FLR 762.

27 *S v. S; W v. Official Solicitor* above n. 24.

28 Code Civil, art. 16-11: 'L'Identification d'une personne par ses empreintes genetiques ne peut être recherchée que dans le cadre de mesures d'enquête ou d'instruction ordonnée par le juge saisi d'une action tendant soit a l'établissement ou a la contestation d'un lien de filiation, soit a l'obtention ou a la suppression de subsides. Le consentement de l'intéresse doit etre prealablement et expressement receuilli.' See F. Granet, 'Reflexions Sur La Preuve Scientifique de la Filiation', *Actes du Colloque IRCID* du 9 au 11 fevrier 1995.

29 Information received from Professor Ake Saldeen, Uppsala University, Sweden.

30 The Convention is enforced by the Committee on the Rights of the Child: see L. Le Blanc (1995) *The Convention on the Rights of the Child*, University of Nebraska Press.

31 Above n. 12.

32 C. Barton and G. Douglas (1995) *Law and Parenthood*, Butterworths, pp. 56-57.

[33] When discussing a mother's knowledge of the paternity of her child, it is important to distinguish practicalities from law. Most mothers will know who the father is, although some may not. The law looks to the mother for information as to the identity of the father. The agreement of the father to registration on the birth certificate is necessary, where he is not married to the mother.

[34] B. Hoggett, D. Pearl, E. Cooke and P. Bates (1996) *The Family, Law and Society*, Butterworths, p. 477; John Illman, 'Negative Proof of Paternity', *The Guardian* 9 July 1996: 'In one extraordinary study designed to investigate antibody formation, it was found that some 30 per cent of the married couples in the study had one or more illegitimate children, probably without the husbands being aware of it.'

[35] G. Van Bueren, 'Children's Access to Adoption Records - State Discretion or an Enforceable International Right?' (1995) 58 *Modern Law Review* 37, p. 43.

[36] The author carried out interviews with two laboratories offering DNA paternity testing services in June 1995: University Diagnostics Ltd and Cellmark Diagnostics (set up in 1987 by ICI, and part of Zeneca Ltd).

[37] University Diagnostics worked only with blood at the time of the interview. They are reluctant, for reasons of scientific reliability to test a child and only one parent. For consent, they look to the person with parental responsibility. Cellmark saw consent of the parties as their main ethical concern, and insist on parental responsibility consent. In establishing their procedures they took advice from the Medical Defence Union. They are prepared to work with other forms of tissue, but reluctant to work with only one parent, for reasons of scientific reliability.

[38] Criminal Justice and Public Order Act 1994, ss. 54 and 55.

[39] University Diagnostics Ltd offer a 'home test' kit for self testing for the cystic fibrosis gene. In the United States there is a similar test available for some breast cancer genes. See L. Goodman, 'Breast Cancer Mutation Screening' (1996) 13 *Nature Genetics* 17.

[40] *Re H*, above note 6; *Re F* [1993] 3 All ER 596; *Re CB* [1994] 2 FLR 762; *Re JS* [1980] 1 All ER 1061.

[41] Article 3(1) provides: In all actions concerning children, whether undertaken by public of private social welfare institutions, courts of law, administrative authorities or legislative bodies, the best interests of the child shall be a primary consideration.

[42] French family law contains the idea of the 'patrimoine' which is a property entitlement of children, not dependent on a testament. For this reason, the presumption of paternity is not easily displaced, and the mechanisms for so doing are restricted.

[43] Access to Health Records Act 1990 s 5(1)(a)(i).

[44] Child Support Act 1991.

[45] Above n. 5.

46   *Re F* [1993] 3 All ER 596; *Re CB* [1994] 2 FLR 762; *Re JS* [1980] 1 All ER 1061.

47   J. Fortin 'Re F: The Gooseberry Bush Approach', (1994) 57 *Modern Law Review* 296. *Re T* [1993] 1 FLR 901.

48   K. O'Donovan, 'A Right to Know One's Parentage?' (1988) 2 *International Journal of Law and the Family* 27.

49   [1993] 3 All ER 596.

50   [1996] 2 FLR 65.

51   *Re CB* [1994] 2 FLR 762.

52   *Re F* [1993] 3 All ER 596 at 599 (Balcombe LJ).

53   ibid.

54   Berry, above n. 2.

55   *Re J* [1988] 1 FLR 65 'virtual certainty'; *Re A* [1994] 2 FLR 463 'positive certainty'.

56   *Re F* [1993] 3 All ER 596 at p. 601.

57   The direct exercise by a child of rights is problematic, for reasons of knowledge, legal status, access to courts, resources. But if we are to say that these rights only crystallise at the age of majority, we cannot then refer to 'the rights of the child', but rather to the rights of adults in relation to their childhoods.

58   Fortin above n. 47 at p. 305.

59   There is an ambiguity in the language of the judgment of Ward LJ in the Court of Appeal in *Re H*. A distinction appears to be drawn between 'welfare' and 'interests' of the child. It has been common practice for commentators on English law to use these terms interchangeably. The Children Act 1989 uses the term 'welfare', whereas the UN Convention on the Rights of the Child, above note 41, uses the term 'best interests'. Ward LJ states that the 'welfare of the child is not the most important factor when deciding whether to direct' a scientific test of paternity; 'instead, the court should refuse a test if it is satisfied that it would be against the child's interests to order it'. This language appears to make a distinction between 'welfare' and 'best interests'.

60   See K. O'Donovan, 'The Subject of Human Rights: Abstract or Embodied?' (1995) 46 *NILQ* 353, at pp. 359-360.

61   (1980) 12 EHRR 36.

62   ibid.

63   I am indebted to my colleague Geraldine Van Bueren for this point.

64   My thinking on this point has been influenced by comments made by my colleague Wayne Morrison at a staff seminar based on a presentation of some of the ideas in this paper at Queen Mary and Westfield College in October 1995.

13 Crimes of War, Culture, and Children's Rights: The Case of Female Palestinian Detainees under Israeli Military Occupation

NADERA SHALHOUB-KEVORKIAN

Introduction

The adoption of the United Nations Convention on the Rights of the Child has raised new issues in the context of the advocacy of human rights strategies for the promotion of greater participation and empowerment of children. These issues are of relevance to those who are concerned with realising children's rights in all parts of the world. They are basic and unless resolved, may create constraints that will render international statements on children's rights mere political rhetoric. Attention should be drawn to problems that can arise in this regard within a multi-cultural context, particularly those which are voiced in societies in which gender discrimination and female subordination exists in a very strong and profound way.

This paper will discuss the relationship between children's rights and social justice, and its implementation within certain cultural contexts. It addresses the limits of universal legal intervention in children's rights and argues that female children are dealt with in a gender-discriminatory manner. The case of violations committed against Palestinian female children detainees' rights, particularly during the *intifada* (popular uprising), will be presented. It will attempt to demonstrate that the Israeli authorities knowingly committed these violations although they were aware of the international conventions prohibiting such practices. Furthermore, the paper will emphasise the intricacies that transpire in the context of any discussion on female children's rights, particularly in the Arab/Palestinian case. The analysis of human rights violations against females in Palestinian society (Arab/Islamic and patriarchal), particularly within the context of political struggle, presents an interesting discourse for both human right activists and policy makers. In order to initiate such a discourse, I will first give an overview of the political background of the Israeli/Palestinian national struggle. Then I will address gender and children's rights in Palestinian society; special emphasis being placed on the relationship amongst gender, patriarchy and political activism of Palestinian girls. The socio-cultural patterning of the fear of rape will be briefly discussed to help in conceptualising the problem of abuse of gender during political struggle, followed by an extensive explanation of the case study of Palestinian girl-detainees.

  This article has both theoretical and practical connotations. It will pose questions regarding the interrelationship between the concept of female children's rights and cultural determinants when the culture is faced with state organised violence. It will also help us to a better understanding of the dilemmas faced by mental health professionals and human rights advocates when dealing with female children detainees. The study is confined to the limited documentation available on the subject matter and to interviews conducted with female children who became victims of such practices. Hence, it should be considered as exploratory in nature. The paucity in documentation and media coverage of girls and women abuse may be attributed to two main factors: abuse of females by one's political enemy is not considered a personal/individual violation only, but a violation against the collective identity of the nation. Hence, it is difficult to acknowledge an onslaught which targets the collective perception of the self. Furthermore, the conservative and patriarchal nature of society dictates that such 'calamities' should remain undisclosed.

Historical Background

State terrorism has undeniably marked the socio/political climate in the Middle East within the past century. In discussing the national struggle of Palestinian society, we may observe that the establishment of the state of Israel has caused hundreds of thousands of Palestinians to become refugees or internally displaced persons.[1] The invasion and occupation of the West Bank and Gaza strip in 1967, along with the extreme measures the Israeli military authorities practised on the Palestinians during the *intifada*, inflicted tremendous psychosocial trauma and hardships.[2] Palestinians have been suffering, from political, economic, and social repression since the Ottoman period.[3] It was this repression, poverty, and subjugation which led Arabs living within the Arabian peninsula and the fertile crescent (Syria, Trans Jordan, and Palestine) to join forces with the British at the beginning of this century to end Ottoman rule.

In the case of the Palestinians, Ottoman rule was exchanged for British rule rather than achieving the promised independence. Britain's famous Balfour Declaration 'promising' world Jews to help them establish a homeland in Palestine was the first major national trauma to which the Palestinians were subjected. The cumulative tragedy and trauma inflicted on the Palestinians was exacerbated in 1948 with the creation of the state of Israel and the consequent expulsion of the Palestinians from their homeland. Within a span of merely thirty years (1917-1948), the Palestinians had to endure the evaporation of their hopes for independence from Ottoman rule and the loss of their homeland to an alien population. After the 1948 Arab-Israeli War and by the time of the 1949 ceasefire agreement, Arab areas had shrunk to 23 per cent of the total area of Palestine (the Gaza Strip and the West Bank). More than 400 Palestinian villages were razed to the ground by the Israelis as a prelude to the expulsion and exodus of Palestinians from their ancestral homeland.[4]

The third major trauma the Palestinians were subjected to occurred in 1967 when they saw the remaining part of their homeland coming under Israeli occupation. Hence, Palestinians were subjected to another trauma that increased tension to boiling point at the end of 1987 when the *intifada* broke out. Given that the major participants in the *intifada* were children, and given that Israel was determined to crush this resistance, it is not surprising to discover that egregious human rights violations were practised on Palestinian children during this period.

The case studies presented in this study are a reflection of the extent of these violations. The socio-economic status of Palestinians, and the lack of Arab and international support, exacerbated the situation.[5] The extent of human rights violations and political oppression practised by the Israeli military authorities in the occupied territories, especially during the *intifada,* permeated all aspects of life and daily living conditions. Schools and universities were closed for protracted periods, curfews and house break-ins became a daily occurrence, imprisonment touched every family, and injury and death reached outrageous levels. During the period between December, 1987 and December, 1992, the scale of the trauma suffered by the approximately two million Palestinians in the Occupied Territories was extensive. At least 1,119 Palestinians (nearly 300 children) were killed, 127,000 injured (20,000 under the age of 16 were injured in the first year of the *intifada*), more than 100,000 were arrested, imprisoned, or detained without trial, and over 2,200 houses were demolished. Collective punishments in the form of economic repression, curfews, house raiding, and school closures were common practices.[6] Although local and international human rights organisations and UN agencies have invested tremendous efforts during the last few decades to protect children's human rights, Israel was cited repeatedly by such organisations for its continuous violation of the human rights of the Palestinians (children being included) living in the territories it occupies. Although Israel ratified the UN Convention on the Rights of the Child, it refused to declare explicitly that its adoption of the Convention applied to children living in the Occupied Territories. Given that the West Bank and Gaza Strip prior to the establishment of the Palestinian National Authority were considered occupied territories, children living within these territories were under the jurisdiction of the occupying power (Israel), which was responsible for the protection of their human rights according to The Fourth Geneva Convention of 1949.

Victimisation of Children as a Tool of Political Oppression

Although data on and documentation of the direct victimisation of children in situations of political repression exists, there has been no concerted effort to organise it in a consistent fashion, especially within the Palestinian context.[7] Furthermore, the *indirect* victimisation of children (e.g., witnessing violence, being the child of a martyr, or of an injured, or deported person) has also not received the attention it deserves. The problem of the direct and indirect victimisation of children is too important to be ignored, despite the fact that it cannot be extensively documented.

International human rights law and United Nations policy documents emphasise the need for special protection of children from any type of repression, especially from violence. Toamasevski has stated that

> The UN summary of data on grave and persistent violations of the rights of detained persons [details] such practices as torture and other cruel, inhuman or degrading treatment, arrests and detentions on vague grounds or no ground at all, detention incommunicado, forced disappearances, unfair trial procedures, abuse of executive and

preventive detention, death during detention, extrajudicial and summary executions, ... children are not spared any violations reported.[8]

Testimonies of children who survived torture, mistreatment, and other forms of practices associated with political oppression have been found in numerous countries all over the world. Reports show mass executions of children in countries such as Colombia, Iran, Latin America, Africa, and India.[9] Cases of children and baby disappearances have been found in Peru and Argentina, while torture and ill-treatment of children was reported in Guatemala, Zaire, Paraguay, Pakistan, and Bangladesh. Political arrests, detentions, trials and imprisonments were documented on Palestinian and Lebanese children. Mass arrests of secondary school children have been reported in Morocco, Zaire, Bangladesh, Pakistan and the West Bank. Furthermore, occasional references may be found to female children as victims of torture, political trials, and disappearances.[10] Although political persecution of children is deplorable, it has rarely been argued that children, particularly female children, have the right to protection which goes beyond the human rights of adults. I argue here that children in general, and female children in particular and as a distinctive group (this issue will be explored later), have the right to be protected from abuses resulting from their vulnerability and inability to secure their own rights and interests.[11]

Gender and Children's Victimisation

The deliberate and systematic attempts to break down political opponents physically and psychologically are well known practices, although little is known about sexual traumatisation. Bustos[12] has claimed that we know very little about the use of sexuality as a political repressive tool, although there are groups (e.g., Chilean ex-prisoners, Iranian exile groups) that have begun to break 'the conspiracy of silence'. The aim of such repression is to shatter the victim's psychological and physical entity in order to break her/him down and humiliate her/him.

A major issue in discussing female children's rights concerns violence and exploitation. Very little material has been specifically written about the victimisation of girls, although such victimisation and human rights violations are embedded in the literature on women's victimisation. The growing recognition among Third World women of the link between violence and class, race, and patriarchy, along with political and economic dimensions, renders female children and women the group most vulnerable to sexual and labour exploitation and violations of human rights.[13] In such societies, victims of violence, including genital mutilation, rape, murder of girls and women in the attempt to control sexuality, are often further victimised by the legal system and by the cultural reaction to such victimisation. Political and human rights violations are another form of violence. Women and girls are not excluded from political repression. The extent of torture, abuse and imprisonment of girls and women for political reasons has only recently been documented, and it can be shown that violations of individual human rights are linked to larger issues of social, economic, and cultural rights.

Gender, Children's Rights and Violations in Palestinian Society

Laws concerning children's rights, when based on the best interests of the child, provide an important national framework and point of reference for the better protection of children. Palestine, like many developing countries, is affected by old colonial laws written when the concept of the rights of the child was undeveloped.[14] As a result these laws are deficient in the protection they give to children.

In Palestinian society, children are still perceived as parental property rather than as individuals having rights of their own. Hence, practices such as arranged and early marriages (especially for the girl) continue. The powerlessness of girls and their exploitation by way of practices that stem from the power of patriarchy (e.g., female child marriage and dedication to family honour) cause trauma, suffering, and female victimisation.[15] The birth of a female child in communities which prefer males renders the female child helpless in terms of choosing her own destiny. Hence, when a girl child faces abuse or violence that causes her victimisation, she is doubly jeopardised because she is considered to be of a lower status than her male counterpart. She is thus denied her right to protection, understanding and support.[16]

On the political-national level, Palestinian society was fully aware of the needs of its children and Israeli efforts to stifle them. Abuses not connected with the Israeli occupation (child abuse, battering, incest) were also not addressed from a human rights perspective. Children's victimisation due to family violence, incest, rape, and battering was discussed and dealt with as a private, individual, or family matter due to social reaction and coping strategies influenced by traditional cultural codes.

Palestinian women are part of a larger group of women in the Arab world who suffer from gender discrimination. Women's status as reflected in the cultural, legal, economic, social, political and other fields is lower than that of men. Despite recent changes in the perception towards women's role in the public/political sphere, and despite the active participation of women in national struggles hand-in-hand with men, women still face inequality, and sexism in the private as well as the public sphere.[17] Most constitutions of Arab countries proclaim that all citizens are equal in their public rights and duties, and hence equal before the law. A careful reading of such constitutions reveals that this equality is a facade. The equality is only in the public sphere, while there is a clear division between public and private. For example, the labour laws may give women equal rights to work, yet they cannot actually exercise this right because of the marriage laws, for it is the women's husband who has the right to make decisions on this matter. As Al-Sadaawi stated 'Thus, in the Arab nations, women are under the authority of two contradictory laws. The first is the public law which does not distinguish between citizens on the basis of sex and religion, and gives them human and civil rights - hence the right to work, the right of freedom of movement and other human rights. The moment that a woman crosses the threshold of her home, she is ruled by another law, based on the division and distinction according to sex and religion.'[18]

The fact that there is a schizophrenia in the laws, culture and values places Arab women in a very vulnerable position. The duality in perceiving women is manifested in phenomena such as the veil,[19] preserving and/or risking the family honour, protecting female virginity, female circumcision etc. Such duality could be explained by what Ahmad termed Arab society's fear of losing its Arab identity and cultural authenticity in this changing world.[20] Therefore, women are perceived as the ones who, despite the changes in the economic, political, international level, should protect and keep the family honour and values.[21]

A major issue facing Palestinian women is custom and religion. This is particularly critical due to the religious fundamentalism which contributes to the public/private dichotomy that has played a major role in circumscribing the status of women. A woman will often opt for her cultural heritage over her own rights so as not to lose or challenge her identity as member of the group. This preservation of acceptable customs, and cultural belonging pose a challenge to developing approaches which creatively confront the contradictions they present. It also crystallises the veiled reality that women's sexuality was and still is abused during political struggles.

The Socio-Cultural Patterning of the Fear of Rape

The abuse, harassment and rape of girls and women during warfare appear to be a common practice.[22] This has become evident particularly after the media coverage of the events in the former Yugoslavia.[23] The history of nations shows that sexual rape and abuse of females in war time has occurred in the Philippines, the north India state of Kashmir, Sri Lanka, Bangladesh, Namibia, Mozambique, Uganda, and Peru. However, no exact figures or in-depth studies are available. Rape and other forms of abuse against women are used to regulate power between sexes and or between competing groups, and as Richters states 'its frequency is a function of socio-cultural circumstances'.[24] Women are vulnerable to various forms of abuse which are gender based. Society's construction of female sexuality and its role in the social hierarchy are based on the society's concept of a female as the property and dependent of a male protector such as the father, husband, son, or uncle. This perception of females converts their abuse, rape, and brutalisation into a means of humiliating the community to which they belong. All these issues are power- and gender-related. They are embedded in the cultural, social, economic, and political contexts of a society. This hierarchical power relationship gives legitimacy to violence against women.[25]

Gender, Patriarchy, and Political Activism of Palestinian Girls

Girl political activists constitute a distinctive group in Palestinian society. Girls as well as women took part in the active national struggle against the Israeli occupation. In doing so, they challenged the social and cultural definition of female roles in society. As was mentioned previously, Palestinian society is a patriarchal, traditional one which discriminates between genders. Therefore, the public sphere, control of resources and power belong to men, while the private sphere which emphasises the need to protect family honour, female modesty, and preservation of moral values belongs to women. Thus any violation of women's purity was considered to be an insult and injury to the entire family.

Girls' political activism raised a serious dilemma. While their contribution to the national political struggle was crucial, it contradicted the traditional cultural beliefs that dictate the need to preserve and protect women's honour. Participation in demonstrations which ended in imprisonment of young girls raised the most complicated dilemma. Despite the fact that political activism and political imprisonment was considered a heroic, praised and respected action, it was also viewed as a moral failing of females. Girls were confronted with a dilemma, particularly during the *intifada*. The general mood in Palestinian society reflected the need to end oppression and suppression. Girls were members of a society which was engulfed in a revolutionary atmosphere, and therefore, acted accordingly. Their dilemma stemmed from the need, on the one hand, to participate in this revolution, but also on the other, to protect their honour by safeguarding their personal and family reputation.

Despite the fact that Palestinian society tried to cope with this dilemma by labelling female activists as heroines, and describing them as *'ucht al-rajal'* (sisters to men), or *'mara bmit zalame'* (one woman is worth a hundred men), the power of traditional and cultural codes prevailed and influenced societal reaction. Political activism meant that female participants were more exposed to interaction with men, a situation which raised the possibility of being abused by them. The fact that Palestinian/Arab society places a high priority on female sexuality and preservation made the political participation of girls more complex. Furthermore, imprisonment raised additional challenges to the traditional cultural mores. Being imprisoned meant being beyond the control of the community or society. Particularly, it raised the concern of society about the possibility of the sexual assault and abuse of girls, loss of virginity, rape, and harassment - meaning in cultural terms, damage to *'ard'* (sexual honour) and being exposed further to more complicated dilemmas. The young age of the girls led to parental fears of shame from societal reaction, feelings that they had lost control over their daughters, and feelings that they could be held responsible for such a failure. In order to protect their social reputation and good name, parents tended to react in a very radical way by preventing their daughters from going outside the home, withdrawing them from school, or marrying them at an early age. It is worthy of mention here that not all parents reacted in the same manner, although they all faced the same intricate dilemmas. Societal reaction to women political prisoners reflects the degree of willingness to change the cultural code for the sake of the political struggle, although the attitude of society toward this phenomenon remains in a state of confusion.

The following analysis introduces some empirical data on Palestinian female children who were arrested and imprisoned by the occupying Israeli authorities to illustrate the use of sexuality as a political weapon against children. The recorded cases are very limited due to the general taboo associated with female sexuality, although it is reasonable to assume that the number of cases in this study is adequate. It should also be noted that the recording procedure itself is not based on any strict definition of female child sexual abuse. Hence, a reservation must be made with respect to the recording frequencies.

The Case-Study of Palestinian Female Detainees During the *Intifada*

The Palestinian national need to preserve its identity, legacy, and culture, and to strive for independence became ingrained into the Palestinian collective consciousness and psyche. Hence, participation in the national struggle became an attractive call for young Palestinians of both sexes. Despite the traditional nature of Palestinian society, some girls decided to participate in the national struggle, although fully cognizant of the contradiction created between cultural and national struggle values. The importance of the traditional cultural need to protect family honour, and the risk of this being compromised by the act of imprisonment of girls was abused by the Israeli authorities. Thus, society in general, and parents in particular, were more tolerant towards and willing to accept the imprisonment of males than females, and girls who were subjected to imprisonment, risked jeopardising their social status. While male children released from prison were considered heroes, and were praised by family members for being politically active, female children frequently faced cautious and suspicious social reactions upon their release.

During the earlier stages of national struggle of Palestinians against Israeli occupation, Palestinian women and girls in the West Bank, Gaza Strip, and East Jerusalem were not affected as much as their male cohorts in terms of arrests, administrative detentions, deportations, and house arrests. Following the *intifada*, girls and women became more active in the struggle; thousands took to the streets in protest. Although the average number of Palestinian women political prisoners never exceeded 18 prior to the onset of the *intifada*, it reached 1,000 during the period from December, 1987 to August, 1989.[26]

The participation of girls under the age of 18 in political activities, demonstrations, strikes, and sit-ins led to their arrest, interrogation, and imprisonment for periods that extended from hours to months. For the overwhelming majority of these girls, this was the first time they had been separated from their homes and families. Many had to endure difficult interrogation experiences, while others were subjected to heavy fines or bail before their release. The Women's Organization for Political Prisoners (WOFPP) reported 164 women detainees in the Russian compound (Israeli police station and prison in Jerusalem) between December, 1988 and December, 1989. Augustin[27] reported that 44 per cent of the females arrested were minors under the age of 18. B'Tselem reported that Israeli interrogation procedures and imprisonment conditions did not meet minimal standards.[28] The girls were subjected to intensive night-long interrogations, put into overcrowded cells, and subjected to violence, sexual threats, and intimidation. Furthermore, health care was inadequate, the food served being neither nutritious nor palatable, and necessary articles (e.g., toilet supplies, sanitary towels) unavailable. Some girls were reported to be subjected to torture techniques and sexual harassment. Matzpen, for example, reported that 'It has been found that in addition to torture and humiliation, physical abuse and beating, the Palestinian women detainees also suffer systematic and consistent sexual harassment'.[29] Moreover, Thornhill states that in addition to food and sleep deprivation, detainees had to cope with a

> barrage of verbal sexual taunts, sexual threat and in some cases, sexual assault ... this probably reflects a calculated attempt to exploit the traditional Arab notion of female honour or sexual purity ... that is still regarded as her most precious attribute. Violation of it is seen as a disaster for the woman's family as well as herself (and if she is single, for her marriage prospects). Thus sexual harassment of Palestinian women is seen as a particularly effective way to get them to confess.[30]

The ambiguous social reaction towards arrested and imprisoned females made it difficult for them to develop a clear stand-point as to how far to divulge their experiences following their imprisonment. They were afraid to reveal the details of their suffering and torture for fear that their parents would adopt a stricter position towards their political and resistance activities. I will present three case studies to elaborate on this theme. The first case study is taken from a testimony quoted by Augustin and collected by the Women's Organization for Political Prisoners.[31]

Case-Study Number One

Laila was sixteen and a half years old. She is from El-Azaria near Jerusalem, and was arrested on 13 February 1989. She was accused of throwing stones at a bus on Salah al-Din Street. She was detained until her trial, and sentenced on 7 July 1989 to one year in prison suspended for eighteen months. Due to her young age, her sentence was reduced by three months. Her testimony was given to her lawyer while she was detained in the Russian Compound.

> I was standing on a side road, when I saw several girls running and four civilians carrying pistols chasing them. I was afraid and started to run too, but fell. I was caught and put in a car, where I met a girlfriend from school who had been caught just before me. In the car the men ordered us to open our legs, and they beat us between our legs; they even tried to penetrate me with their clubs. When I resisted, they tore the zipper off my pants. One of the soldiers had a metal wire. He bent the edge and placed the wire around our necks, pulling our heads back and forth. During interrogation my hands and legs were put in handcuffs, and my wrists started to bleed. When I refused to sign a form in Hebrew, the contents of which were not translated to me, a woman interrogator named Marcelle hit my fingers with a metal ruler until they bled.
>
> One day while I was held in a regular cell, my friend was removed. After a while we began to worry, and asked a policewoman called Ruhama what had happened to her. Ruhama told us our friend had died. We continued to ask her, until she took me to a dining room. My feet were cuffed, and my hands were tied to an iron railing above my head, my face touching the wall. Ruhama and a number of policemen beat me violently.
>
> The night before my trial. I was taken into a small room. Three men threatened to rape me, unless I confessed to throwing stones. They brought a wire and threatened to insert it into my vagina, unless I confessed. On the day of the trial, while we were walking along the corridor to the detention centre, one of the soldiers tripped me. When I fell down he started to 'ride' on top of me.

Case-Study Number Two

The following is a story of a 15 year old girl from the West Bank. She was arrested in the Winter of 1990 following her participation in a student demonstration against the Israeli occupation.

My whole future was affected because I was arrested and spent a night out of the house. I was 15 years old and my friends informed me that a student rally would be held in my area. My schoolmates decided to participate in the rally to demonstrate against Israeli violations of human rights, mass arrests, and house demolition in my area. The soldiers threw tear gas bombs, and I stood on the side, unable to breathe. When I was standing there, a soldier caught me, forcibly dragged me by my hair to his jeep, and prodded me with his stick every now and then to make me walk. He got me in the jeep with other girls from my school. Some of the girls that were arrested were younger than me. We were very afraid, but tried not to show it. On our way to prison, soldiers started calling us names, cursing and threatening to rape us. One of the soldiers told me that he wanted to do it to me by himself. He even tried to explain in his broken Arabic how he was going to do it. My friends started screaming at him, but we were all afraid that they would do it..

It was a very cold winter night and they put us in one room without mattresses on the floor. We stood up all the time because the room was crowded with girls. Soldiers kept calling us names, scaring us with the threat of rape. Female soldiers were even worse than the male ones. One of them came to our room. She looked at me and called me a whore. I said 'I am not; maybe you are.' She then took me with another 14 year old girl and made us spend the night outside in the cold weather. She did not allow us to sit all night. All she said was that we would regret doing any political activities from now on, and she was going to teach us a lesson that we would never forget as long as we lived.

In the morning, my parents came and bailed me out. On our way home, I was beaten first by my father, then my brother. When we reached home, my uncle started beating me in a very aggressive way. All of my family members were angry. Since then, they keep blaming me for doing what I did.

The rumours in the village were that I was raped by the Israelis. Everybody came to see me, but I felt they pitied me. They all thought that I had lost my virginity. Following the rumours, my father decided that I should stay at home, and not go back to school. He thought that this was the best way to protect me. Moreover, and since then, men in the village keep sexually harassing me.

No one came to ask for my hand from my father. I have no friends because girls are afraid to come close to me for fear of being accused of the same accusation. Even my own mother keeps telling me that if I had not been imprisoned, I would have got married, but I ruined my future, victimized myself, and I will always be a burden on my own family.

Case-Study Number Three

Salma was 14 years old when she was arrested. She was taken from her school playground together with three of her schoolmates. She remained in the detention centre for seven hours, during which she underwent interrogation and signed a paper in Hebrew (a language that she does not know) confessing that she threw stones two days earlier. In reality, she says that she was visiting her aunt in Hebron that day.

> When arrested, I didn't stop crying. No one touched me or used any physical violence, but they slapped the other girls. I stayed there seven hours and my parents released me after paying bail, which they borrowed from relatives. I come from a very poor family.
>
> When I got home, everybody cried and was happy that I was back. My grandmother asked me to go with her. She took me to her room, and together with my mom and aunt, they undressed me and opened my legs. As my mom and aunt held my legs apart, my grandmother checked to see if I was still a virgin. They also asked me whether I was raped, or sexually abused. I said no, not at all.
>
> Since that day, my parents have become very cautious; my whole style of life changed. For them I am no more a child, and I have no right to go anywhere - even to the friends that I always visited. My parents were very strict with me, and they treated me as if I committed a sin. I didn't surrender. I talked about my imprisonment in a very proud way, like my brother who also was arrested . He was proud of his activities, and I was also proud of myself. My other friends who were with me in prison suffered a lot, and their parents made them leave school and forced them to marry men they did not want. I got married to the man I loved, but my imprisonment still affects my family and my husband's behaviour. They don't trust me in times of political tension, and forbid me to leave the house.

Discussion

The adoption of the UN Convention on the Rights of the Child means that the international community has accepted a statement of children's rights, and it is a binding international treaty for more than 180 countries. As such, it offers a special opportunity to approach an important human rights challenge in terms of planning public policy. To foster more effective rights awareness initiatives, Article 42 offers considerable potential: 'States parties undertake to make the principles and provisions of the Convention widely known, by appropriate and active means, to adults and children alike.' In many countries the challenge is to set standards and objectives for measuring performance in some key areas of children's rights.

The present case study has shown that on the broader human rights front, it appears that, independent of the degree of international consensus there may or may not be, an understanding of the complexity and special nature of the violation of female children's rights is needed. Just as theories and practices should be sensitised to female children's rights concerns, so children's rights work, including for females, needs to be enriched by the sort of social planning and public policy approaches which take into consideration the socio-cultural as well as the political context of the child. When dealing with the case of female detainees and sexual harassment and exploitation in the Palestinian-Israeli struggle two questions arise on which discussion should be focused. The first question is why such practices occur, and what is their function? The second relates to the effect traditional/cultural values have in shaping social reaction, particularly in the victimisation of girls and their effect on implementing children's rights.

Legitimate/Illegitimate Crimes

This paper has awakened us to an old, but unvoiced practice, the physical and sexual abuse of girls and women as a weapon used against political opponents. Moreover, it has shown that despite the fact that officially (and theoretically), governments comply with international codes of preserving children's rights, in practice they violate the basic philosophical principle on which it is built and based. The strategic selection of the means to fight political opponents, in our case study the use and abuse of the issue of family honour and reputation (that is considered a taboo in Palestinian society), renders the 'hidden war' more complex. Furthermore, this is abuse of the most vulnerable members of society, female children, in order to combat the enemy. The case-study shows that mores, morals and values of the local indigenous population were far from being taken into consideration by the Israelis. Girls not only were treated in a discriminatory way as compared with their male counterparts, their future was also deeply affected. The fact that the Israeli authorities prevented the Palestinian female child from enjoying her rights and freedoms, as recognised and internationally guaranteed, affected and reflected on her life and future. Violations such as school closure, collective punishments, curfews etc. hindered the promotion and development of the child's personality, talent, mental and physical abilities, in addition to the practices aimed at weakening the morals, traditional values and culture of the Palestinian society. The use and abuse of female child detainees inhibited the promotion of the Palestinian child's feelings for unity, solidarity and identity, even apart from the fact that the abuse of Palestinian detainees during their imprisonment prevented the child from enjoying physical, mental, and spiritual health. Hence, the lack of proper conditions in prison prevented children from having necessary medical assistance, adequate nutrition, hygiene and environmental sanitation.

Israeli practices against female children not only affected the particular victimised child, but also victimised the family unit. They weakened the family's power to protect and safeguard the physical and mental health of the child. The political reality of Palestinians during the *intifada,* the lack of proper communication between family members and relatives, the high risk involved in moving from one area to another, the lengthy curfews, the poor economic conditions, and all the other measures aimed at shattering Palestinian society and destroying its ability to continue the political struggle - all these rendered the capacity of the family to confront girls' imprisonment extremely limited. One of the responses to girls' detention, particularly among more vulnerable families, was the use of traditional/cultural codes. Such codes, as shown in the case-studies, further victimised the victim.

The fact that such practices have been sparsely documented, raises the need for a more careful look of the situation of children, particularly female, in political struggles. Moreover, the policy of inaction and silence in the wake of such abuses should be addressed. The need to document, study, act and react to such criminal practices is a challenge not only to Israeli human rights activists, but also to the international human rights community. Moreover, effective procedures for establishing special monitoring units to provide support for children in general and female children in particular is needed. That should be achieved through the creation of different forms of prevention and identification, reporting, referral, investigation, treatment and follow-up of instances of female child physical, psychological, and sexual abuse.

Culture and Female Children's Rights

This article has shown that patriarchal ideologies, and patterns of gender discrimination are found to be very powerful in defining, affecting, and planning girls' futures and destinies. The fact that the cultural position of girls and their role within the family structure is subordinated to that of men, increases their vulnerability. Socio-cultural discrimination is used and abused during wartime and political struggles to attack the cultural infrastructure of the enemy.

In Palestinian society, the power of patriarchy is very strong. Women in Palestinian society share a very similar status to that of their sisters in the Arab world. The status of women in such society reveals a strong and organic link between the public/political challenges facing Arab women, and the private/family related challenge. The public political challenge cannot be separated from the private/individual one, and there is no way to confront one without facing the other. The danger of being a female detainee lies in the fact that Palestinian society is a patriarchal one that contains a well defined place for women in terms of their socio-cultural role in protecting and preserving family honour. Yet, as Holt[32] has noted, the *intifada* brought about a culture of resistance, a phenomenon which has had two significant outcomes. The first was the Israeli attempt to subvert the national struggle by targeting Palestinian women and girls. The second was that some families began to take measures to limit the dangers to which they felt their daughters and sisters were being exposed. These resulted in the drop in marriage age for girls and also attempts by various segments of the community to 'protect' their women by hiding them away and curbing their activities. (It is worth mentioning that the socio-economic and political conditions in the area were also considerations that encouraged Palestinians to build 'protective measures' in an attempt to safeguard girls, regardless of the long term effect on girls' education, and socio-political power.)

The case studies showed that girls were targets of gender crimes during the period of political/national struggle. Gender violence committed by the Israelis reinforced traditional relations of domination and subordination between the sexes, and which is derived basically from conservative representations of femininity and masculinity in Palestinian society. The over-idealization of the female/mother figure justified any social reaction or deed to protect the most sacred 'family honour'. Retreat into the family sphere became the only socially significant and normatively valid option for women.

This abuse of culture by the Israelis, in addition to the patriarchal culture of Palestinians, reinforces the culture of silence and poses new questions. If one wants to understand girls' inability to raise their voices in protest despite the dangers involved, one needs to understand the relationship between the gender specificity of personal trauma and the gender specificity of the socio-political trauma. Outside supporting agencies when dealing with such traumas, should be aware of the additional problems, and of the enduring effects girls have to cope with after being victimised.

The aim of this paper was to verbalize and document the unvoiced rights of girls. Three main conclusions can be drawn from this study. The first is a theoretical feminist one. The female struggle for equality is necessarily linked to the varying political and economic realities of the Third World countries where these struggles unfold. Hence, the understanding of female children's rights should be based on such a context. These contextual differences help us to understand the variation of strategies women adopt in order to achieve *de jure* and *de facto* equality, and their relative success and failure. The nature of achieving the task of equality differs if the country is currently engaged in nationalistic struggle, which is the case of Palestinian society.[33] Only a political understanding of the context can enable the political, national (Israeli), patriarchal, class, and ethnic biases, that serve to exclude women from development, to be identified. Recognising the problem areas and limitation of women's empowerment within a given context can guide the design of legal strategies that get to the heart of the problem.

The second main conclusion relates to the effect of such practices on female children. It is argued here that in addition to the actual pain of being sexually and physically abused and harassed by the political opponents, Palestinian girls faced additional pain from their own so-called protective net. The question is what are female children learning from observing or experiencing such abuses? Social development theories posit either that children learn by internalising adult views, or that children grow through developing cognitive capacities and views that are affected by adults' ideas, but stem from the child's own effort. The argument is that parental and social reaction toward female children's victimisation bring them to accept social values that dehumanise and devalue them. The female child, through her observation or personal experience, understands the enormous power of political opponents to destroy or dictate her future. She also understands the way culture further subordinates her status. The culture of the socio-political situation has offered an illusion of protecting and defending children's rights, and an illusion for the need for freedom of expression. It has resulted in a large group of female children who have become increasingly marginalised, most fundamentally in their access to education, freedom of expression, and self-actualisation.

The third main conclusion relates to the subject of protecting children's human rights. It is claimed here, that in order better to understand and help children all over the world, we ought to understand the context in which each group of children is situated. This understanding, as was exemplified in this article, showed that the political versus the traditional context and its relation to a gender context added new issues and meanings to the understanding of children's rights from a curative and preventive level. The context may be sex, age, gender, ethnicity, race, or mental state. Whatever the relevant context, it has to be carefully studied in order to facilitate prevention and intervention strategies in situations where the violation of children's rights occurs.

Notes

[1]   Abu-Lughod, I. (1982) *Palestinian rights: Affirmation and denial.* Wilmette, III: Medina Press. Hadawi (1988); Khalidi, W. (1991) *All that remains: The Palestinian villages occupied and depopulated by Israel in 1948* Berkeley, University of California Press; UN Division for Palestinian Rights *The origins and evolution of the Palestinian problem 1917-1990,* p. 278.

[2]   Baker, A.M. (1991) 'Psychological response of Palestinian children to environmental stress associated with military occupation' *Journal of Refugee Studies,* 4(3), 237-247; Baker, A.M., and Kevorkian, N. (1995) 'Differential effects of trauma on spouses of traumatized household' *Journal of Traumatic Stress,* 8, 61-74; Punamaki, R.L. (1987) 'Psychological stress of responses of Palestinian mothers and their children in conditions of military occupation and political violence' *Quarterly Newsletter of the Laboratory of Comparative Human Cognition* 9(2), 76-84.

[3]   Said, E. (1990) 'Reflections of twenty years of Palestinian history' *Journal of Palestinian Studies* 20(4), 5-22; Smith, P.A. (1984) *Palestine and the Palestinians 1986-1983* New York: St. Martins Press, p. 279; Aruri, N. (1989) *Occupation: Israel over Palestine* (2nd. ed.) Bellmont, Mass: Association of Arab-American University Graduates Press (AAUG); Aronson, G. (1990) *Palestine and the intifada: Creating facts on the West Bank* London: Kegan Paul International.

[4]   Abu-Lughod, I. (1971) *The transformation of Palestine* Evanston, Ill: Northwestern University Press. Khalidi, W. (1991), op. cit.

[5]   Nassar, J. and Heacock, R. (1990) *Intifada: Palestine at the crossroads* New York: Praeger Press; B'Tselem *Violation of human rights in the Occupied Territories 1990/1991* Jerusalem, 1992.

6   Al-Haq *A Nation Under Siege* Al-Haq Centre, Ramallah, West Bank,1989.
        See also Al-Haq's report: *Protection denied: Continued Israeli human
        rights violations in the OPT* in 1992 and the report by the Palestinian
        Human Rights and Information Centre (PHRIC), *Major Israeli human
        rights violations in the Occupied Territories in 1992* and *Comparison of
        Israeli Human rights violations during the Shamir and Rabin
        administrations in 1992-1993.* PHRIC, Jerusalem, February, 1993.

7   Al-Haq, op. cit.; B'Tselem, op. cit.; PHRIC, op.cit. See also U.S.
        Department of State report, 'Country Report on Human Rights Practices for
        1992: Israel in the Occupied Territories' which also appeared in the
        Journal of Palestinian Studies 23(1) (Autumn 1993), 125-136.

8   Toamasevski, K. (1986) *Children in adult prisons: An international
        perspective* London: Frances Pinter at p. 39.

9   Ibid.

10   See United Nations Documents No. E/CN.4/1984/28,29 February, 1984,
        paragraphs 36 and 38, and No. E/CN.4/1984/NGO/1,2 February, 1984, pp.
        2-3.

11   See Freeman, M.D.A. (1983) *The Rights and wrongs of children* London:
        Frances Pinter.

12   Bustos, E. (1988) 'Sexualitet och exil hos traumatiserade flyktingar. En
        psykodynabisk forstaele' [Sexuality and exile in traumatized refugees. A
        psychodynamic understanding] *Nordisk Sexologi* 6:25-30.

13   A'Haleem, A.M. (1992) 'Claiming our bodies and our rights - exploring
        female circumcision as an act of violence' (Sudan); Kelkar, G. (1992)
        'Stopping the violence against women - fifteen years of activism', in
        Schuller, M. (1992) *Freedom from violence: Women's strategies from
        around the world,* Women Law and Development, OEF International, New
        York, pp. 141-157. Davies, M. (ed) (1987) *Third World - second sex* (vol.
        2). London: Zed Publication.

14   Abu-Lughod, I. (1982) 'Israeli settlements in the occupied Arab lands:
        Conquest to colony' *Journal of Palestine Studies,* 11 (Winter), 16-54.

15   Fortuyn, M.D. and de Langen, M. (1992) *Towards the realisation of human
        rights of children* (Defence for Children International, The Netherlands
        Section, Amsterdam).

16   Kevorkian-Shalhoub, N. (1993) 'Fear of sexual harassment: Palestinian
        adolescent girls in the Intifada' In E. Augustin (ed), *Palestinian women:
        Identity and experience* London: Zed.

17   Afshar, H. (1993) *Women in the Middle East: Perceptions, Realities, and
        struggles for liberation* London: Macmillan; Augustin, E. (1993)
        'Development of Palestinian women's movement during the Intifada' in
        Augustin, E. (1993), op. cit.; El-Mernissi, F. (1988) 'Democracy and moral
        disintegration: The contradiction between religious belief and citizenship as
        a manifestation of a historicity of the Arab identity' in Toubia, N. (1988)
        Women of the Arab World London, Zed Publication; Giacaman, R. and

Odeh, M. (1988); 'Palestinian women's movement in the Israeli-occupied West Bank and Gaza' in Toubia, N. (1988) *Women of the Arab World* London: Zed Publication.

[18] Al-Saadawi, N. (1988) 'Introduction' in Toubia, N. (1988) *Women of the Arab World* London: Zed publication, (p. 10).

[19] Zakaria, F. (1988) 'The standpoint of contemporary Muslim Fundamentalism' in Toubia, N. (1988) *Women of the Arab World. London: Zed Publication.*

[20] Ahmad, L. (1992) *Women and gender in Islam: Roots of a modern debate.* New Haven, Ct.: Yale University Press.

[21] Afkhami, M. (1995) *Faith and freedom: Women's human rights in the Muslim world.* Syracuse, N.Y.: Syracuse University Press, Makia, K. (1993) *Cruelty and silence: War, tyranny, uprising, and the Arab world.* London: Norton.

[22] Porter, R. (1989) 'Rape - does it have a historical meaning?' In S. Tomaseilli and R. Porter, (eds) *Rape - an historical and social inquiry* pp. 216-237 Oxford: Basil Blackwell. Also see Sanday ibid.

[23] Seifert, R. (1993) *War and Rape - Analytical approaches* Geneva: Women's International League for Peace and Freedom.

[24] Richter, A. and Mugyenyi, M. (1993) *The mental health of Ugandan women in the context of organized violence - research, training and counselling* Project proposal, Leiden: VENA.

[25] Schuller, M. (1992) *Freedom from violence: Women's strategies from around the world* Women. Law and Development, OEF International, New York.

[26] See 1994 Palestinian Academic Society for the Study of International Affairs (PASSIA), Jerusalem.

[27] Augustin, E. op. cit.

[28] See B'Tselem document, 'Violence Against Minors in Police Detention', July, 1992. B'Tselem, Jerusalem.

[29] See information paper by Matzpen (translated by Israel Shahak) and published by WOFPP, Jerusalem in April, 1989.

[30] Thornhill, T. (1993) 'The interrogation of women "security" detainees by the Israeli general security service' in Afshar, H. (1993) *Women in the Middle East: Perceptions, realities and struggles for liberation* London: Macmillan, (p. 196).

[31] Augustin, op. cit., pp. 194-195.

[32] Holt, M. (1996) *Women in contemporary Palestine: between old conflicts and new realities* Jerusalem, PASSIA (Palestinian Academic Society for the Study of International Affairs).

[33] Schuller, M. op. cit.

14 Protection for Whom and from What? Protection Proceedings and the Voice of the Child at Risk

YA'IR RONEN*

Introduction

Article 12 of the UN Convention on the Rights of the Child presents a difficult challenge of implementation. Contrary to the intention of the Article, children typically play a minor role in decision-making processes related to their own protection.

In these pages, I contend that child advocacy, stemming from a procedural-formalistic approach to children's rights and acceptance of the rights-protection dichotomy, may perpetuate the disempowerment of the child at risk and the historical inertia of 'saving' and protecting children from 'themselves' and their meaningful relationships. The paper explores how a blurred concept of child protection may lead to the pitfall of protecting public order in the name of child protection. I propose a conception of advocacy which emphasises the child's right to be an active participant in the determination of his best interests.

The Child's Evolving Capacities in Context - Adult Guidance and State Protection

The UN Convention on the Rights of the Child (hereafter: the Convention) mandates in Article 12 the hearing of the child 'who is capable of forming his or her own views' and giving 'due weight in accordance with the age and maturity of the child' to those views 'in all matters affecting the child'. The Convention unequivocally supports an emerging image of the child as an autonomous - though not independent - human being; no longer a passive object of care.[1] State protection, by its essence, carries with it the risk of becoming a tool to control the life of the protected person by the State,[2] and so is in potential conflict with human rights such as the right to personal autonomy and self-determination. Therefore, ratification, wherever it carries legal force in domestic law, may further intensify an already tense conflict between two needlessly dichotomised outlooks: the 'child protection' outlook and the 'children's rights' outlook. In order for child advocacy to be more than a catch-phrase[3] justifying all kinds of power struggles between competing systems and professional disciplines one needs to offer a conceptual basis for advocacy action. This paper attempts to offer such a basis.

The Convention affirmed the child's right not only to be heard but also to be listened to, i.e., his opinions must now be sought so that he can become an active participant in the determination of his well being and his opinions are given due weight. What are the implications of the Convention's wording in Article 12 mandating that 'the views of the child' be 'given due weight in accordance with the age and maturity of the child'? It seems that a reasonable implication is that once the child is mature enough the decision-making power should be in his own hands and adult involvement should be only in the form of advice.[4] The matter is further elucidated through examination of Article 5 to the Convention. This Article introduces a concept novel to international children's rights law - the concept of the child's evolving capacities. It states that :

> State Parties shall respect the responsibilities, rights and duties of parents or where applicable the members of the extended family or community as provided for by local custom, legal guardians or other persons legally responsible for the child to provide in a manner consistent with the evolving capacities of the child appropriate direction and guidance in the exercise by the child of the rights recognised in the present Convention.

The Convention adopted *inter alia* the position that since the child's capacities are continually evolving, partial incapacitation under domestic law does not necessarily imply that the child is considered intrinsically less worthy of human dignity or human rights under such law: one whose *de facto* capacities are evolving is not necessarily discriminated against by partial incapacitation *de jure*.

Furthermore, it is relevant to remind ourselves that the concept of evolving capacities is not a legal fiction created by the drafters. I would claim that it is a self-evident truth universally within judicial knowledge. However, one need not rely solely on such reasoning: the concept is firmly anchored in present day knowledge in child development.[5] Therefore, loyal to the Convention's position, one has to concede that child protection is 'here to stay', under any theory of human rights which accepts that human rights must serve the well-being of the individual, and that equality, not only in one's eligibility to rights but also in their actual exercise, should be aspired to: A child at risk, whose capacities are not in their full bloom but only evolving, may need protection in order not to remain powerless and stripped of human rights in the face of adversity (such protection may be considered as child advocacy as shall be explained below).

The rights guaranteed under the Convention are not only civil liberties but also social rights such as the right to education, health and welfare. This paper likewise does not demote such social rights to an inferior position. It is therefore proposed, that when preparing a preliminary 'check list' evaluation of protectionist intervention one should be careful to examine its impact on the implementation of *all* the child's rights and not only his civil liberties.

However, the relationship and balancing between child protection and the child's liberties needs further elucidation: The child is guaranteed under Article 5 of the Convention a negative freedom[6] from State intervention in the privacy of his family life as long as parental guidance and direction are deemed 'appropriate'. I assume that 'appropriate' in this context means residing within culture-sensitive boundaries of reasonableness. Under the wording of the Article, it is clear that the innovative reference to 'local custom' does not justify abusive traditions that belittle a child's capacities: The Article gives freedom to 'members of the extended family or community as provided by local custom' to guide the child. However, such freedom is clearly not limitless. Whenever such guidance is given in a manner inconsistent 'with the evolving capacities of the child', it no longer enjoys the Article's protection against State intervention. Whenever adult involvement ceases to be justified by the child's need for guidance and direction as a growing person, he is entitled to State protection from such involvement.

Bearing in mind the widely accepted axiom that parents are the most trusted proxy decision-makers on their child's behalf, it becomes even clearer why the State's power as *parens patriae* should not exceed that of the parents. A human rights analysis of the child's status rests on his fundamental humanity, on a rejection of his depersonalisation to an object of care.[7] It therefore cannot justify discrimination against biological parents

252 Children's Rights and Traditional Values

and other meaningful adults in favour of an imposed impersonal *parens patriae*. The State cannot be given more power to curtail the child's rights than parents whose naturally developed bonds to the child may precede and go beyond legal regulation.[8] Therefore State protection, like parental guidance and direction, must also be provided 'in a manner consistent with the evolving capacities of the child'. Furthermore, State protection can no longer be understood as an act of benevolence carried out through professional recognition of the child's needs. Rather the Convention frames it as a social right in itself which may as such be invoked by the child right-holder when he reaches sufficient age and maturity.[9] Protectionist intervention failing to take into account the child's evolving capacities or the guidance given by the extended family or community may thus be seen as *ultra vires* under the terms of the Convention.

In summary, it is often accepted without question that child protection is in potential conflict with the child's human rights. It has been proposed here that child protection is a right of the child derivative of a human rights concept which is its *raison d'être* .

On the Incentives to Dichotomise Between Children's Rights and Child Protection

Risk of abuse or neglect is not easy to define, detect, prevent or treat while the pressures to 'do something' persist.[10] Therefore the temptation to produce 'oracle statements' through reification of reality and insulation of professional boundaries is great. The undercurrent of much interdisciplinary discourse seems to be 'let's agree that we cannot agree since we have different concerns and talk in different languages. Otherwise, we may get confused.' The dichotomy between 'children's rights' and 'child protection' may thus be seen as serving the desire of professionals for unthreatened and distinct professional roles and decision-making power.

Why Do We Need to Clarify for Whom and from What We Seek Protection?

Child protection carries with it the real risk of becoming protection of social order, i.e., protection of 'orderly' society from the initially at risk and now also somewhat 'deviant' - 'disturbed' - 'different' child in need of control. The differentiation between the protection of the child and that of society is not an easy task.[11] It necessitates reflective practice that is not common.[12]

Especially when the child is breaking social norms, unconscious, preconscious and conscious factors may come into play that may promote the protection of social order under the guise of disciplining - educating - protecting the child or without such a guise.[13] However, awareness of the pitfall of protecting orderly society in the name of child protection is not consistently mirrored in legal norms.

An historical remnant of an undifferentiated blurred concept of child protection may be found in one of the the provisions of the Israeli Youth (Care and Supervision) Law of 1960, which states that a 'minor is in need of protection if ... he has done an act which is a criminal offence and has not been brought to trial' (section 2(3)). It can be presumed that the clause was intended by the Israeli legislature to apply to the population of minors under the age of criminal responsibility - age 12 in Israel.[14] However, such an intention is not explicit in the wording of the law and this clause has been used to justify the institutionalisation of adolescents up to the age of 18 together with offending minors in secure facilities solely in the name of their own protection. This is done on the basis of hearsay evidence introduced into protection proceedings through social welfare reports. In other words: the police may have no intention even to interrogate the youth who therefore continues to be presumed innocent under law. However, it is not uncommon for a child protection worker to request that the court curtail the child's liberties to an extent that exceeds by far the expected criminal sanctions which would have been imposed on the child, had he been charged and convicted of the offence allegedly committed.

Another example of an undifferentiated blurred concept of protection is the criminal prosecution of children at risk who run away from institutions. Having disobeyed a court protection order such children may be punished under the criminal law. Although theoretically every child has a right to approach the juvenile court and request a change in placement, rarely is this right exercised. A child often explains that he ran away from an institution because nobody in the institution would heed his complaints about maltreatment, his feelings of alienation and isolation or his longing for home.

The harsh public response demonstrated by criminal prosecution inevitably silences many children by reframing their legitimate objections to their placement as futile attempts to resist 'what is good for them' and to disobey their 'superiors'. It is hoped that this route of criminal prosecution of runaways will be abandoned soon. It is anticipated that such a development will empower children and will facilitate a more egalitarian dialogue between them and the professionals working with them.

Towards a Definition of Child Advocacy

How do such phenomena of misguided protection relate to the role of child advocacy? Child advocacy is not a role or a vocation limited to jurists by definition.[15] Hornby's dictionary definition of 'advocate' is as follows:

1.   A person who speaks in favour of somebody or something (especially a cause)
2.   legal person who does this professionally in a court of law.[16]

We learn that the primary use of the word does not limit its scope to professionals nor to the legal arena. Advocacy is defined as: 'pleading in support (of a cause or somebody)'.

In the United States advocacy in its wider meaning is common-place in the political arena. Such a form of advocacy is somewhat foreign to Israeli society and most probably to many other societies. Widening the socially accepted meaning of advocacy may be seen as an important landmark in the development of truly participatory democracy: In such a democracy it is clear that 'pleading in support of a cause or somebody' does not require special qualifications. What child advocacy does necessitate is a value-laden commitment to making the specific child's interests paramount in conflicts relating to him and to a primary ethical accountability towards the child.[17] Both laypersons and professionals working with children (such as social workers, psychiatrists and psychologists) who take upon themselves such a commitment may therefore justifiably see themselves as child advocates. Making the specific child's interests paramount minimises the power of the organisation over the professional as he struggles to define and promote his own independent and differentiated position as to the child's best interests and inevitably 'dethrones' systemic considerations when they do not coincide with the specific child's best interests.[18]

Most human beings tend to be followers. The individual adult decision-maker in any group has a natural tendency to 'hand over his maturity' as a decision-maker to a group leader.[19] What happens when an organisation is criticised for failing to protect a child? Failure to protect the child by an organisation whose leader is unable or unwilling to use such failure for self examination may lead to efforts on his part to bolster group cohesiveness by attacking the criticism and the critics. The organisation's workers will typically follow his lead. When an individual worker advocates a 'different truth' - acknowledging the failure - he may be perceived as a threat to the power of the organisation to define legal truth and thus as joining 'the enemy', i.e. the critics.[20] His position may create turmoil in the organisation. If others join his position (in what may be perceived by some as a crusade) he may bring about a transformation in the personal level of commitment to children by the organisation's workers.[21] In the long run, the organisation, as a system serving children, is profoundly benefited by such a commitment of its workers to accountability to the child. Through such accountability, the optimisation of services becomes less an issue of supervision from above and more an issue of shared professional-client dialogue and power arising from within the system.

What is to be Advocated - Or What are the Best Interests of the Child?

In the past, contradictory positions and strategies were justified in the name of protecting children, causing the principle of the best interests of the child to be severely criticised by some as a hollow, meaningless and dangerous principle.[22] An easy escape from this predicament is the adoption of a formalistic understanding of children's rights focusing only on procedure as if justice is no more than procedural rights. It is an escape and an easy one because it does not face squarely the prevalent inclinations towards 'welfare from above' and the dichotomisation of professional roles and concerns. Procedural rights are a gateway to influence in the child's world; they are essential for justice but simply do not go far enough. A formalistic understanding may perpetuate a reality in which children are excluded from decision-making processes concerning them,[23] or, to use Nils Christie's wording: their conflicts are stolen from them.[24] Children were passive participants when it was well accepted that helping professionals advocated their best interests through learned diagnosis of their deficiencies which they did not understand and through formulation of therapeutic aims to which they were not party. Children may remain in such a passive role when they are hidden behind legal advocates who struggle for their procedural rights using professional language still incomprehensible to the child, and with aims they do not understand derivative of the advocates' 'specific brand' of human rights ideology.

Jargon and ideology may change without changing the reality of the child's participation. The child may remain an outsider, at best trusting his advocate's proclamations of loyalty though feeling somewhat uneasy at not being genuinely heard. A formalistic-procedural conception of children's rights does not minimise the hollowness of the best interests principle but rather acts as its antidote, minimising its impact: It does not attempt to define the principle's substance but rather to curtail its legal implications through procedural safeguards.

Through such a conception different professionals might be channelled not to see the child as a whole person but rather those aspects of him that 'live in peace' with the professional's perceived tasks. Thus the same child may be described as a 'mature intelligent' ten year old - therefore able to understand the duty to tell the truth - and at the same time as a 'sad confused and traumatised child torn between conflicting loyalties to mother and father' and therefore not to be involved in any way in the legal process.

Such a conception would lead one to focus only on legal questions such as:

Was the protection worker's order legally valid?
Did he serve the child and his parents notice of the proceedings as legally required?
Did the term of confinement in a closed institution exceed the specification in the judge's decision?

Other questions may be put aside: Those are questions that directly embody legal principles and therefore verification of one's adherence to the principles they embody cannot be exhausted through examination of compliance to procedural rules.[25]

The following are examples of such questions:

Was the least restrictive-placement necessary chosen?
Was the child's input given due weight?
Were the child's relationships with his psychological parents and other meaningful adults given due weight ?
Did the professional clarify his personal values, those of the child and family and how their interaction and relationship to professional knowledge and know-how led to his decision or opinion?

A narrow formalistic conception of children's rights strips the non-legal professional of his responsibility to advocate the child's right to be an active participant in decisions related to him and correspondingly strips the legal professional of the responsibility to scrutinise the substance of decisions related to the child's protection including the weight given to the child's preferences and feelings. Both disciplines are liable to be prevented from deciphering the child's authentic experience and from relating to his suffering due to preoccupation with over narrowly defined professional goals and concepts.

Lopez[26] explains that human rights advocates may learn to play the hardened professional role, not wanting to hear from others. He explains that in the face of difficulties, disappointments and contradictions in the field one may search for an easy way out, doing work without involving the client. His analysis seems relevant to all professionals who have to apply theoretical schemata to complex live-world situations.[27] When insulated from the subjective and unique child, theoretical frameworks imposed on the child's reality may prevent all those involved in the child protection process from understanding the child's experience and responding to his worries. At its extreme, theoretical objectification of the child may lead to his depersonalisation, to seeing him as an object.[28] When professionals are preoccupied with narrowly defined goals and concepts in such a detached way, the substantive considerations leading to a decision as to what and whom a child must be protected from and how he should best be protected are liable to remain implicit and unquestioned.[29]

The exercise of the child's right to be heard may potentially contribute to the child's feeling of self esteem[30] and therefore is an end in itself. However, it should mainly be seen as a tool to facilitate the child's substantive influence over the decision concerning him. Otherwise, Article 12 may be emptied of meaning to a large extent, as professionals may continue to act as they did before the ratification of the Convention, only now justifying post-factum some of their decisions by the child's expressed wishes. Empowerment of children entails active advocacy, meaning the development and pursuit of mechanisms aimed at maximising the child's evolving influence over decisions related to him,[31] i.e., the development of an array of culture- and age-appropriate tools such as work with a children's ombudsman, play therapy, family mediation, hearing the child in chambers and the appointment of trained independent social workers or lawyers as guardians *ad litem*.[32]

Endnote: The Voice of the Child at Risk - What Do We Make of It?

It seems that one cannot separate the implementation of Article 12 true to its spirit from its underlying assumption - historically rooted in the basic notion of humanistic psychology and now commonly accepted by different schools of psychotherapy - that one must show trust and encourage the individual's intrinsic growth factors.[33] Such an assumption has far reaching consequences for the practice of protection proceedings: professionals may no longer assume and claim as a first choice of interpretation that the child's objection to their professional position as to his welfare is rooted in 'resistance'; children's complaints against their carers and therapists and their positive appraisal of meaningful relationships may not be seen as prima facie unreliable or attributable to 'pathology' or 'disturbance' and may not be explained as a general rule by their inability to face their own shortcomings. Such consequences may be seen as a guarantee of what is widely accepted as optimal child care practice.[34]

The role of child advocates, in their different professional roles, is to attempt to promote 'good enough' professional opinions and treatment plans, i.e., such that make sense of the child's wishes and feelings in context and that substantiate the child's realistic perceptions of risk and well-being. No doubt, the child's views may justifiably be characterised at times by their inadequate - childish-unrealistic-unhealthy - aspects and his family's and community's child rearing traditions as risky or abusive. However, one must be able to tackle tendencies to pathologise the child and his family and exclude them from normative society in overemphasising such aspects.[35] Diagnostic prescribing of pathology may make the decision-maker feel more secure and protected as he can attribute his understanding and line of action to seemingly objective knowledge.[36]

Implementation of the child's right to be heard entails a departure from practices that aim primarily at saving the child from 'himself' including his meaningful relationships. Children at risk sometimes endanger themselves, therefore professionals working with them need to be careful of adopting the stereotype that the child at risk is a risk to himself. Adoption of such a stereotype naturally leads to a tendency to curtail and control the child's behaviour.

A basic attitude of trust and respect for the child brings about a search for ways to respect the child's wishes, feelings and relationships while enhancing his well-being. Programmes that enable the optimal influence of the child's input are thus advanced. Such an attitude, inevitably, abandons a superficial conception of the child as an isolated atomistic unit and can see the web of familial and community relationships and traditions sometimes surrounding the child as potentially worthy of protection. It is widely accepted that minority and poor children are over-represented on at-risk registers in developed countries, potentially causing the penalisation of their parents. However, the relevance of such an attitude goes well beyond these groups of children who are often marginalised from mainstream society. The proposed attitude bears on children from all segments of society and minimises the risk of punitive reactions to their parents. For example, recognising the importance of protecting the child's relationship with a helpless yet caring mother may divert energies from efforts aimed at ensuring her criminal conviction for failure to prevent physical abuse by the father to efforts aimed at enabling her to insure safety for her child.[37] Such an attitude necessitates the acceptance of a degree of uncertainty, ambiguity and dynamic change as inherent in decisions pertaining to the best interests of children at risk.[38]

Attempts have been made in different countries, including Israel, to translate the child's right of participation into working guidelines aimed at evaluating and guiding child care practice. For example, The International Initiative, a foundation established in 1992 in Holland, has set out six guidelines based on experience of practitioners and evaluation of working programmes from different countries.[39] Three of these guidelines relate most closely to the subject matter of this paper:

[1] The child and the parents should be allowed to set the agenda and not the professional, who should be working with them rather than for them;

[2] The professional works only with what the family knows or is able to understand at each stage;

[3] The professional should build on strengths rather than emphasising problems, focusing on the possibilities and resources of all persons involved.

Inevitably, adherence to such guidelines cannot be dogmatic if the child's well-being is to be guarded as the paramount consideration in each and every protection case: indeed, they can only serve as guiding principles to be weighed and balanced together with other principles and not as prescriptive rules (e.g., some parents cannot be allowed to set the agenda as that would inevitably endanger the child). However, such efforts do offer a path towards the implementation of the child's right to be heard, listened to and understood. The child at risk may thus become more influential in the determination of his own best interests.

Notes

*   Revised version of a paper presented in the author's name at the Eleventh
       International Congress on Child Abuse and Neglect, Dublin, Ireland, 20
       August 1996. I thank Judge Philip Marcus, Prof. Jona Rosenfeld, Dr. Mili
       Mass and Ms. Aliya Kedem for their valuable comments. The editors'
       comments were also very helpful. Of course, I bear sole responsibility for
       the views expressed and any mistakes. Please address comments to the
       author at PO Box 6443, Bet Shemesh, Israel 99531.

1   Verhellen, E. (1992) 'Changes in the Images of the Child' in Freeman, M.
       and Veerman, P. (eds) *The Ideologies of Children's Rights* Dordrecht:
       Kluwer, 79.

2   Sebba, L. (1981) 'Legalism Versus Welfarism in Israel's Juvenile Justice
       System' *Is. L. Rev.* 16, 461. Qvortrup, J. (1991) *Childhood as a Social
       Phenomenon - An Introduction to a Series of National Reports,* Vienna;
       Parsloe, P. (1996) 'Some Issues for Social Work Education' in Parsloe, P.
       (ed.) *Pathways to Empowerment.* Birmingham: Venture Press.

3   See Sebba op. cit. n. 3.

4   Abramson, B. (1995) 'The Invisibility of Children and Adolescents: The
       Need to Monitor our Rhetoric and our Attitudes'. *Revised version of a
       paper presented at the European Conference on Monitoring Children's
       Rights,* 1994, Ghent, Belgium.

5   Goldstein J., Freud, A. and Solnit, A. (1996) *The Best Interests of the
       Child: The Least Detrimental Alternative,* New York: Free Press; De
       Winter, M. (1997) *Children and Fellow Citizens: Participation and
       Commitment* New York.

6   Oakes, J. (1996) 'What's Wrong with "Negative Liberty"?' *L. and Social
       Inquiry,* 21, 79.

7   Cohn, H. (1991) 'A Human Rights Theory of Law: Prolegomena to a
       Methodology of Action' in Barak, A. and Gavison, R. (eds) *Haim Cohn
       Selected Writings.* Tel Aviv: Bursi 17.

8   See Goldstein et al, op. cit.; n. 5; Szasz, T. (1977) 'The Child as
       Involuntary Mental Patient: The Threat of Child Therapy to the Child's
       Dignity, Privacy and Self Esteem' *San Diego L. Rev.* 14,1005; King, M.
       and Trowell, J. (1992) *Children's Welfare and the Law - The Limits of
       Legal Intervention* London, Sage.

9   On the move from a needs framework to a rights framework see e.g. Braye,
       S. and Preston-Shoot, M. (1994) 'Partners in Community Care? Rethinking
       the Relationship between the Law and Social Work Practice' *J. of Social
       Welfare & Fam. L,* 163; Rosas, A. (1995) 'The Nordic Welfare Model:
       Moving from Welfare "From Above" Towards a System Based on Rights'
       Nordic J. of Int L., 369. Ramalingawami, V. (1996) 'Commentary :The
       Asian Enigma' in *The Progress of Nations 1996.* Paris: UNICEF.

10   Aldgate, J. (1996) 'Child Abuse and Child Protection: An Overview of Recent Research' *Paper presented at the International Conference on Protecting Children by Strengthening Families: Partnerships for Safety*, Oslo. Best, J. (1989) *Threatened Children - Images of Issues*. Mass, M. (1995) 'The 'Best Interests' of the Child: Ideological Aspects and the Role of Experts' *Society and Welfare*, 15, 415 (Hebrew).

11   Queloz, N. (1991) 'Protection, Intervention and the Rights of Children and Young People' Ch. 2 in T. Booth (ed.) *Juvenile Justice in the New Europe* Sheffield.

12   Schon, D. (1983) *The Reflective Practitioner: How Professionals Think in Action*. New York

13   Winnicott, D.W. (1985*) Deprivation and Delinquency* (Winnicott, R. Sheperd and M. Davis eds). London and New York: Tavistock; Miller, A. (1988) *For Your Own Good - The Roots of Violence in Child Rearing*. London: Virago; Rogers, C.R. (1989) *Carl Rogers on Personal Power - Inner Strength and its Revolutionary Impact*. London: Constable; De Winter, op. cit. n. 5.

14   See also Sebba op. cit. n. 2.

15   Flekkoy, M. (1991) A *Voice for Children - Speaking Out as Their Ombudsman*. UNESCO; Gavison, R. (1982) 'Introduction' in Gavison, R. (ed.) *Civil Rights in Israel - Essays in Honour of Haim H. Cohn* (Hebrew), Tel Aviv: Association for Civil Rights in Israel.

16   Hornby, A. (1974) *Oxford Advanced Learner' s Dictionary*. Oxford: Oxford University Press.

17   Blass, L. (1991) 'Accountability' *Society and Welfare*, 11, 214. (Hebrew).

18   Fromm, E. (1964) *The Heart of Man- Its Genius for Good and Evil*. New York: Harper & Row; Peck, S. (1985) *People of the Lie - The Hope for Healing Human Evil*. New York: Touchstone; Mearns, D. and Thorne, B. (1989) *Person Centred Counselling in Action* London: Sage; Rogers op. cit. n. 13.

19   Peck, op. cit. n. 18

20   On the potential discrepancy between factual and legal truth see e.g. King and Trowell, op. cit. n. 8; Cooper, A , Hetherington, R., Bainstow, K., Pitts, J. and Spriggs, A. (1995) *Positive Child Protection - A View from Abroad*. Dorset: Russel House.

21   See Fromm op. cit. n. 18 and Peck op. cit. n. 18.

22   For criticisms see e.g. Alston, P. and Parker, S. (1994) 'Introduction' in Alston, P., Parker, S. and Seymour, J. *Children, Rights and the Law*. Oxford; Eekelaar, J. (1994) The Interests of the Child and the Child's Wishes: The Role of Dynamic Self Determination in P. Alston (ed.) *The Best Interests of the Child - Reconciling Culture and Human Rights*. Oxford: Clarendon; Freeman, M. (1996) 'The Best Interests of the Child - Is The Best Interests of The Child In The Best Interests of Children?' *Lecture given at an international conference on 'In The Best Interests of*

The Child: Contemporary Perspectives'. The Sigmund Freud Center. The Hebrew University of Jerusalem, November 6-7, 1996; Kline, M. (1992) 'Child Welfare Law, "Best Interests of The Child", Ideology, and First Nations' *Osgoode Hall L. J.*, 30, 375; Shamgar-Handelman, L. (1994) 'To Whom Does Childhood Belong?' in Qvortrup, J., Bardy, M. Sgritta, M. and Winterberger H. (eds) *Childhood Matters: Social Theory, Practice and Politics,* Aldershot: Avebury, 249-265.

[23]   Queloz op. cit. n. 11.

[24]   Christie, N. (1977) 'Conflicts as Property' *British J. of Criminology*, 17, 1.

[25]   On the distinction between principles and rules see e.g. Raz, J. (1972) 'Legal Principles and the Limits of Law'. *Yale L. J.*, 81,823.

[26]   Lopez, G. (1996) 'An Aversion to Clients: Loving Humanity and Hating Human Beings' *Harvard Civil Rights - Civil Liberties L. Rev.* 31, 315.

[27]   See also Schon op. cit. 1983 and Rosenfeld, J., Sikes, I. and Schon, D. *Out From Under: Lessons from Projects for Inaptly Served Children and Families.* JDC - Brookdale Institute (Jerusalem, 1995).

[28]   Coan, R. (1987) *Human Consciousness and Its Evolution.* New York: Greenwood.

[29]   See also Mass op. cit. n. 10; Minow, M. (1996) 'Comments on "Suffering, Justice and the Politics of Becoming" by William E. Connolly, presented as the Roger Allan Moore Lecture, May 11, 1995' 20 *Culture, Medicine & Psychiatry* (1996) 279; Minow, M. (1996) 'Political Lawyering: An Introduction' *Harvard Civil Rights - Civil Liberties L. Rev.*, 31, 287; Wood, N. (1995) 'Professional Dangerousness' *Children - A Newsletter from the Office of the Commissioner for Children*, 18, 5; Wyness, M. (1996) 'Policy, Protectionism and the Competent Child' *Childhood - A Global J. of Child Research* , 3, 431.

[30]   Flekkoy op. cit. n. 15; Szasz op. cit. n. 8.

[31]   See Eekelaar op. cit. n. 22.

[32]   See e.g. Drapkin, R. and Bienenfeld, F. (1985) 'The Power of Including Children in Custody Mediation' *J. of Divorce*, 8, 63; Flekkoy op. cit.

[33]   Eekelaar op. cit. n. 22.

[34]   Rosenfeld et al, op. cit. n. 27; Timms, J. (1992) 'The Development of Children's Rights' *Quarterly Journal for Guardians ad litem, Reporting Officers and other Child Care Professionals*, 5, 1.

[35]   Cooper et al, op. cit. n. 20; Jack, G. and Stepney, P. (1995) 'The Children Act 1989 - Protection or Persecution? Family Support and Child Protection in the 1990s' *Critical Social Policy*, 26; Kufeldt, K. (1993) 'Listening to Children: An Essential for Justice' *Int. J. of Children's Rights*, 1, 155; Rogers, C.R. (1957) 'The Necessary and Sufficient Conditions of Therapeutic Personality Change' *J. of Consulting Psychology*, 21, 95; Saleebey, D. (1994) 'Culture, Theory and Narrative: The Intersection of Meanings in Practice' *Social Work*, 39, 351.

[36]   Rogers op. cit. n. 35.

[37] Davidson, H. (1995) 'Child Abuse and Domestic Violence; Legal Connections and Controversies' *Fam. L.Q.*, 29, 359; Schechter, S. and Edleson, J.L. (1994) 'In the Best Interest of Women and Children: A Call for Collaboration Between Child Welfare and Domestic Violence Constituencies'. *Paper prepared for the Conference 'Domestic Violence and Child Welfare: Integrating Policy and Practice for Families'*, Racine, Wisconsin, June 8-10, 1994.

[38] Aldgate op. cit. n. 10; Eekelaar op. cit. n. 22.

[39] The International Initiative (1992) *Rebuilding the Family from Within* Cheshire: David Lewis.

15 The Child's Right to Make Mistakes: Criminal Responsibility and the Immature Minor

GILLIAN DOUGLAS[*]

Introduction

> For a young offender to accept responsibility for his or her offence and face up to the harm which they have caused to the victim is both a valuable moral lesson and a first step to rehabilitation.[1]

In this paper, I discuss children's criminal responsibility in English law, and attempts, most recently by the Labour Government elected in 1997, to extend this through abolition of the '*doli incapax*' presumption, under which a child aged between 10 and 14 is presumptively regarded as incapable of committing an offence. I argue that these attempts reflect a desire to promote a particular version of society which is presented as a return to the traditional values of a more stable past, but that this is no more than a myth. I also suggest that the *doli incapax* presumption should be seen as an important right of a child which, far from being abolished, should be preserved and possibly extended.[2]

The Age of Criminal Responsibility

David Garland has argued that

> penal practices exist within a specific penal culture which is itself supported and made meaningful by wider cultural forms, these, in turn, being grounded in society's patterns of material life and social action.[3]

264

This would appear to be borne out when examining the age of criminal responsibility. In English common law, the minimum age at which a person could be convicted of a crime was 7. The current minimum age is 10.[4] Below this age, there is an *irrebuttable* presumption of law that the child is *doli incapax* - incapable of wrong. The position in a range of other European jurisdictions is currently as follows - 7 in Cyprus, Ireland, Liechtenstein and Switzerland; 8 in Scotland and N Ireland; 9 in Malta; 12 in Greece, Israel, Netherlands, San Marino, Turkey; 13 in France; 14 in Austria, Bulgaria, Germany, Hungary, Italy, Latvia, Lithuania, Romania, Slovenia; 15 in Czech Republic, Denmark, Estonia, Finland, Iceland, Norway, Slovakia, Sweden; 16 in Andorra, Poland, Portugal and Spain; 18 in Belgium and Luxembourg.[5] Such a wide range of ages must reflect the extent to which attitudes to children are historically and culturally specific, even within one relatively homogeneous region. Yet, despite changes in cultural patterns over time, it has proved perhaps surprisingly difficult to raise the minimum age in the United Kingdom, as will be demonstrated below. One reason may be because there is an ambivalence in societal attitudes towards children which is reflected in many aspects of the law, with criminal justice as perhaps one of the sites of greatest tension. On the one hand, there is increasing recognition that children may be capable of making quite sophisticated and important choices in their lives (such as to consent to medical treatment, for example), at relatively young ages, while on the other, there is a wish to protect them from the full consequences of actions which can often seem highly irrational and unreflective (such as committing violent criminal acts). Another possibility is that, as Garland points out,[6] there are also contradictory conceptions of justice - individualisation or consistency? punishment or welfare? - within modern culture. These are explored below.

The *doli incapax* Presumption[7]

Between the ages of 10 and 14, there has long been a *rebuttable* presumption in English law, that the child did not know what he was doing was wrong and therefore cannot be convicted of the crime without positive proof of such knowledge, or, as it may be referred to, a 'mischievous discretion'.[8] The eighteenth century jurist, Hale, regarded the test as being satisfied where it could be shown that the child could 'discern between good and evil at the time of' the offence.[9] The modern test was said, in *JM (A minor) v Runeckles*[10] to be proof that the child knew what he was doing was 'seriously wrong' - not morally or legally wrong, but more than mere naughtiness. There must be discrete evidence to rebut the presumption; it is insufficient to let the facts of the offence speak for themselves in an attempt to provide evidence, and the mere fact of the child running away from the scene is insufficient.[11] Evidence can be supplied from what the child said or did at the time of the offence or when interviewed later, from psychiatric examination, from covering up the crime, from his background and from his upbringing.[12]

As thinking about juvenile offenders has changed over the years, the desirability of retaining the presumption has been called into question. Most recently, in the wake of the murder of the toddler, James Bulger, by two 10 year old boys, and the enormous media coverage which followed this,[13] a considerable shift towards a more punitive stance has been discernible in the political sphere.[14] Unusually perhaps, the political response was mirrored by an attempt to remove the presumption in the courts, in an important judgment of the Queen's Bench Divisional Court in 1994.[15] This judicial response may be seen as an example of what Colin Hay has described as 'the judicial internalisation of the discourse of moral panic'. He argues that once the media have created a moral panic over a particular social problem, here, the murder of a child by other children, the judiciary may feel compelled to respond by echoing the fears thus created:

> This is at least in part a consequence of the media's presentation of each 'moral panic case' as a trial not so much of those charged (whose guilt is assumed unquestionable) as of British Justice *per se*. Trial by *jury* of those directly accused, becomes trial by *press* (on behalf of 'the British people') of British Justice. The latter can only demonstrate its resilience in the face of the degeneration of tradition, respect and authority by out-competing the tabloid press in the tone of its *authoritarian populism*.[16]

The House of Lords rejected the attempt,[17] but called for the issue to be thoroughly investigated by Parliament. The Home Office (the government department responsible for criminal justice policy) examined the issue,[18] the Labour Party announced that it would abolish the presumption as part of its stance on youth crime in the run-up to the 1997 General Election, and confirmed this stance after taking power.[19] Certainly, removal of the presumption would fit well with the current political climate, which is explored further below.

What is the Rationale for the Presumption?

The *doli incapax* presumption represents perhaps the earliest recognition of what today in English law would be understood as the test of *Gillick* competence,[20] i.e., that children mature, and grow in intellectual and emotional understanding, at different rates and that allowance should be made for this when assessing whether a child's act, or choice, should be regarded as made with full appreciation of its implications. It is true that the *Gillick* test has arisen in the context of child decision-making, but the basis of criminal responsibility under English law is in the assumption that only those capable of understanding their own actions - and the consequences of those actions - can be held liable for them. It is this very focus upon individual criminal responsibility which justifies the retention of the presumption in the law, and explains the criticisms which have been made of it in the past.[21]

Blackstone traced the presumption back to the time of Edward III, and embraced a *Gillick*-type approach when explaining it thus:

> the capacity of doing ill, or contracting guilt, is not so much measured by years and days, as by the strength of the delinquent's understanding and judgment. For one lad of 11 years old may have as much cunning as another of 14; and in these cases our maxim is that '*malitia supplet aetatem*' ... under fourteen, though an infant shall be prima facie adjudged to be *doli incapax*; yet if it appear to the court and jury that he was *doli capax*, and could discern between good and evil, he may be convicted...[22]

The historical necessity for the presumption has been explained by modern writers noting how, before the mid-nineteenth century, there was no separate treatment of juvenile offenders. If they were regarded as being *doli capax*, they were in no different position from an adult, and they suffered the same penalty as an adult. Morris and Giller,[23] for example, note how, on one day in 1814, 5 children aged between 8 and 12 were hanged for petty larceny. (The assumption at that time was that, if children were treated more leniently than adult criminals, there would be an incentive to use them as agents of crime). The presumption, therefore, served as a means of showing some mercy to children (but it seems that it may not have been very difficult for the prosecution to rebut the presumption and prevent this) in a very harsh system where capital punishment was frequently the only penalty.

Glanville Williams,[24] reviewing the presumption in the 1950s, argued that

> the test ... is bound up with retributive punishment and the mystical theory of moral responsibility. According to the theory of moral responsibility, the only persons capable of acting wrongly are those of a certain intelligence or intellectual accomplishment... The retributive theory of punishment imports the doctrine of moral responsibility into the law, because no one can justly be punished unless he is morally responsible ... In the case of children, the law recognises a twilight zone ... in which they are morally responsible not as a class, but as individuals, when they know their act to be wrong.[25]

In modern times, the United Nations Standard Minimum Rules for the Administration of Juvenile Justice, the 'Beijing Rules', adopted by the General Assembly in 1985, propose, in rule 4, that the beginning of the age of criminal responsibility 'shall not be fixed at too low an age level bearing in mind the facts of emotional, mental and intellectual maturity.' So the minimum age of criminal responsibility, and the *doli incapax* presumption, serve to ensure that only those children who are morally responsible for their acts, are met with the force of the law.[26]

What Sort of 'Right' might the Presumption Be?

At first sight, it might seem odd to describe the *doli incapax* presumption as a right of the child. Adopting Michael Freeman's[27] useful classification, children's rights may be divided into four categories: rights to welfare, or human rights, such as those enshrined in the UN Declaration (and now many of the rights in the UN Convention on the Rights of the Child) and which may be seen as rights against everyone; rights to protection from abuse or neglect, imposing a corresponding duty primarily upon parents or other care-givers; the right to be treated like adults, a form of social justice akin to non-discrimination on grounds of race or gender; and the right to autonomy in decision-making.

Interestingly, although Freeman discusses the 'rights of children who do wrong' extensively in the book in which this four-fold classification is set out, he does not consider the age of criminal responsibility in any detail. His focus instead is on the need to ensure that children receive the same due process rights as adults i.e., he focuses on the third class of rights he has elucidated. I would suggest that the presumption should be seen as a right in his second category - the right to protection. In requiring the prosecution to prove that the child knew he was doing wrong, the child is protected from being stigmatised by the criminal justice system before he or she is mature enough to accept responsibility and to learn from his or her mistake (as the United Nations Declaration of, and the Convention on the Rights of the Child both put it, 'the child, by reason of his physical and mental immaturity, needs special safeguards and care, including appropriate legal protection').

Article 40(1) of the Convention on the Rights of the Child goes on to provide that

> States Parties recognise the right of every child alleged as, accused of, or recognised as having infringed the penal law to be treated in a manner consistent with the promotion of the child's sense of dignity and worth, which reinforces the child's respect for the human rights and fundamental freedoms of others and which takes into account the child's age and the desirability of promoting the child's reintegration and the child's assuming a constructive role in society.[28]

This formulation recognises both the need to consider the child's level of maturity when applying the penal law, and the desirability of reintegration rather than punishment as an aim in responding to the child offender. Geraldine Van Bueren[29] has noted that, during the drafting of Article 40, the concept of reintegration into society, rather than rehabilitation of the child, was incorporated, for two main reasons. First, there was concern that rehabilitation may be abused as an undesirable form of social control; secondly, it was considered that rehabilitation implies that responsibility rests solely with the offender who is to be 'treated', 'cured' and then placed back in society. Reintegration, on the other hand, was said to focus upon the child's social environment and upon the role of the community in helping the child to become a responsible member of society. It is arguable whether such a distinction needs to be drawn between the two concepts. Nonetheless, what is important in this view of children's rights is the recognition of the right *to be a child*, i.e., *not* to be treated as an adult. In this respect, although the *doli incapax* presumption operates as a type of *Gillick* competence test, it is intended to protect the child who *lacks* competence, not the child who *has* it. It can be seen as the opposite of the autonomy right of children, which has been characterised by John Eekelaar, in commenting upon *Gillick*, as 'that most dangerous but most precious of rights: the right to make their own mistakes'.[30]

It can also be argued that there is, in any case, a strong utilitarian value to society in recognising an 'incompetence right' in the criminal justice sphere. Edwin Lemert has argued for the need for 'judicious non-intervention' in responding to juvenile offending, on the basis that offending is a relatively normal part of growing up, which most offenders will grow out of as they mature.[31] The stigmatisation associated with involvement in the criminal justice system may make it much harder for a person to avoid offending in the future. Thus, the right of a child to make mistakes and *not* to have to suffer the consequences which would be visited upon an adult is more likely to keep the child from being drawn into long-term criminality.[32] This rationale has been accepted in the international sphere. The Beijing Rules and Article 40(3)(b) of the Convention on the Rights of the Child both refer to the need to promote mechanisms outside the judicial system for dealing with child offenders, and the Council of Europe, in its Recommendation on Social Reactions to Juvenile Delinquency, encourages the use of diversion.[33]

Changing Attitudes to Juvenile Responsibility and Juvenile Crime

It has been argued[34] that concern about juvenile delinquency grew in the nineteenth century as a by-product of a growing awareness of the concept of childhood as a distinct phase of development of the person. At that time, (as in earlier and more recent times), the fear of disorder in society was regarded as being linked to poverty, poor public morals, and unruliness of children. If people, during their formative childhood years, could be inculcated with the appropriate attitudes and mores, there would be less risk of disorder.[35] Of course, parents are supposed to provide the most important influence upon children's socialisation, but with more complex industrial societies requiring a more disciplined work-force, parents could not always be trusted to do what was needed. The requirement upon parents to ensure that their children are educated, almost always in a school which is then either run by, or inspected by, the state, with consequential sanctions for failure to do so, can be seen as the main societal mechanism intended to ensure that children are brought up imbued with appropriate values and modes of behaviour. The tension between parental freedom to bring up one's child according to one's own values, and the need of the state to have a population which shares common values, has produced disputes as regards state control over schooling,[36] but is also reflected in attitudes to parental responsibility for children's offending. The link between criminal conduct and poor education/upbringing has been made since Tudor times,[37] but came to the fore in the nineteenth and twentieth centuries when it became allied with belief in either the welfare or treatment models of penology.

The development of special juvenile courts[38] and of special dispositions for juvenile offenders (from the first separate prison at Parkhurst in 1838 and the innovation of reformatories and industrial schools, originally charitable, to the range of penal measures such as curfews, attendance centres and intermediate treatment today) has been described as the advent of a welfare approach to juveniles,[39] whereby they are seen as requiring separate provision from that for adults, in order to reflect the need for them to be given the care and education which will divert them from crime. The concern to reform the child developed into a 'treatment' approach at the end of the 19th and beginning of the 20th centuries; the criminality of the offender was to be cured by whatever means were required - education, psychological approaches, for example.[40]

The main assumption of reform proposals from the 1920s onwards was that criminal behaviour is a symptom of some sort of disruption or failure of parental upbringing, in much the same way that abuse or neglect are. Hence, the child is a victim of this failing and requires care, education or treatment to put right what has gone wrong and there is little or no distinction to be drawn between the deprived and delinquent child. Note, for example, the view of the Molony Committee in 1927,[41] which carried out the first review of the English juvenile courts, that

> It is often a mere accident whether [the child] is brought before the court because he is wandering or beyond control, or because he has committed some offence. Neglect leads to delinquency and delinquency is often the direct outcome of neglect.[42]

However, this view conflicted with a continuing belief in the value of punishment, either as reformative in itself, or as a deterrent or retributive act. The tension between these approaches has led to a continuing ambivalence in attitudes to juvenile offenders. How far should the criminal justice system seek to 'save' young offenders from a life of crime, through diversion, care and education, and how far should it remain a criminal *justice* system, concerned to ascribe responsibility for wrong-doing and to bring proportionate punishment to the wrong-doer? The English juvenile court system (first placed on a statutory footing by the Children Act 1908) has long represented an uneasy compromise between notions of welfare and due process. For example, there is a statutory duty to have regard to the offender's welfare when deciding on a disposition:

> Every court in dealing with a child or young person who is brought before it whether as an offender or otherwise, shall have regard to the welfare of the child or young person and shall in a proper case take steps for removing him from undesirable surroundings, and for securing that proper provision is made for his education and training. [43]

On the other hand, the English system never moved wholesale to an indeterminate system without due process rights, as the American system did until the Supreme Court decision of *In Re Gault*.[44] Indeed, magistrates administering justice in the juvenile courts remained influential in ensuring that concerns about punishment and proportionality were heard and addressed. Allison Morris and Henri Giller to a considerable extent blame magistrates for the 'failure' of the Children and Young Persons Act 1969 - the high point of reformist attitudes to juvenile offenders in English legislation - by showing how they insisted on imposing penalties and measures more allied to discipline and control of the offender rather than entrusting juveniles to the more 'caring' approach of social services departments.[45]

One of the most telling criticisms made of the welfare/treatment approach to dealing with offenders has been that the rhetoric of reform disguised the extent to which punitive treatment was in fact meted out, and punitive effects suffered, not just by those who might, if one instead adopted a retributive approach, be said to 'deserve' it because of their wrong-doing, but also by those swept up into a system which did not distinguish between the causes of the anti-social behaviour (which might, at one end of the spectrum, be begging on the streets because of destitution or abandonment, and at the other, involvement in organised criminal activity).[46] In addition, the lack of due process safeguards and the possibility of indeterminate length of incarceration, release being judged by 'experts' when satisfied that the child had been cured of his criminality, came under strong attack in the 1970s, especially in the United States.[47] In England and Wales, the public 'respectability' of a punishment approach was revived (not that it had ever really gone away) through a variety of factors. There was the general loss of confidence in the ability of reform measures to achieve results. There was a developing view that, contrary to earlier opinion, there *is* a distinction between the deprived and the depraved child, and that measures to deal with children ought to be differentiated.

This view stemmed as much from concern for the neglected or abused child as from a renewed faith in punishment as the appropriate response to crime. Such a child might be placed in the same children's home as the juvenile offender, and be stigmatised accordingly. Even more gravely, there was a fear that children in need of care or protection were not being protected precisely because of the strict rules of evidence and requirements of satisfaction of proof imposed in proceedings for compulsory care measures which extended to juvenile offenders.[48] More recently, the focus has partly switched to *parents'* responsibility for their children's misbehaviour, with proposals both to punish parents if their children offend, and to (re-)educate them in how to bring up a child 'correctly'.[49]

The Current Position Regarding Under-14s in the Criminal Justice System

The pendulum shift towards a more retributive stance resulted in further legislation designed to strengthen the possibility of juvenile courts imposing punishments upon young offenders.[50] Yet alongside this rhetoric, the recognition of the need to divert juveniles (and indeed, adults as well) from the criminal justice system altogether resulted also in a huge increase in the use of formal and informal police cautioning instead of court proceedings. In 1984, 10,900 *males* aged 10 to 13 were sentenced for indictable offences; by 1993, the total had fallen to 2,300.[51] Where offenders in this age group *were* sentenced, the most usual disposal was a discharge (52 per cent of those sentenced in 1994). A discharge may be ordered by the court where it considers that it is unnecessary to punish the offender. It may be absolute, which imposes no restrictions on the offender at all, or, more usually, conditional upon the offender's good behaviour (i.e., no further conviction) within a period not exceeding three years. Where something more than a discharge was deemed necessary, the next most usual disposal was supervision (23 per cent) where the emphasis is upon the offender's rehabilitation rather than punishment. Only the third most usual disposal (19 per cent), the requirement to visit an attendance centre to take part in activities on Saturdays, could be regarded as retributive in nature, since it is intended to deprive the offender of leisure time which might otherwise be spent in offending. But the numbers are very small - around 500 children.[52] The fine is the most common punitive sentence given to all offenders, but even though parents are normally required to pay their children's fines, only 48 parents, of girls *and* boys, were ordered to pay the child's fine in

1994. A higher number (307) were required to pay compensation, which is another way of fixing responsibility, but this is not intended, in the same way as a fine, to bring home to the offender (or the parent) the state's judgment that he or she is deserving of *punishment* as such.[53]

Why is it that the majority of children who are regarded as deserving of a court appearance are yet considered not deserving of any punishment? It may be that the need to bring home to the offender his or her responsibility for wrong-doing, which the *doli incapax* presumption is intended to stress and which will have been rebutted in each case[54] (albeit that the majority of offenders will have pleaded guilty and so admitted they were *capax)*, may be regarded as of less importance in most courts than the need to try to prevent further offending by the child. Alternatively, it may be that the shaming of the child, by being brought before a court, is regarded as sufficient to bring home the child's responsibility for his acts.[55] It should also be borne in mind that the statistics referred to above relate to *indictable* offences - those which are more serious and could be tried by a jury in an adult court.[56] In fact, the *gravest* crimes committed by children *are* still tried in the Crown Court with a jury, rather than in the youth court. Offences of murder, manslaughter, those carrying a possible sentence for an adult of 14 years or more (e.g., robbery, arson), indecent assault on a woman, offences of causing death by driving (unlikely, one would have thought, to be committed by a child, but not impossible), and offences where the child is charged jointly with an adult, are all dealt with at the Crown Court. This may well be in order to stress the severity of the offence, but it is likely to be challenged as contrary to the European Convention on Human Rights.[57]

The political desire to permit courts to react punitively to child offenders was further demonstrated by the introduction, in the Criminal Justice and Public Order Act 1994 s. 1, of a new sentence, the 'secure training order', a custodial determinate sentence of between 6 months and 2 years, with half the sentence served in the community under supervision. This provision, which was not to be brought into force until the appropriate accommodation was made available, applies to 12 to 14 year olds who have already been convicted of three or more imprisonable offences and who have re-offended during, or been in breach of, a supervision order. The objective is to deal with recidivist children who, in a further example of media panic, were blamed in the media for 'mini crime waves' of shop-lifting, burglary, vandalism, and car crime which, in the eyes of police and magistrates, could not be prevented because of the lack of any action which could be taken to lock such children up. It seems doubtful whether the measure will prove effective, and its introduction would appear to be a political symbolic gesture to be seen to be 'doing something' about persistent young offenders.[58]

Secure detention of children has hitherto not been permitted other than for the gravest offences, such as murder and manslaughter, and in the same Act, provision was made for the very few children convicted of these and other grave crimes to be detained for up to the adult maximum length of imprisonment for their offence. Children guilty of murder have long been required to be sentenced to be detained 'during Her Majesty's Pleasure'. This form of indeterminate sentence was introduced by the Children Act 1908 to replace the death penalty for juveniles convicted of murder (now the life sentence in the case of adults), and was intended to be rehabilitative rather than punitive.[59] It has been held, in relation to the Bulger murderers, that while punishment and deterrence are relevant considerations in determining how long a juvenile should serve in such detention, they do not carry the same weight as would be the case for adults, and length of detention must be kept under constant review.[60] And where there is a discretion as to sentence, despite the political emphasis upon retribution and concern about public reaction, courts may take a different approach. In one highly publicised case[61] where an 11 year old boy was convicted of manslaughter after he threw a concrete slab from the roof of a tower block, killing a woman walking below, the judge sentenced him to three years' supervision. The media noted that both the police and the relatives of the victim supported this approach, which suggests that, in individual cases where the facts and background are actually known, rather than when presented with media portrayal of juvenile crime in general, a punitive response may not be uppermost in the mind of the public.

This difficulty of finding a balance[62] between welfare and justice (in the sense of retribution) has been perceived not just in England and Wales, of course. Leslie Sebba has noted the inconsistencies and confusions which underlie internationally agreed standards and which illustrate the dilemma.[63] In 1989, the European Committee on Crime Problems issued a Report on Social Reactions to Juvenile Delinquency[64] in which the Committee were concerned to find a means of integrating the due process and welfare approaches. They considered that education of the minor should continue to be the main purpose of the system, because what is needed is to help young persons 'who are at a stage of physical intellectual and psychological development particularly important for shaping their personality' to ' face up to the real world without committing offences and take their place in society'.[65] Wider international uncertainty about the aims of the juvenile justice system was noted in the Commentary to the Beijing Rules,[66] but a conclusion in favour of reintegration rather than retribution or deterrence was arrived at in the Convention on the Rights of the Child, as we have seen above.

Criticisms of the Presumption

These shifts in attitude towards juvenile offenders, demonstrated both in England and Wales and internationally, are clearly reflected in views taken within this jurisdiction of the *doli incapax* presumption, usually as part of wider reviews of juvenile justice policy over the years. Until the decline in confidence in the efficacy of penal measures which grew from the 1960s, a much more positive view of the capacity of society to do something about juvenile crime was reflected than is prevalent today. Thus, the old criticisms of the presumption were related closely to a view that juveniles require treatment or reformation and not punishment.

For example, the Molony Committee, referred to above, pondered whether the juvenile court system should not become a much more welfare-oriented one, along American lines, but concluded that it was essential, at the adjudication stage, to demonstrate to the offender, and to society, the link between the offence committed and responsibility for it. Once guilt had been established, however, the committee saw little difference between the deprived and the depraved child, and argued for dispositions which would best reform the child. As far as the presumption was concerned, therefore, the Committee recognised the desirability of continuing to ensure that the child was truly responsible for his or her criminal act, through the retention of the presumption. Indeed, the committee wanted the minimum age of criminal responsibility raised to reflect society's greater understanding of the needs of juveniles; they said[67]

> The age [then seven] was adopted hundreds of years ago and the whole attitude of society towards offences committed by children has since been revolutionised. We think the time has come for raising the age...

and their bold recommendation was that the age be raised to eight![68]

Similarly, Glanville Williams, in the article referred to above, went on to criticise the 'moral responsibility' approach as outmoded:

No one whose opinion is worth considering now believes that a child who does wrong ought as a matter of moral necessity to expiate his wrong by suffering. Punishment may sometimes be the best treatment, but if so it is because this is the only way in which the particular child can be made to see the error of his ways... Merely retributive punishment is ruled out. [69]

He criticised the presumption as operating as a barrier between the child and the availability of help or treatment - 'It saves the child not from prison, transportation, or the gallows, but from the probation officer, the foster-parent or the approved school.' [70]

The argument that the *doli incapax* presumption enables those most in need of help or control to escape it was also made by Laws J. in the Divisional Court, in *C v DPP*:

delinquents under the age of 14, who may know no better than to commit antisocial and sometimes dangerous crimes, should not be held immune from the criminal justice system, but sensibly managed within it. [71]

On this reasoning, children need the intervention of the criminal justice system so that they can be offered the appropriate treatment to put them on the right track. The problem with it is that such an attitude ignores the potential for stigmatisation in being caught up in the system, and the class- and race-based operation of the system, a concern which can be traced back to no less a role-model than Winston Churchill, cited by Rutherford: [72]

I am sure that the House [of Commons] will support me in any steps that may be taken to prevent this unnecessary imprisonment. It is an evil which falls only on the sons of the working classes. The sons of other classes may commit many of the same kind of offences and in boisterous and exuberant moments, whether at Oxford or anywhere else, may do things for which the working classes are committed to prison, although injury may not be inflicted on anyone.

Laws J. put forward a further reason for regarding the presumption as out-dated. He argued that the presumption stemmed from an age before there was compulsory education, and when children did not grow up as quickly as they do nowadays. [73] It was therefore, he implied, contrary to common sense to pretend that ten year olds in today's society did not know the difference between right and wrong. Yet Morris and Giller[74] suggest that, it was precisely those working-class children who 'grew up' quickly, by joining the labour force - and street life - at a young age, who were most perceived as a threat to order and needful of intervention. Laws J.'s argument may therefore not reflect the historical reality.

Interestingly, a more overt, but still un-selfconscious, appeal to class arguments was also put forward by Laws J.:

> The rule is divisive and perverse: divisive, because it tends to attach criminal consequences to the acts of children coming from what used to be called good homes more readily than to the acts of others; perverse, because it tends to absolve from criminal responsibility the very children most likely to commit criminal acts.[75]

In other words, the problem with the presumption is that those children from the most unsatisfactory families, with the worst upbringing, (i.e., those from the poorest classes, sometimes known these days as the 'underclass') will be most likely to be able to take advantage of its operation to avoid criminal sanctions. This objection reflects the long-held view that juvenile delinquency is due to parental shortcomings, especially of working-class parents. Lord Lowry, in the House of Lords, attempted a half-hearted rebuttal of the argument, suggesting that

> One answer ... (not entirely satisfying, I agree) is that the presumption contemplated the conviction and punishment of children who, possibly by virtue of their superior upbringing, bore moral responsibility for their actions and the exoneration of those who did not.[76]

But it could be argued that it is precisely those children who have proved unamenable to *good* parenting and social conditioning, whom society is most in need of dealing with; those who have never benefited from such upbringing can be dealt with outside the criminal justice sphere because, by definition, they lack the moral responsibility for their acts which is the hallmark of that sphere.

Other official references to the *doli incapax* presumption have been in the context of general reviews of the treatment of juvenile offenders. For example, the Ingleby Committee, in 1960,[77] would have abolished the presumption as a consequence of raising the age of criminal responsibility to 12 or eventually 14, with children under that age dealt with through care proceedings, whereby they would be entrusted to local authority social services departments just as abused or neglected children are. Government reluctance to be so bold led only to the raising of the age from eight to ten in the Children and Young Persons Act 1963. However, a bolder approach was taken with the enactment of the Children and Young Persons Act 1969, which permitted (and encouraged) a court to make a care order in respect of a child found to have committed an offence.[78] The Act also contained provision for raising the age of criminal responsibility to fourteen, and abolishing the *doli incapax* presumption in consequence. These latter changes were not implemented due to the change of Government in 1970 noted above.

Although the Law Commission, in their draft criminal code[79] in 1985, stated that there was no case for survival of the presumption, they drew only on the criticisms of Glanville Williams who, as we have seen, was concerned to ensure that adequate treatment could be given to juvenile offenders, and who was not an adherent of a just deserts approach to crime. The reverse was the case; he argued that, since juvenile courts made findings of guilt, rather than convictions, they were not concerned with ascribing responsibility anyway, and '[i]t seems absurd that a child who indulges in a series of annoying peccadilloes can set the magistrates at defiance, for the reason that none of his acts is gravely wrong'.[80]

We know now that one of the most dangerous aspects of the welfare approach to juvenile offenders has been the loss of proportionality and fairness in treatment. The presumption can be seen as a vital safeguard in limiting the possibility of the child being at the mercy of a relentless system which is going to 'treat' him or her regardless. Thus, contrary to the views of the reformists such as Glanville Williams, the presumption appears to be justifiable even if we retain a commitment to a reform/welfare approach. It is certainly still necessary if we embrace a just deserts philosophy. The Conservative Government, in 1990, recognised this. In the White Paper, *Crime, Justice and Protecting the Public*,[81] it sought a balance between imposing responsibility upon the parents, for failing to bring up the child properly, and upon the child as he or she reaches an age at which responsibility ought to be imposed.

> The criminal law is based on the principle that people understand the difference between right and wrong. Very young children cannot easily tell this difference, and the law takes account of this ... these arrangements [the presumption] make proper allowance for the fact that children's understanding, knowledge and ability to reason are still developing.[82]

By contrast, the Labour Government elected in 1997 appears to have decided to remove the presumption because it 'flies in the face of common sense' to think that a child aged between 10 and 13 cannot differentiate between right and wrong.[83] Criticising the presumption as archaic, illogical and unfair in practice, they outlined two alternative reforms. First, they proposed outright abolition, which they favoured on the basis of simplicity and symbolic clarity. Alternatively, they mooted reversing the presumption and leaving it open to a child defendant to argue that they were *incapax*. However, they considered that this might simply lead to the defence being pleaded in every case, and 'the prosecution would once again be set the task of proving, beyond reasonable doubt, that the child knew the seriousness of his or her act'. This criticism seems to reflect an ignorance of the whole point of reversing the presumption, which is precisely to place the burden of proof on the defendant rather than the prosecution. It is clear that removal of the presumption is seen as part of the package of measures introduced to demonstrate the Government's determination to show that it is 'tough on crime', regardless of the substance of the arguments for or against.

Traditional Values

What traditional values could it be said that the *doli incapax* presumption serves either to uphold or to undermine? The European Committee on Crime Problems,[84] in tracing the change in approach to crime policy over the previous twenty years, characterised it as a move towards a 'traditional' model. They identified two principal characteristics of this traditional approach as being first, an emphasis on 'just deserts', i.e., where the punishment should be strictly proportional to the crime. They commented that this 'ignores the principle whereby the court makes the punishment fit the individual, having regard to the circumstances of the crime and the offender's personality.'[85] They defined the second characteristic as 'the principle of incapacitating or neutralising the offenders, that is to say simply parking them in a prison so that, at least while they are there, they will not be committing crimes'.[86] This 'traditional' model presumably dates back to the eighteenth century theories of Beccaria and the other 'classical' theorists, but David Garland has noted how difficult it is to determine what was 'traditional' thinking about crime, and how far attempts to classify different writers and theories as fitting within distinct 'schools' of thought are misleading.[87] Indeed, it might be thought that, in fact, the just deserts/due process model outlined is less 'traditional' than the welfare approach, since it is the latter which has dominated thinking (if not day to day practice) in the system dealing with juvenile offenders since the turn of the century. So we cannot be confident that the Committee, in their review of European developments, correctly identified what is really the 'traditional'.

Andrew Bainham[88] has drawn attention to the problem of identifying any shared values at all in a diverse society such as Britain. It is even harder to identify *traditional* values, in a society where only a minority of the population practise the nominal State religion (Anglican Christianity); where increasingly, there is no overwhelming norm of family structure; and where there is acrimonious debate over how children should be educated. Bainham was writing in the context of discussing the government's ill-fated attempt to start a moral crusade called 'Back to Basics' in 1994 which exhorted people to revert to so-called 'traditional' family structures and practices - i.e., to raise children within marriage, to remain faithful to one's spouse, and to impose strong discipline on one's children. This picture drew upon a mythical stereotyped image of the 1950s, when most government ministers were growing up, and was contrasted with the permissive 60s which have been blamed by the government for the collapse of society.[89] The political portrayal of children and their 'proper' sphere within society is also mythological. Children's alleged lack of respect for their elders, their lack of obedience to authority, and their lack of concern for others, are bemoaned and contrasted with earlier times when the saying that 'children should be seen and not heard' guided adults' behaviour towards them. There is some truth in this view of the past, in so far as children were not recognised as having a legitimate voice to *be* heard. But such inaccurate nostalgia for the good old days is a feature of every epoch.[90] Perhaps this harking back to the past is itself a 'traditional' British value; it is certainly an enduring feature of British popular culture.

Modern views of children in Britain are confused, to say the least. On the one hand, children are seen as maturing earlier, due to the influence of compulsory education and, in particular, their exposure to all aspects of life as revealed by television and other mass media, especially video films. On the other hand, children are seen as increasingly unmanageable, unsusceptible to reasoning and beyond their parents' control. Interestingly, perhaps the one issue on which most parents and adults agree, is on the use of limited physical punishment of children as an acceptable form of discipline.[91] But the suggestion[92] that under-10 year-olds should be subjected to evening 'curfews' to prevent them causing mischief in their neighbourhoods reveals a profound fear of young children (we are talking about those who are, even under New Labour, irrebuttably presumed incapable of committing crimes!) and a bankruptcy of ideas on how to deal with them, which does not say much for what their apparent 'maturity' amounts to. And punishing children for their wrong-doing, while at the same time seeking to punish and control parents because of their failures of supervision, appears somewhat illogical. The reality for most children is more complicated than this. No more than 10 per cent of British children now go to school unaccompanied by an adult,[93] due to fears of abduction, and children may be the *victims* of violent crime at least as often as they are its perpetrators. Politicians might reflect upon their own childhoods when they probably had far more freedom to play with their peers and get up to mischief out of sight of adults, than is the case today. It could be argued that what children need, instead of further containment and punishment, is the possibility of behaving more like the popular hero of English children's literature, William Brown, who appeared in a series of books written in the 1920s to 1940s portraying a picture of middle-class children safely roaming their towns and streets in gangs which caused mischief rather than mayhem. Such freedom is increasingly inconceivable for today's children.

Conclusion

The issue of how to respond to juvenile offenders has long taxed policy-makers and law-enforcers. Since the turn of the nineteenth century, there has been a growth in the desire to reform such offenders, through 'treatment', 'education' or 'punishment', but a continuing uncertainty as to how to do this, and how to reconcile it with retribution. While the reality of what happened to the juvenile offenders (or neglected children) swept into the system of, first, reformatories and later approved schools and children's homes may have fallen very far short of what was claimed for these, the *intent* was reformative and rehabilitative. The current more punitive attitude to offenders, especially juveniles, in Britain, is a part of an attempt to establish, not re-establish, a golden age of moral responsibility.

  In the United States, cases involving children as young as six who may have killed even younger children, have received publicity and are apparently being dealt with through the criminal justice system.[94] Killing by children is, of course, very rare,[95] and cannot be used to make broad generalisations about juvenile offending. Similarly, the *doli incapax* presumption is merely a small facet of the wider picture concerning how the law responds to juvenile offenders. Both, however, mark out sharply that it is the issue of *responsibility* for one's acts which lies at the heart of a criminal *justice* system. The age at which a state determines that a child can be held responsible for a crime reflects its attitudes to children, and to offending. In a civilised society, it seems hard to explain how children as young as six or ten can be regarded as morally, and thus legally, responsible for their wrong-doing. The *doli incapax* presumption remains an important symbolic recognition of children's *immaturity*, of their need for, and right to, protection, which cannot safely be jettisoned until the age of criminal responsibility is substantially raised.

Notes

*   I am grateful to Leslie Sebba, and to my colleague Stewart Field, for their helpful comments on this paper.

1   Home Office, *Tackling Youth Crime* (1997) para. 1.

2   Paul Cavadino also argues against abolition of the presumption in 'Goodbye doli, must we leave you?' (1997) 9 *Child and Family Law Quarterly* 165.

3   Garland D, *Punishment and Modern Society: A Study in Social Theory* Clarendon Press, Oxford (1990).

4   Children and Young Persons Act 1933 s 50, as amended by the Children and Young Persons Act 1963 s 16.

5   Cavadino op. cit. p. 171 and also see (1995) NLJ 1771.

6   Op. cit. p. 207.

7   See Penal Affairs Consortium, *The Doctrine of Doli Incapax* London (1995).

8   There is no such presumption in Scottish law: Morris, A. and McIsaac, M., *Juvenile Justice?* (1978) p. 1.

9   Hale *The History of the Pleas of the Crown* Vol 1 (1736) 630.

10   (1984) 79 Cr App R 255.

11   *A v. DPP* [1992] Crim LR 34; *JBH & JH (Minors) v O'Connell* [1981] Crim LR 632.

12   Card, R., *Card, Cross and Jones Criminal Law* 13 ed (1995) para 9.2; Allen, M., *Textbook on Criminal Law* 3d ed, (1995) para 5.2.

13   See Hay, C., 'Mobilization through Interpellation: James Bulger, Juvenile Crime and the Construction of a Moral Panic' (1994) 4 *Social and Legal Studies* 197. For an analysis which departs from the 'moral panic' model, see King, M., *A Better World for Children: Explorations in Morality and Authority* Routledge, London (1997) Chapter 5.

14   Both main political parties have adopted a 'get tough on crime' stance and have sought to outdo each other in their proposals to tackle criminals. See, for example, the abolition of the suspect's right to silence under the Criminal Justice and Public Order Act 1994 Part III, ss 34-39 and attempts to introduce mandatory life sentences for repeat violent offenders by the Government, and proposals by the Labour Government to place children under 10 under 'curfew' at night: see Home Office, *Tackling Youth Crime* (1997).

15   *C v. DPP* [1994] 3 WLR 888, discussed by Ashworth, A, 'Abolishing the presumption of incapacity: C v. DPP' (1994) 6 *Journal of Child Law* 174.

16   Hay, above, at p. 200.

17   *C v. DPP* [1995] 2 WLR 383; Ashworth. A,, 'The presumption of incapacity restored - C v DPP' (1995) 7 *Child and Family Law Quarterly* 158.

18   Reported in *The Times* 25 September 1995.

19   See the speech by the Home Secretary, Jack Straw in Hansard, HC Debs, 19 May 1997 at col 390 and Home Office, *Tackling Youth Crime* (1997).

20   *Gillick v. W Norfolk and Wisbech Area Health Authority* [1986] AC 112.

21   Indeed, it can logically be argued that on this basis, the *doli incapax* presumption should apply to adults as well, since many of these show signs of lack of comprehending the implications of their acts. The courts have certainly proved willing to assume that adult women lack the necessary competence to veto medical treatment in pregnancy (see, for example, *Re S* [1993] Fam 123), so there is a precedent for extending the protection given to children, to adults as well.

22   Blackstone, *Blackstone's Commentaries on the Laws of England*, Book IV 1st ed (1769) pp. 23-24.

23   *Understanding Juvenile Justice* (1987) p. 6.

24   'The Criminal Responsibility of Children' [1954] *Criminal LR* 493.

25   At p. 494.

26   See Van Bueren, G., *The International Law on the Rights of the Child* Martinus Nijhoff, Dordrecht, (1995) Chap. 7 and 'Child-Oriented Justice - An International Challenge for Europe' (1992) *International Journal of Law and the Family* 381.

27   *The Rights and Wrongs of Children* (1983) Chap. 2.

28   The wording reflects that used in Article 14(4) of the International Covenant on Civil and Political Rights (1976): 'In the case of juvenile persons, the [criminal justice] procedure shall be such as will take account of their age, and the desirability of promoting their rehabilitation.'

29   Van Bueren op. cit. at p. 173.

30   Eekelaar, J., 'The Emergence of Children's Rights' (1986) *Oxford Journal of Legal Studies* 161 at p. 182.

31 Lemert, E., *Instead of Court: Diversion in Juvenile Justice* National Institute of Mental Health, Maryland (1971). See also Audit Commission, *Misspent Youth: Young People and Crime* (1996).

32 Graham, J. and Bowling, B., *Young People and Crime* Home Office Research Study 145, London (1996).

33 Discussed fully by Van Bueren loc cit.

34 Morris, A. and Giller, H., *Understanding Juvenile Justice*, Croom Helm, London (1987) Chap. 1.

35 Foucault, M., *Discipline and Punish* Allen Lane, London (1977), Donzelot, J., *The Policing of Families* Hutchinson, London (1979).

36 See Goldstein, S., Chap. 8 above, and Hamilton, C., *Family, Law and Religion* Sweet & Maxwell, London (1995) Chaps. 7,8.

37 Pinchbeck, I. and Hewitt, M., *Children in English Society* Vol 1 Routledge and Kegan Paul London (1969) p. 95.

38 They are now called youth courts: Criminal Justice Act 1991 s. 70.

39 The history of penal measures for juveniles is traced extensively by Morris and Giller op. cit., and, in a more recent review, by Rutherford, A., *Growing out of Crime: The New Era* Waterside Press, Winchester (1992) Chap. 3; Gelsthorpe, L. and Morris, A., 'Juvenile Justice 1945-1992' in Maguire, M. et al (eds) *The Oxford Handbook of Criminology* Clarendon Press, Oxford (1994).

40 Scepticism as to the extent to which 'reform' as opposed to punishment actually went on under a treatment approach was expressed as early as the 1890s by the then head of the Home Office, Sir Godfrey Lushington: See Rutherford op. cit. pp. 44-50.

41 *Report of the Departmental Committee on the Treatment of Young Offenders*, (1927) Cmd 2831 HMSO, London.

42 Op. cit. at pp. 71-72.

43 Introduced by the Children and Young Persons Act 1933 s. 44. It may be noted how this provision associates welfare with removal from an unsuitable home, and with provision of education.

44 387 US 1(1967).

45 Morris and Giller op. cit. Chap. 4

46 Morris and Giller ibid.

47 For discussion and a diagrammatic portrayal of the changing ideologies affecting the American juvenile court system, see Mahoney, A.R., *Juvenile Justice in Context* Northeastern UP, Boston (1987) Chap 2. and Figure 2.1.

48 See Bainham, A. with Cretney, S.M., *Children: The Modern Law* Family Law, Bristol (1993) at p. 29.

49 Slapper, G., 'Stepping behind the family' [1997] NLJ 11; Audit Commission op. cit.; Labour Government proposals to allow courts to make 'parenting orders': Home Office, *Tackling Youth Crime* (1997).

50 Most notably through a supposedly revamped 'short sharp shock' administered in a detention centre: Criminal Justice Act 1982 .

51   *Criminal Statistics England and Wales 1994* (1995) Cm 3010 Home Office, para. 7.15. But the Government's determination to appear firm on crime led to a revision of the policy on cautioning in 1994 which appeared to lead to an immediate increase to 2,900 offenders sentenced in that year. See Morrison Chap. 16 below.

52   Ibid. Table 7.6.

53   Ibid. Table 7.21.

54   But it may be noted, in the case referred to in the next paragraph, that the judge, in sentencing the juvenile, said 'You may not have understood everything that has gone on here, but you do understand that there are now a lot of people taking a very serious interest in you, because of this very serious thing that has happened'. *The Guardian* 14 June, 1996.

55   Braithwaite, J., *Crime, Shame and Reintegration* Cambridge University Press, Cambridge (1989).

56   Although it should be noted that the majority are in fact offences 'triable either way', i.e., can also be tried by the magistrates if the defendant so wishes and the prosecution does not object.

57   See Bandali, S., 'Tariffs and Children Who Murder' *Childright* June 1996, 19 at p. 20.

58   The difficulty of identifying and dealing with such children was emphasised in a study of 531 repeat offenders between 1992 and 1994. No consistently reliable indicator was found to identify them as likely repeaters, and half were already known to social services: Hagell A and Newburn T, *Persistent Young Offenders* Policy Studies Institute, London (1994).

59   Bandali op.cit.

60   *R v. Secretary of State for the Home Department ex parte Venables and Thompson* [1997] 3 All ER 97 (HL).

61   See note 53 above.

62   Though King, op. cit., argues that justice and welfare cannot be 'balanced' since they are concepts deriving from different social systems - law on the one hand, and 'science' on the other.

63   'Juvenile Justice Policy: Mapping the Criteria' in Freeman, M. and Veerman, P. (eds) *The Ideologies of Children's Rights* (1992).

64   Recommendation R (87) 20.

65   At p. 39.

66   Van Bueren, op. cit. at p. 183.

67   At p. 21.

68   Parliament did so in the Children and Young Persons Act 1933.

69   At p. 495.

70   Ibid.

71   At p. 896A.

72   Op. cit. p. 39. And see Morris and McIsaac op. cit. Chap. III.

73   At p. 894F. The Government echoed this argument in *Tackling Youth Crime* (1997) para. 8.

74   Op. cit. pp. 20-22.

75   At p. 895H.

76   At p. 399D.

77   *Report of the Committee on Children and Young Persons* (1960) Cmnd 1191 HMSO, London.

78   As we have seen above, magistrates dealing with child offenders proved reluctant to make use of this measure and preferred more overtly punitive responses.

79   Law Commission No 143 *Criminal Law: Codification of the Criminal Law: A Report to the Law Commission* (1985) HMSO, London.

80   At p. 496.

81   Home Office (1990), Cm 965 HMSO, London.

82   Paras. 8.3,8.4.

83   *Tackling Youth Crime* para. 3, and see paras. 3-18.

84   Above.

85   p. 24.

86   Ibid.

87   Garland, D., 'Of Crimes and Criminals: The Development of Criminology in Britain' in Maguire, M. et al (eds) *The Oxford Handbook of Criminology*, Clarendon Press, Oxford (1994).

88   'Family Law in a Pluralistic Society: The View from England and Wales' in Lowe, N.V. and Douglas, G. (eds) *Families across Frontiers* Martinus Nijhoff, The Hague (1996).

89   The Conservative Party Annual Conference is the usual platform for the announcement of such ideas and was used in the autumn of 1994 and 1995 for this purpose.

90   See Pearson, G., *Hooligan: A History of Respectable Fears* Macmillan, London (1983).

91   See, for example, Law Commission, *Criminal Law: Consent in the Criminal Law: A Consultation Paper No 139* (1995) London HMSO paras. 11.13-11.20.

92   See Home Office, *Tackling Youth Crime* (1997).

93   *The Times* 26 June 1996.

94   See eg *The Guardian* 30 April 1996.

95   See Abu-El-Haj T, 'Children and Homicide: A New JUSTICE Report' *Childright* April 1996 15.

16 Traditional Values, Children's Rights and Social Justice: English Youth Justice in the 1990s

WAYNE MORRISON

Introduction: A Hostile Relationship?

Children and youth provide practical and theoretical problems for the liberalist criminal jurisprudence of western modernity. Hobbes[1] founded modern political liberalism upon three sources: (i) the ethics of self-assertion; (ii) an agreement that the political and legal institutions of civil society must be legitimated by secular rational discourses concerning the human condition and not traditional values; (iii) the acknowledgment that 'modern' institutions and societies were artefacts, products of the social and cultural energies of humans, and not a reflection of any 'natural law or design' independent of human volition and logical analysis.

In modernity individuals relate to others and their environment as means to their self-advancement. The environment becomes a site for mastery and control - resources must be determined and exploited, opportunities seized. Similarly modern individuals must learn to appraise themselves, come to understand their position and emotions, to control their desires and impulses; but first they must be created. Modern societies need modern subjects. Whilst, in the pre-modern condition, an 'autonomous individual may be conceived of only as an excess, a surplus, an uncontrolled effluent of the discourse of control; he is, one may say, an 'unfinished business' of the ordering scheme'[2], through a process of dis-association and disembeddment modernity creates the 'autonomous individual'. Autonomy, however, is always social and cultural. One of the concepts that enables the reassociation of the 'modern' person/individual within a diverse set of social formations is that of rights. Rights are a specifically 'modern' judicial technology furthering the process whereby tradition is replaced by reason, and a social life according to roles and expectations - as laid out by the body of duties under various ideas of 'natural law' - is rejected in favour of an individualist social space made possible by the possession of legal, cultural and social rights. Rights replace traditional values. The process, however, is not straightforward. Whilst modernity is flux and mobility, it is also disparate attempts to create stable social structures, structures which require the forms of social bonding traditional values allow to hide their contingency, to prevent their continual deconstruction. Modernity is paradoxical. In that it reflexively understands itself to be an artefact, a contingency, it dooms its human inhabitants to a process of continual dissatisfaction and existential doubt. The mere possession of rights does not guarantee happiness or an existentially satisfying life: quite the converse. The search for the just society is conducted with the knowledge that no such stable social order can be constructed. All answers to the question 'what is social justice?' are open to reflexive self-doubting.

What then is the position of justice discourse in contemporary conditions? On one hand it appears easy to claim that we have tired of the idea of social justice; control of the allocation and distribution of rewards and identities has increasingly been handed to the market. But on the other hand, the appeal to the transcendental yet particular idea of human rights - an idea we reflexively know is founded only in procedure and rhetoric but has resulted in tremendous practical consequences - may have taken over from taking sides in the clash of competing epistemologies. The battle between the two grand narratives of social structure in middle modernity - that between liberal-capitalism and organised socialism - having been resolved in favour of capitalism, the universality of the human rights idea offers itself as a transcendental signifier above the specificity of any particular national jurisdiction with its local traditions and interpretations. The development of a children's rights discourse and movement, and the arrival of children's rights into various national jurisdictions in relevant statues (for example, in England and Wales in the Children Act 1989), is indicative of the need for some criteria which will provide a standard of just procedure and aid in legitimation in the context of a late-modernity where multiple perspectives reign.

Market Eligibility: The Criteria of Late-Modern Social Justice?

How do we describe our position as we approach the end of the twentieth century? Are we in the midst of a radically new set of social transformations and processes - the advent of post-modernity? Or do we witness the intensification of the process of modernity moving us into a hyper- or late-modernity?[3] What are the consequences for our networks of social control?

Juvenile justice systems were born in the height of industrialisation and have operated as a social control network - officially of last resort - situated beneath the 'failings' of the disciplinary mechanisms which positioned subjects into the roles and class-structured expectations of industrialised society. In recent decades, however, western societies have 'post-industrialised'. Relatively stable socio-economic life patterns based around Fordist production have given way to a complex situation where various 'service industries' and small-scale 'high-tech' production units which demand high skills and flexibility from their workers, co-exist with high levels of unemployment and the disappearance of traditional working class employment particularly for males. The past two decades have seen a widening income gap between the rich and poor. At the same time a mass consumer society inhabiting a globalised economy and rapidly changing communication networks has sprung up. Consumption power, rather than location in the structure of production has come to be a major ascriber of identity/class. The pace of social change has intensified and it is very difficult to tell coherent stories about the direction of social change or judge qualitatively the nature of our social institutions. In *Legislators and Interpreters*[4], Bauman suggests that while modernity tried to construct a thoroughly rationalised society, we inhabit its failure. What then is the status of our knowledge and the knowledge seeking professions? If early modernity asked for intellectuals to act as legislators, and middle modernity demanded knowledge for bureaucracy, the contemporary demand is for knowledge as technology; the authorities are no longer looking for the counsel of intellectuals and philosophers to build the just society. There are philosophers desperately trying to offer the discourses necessary to construct communities and argue for an ethical social life, but the market appears as the dominant criterion for ascribing values. The result is a new dialectic of social control. On the one side we have *those who are tuned into the market who become seduced by its items and messages*; a group of people who are now effectively and efficiently integrated through a new cluster of mechanisms of public relations, advertising, growing needs, institutional and individual bargaining.[5] Opposed to these, Bauman suggests, are the new poor who are not really consumers since their consumption does not matter much for the successful reproduction of the capital (they often consume low quality produce). They are not the core members of the consumer society and are not keyed into its institutions. The market provides the acid test of eligibility for membership of the late-modern consumer society. The market appears thoroughly democratic - it ranks people according to ability (IQ, for example) - and it reaches out to anyone who would listen, and everybody is encouraged to listen or forced to hear. Which implies that potentially, everybody is encouraged to listen or forced to hear and potentially, everybody is seduced or seducible. The democracy of the market, however, is that of the Ritz hotel; all a person needs is good dress sense and/or money to enter. But many have neither. Thus contrasted to those tuned into the market, we have *those who have to be disciplined by the combined action of repression, policing, authority and normative regulation*. Bauman suggests they are not part of the 'cultural game', even 'if, stupidly, they think otherwise', but this is the point: they do think so. While the second group - those without resources to play successfully the games of the market, at least by the rules - are excluded, the pressure to play the multiplicity of games is intense.

But can satisfaction be achieved? The burden falls most on those with least resources: the concept of the underclass has arrived.[6] The underclass may feel the burden of performance but experience failed attempts at success and live daily humiliations the most; moreover they are the subject of the most severe labelling processes. Nothing can be allowed to cast doubt upon the validity of the market; hence failure must be defined as the result of either the constitution, the inadequate socialisation, or the sub-culture of those who do not succeed.

We are told that we are all members of consumer society, yet we are not equally located structurally. This is a more complicated set of messages and social strains than Robert Merton envisaged in his classical writings on anomie, and difficult to feel secure within. Moving to the consumerist dance, many young people soon discover that the goods they covet, although attractive to everybody, bring happiness only to some; many individuals know they are not among those 'some'. The consumer society creates a circle of desire and the need to possess a commodity; but gaining the commodity does not cause satisfaction - a continuous process of desire, consumption and dissatisfaction is set in motion in which the game itself is the only reward, offering as it does the ever renewed hope of winning. But to reap this kind of a reward, one must be able to go on playing without end, so that hope is never allowed to die and defeat always means losing a battle, not the war. Once you stop playing, the hope disappears, and you know that you have lost, and that there will be no next stage at which you win. But many young people living in England know full well that the game is loaded against them; many understand that there is little reason for them to keep any mythical social contract since there is little chance of their legitimately enjoying a full range of consumer goods. How then can a coherent operational justice be constructed which could legitimate the juvenile/youth justice system?

The Dilemma of Contemporary Juvenile/Youth Justice Practice[7]

> We know the families of virtually every juvenile who comes before us. Their families' lives are throughout the files of social services - families at risk, clients, dependants - the different terminologies don't really matter; the fact is that certain families can be seen as our client base. We know the social reality. There is no secret. (Head of a Social Services Youth Justice Section, 1993)

> Justice? We [i.e. the youth justice teams] are the only real justice they are getting. All we can do is prevent further injustice. (A Team Leader, 1993)

> We do not support the system; we keep the system from the kids. (A Team Leader, 1993)

In the 1980s much of the rhetoric of British penal policy was structured by the politicisation of law and order which had become apparent in the 1979 general election. Practice, however, contained a more complicated set of ebbs and flows. Although certain voices openly espoused harsh treatment for young offenders - epitomised by the debacle over the 'short sharp shock' of detention centres - juvenile justice professionals were also encouraged to increase cautioning and develop alternatives to incarceration. As a response juvenile justice professionals created a separate working definition of social justice somewhat at odds, but accommodated with, government bureaucracy. This approach was to radically reduce the use of custody and - clearly under the influence of labelling theory - change the operational ethos of grass roots juvenile justice from a vaguely rehabilitative approach to one of protecting the young person's rights[8], defending the young person against the system, and relying upon 'natural' processes of maturation to result in the young person growing out of crime.[9] The 1980s witnessed a quite dramatic although rather unnoticed transformation in juvenile justice. At the international level there was growing recognition of the rights of the child, and, as one author put it: 'international law is beginning to reject the unfettered discretion on authorities to rehabilitate children in their best interests and to involve children at the earliest of stages in the reintegration into society'.[10] Academic writing on juvenile justice became more critical and attempted to escape from wiggish readings of progressive civilisation; it was rather seen more as an arena of many conflicting pressures, philosophies and political contingencies. Commentators described juvenile justice as an arena of activity without any secure criteria of performance and thus legitimation. In the leading work on juvenile justice in England for the 1980s, Morris and Giller argued that expecting too much out of the juvenile justice system blinds us to the fact that it is only called into play when other institutions of social control and socialisation, such as the family, schools and employment, fail.

> Systems of juvenile justice cannot resolve such difficulties. Remedies lie within other social policy areas and demand a political will (and financial commitment) to change the life opportunities of the young. But different forms of juvenile justice systems expose rather than conceal these pressures on the young. A different kind of political exercise from the rhetoric of 'law and order' is now necessary: an evaluation of the role of juveniles in society. Juvenile justice policy and practice in England has yet to address this.[11]

But whereas juvenile justice policy and official rhetoric may not have addressed this, certain elements of practice changed as a result of the implicit recognition of grass roots professionals of these very concerns and the leeway allowed these practitioners by the decline of rehabilitation, the mistrust of welfare ideologies to serve the child's best interests (hence the decline of care orders), and the desire by government to lower costs and divert the less serious offenders from custody.[12] As a result the 1980s saw the development of an approach which came to be labelled a *systems management* approach based around a multi-agency interaction by social services, probation, the voluntary services, the police and crown prosecution service to lower the amount of individuals processed into the most intensive parts of the juvenile justice network.

The systems management approach had several features, two of which are: (i) the encouragement of a multi-agency approach to young peoples offending; and (ii) an active campaign by a range of professionals - and the remainder of this chapter will concentrate upon local authority social services juvenile/youth justice teams - to prevent young people's deeper involvement with the justice system as much as possible.

Several factors contributed to its set up:

1. The influence of labelling theory with its lesson that the intervention of social services and other welfare agencies, as much as that of the punitive arm of justice, could have harmful unintended consequences for juvenile offenders. Formal intervention should therefore be avoided as much as possible and the intrusiveness of intervention kept to a minimum. The rise of the 'back to justice' or 'rights' movement contributed by providing the criteria that no intervention greater than the seriousness of the offence should be permitted.

2. The overwhelming conclusion that custodial and institutional measures were especially damaging to young people and should be avoided as much as possible.

3. A movement towards community-based schemes which aimed to strengthen and support juveniles' links with the home, school and the workplace; these schemes were also thought to provide effective ways of dealing with serious and persistent offenders. Such schemes should, however, contain proper levels of supervision. Moreover, it was increasingly felt that responses to juvenile delinquency should be locally focused with a series of community-based schemes run by local authority social services departments. Two further conceptions grew out of this:

4. The way in which juvenile offenders are dealt with depends on a series of decisions made by the agencies which comprise the local juvenile/youth justice system. Developing new methodologies can be achieved by influencing these decisions at key points in the process.

5. The collection of information about what happens to juveniles/youth in the local system is necessary to identify where to intervene in order to produce the desired change. The impact of change needs to be continually monitored to allow any adjustments to be made in policy and practice.

We can summarise the systems model in the following principles:

minimum formal intervention in the life of the young person, commensurate with the seriousness of the offence;

diversion from crime, from prosecution and from care and custody;
the need to deal with offenders in the community;
the importance of collaboration at local level between all the agencies
involved in the juvenile justice system;
the importance of clear policy and procedures;
the value of sound, up-to-date information from a continuous, detailed
monitoring of the system;
the necessity for 'gate keeping' at every major point in the system.[13]

Such a model would have various important points of interaction
and opportunities for decision-making, for example: (i) the initial encounter
between Police and youth; (ii) the conduct of interviews and the grounds for
holding the young person; (iii) deciding on prosecution or cautioning; (iv)
working out an appropriate sentence or disposition; and (v) the conduct of
that sentence[14]

The most dramatic change in policy was the widespread adoption
of cautioning used by the police as an alternative to charging a young
person with an offence. Whether or not the police give a caution is, at the
end of the day, up to them. Normally, however, three formal criteria must
be met before the police will administer a caution. These were laid out in
Home Office circular 14/1985[15] as:

(a) The evidence available must be enough to prosecute the young person;
   cautioning should not be used as a substitute for a weak prosecution
   case;
(b) The young person must admit the offence, moreover, he must not only
   admit the facts which constitute the offence, he must recognise his guilt.
   If there is no such admission in circumstances in which otherwise there
   would have been a caution, the proper course is to take no further
   action;
(c) The parents or guardian agree to the caution being administered, but
   parental consent should only be sought after it has been decided to
   caution.

In the changed climate the views of the victim, which had earlier
been a major factor in the decision to charge, were still seen as important
but not paramount.

If neither one of these conditions was fulfilled, then a caution was
not used - the options are then to prosecute (if the evidence is strong
enough) or drop the matter. Even if all these conditions were met the police

could still prosecute. Practice varied from police authority to authority. In many areas the decision was usually referred to a Juvenile Bureau who made further enquiries about the young person's background.[16] They may visit the young person's parents, or make enquiries with the social services or education department before recommending a caution or charge.[17] In general, the policy of increasing cautioning was regarded as a success.[18]

The Aims of Juvenile/Youth Justice Teams and Interaction with Other Agencies

The rise of cautioning was linked to encouraging inter-agency discussion and co-operation as was the desire from the Children and Young Persons Act 1969 onwards to replace institutional-based programmes with community-based programmes, particularly Intermediate Treatment, the responsibility for which rested with local authority social service juvenile justice teams. Local authority social services departments came to run juvenile justice teams which both represent the social services department in courts where juveniles appear and provide an Intermediate Treatment service for juvenile offenders within each authority. The policy of such teams is clearly influenced by labelling theory[19], as one authority's Introduction to its team stated:

> **The policy of the team** is based on the wealth of research that indicates that the peak age of offending is 16 years. All recent Home Office papers acknowledge that this offending period can be negatively influenced by the experience of court or custody. We therefore at present have a policy of focusing on that minority of young people most 'at risk' of re-offending, with a view to increasing their self-reliance and respect for others, through gaining a greater understanding of those factors that have influenced their decision to offend and the effects that such decisions have both on themselves and on their victims and families.
>
> **The aims of the team** are to:
> (a) Safeguard the rights of the young person involved in the criminal justice system.
> (b) Encourage and develop constructive responses to juvenile offending in the community.
> (c) Reduce the use of care and custodial institutions for juvenile offenders.
> (d) Develop programmes that:
>   can be offered to the court and young people as realistic alternatives to custody and care;

restrict the liberty of young offenders whilst allowing them to remain in the community;

place emphasis on encouraging the young people to examine the issues relating to offending behaviour and its consequences;

attempt to break patterns of offending behaviour and thereby reduce the possibility of further involvement in crime;

provide and introduce constructive leisure pursuits;

give support and guidance concerning home, school, employment, racism, drug abuse, personal problems etc.;

put the council's equal opportunities policy into practice.

As the mission statement of another local authority's youth justice section (1994) put it, the aim is: 'To provide high quality and comprehensive community services to young people aged 10 to 18 years to prevent their progression in the criminal justice and local authority looked after systems.' The same local authority's youth justice section had three teams with different areas of activity: (i) The youth justice duty and court team which provides 'crisis intervention, assessment and short term work for young people in the criminal justice system. Staff also service the X Youth Court'. The team members work with the police on appropriate adult roles, interact in the juvenile Bureaux on decisions to prosecute or caution, assess youths before court appearance, and work with colleagues to come up with schemes for suggestion to the court for effective supervision orders. (ii) The youth justice community services team, which provides social work supervision for young people aged 10 to 18 (i.e., the schemes which were once Intermediate Treatment) under the supervision order sanction of the juvenile/youth court. (iii) The youth justice community team, which provides social work intervention for young persons aged 10-18 'to avoid their progression within the criminal justice or the local authority looked after systems'.

The Home Office actively encouraged inter-agency work. For example circular 59/1990 structured the consultative process between the police and local authorities:

Participation by other agencies in the decision-making process can do much to improve the quality and consistency of cautioning decisions. It is the view of the Secretary of State that chief police officers may find it helpful to consult other agencies at two different levels:-

a. At the policy level, to discuss broad cautioning strategy and objectives, particularly in respect of young offenders, with local agencies including the Probation Service, the Social Services and the Crown Prosecution Service.

b. In the making of cautioning decisions 'chief officers should consider inviting juvenile liaison panels ... to review any case where the police are in doubt whether or not to caution a juvenile.

The 'Justice' of Operational Juvenile/Youth Justice in Late-Modernity

The difference between the working ideology of the juvenile justice teams and the then government policy was perhaps the difference between a humanitarian and rights-orientated management model and a bureaucratic managerial model. The working ideology of the juvenile/youth justice teams incorporated a pragmatically feasible, if defensive, 'operational justice'. This image of an operational justice is visible in the printed set of assumptions 'underpinning youth justice practice', which one social services department gave to all their staff and which were five in number:

1. Most youth crime is relatively minor.
2. Custody does not work.
3. The criminal justice system does not deal equitably with individuals.
4. A purely welfare orientation to young offenders may have unintended consequences.
5. Young people spontaneously desist.

As apparent from previous quotes, many team leaders held a somewhat cynical and realistic view of their role and the prospects for the youth they were called upon to deal with. They were clearly concerned about the development of a British underclass, although the term might not be used, which was providing the majority of their client base:

> While many of the kids [in the area] may get into trouble once or twice, and we have relatively little trouble with the police in deciding that cautions are used, with a[nother] group, we know that we are going to see them for years. (A Team Leader, 1993)

What makes this group so visible?

> Bad home conditions, overstretched schools that don't have the resources or the teachers with the time to devote to kids whose parents, if they have both, don't have the time or the inclination to devote

attention to them, and colour ... colour makes the system pick them out. (A Youth Section Head, 1993)

While teachers may wash their hands of troublesome pupils, the police may be even more unjust:

> As for the police ... well I don't have any problems with 'Y' [the Community Police Officer]. He is a reasonable and sincere individual ... but he's not the officer on the beat. Many of the officers on the beat continually pick on the black youngsters. And the vans! The guys [in the vans] are bored most of the time ... sitting and driving around waiting for something to happen. They stop some black kids and wind them up. Wait for the kids to crack, start swearing or spitting at them ... and they can't stand the kissing [black young males pretending to kiss the police officers]. That really gets them ... then all hell breaks loose. If they want to pull them in they find a way. (A Youth Section Head, 1993)

But if police boredom is a cause of unjust harassment, the aimlessness and boredom of the youth's lives lead them into creating situations which call for police reaction.

> Some of the kids set fires to the rubbish bins of the estates, this gets the Fire Brigade called out. Lots of flashing lights and sirens sounding. Then they taunt the officers. A good lark is to steal a motor [car] race it around the estate until the police van arrives, then scatter ... watch the police chasing. The police get mixed up with who they think was in the car and those who were only watching. Kids are yelling at them from all directions. They [the police] want to grab somebody but know they can't make anything stick. The kids have them [frustrated] most of the time. (A Youth Section Head, 1993)

How holistic ought the team members' awareness of social justice be? At what point would asking questions as to the justice of contemporary society necessitate recourse to prozac and the gin bottle to simply get through the day?

> We're left with the crap that failed social institutions have created. Some of the time I think we are refuse cleaners ... as long as we keep the failings of the society becoming too visible everything can go on as usual. (A Youth Section Head, 1993)

> Often these kids have entered into our files as children in need of care and protection - as the phrase used to have it. In the conditions they're grown up in ... they've been on the receiving end of loads of trouble ... now they are going to give trouble ... (Youth Team Member, 1993)

If philosophical liberalism works on the assumption of equality before the law, team members know that 'there ain't no level playing fields round here' (Team Member, 1993). Differential access to social, intellectual, and economic resources means that young people differentially possess the skills necessary to negotiate the life games of late modernity.[20] In a social order where dominant messages are of success, self-motivation and control of one's life, many young people are anything but in control of their situation or their 'selves'.[21] What ideology can legitimate rehabilitation in the conditions of an emerging post-modernity? It is difficult to see how rehabilitation - as traditionally conceived - could retain legitimation. Whereas the discourses of positivist criminology (broadly conceived) could create a new or modernist traditional value for the system in notions of welfare and rehabilitation, this can no longer be believed in. How could it, since its practical reality was to reinforce the processes of accepting one's place in the patterned division of labour, and that pattern of stratification - the modern division of labour - can no longer be accepted as 'natural'. Whereas even Durkheim appeared to postulate that people would find their natural place in the stratified division of labour, which could be presented as corresponding to functional lines, the Youth Justice Team members know too much about the reality of everyday life to believe in any channelling of life chances through natural or inevitable functional lines. Contingency - the mere accidental fact of one's birth as black or white, as wealthy or poor - replaces the functionality of modernity.

> The kids, all of them know there is no reason why they should not enjoy the things and the life style they see others, even if only on the TV, enjoy. And I can't tell them that I can't enjoy things without working hard, because, if the truth is told, I also feel that there is no real reason why I should have to struggle so hard while some others get it easy. But if I tell them: 'that's simply the way of this world. You have to put up with it and work hard', then I have no answer if they come back and say, 'you're just a coward. We are not playing that game'. For why should they? You tell me ... why should they? They know their position ... it's bad. There is no good future for many of them. (Team Leader, 1993)

So what can the team members do? How is it possible to act justly knowing these 'social realities'? Two concerns were apparent:
(i) The system must be prevented from creating future criminals out of the youngsters:

> What are we doing? Preventing the system creating more injustice. Preventing more of the labelling process. Trying to stop the creation of criminals out of the kids we have to deal with. ... Trying to treat them decently and honestly ... (Youth Section Head, 1993)

The hope is that 'if we prevent the system messing them up, then they will grow out of it'[22]
(ii) Some positive image of intention must be created. While rehabilitation - in the sense of disciplining the young person into a fit entity for a settled social structure - cannot be believed in, helping the youngster realise his position and better articulate the feelings and emotions he experiences is perceived as useful.

> Our supervision programmes aren't an easy ride. Confronting the youngsters' patterns of behaviour, attitudes and views on what is possible is hard. And frustrating ... you have to be an optimist to survive long in this job. (Team Leader, 1993)

One principle underlying practice can be termed *the principle of methodological optimism*. There are no grand illusions. Team members work within a context which is one of conflicting and complex demands and social pressures on themselves and the youth they deal with. They realise it is difficult to judge the 'justice' of the situation. Team members strive for damage limitation and small gains in the youth's self-esteem and increases in their confidence and ability to articulate their needs and realise the consequences of offending. Put another way, the concern of the juvenile/youth justice team leaders is to act justly in conditions where they realise that no pure justice is possible. Working within this understanding practice is subject to various tensions, among them:

1. The fact that their interaction with the youngster takes place because of intervention by the youth justice system

Thus the young person, even if he/she has officially agreed to the programme, perceives it as 'forced'. There is an inevitable tension between the operation of a penal sentence or 'diversion', and the opportunity for critical analysis of the young person's self-identity and views of the world. The team members are committed to developing programmes which are progressive for the young person. The youth justice team members realise that their supervision and contact is seen by the young person as an imposition, the youth is forced to engage in something imposed upon him/her, but it also provides the situation for a process wherein the young person may be encouraged to better understand his/her position. Juvenile justice officers recognise the illegitimacy of the demand for punishment mandated by a legal justice which claims the philosophical equality of the rule of law when it operates in a socially unequal terrain, but recognise also the impossibility of rehabilitation as a legitimating criterion. Instead the target is greater self-awareness and self-control on the part of the young person.

Note: there is little support for the claim that supervision, or other measures for that matter, can stop offending but the interactional process can be a positive influence in terms of aiding problem solving and identification of problems, as well as providing some practical care and support. The team members, however, face a tension in their own self-images.

2. Are team members agents of coercive discipline or facilitators of a process of growing self-awareness and self-expression by the youth?

As one team member put it:

> I've read my Foucault. I don't want to be an agent of some super discipline. But without discipline nothing is possible today. What I'm trying to get across is that without self-discipline you [the young person] are nothing .... Powerless ... you are getting pushed around by all the contingent forces these guys are located in. (Team Member, 1993)

Coercive discipline, which has traditionally been at the end of toughness, punishment and confrontation in the supervisory process of juvenile justice in modernity, is seen as something to be avoided. However, the issues of exploring the self, and raising self-esteem, are engaged in an official environment, and under the overall guidance of a Home Secretary who believes in 'punishment first'.

> ... a lot of the practical projects have to do with encouraging the self to explore, to achieve little things and [get the young persons to] feel

> better about themselves. But the feeling persists that what the young
> men need is jobs - they need to earn their own living and feel valued
> through work and participation. But that's simply not available for
> many of them ... won't be in the future. (Team Leader, 1993)

Thus a pessimism always threatens to break through the principle of
methodological optimism the youth justice teams operate with. It is at this
stage that adherence to a rights perspective is helpful. There are two further
dilemmas which rights help to alienate.

3. The dilemma of handling multiple expectations

Juvenile/youth justice is the site of various interactions. The team member
is subjected to feelings of negativism, opposition and despair transferred by
the youth, while he/she must maintain the confidence of the interacting
parties - namely, the police, education officers and the youth courts - while
he/she is subjected to the demands of the outside bodies - local authorities,
the Home Office, representatives of 'community'.[23] Rights aid in that they
provide a stable reference point; for example all parties - the police, the
young person and the team member - can use the idea of rights in the
conduct of the 'appropriate adult' role in interviews to position the various
persons in the process.

4. The dilemma of communication in the performance of a penally-related role: preaching to the offender or educating him/her in the reality of being a rights-bearing person?

One of the neglected features of the tradition of rehabilitation has been the
ethics of communication. To avoid being cast as coercive discipline from
the outside, those who believed in rehabilitation implicitly assumed the
reality of a communication process, but this was mostly a facade.[24] Much
of traditional rehabilitation consisted of the therapist or counsellor trying to
get the offender/client to see 'social reality' and his/her position in it as the
therapist did. It was a top-down process, but the suspicion was always
there: what if the client/offender inhabits another social reality to the
therapist? Team members realise this:

> You can't just lecture them ... that gets nowhere. And it's so difficult to
> get them to talk ... I mean really talk ... they soon realise what you
> would like them to say and there's always the danger that they'll simply
> say those things. You have to treat them firmly but decently. Treat them

> according to their rights and ask to be treated likewise. That's the only
> framework. (Team Leader, 1993)

Rehabilitation conjured up a metaphysics of totality which cannot be believed today - to what is one to be rehabilitated in today's metaphysics of pluralist differentiation? Into what can one be reinserted and made a part of, if it no longer makes sense to talk of 'society' or the 'social structure' and instead we acknowledge the immediate locality as 'fragmented (non)communities in globalising processes'? Or if 'society' has become a complex set of processes, and if all attempts to reduce them to one master logic (such as capitalism) immediately become apparent as the choice of the analyst? Perhaps only the imaginary concept of a self in control of itself: the myth of a radical wholeness of a self which can create narratives of possession in the face of a multiplicity of disorientating and destabilising forces. To what narrative can the team members appeal if they realise they are in large part in different social worlds than the young people they are dealing with?

> I can sympathise with him, but I don't really know what it's like to
> grow up black in Tottenham, living in that street, coming from that
> family. If I pretend to I am insincere. (Team Leader, 1993)

What then can provide a foundation for meaningful interaction? Perhaps bridges could be built through the concept of decent treatment and the idea of encouraging self-respect and self-esteem:

> Well I don't know ... I'm not a trained psychologist ... but I suspect
> many of these youngsters have no meaningful sense of worth or self-
> respect. They are so used to being pushed about, that whatever else
> happens it's just added on ....
>
> The trouble with X is that he has no sense of self ... (Team Member,
> 1993)

What of the youngster's accounts? One can only hint at the existential world of the youth - talking about it on intensive supervision schemes turns the strange mixture of the mundane and the desperate need for excitement into a stale discourse. Humiliation, powerlessness and the search for trips, for moments of power are themes running through the youngsters' accounts. There is little firm data on this. Elsewhere I have argued - partly as a result of the conversation and interviews conducted with the youngsters on the schemes visited - that offending offers moments of power and transcendence of the powerless which runs through the routines of most of these youngsters' existence.[25] The conditions which intensify this pressure may be increasing.

The Collapse of Systems Management in the 1990s?

The 1980s may appear as a little known success story in the history of British Juvenile Justice. At the beginning of the 1990s the amount of recorded juvenile crime was half that of the late 1970s and the numbers receiving custodial orders was similarly lower. Changing demographical characteristics were only a partial explanation. The 'system' appeared to have made a significant impact. Were the 1990s then to be a time of congratulations and for the lessons gained to be spread to other parts of the Criminal Justice networks? It seemed not. A series of moral panics overtook events.

The principle of methodological optimism may also be misplaced. There are various reasons, some external to the system some reflecting changes in government policy.

1. Changing social stratifications

Talk of an underclass refers to real processes. A recent Home Office Research Study[26] argues that a significant portion of young people are not maturing in the way expected and are remaining outside the normal pattern of jobs and family. In the mid 1990s over 70 per cent of young persons aged between 16-17 arrested by the police are unemployed; 31 per cent of children born in the UK are born out of wedlock. What makes the development of an underclass so different from the previous poor of the Victorian society? The new factor which places the client group of juvenile justice in a unique position is that *production has largely become divorced from labour*. The economist Jeremy Rifkin entitled his latest book simply: *The End of Work*.[27] The underclass does not have property. The underclass does not even have the one thing that the old working class or the reserve army of labour had, namely, the fact that others needed them to exist to be exploited. There is no point in exploiting the underclass - except perhaps sexually (although virtual reality machines may soon remove even their need to exist for sexual exploitation) - as we do not need their labour. There simply is no need for them.

2. The fragile accommodation between government and grass roots personnel in juvenile justice came under intense strain by the mid 1990s

This was due to a variety of factors, not the least being the personality of the then current Home Secretary who pushed the politicisation of his department to new heights. The opposition Labour Shadow Home Secretary (who was to become Home Secretary following the Labour victory of 1997) followed suit. The perceived target was the 'persistent young offender(s)', for whom cautioning and other measures was believed to be encouragement to further offend.

3. The James Bulger murder

The moral panic surrounding the killing of 2 year old James Bulger by two 10 year old boys in February 1993 who had taken James from a crowed shopping mall recorded by closed circuit video cameras and took him more than two miles witnessed by more then 40 people who remembered the two boys forcing the child along before they killed him.[28] This incident added to the images of joyriders who seemed to taunt the police and demonstrate the impotence of the youth justice system.

Seizing the popular political way, the Home Secretary introduced through the Criminal Justice and Public Order Act 1994 the secure training order intended for 12 to 14 year olds. Those eligible will be young offenders who have been convicted of three or more imprisonable offences and who have reoffended during, or have been in breach of a supervision order. Juveniles sentenced to a secure training order will be detained in a new system of secure training centres. There will be five centres, each with 40 places. The maximum sentence will be two years, and the sentences will be determinate, with half spent in custody and half in the community under supervision. The centres will be built on Prison Service land, managed by private sector contractors and subject to statutory rules made by the Home Secretary. Overall costs of the order including supervision are expected to be in excess of £30 million a year.

4. The developing climate of penal harshness

This was reflected in a rise in the numbers of young people incarcerated. For example, the number of boys aged 15 and 16 remanded awaiting trial to prisons in England and Wales (the average number of 15 and 16 year old boys in prison on remand more than doubled in the 1990s to an average of around 145). At 31 December 1995, 30 15 year olds and 122 16 years olds were on remand; in the period October 1993 to September 1994 there were 1,478 admissions to prison custody of 15 or 16 year olds awaiting trial. On average these young people spent one and a half months (47 days) in prison. This increase runs directly counter to the stated intention of the government in the 1980s to phase out the remanding of juveniles to prison custody. Successive reports by various boards of visitors and HM Chief Inspector of Prisons highlighted the unacceptable conditions in which they were often held (there were reports of resisted regimes, widespread bullying and intimidation by older prisoners, as well as reports of self-harm, injury and suicides). The 1991 Criminal Justice Act abolished previous procedures and introduced new statutory criteria. The Act required consultation between the courts and the appropriate Local Authority about the use of conditions which could be attached to local authority accommodation. The Act contained provision for courts to remand 15 and 16 year olds of both sexes to local authority secure accommodation instead of a remand to prison custody. The Criminal Justice and Public Order Act 1994 extended the age range for secure remands to include 12-14 year olds.[29] By 1997 a large factor behind the rise in the total number (adult and young people) of persons incarcerated to record levels (over 61,000) was a dramatic rise in youth detention. The system seemed to ignore any optimistic lessons.

Conclusion: Operational Concepts of Social Justice for Juvenile Justice and the Ideology of Children's Rights

If one steps outside the illusions of liberal philosophy any easy assumption of the social justice of modernity and its institutions disappears. In the eyes of a revisionist perspective in which class forms a role, for example, the traditional aims of the juvenile justice system have been (i) to pacify the section of the working class which forms the 'dangerous classes'; (ii) to enable the conditions in which a discourse of delinquency can be formulated in which various pathologies are discussed which differentiate the objects of repressive control from the normal; (iii) to enable institutions of surveillance and control to function. Using the discourses associated with the social theory of post-modernism, the above functions are recognised but subsumed in a dialect of development in which liberty (autonomy) and discipline are intertwined. Thus only those who can exercise full self-control can hope to play the games of late- or post-modernity with any real chance of success. Modernity has been remarkably successful in creating large numbers of basic social units - persons/individuals - who can play legitimate games reasonably adequately; but many cannot. In large part they provide the material for the system of youth justice. Those who staff the system need the constant production of new 'traditional values' to enable them to survive; they also need images of operational social justice(s) to keep their humanity. This chapter has looked at the issues of traditional values, children's rights and social justice as the author has seen them operationalised in youth justice in England in the mid 1990s. In the process I have observed many grass roots professionals refused to play the labelling game, instead they relied upon a thesis of methodological optimism, confronting the young people with their behaviour while trying to help them to come to a better understanding of their position, but they also operated with an image where the system itself contributed to the very harms it was officially meant to remedy. Treating the young people involved as bearers of 'rights' was one way of striving for the participation of the youth in a legitimation of the process. In the situation of the late 1990s, if the pragmatically optimistic message of the 1980s appears to have been overlooked, the system will require a new set of values. Already there is some evidence that a new dialectic of optimism and pessimism may be beginning with some looking towards notions of 'restorative justice' as a way beyond impasse of the traditional values of welfare and punishment. Whatever dialectic will develop, the ideas of both the victims and the offenders as rights-bearing persons will undoubtedly serve as a continual point of reference in a world where the only 'traditional values' recognised by our social institutions are those useful to the system.

Notes

1   Hobbes, Thomas *Leviathan* [1651], Richard Tuck, (ed.) (1991) Cambridge: Cambridge University Press.
2   Baumann, Zygmunt *Intimations of Postmodernity*, Routledge, London 1992, xxvii.
3   Radical changes have occurred over the last 30 years. To describe these changes social theorists have coined various labels including the Media Society, the Society of the Spectacle, the Consumer Society, the Bureaucratic Society of Controlled Consumption, the Post-industrial Society and lately, and most fashionably, the description of post-

modernism. Certain key writers are responsible for this term, among them Jean Francois Lyotard, who, in a well known book, *The Post-modern Condition* (Manchester: Manchester University Press, 1984), coined the term post-modern to reflect changes in the level of science and technology, in particular the development of computers, mass communication and increasing emphasis upon language in social and cultural studies. Others have referred to the Post-Capitalist age and announced that we no longer need labour for successful production: machines, in particular computers have largely, or are in the process of doing so, made mass labour redundant. Thus we appear headed for a world which does not need large sections of its population.

4   Bauman, Zygmunt *Legislators and Interpreters: On modernity, post-modernity and intellectuals*, Oxford: Basil Blackwell, 1987.

5   Bauman (ibid) interprets the (overly optimistic) analysis of Pierre Bourdieu, as suggesting that in some considerable part: 'What ties individuals to society today is their activity as consumers, their life organised around consumption. Individuals do not need therefore, to be repressed in their natural drives and tendency to subordinate their behaviour to the pleasure principle; they do not need to be invigilated and policed. (This function has been taken over by the market - through making information technology the object of private consumption a "surveilling" society has been replaced, as Jacques Attali suggests, by an "auto-surveillance" society.) Individuals willing by submit to the prestige of advertising, and thus need no "legitimation" beliefs. Their conduct is made manageable, predictable and hence non-threatening, by a multiplicity of needs rather than a tightening of norms.'

6   See Morris, Lydia *Dangerous Classes, The Underclass and Social Citizenship*, London: Routledge, 1994; Morrison, Wayne *Theoretical Criminology: from modernity to post-modernism*, London: Cavendish, 1995: Chap. 16.

7   This section draws upon empirical work conducted in 1993 on the operation of Local Authority Social Services Juvenile Justice teams. Various teams were visited and officers and young people being supervised interviewed. That research was funded by a small grant from the Research Fund of the External Programme in Law of the University of London, administered by the Institute of Advanced Legal Studies London. All quotes are taken from interview transcripts from 1993.

8   On the return to justice arguments in the late 1970s and 1980s see Clarke, J. 'Whose Justice? the politics of juvenile control', *International Journal of the Sociology of Law*, 13, 407-21; Giller, H. 'Is there a role for a juvenile court?', *Howard Journal*, 23 (3), 161. (1986); Harris, R. (1982) 'Towards Just Welfare', *British Journal of Criminology*, 25 (1) (1985); Krisberg, B. and Schwartz, I. 'Rethinking Juvenile Justice', *Crime and Delinquency*, 28 (3), 333. (1983); Krisberg, B. et al. 'The watershed of Juvenile Justice

Reform', *Crime and Delinquency*, 32 (1) 5.; Morris, A. and Giller, H. (eds) *Providing Justice for Children*, London: Edward Arnold. (1983); Pratt, J. 'Delinquency as a scarce resource', *Howard Journal*, 24 (2); Rutherford, A. *Growing Out of Crime*. (1986) and revised as *Growing Out of Crime: The New Era* (1992); Garapon, A. 'Paternalism and legalism in juvenile justice: two distinct models', *The Liverpool Law Review*, 12, (1990) 115 - 27.

[9]   As one Team Leader of a local authority youth justice team (1993) explained it: 'Well the rehabilitation ethos is the basis of our desire ... I mean we want to help and do good. We're working on the assumption that Juvenile justice 'ought' to be helpful, solving problems, not punishment. But rehabilitation was naive and meant we were actually carrying out the demands of the system... [Now] we are doing what we think real justice demands. If we can't rehabilitate we can stop the youngster being sucked into the system with all that entails. I mean destroyed life prospects and future offending ... more serious ...'. This view was also expressed at official level. As, for example, in the following extract from a report produced by a Government Inter-departmental Group on Crime in 1983 (Home Office, 1983, *Crime Reduction: Report of an Inter-departmental Group on Crime*): 'All young people go through a difficult period in adolescence and many commit offences of some sort. The great majority grow out of criminality but there is a danger that the wrong sort of reaction to their offences could propel some into further crime.'

[10] Van Bueren, *The International Law on the Rights of the Child*, 1995: 169. The various international Instruments pertaining to the treatment and response to juvenile delinquency are *The United Nations Guidelines for the Prevention of Juvenile Delinquency (Riyadh Guidelines), the United Nations Convention on the Rights of the Child, the United Nations Rules for the Protection of Juveniles Deprived of their Liberty, and the United Nations Standard Minimum Rules for the Administration of Juvenile Justice (The Beijing Rules).* Since most of these instruments are not binding their effectiveness lies not in the judicial actions that can be brought to enforce them but in their ability to function as ethical and principled bodies of guidance. *The Riyadh Guidelines*, for example, is a policy statement of the prevention of juvenile delinquency aiming to keep children out of court. It places emphasis upon the socialisation process in which five factors are important: family, education, community, the media, and government social policy. *The Riyadh Guidelines* is a child centred document and this is an international trend at present. Recent UK legislation, notably the Children Act 1989 and the Children (Scotland) Act 1995, does involve the child in decision-making. Another Convention, *The United Nations Rules for the Protection of Juveniles Deprived of their Liberty*, states it is 'designed to serve as convenient standards of reference and to provide encouragement and guidance to professionals involved in the management of the juvenile justice system'. It stresses 'imprisonment

should be used as a last resort' and the rights of juveniles be respected. The overall intention is to further the respect of juveniles as human beings.

[11]   Morris, Alison and Giller, H. *Understanding Juvenile Justice*, Croom Hill, 1987: 257.

[12]   A note on costs. The Audit Commission Report *Misspent Youth, Young people and Crime* (1996) estimated that public services spend around £1 billion a year processing and dealing with offending by young people. The breakdown was as follows: Police £660m; Social Services £200m; Legal Aid £42m; Crown Prosecution Service £24m; Court £13m; Probation £12m; and Prison £40m.

[13]   As a consequence of the systems management approach it appeared to many by the end of the 1980s that the majority of serious and persistent juvenile offenders can be managed in the community without recourse to institutional care or custody. The extension of the category of juvenile to 17 year olds in the 1991 CJA bears this out and is also a reflection of the decreasing numbers of juveniles processed by the juvenile court as a result of the systems management approach and the rise of cautioning. Indeed a study by Social Information Systems Ltd. - *Justice by Geography* (quoted in the *New Law Journal*, 19 May 1989) noted that 6,000 fewer juveniles came before the courts in 1987 than in 1986 (when there were 48,000). The study suggested in a light vein that if this trend continued there would be nothing for Juvenile Courts to do by the mid-1990s. In fact the court was changed into a Youth Court exercising only criminal jurisdiction with an increased age limit (up to 18). The study also noted the large variations in the use of cautions. For example in Northamptonshire cautions were relied upon twice as frequently as Staffordshire; Dorset and Lancashire used cautions rarely, while Warwickshire made extensive use. The political climate in the early and mid 1990s changed, however, and a series of moral panics associated with fear of joyriders, children who kill (the Jamie Bulger case), and persistent offenders saw an increased concern with making the system more punishment-orientated. See further, Douglas at Chap. 15 above.

[14]   For detailed discussion of the various possibilities see the Audit Commission Report *Misspent Youth: Young People and Crime* 1996.

[15]   Criteria changed in 1994 by circular 18/94.

[16]   In some areas the matter came to be dealt with by a multi-agency panel composed of representatives from the police, social services, the local education authority, the probation service, etc., who discuss whether the young person should be cautioned or prosecuted (the Northampton model came to be the most discussed and researched).

[17]   When the caution is given a form is filled in with the details of the juvenile and the offence and is signed by the officer who gives the caution and the juvenile's parents. The form is kept by the police for at least three years and may be referred to if a court subsequently needs to know about the

juvenile's character. Thus although a caution avoids prosecution and possible conviction, cautions can be read out later if a young person is subsequently convicted of another offence. An early problem was that the forms used often gave the impression of multiple cautions, i.e. on several occasions, where a youth had been cautioned for several offences at one time. One criticism of cautioning is that young people may be persuaded to admit something they have not done in order to avoid being taken to court.

18 The Home Office circular issued in 1990 to the police urged them to caution all first offenders unless there is a strong reason against, and goes on to state that 'a second or subsequent caution would only be precluded where the offence is so serious as to require prosecution; (see Home Office Circular 59/1990). As a result, the cautioning rate rose for male juveniles from 55% in 1984 to 71% in 1989, and for female juveniles from 79% in 1984 to 86% in 1989. In other words, of all boys under 17 who are detected for committing an offence, only 29% were prosecuted, and for girls under 17 only 14% were prosecuted. Research demonstrated considerable variations between police force areas in the proportions of juveniles cautioned, variations which are not explained by the different 'mix' of offences in those areas, and it remains to be seen whether the increasing involvement of the CPS has improved consistency. Relevant literature includes Landau, S. and Nathan, G., 'Juveniles and the Police', *British Journal of Criminology* 23 (1983); Wilkinson, C. and Evans, R. 'Police Cautioning of Juveniles: The Impact of Home Office Circular 14/1985' [1990] *Crim LR* 165; Giller, H. and Tutt, N., 'Police Cautioning of Juveniles: the Continuing Practice of Diversity' [1987] *Crim LR* 367; Gelsthorpe, L. and Giller, H., 'More Justice for Juveniles: Does More Mean Better?' [1990] *Crim LR* 153.

19 If a traditional criminological theory underpinned how the practitioners operated within the systems management approach it was labelling theory. As Tannenbaum's classic definition put the main point of this theory: 'The process of making the criminal, therefore, is a process of tagging, defining, identifying, segregating, describing, emphasising, making conscious and self-conscious; it becomes a way of stimulating, suggesting, emphasising and evoking the very traits that are complained of. If the theory of relation of response to stimulus has any meaning, the entire process of dealing with the young delinquent is mischievous insofar as it identifies him to himself or to the environment as a delinquent person. The person becomes the thing he is described as being. Nor does it seem to matter whether the valuation is made by those who would punish or by those who would reform ... Their [the reformers] very enthusiasm defeats their aim. The harder they work to reform evil, the greater the evil grows under their hands ... The way out is through a refusal to dramatise the evil. The less said about it the better.' (*Crime and the Community*, New York: Ginn (1938) 1951:19-20)

[20] For fuller discussion see Morrison, Wayne *Theoretical Criminology: from Modernity to Post-modernism*, above note 6.

[21] It is no coincidence that the idea of self-control has surfaced in academic writings as the key concept of criminality. See Gottfredson and Hirschi, *A General Theory of Crime*, Stanford, 1990; see the sustained critique of the narrowness of the position in Morrison, *Theoretical Criminology: from modernity to postmodernism*, above note 6.

[22] Youth Section Leader, 1993; also the title of Andrew Rutherford's book *Growing Out of Crime*. As Rutherford explained his position in the preface to his first edition: 'If a young person becomes involved in crime or other troublesome behaviour, it is tempting for parents or teachers to imagine that the responsibility and solution lie elsewhere. By creating a network of criminal justice, welfare and mental health arrangements, public policy holds out the seductive offer of an institutional fix; although the offer may be appealing it is not an answer. If young people are to grow out of troublesome behaviours, the home, school and other developmental institutions must be encouraged and equipped to hold on during difficult and sometimes volatile phases. Formal intervention carries the threat of exile from a normal environment and the consequent inevitable waste of a chance for normal growth and development. Existing policy trends must be reversed so as to direct attention to the everyday and intuitive practice which holds the most promise.' (1986; 2nd ed. 1992)

[23] One of the ways in which these pressures are handled is by team members bearing in mind a checklist the LA Social Service's Department issue them with. One such list is:
What results are you trying to achieve?
Have you control over all the processes involved?
Do you have the authority needed to accomplish the task?
Whose/what support do you need in order to deliver?
How are you going to secure them?What are the potential risks you are trying to avoid?
What are the resource implications?

[24] Note the techniques of neutralisation Sykes and Matza bequeathed us. Sykes, G.M. and Matza, David 'Delinquency and subterranean values', *American Sociological Review*, 26, 1961.

[25] See Morrison, Wayne *Theoretical Criminology: from Modernity to Post-modernism*, above note 6.

[26] Home Office Research Study 145, HMSO, 1995.

[27] Rifkin, Jeremy *The End of Work: the decline of the Global Labour Force and the dawn of the Post-Market Era*, New York: Putnam Books, 1995.

[28] See Young, Alison *Imagining Crime*, London: Sage, 1996: Ch. 5 'The Bulger Case and the trauma of the Visible', for a reading of the various representations of crime by and on children which responded to the case.

[29]   The criteria for secure remands is the same as those for a remand to prison, with the addition that remand to local authority secure accommodation will be available for females, as well as males (the following conditions are thus for prison remand for males 15-16, and to be for secure accommodation for males and females 12-16). The legislation requires that the defendant is legally represented or has had the opportunity to seek legal advice; that a social worker or probation officer has been consulted in court; and that the young person has been charged with or has been convicted of a violent or sexual offence (as defined under s. 31 of the 1991 Act), or an offence punishable in the case of an adult with imprisonment for a term of 14 years or more; or has a recent history of absconding while remanded from local authority accommodation, and is charged with or has been convicted of an inprisonable offence alleged or found to have been committed while so remanded; and in addition the court must be of the opinion that only a remand to custody would be adequate to protect from serious harm from him.

17 Afterword: Choosing Rights for Children

DAVID NELKEN

The concept of children's rights is both ambiguous and highly contested. What do rights for children mean? Who is responsible for asserting them? Many have questioned whether the term rights is even appropriate. For others the self-evident fact that children do have rights is the best proof of the superiority of the so called 'interest' theory of rights as compared to the competing 'will' theory.[1] But how are we at the same time to treat children as capable of exercising rights whilst also emphasising how much they need our protection? It is certainly no easy matter to find one concept capable of integrating with any coherence children's demands for autonomy with the realities of their dependence and vulnerability. As this collection shows, however, despite the multi-faceted, unwieldy, and even contradictory nature of much 'rights talk' (or perhaps because of this?) the idea that children do and should have rights has made considerable progress, and has become central to one of the most successful recent global campaigns, with almost 200 countries having now signed the relevant 1989 United Nations Convention.

The chapters published here report on some current developments and critical issues in this area. Because of the place where the papers were first presented particular attention is devoted to the vicissitudes of children's rights in Israel - a society which offers enough examples of political, religious and cultural differences to put to practical test any new theory of rights. Many of the papers try to see the import of this allegedly universal idea for Israeli society and offer us a rich description of the different ways a concept such as this has and can be marshalled in the contexts of education and family life. Other papers cover a wide range of relevant topics where the aim is to describe or develop principles and practices which make reference to the idea of children's rights. Almost all of these articles (apart perhaps from that by Michael King) can also be considered part of the phenomena they are describing, in so far as the authors are actively engaged in trying to shape the evolution and application of these rights; identifying the need for intervention, developing legislative schemes, analysing judicial decision-making and so on.

There can be no denying the success of promoters of children's rights in beginning to change what is accepted as the appropriate legal and political discourse to use regarding children. But as King has written elsewhere, it is more difficult to be sure of the other social effects of their recommendations.[2] Fortunately, my task in this afterword is not to evaluate the feasibility of the detailed suggestions made by the various contributors but rather the somewhat easier one of trying to bring out the general issues which the papers raise. In particular, I shall discuss the diverse goals children's rights may be thought to serve, the way the concept is used in changing contexts, the strengths and weaknesses of seeking to use rights to improve children's welfare, and the larger significance of our concern with children's rights at this time. What emerges is a Janus-faced image of children's rights: confident and determined where the issue concerns the wrongs done to children in other cultures but rather more uncertain and anxious at home, revealing our frequent doubts about whether we really do know what is good for children - and for us.

The Many Goals of Children's Rights

The literature on children's rights - as well as much already existing national and international legislation - covers both negative and positive rights which range over a number of worthwhile purposes. These include defending children from harm and exploitation, protecting their chances to grow up cared for in a way which is emotionally sound, and ensuring that children receive that to which they are entitled in terms of health, housing, education etc. (on the model of 'welfare rights'). In addition, however, children's rights are intended to recognise and further their autonomy as persons by providing the conditions in which this can flourish, such as by allowing them to participate in and affect decisions which influence their future.

Many of these basic rights to 'protection, provision and participation' are virtually universally acknowledged. The problem is how to enforce them in practice, especially where societies or families are handicapped by economic problems or where States are weak or collusive in relation to those abusing children's rights. But, at the other extreme, some rights are intrinsically controversial, such as the right, discussed by Katherine O'Donovan at Chapter 12, for children born as a result of AID procedures to know the identity of their biological parent. Everyday problems in safeguarding children's psychological and emotional health, however, often have less to do with agreement over goals than with predicting the future. Whilst there are certainly continuing disagreements on what constitute the ideal conditions of emotional health, the main difficulty faced by judges and health and welfare professionals lies in knowing whether their decisions in cases of uncertainty are more or less likely to lead in the right direction. The crucial question is whether the goal of safeguarding children's rights which, as Leora Bilsky discusses at Chapter 9, is increasingly displacing the notion of 'the best interests of the child', can offer a reliable way of signposting that direction.

The diversity of goals of children's rights does not in itself necessarily create difficulty. Some at least of the apparent contradiction between autonomy and dependence may disappear if we distinguish amongst the very different age groups included in the category of children (indeed languages other than English do not all use such an all-embracing term - and it is unfortunate that the United Nations Convention uses the undiscriminating English language word). Alternatively, some of the different goals of children's rights can be considered as merely a means to others, as in the way greater participation in decision-making can be considered a means to advancing their autonomy. The goals of children's rights may also overlap or at least can be made to do so. The idea of protecting children from sexual or economic exploitation can, rightly or wrongly, be relatively easily assimilated to that of protecting children (and parents) from the sectoral interests of welfare professionals, however dissimilar in fact these situations may be.

Nonetheless, it must be conceded that the various aims of children's rights may - and sometimes do - also enter into conflict. Above all there is a fundamental awkwardness about trying both to safeguard children's right to choose and their right to have their interests protected. How far does 'listening to children' have to go? There is considerable scope for giving children much more information about many of the decisions that affect them. There is certainly a case for requiring the consent of some children, rather than merely that of their parents, in decisions regarding adoption or medical interventions. But what is to be done if a child wishes to use her autonomy or participation rights in ways which others consider to be against her interest?

How this conflict is handled depends on the politics of those working to enhance children's rights. Some promoters of children's rights do want to discover what children actually want so as to help them secure this, but many others mean by children's rights only what can be argued to be objectively best for them. Others' positions are even more ambitious, as where the aim sought is actually to create 'choosing subjects'. For example, Sebba and Shiffer (at Chapter 10 in this volume) interpret children's rights to mean that a liberal state should not be obliged to wait until children at ultra-orthodox schools actually challenge the school's value system - a possibility they consider remote. They insist on a core curriculum which exposes children to other ways of life precisely so that they may be able to conceive of the possibility of choosing to 'exit' from their culture.

As these examples remind us, while the addressees of children's rights may sometimes be children themselves, conceived as rights-holders, more often they are those who are supposed to protect them from harm or further their welfare.[3] Whatever the ultimate goal of increasing their autonomy, this means that in the medium term the idea of children's rights necessarily leads to increasing the control of welfare professionals and others over the child. This is consistent with the steady trend towards undermining the control of parents[4] - both mothers and fathers - in favour of the so-called 'psy' professionals. At the same time we should not exaggerate the decline in 'paternalism' as such. This continues to play a large part in our regulation of childhood at all ages and explains our unease with suggestions such as that put forward by James Michael (at Chapter 11 in this volume) who asks us why we are reluctant to abandon the special restrictions on information which are intended to protect children involved in legal processes. On the other hand, Gillian Douglas (at Chapter 15) wants us to resist the pressure to increase children's autonomy by lowering the age of criminal responsibility and advocates the provocative idea of 'the right to make mistakes'. But can it make sense to demand respect for children as persons without also ascribing them equivalent adult responsibilities? Likewise, must children always be required to reason like adults for their opinions to have weight? It depends of course on the content we give to the idea of respecting children.

Adult rights can be said either to derive from claims deriving from one individual in relation to another or from entitlements made available by the state: children's rights tend to be seen more in terms of entitlements. This means that it is more common to see the movement for children's rights as a further instalment in the story of the rise of the 'child savers'[5] rather than as an attempt to set limits to the activities of professionals and charitable interventions on behalf of children. In practice both approaches to rights are employed, for different purposes, without always making a clear distinction between what each implies. Those using the notion of children's rights (like many similar uses of the language of rights for advancing the interests of disadvantaged groups) therefore often blur the difference between an instrumental and a non-instrumental approach to rights. In Dworkin's language[6] we might describe this as the difference between policy-determined entitlements (which depend on resource considerations and can theoretically be withdrawn) and rights-talk as a way of referring to those cases where actions justified in the name of the collective (or the community) must necessarily be subordinated to the priority of the individual. When rights are seen instrumentally they can be easily linked to the search for improving children's welfare (see, for example, Geraldine Van Bueren, at Chapter 2). But they are less able to restrict such a search. Where rights are conceived non-instrumentally, however, they can serve as a guide to principled control over governmental and official interference with such deserts. But, by the same token, they can promise no overall specific instrumental outcomes which increase social welfare.

As suggested at the outset, the variety of goals which can be connected to the notion of children's rights may actually have helped spread its popularity. The 'magical' idea of rights,[7] like other 'magic' words such as community or democracy, may gain consensus precisely because of the way it can be filled with a range of meanings. Where those who otherwise hold different political and social opinions agree on a slogan it may safely be assumed that they do not always have the same goals in mind.[8] The idea of children's rights, like that of women's rights, victims' rights and human rights more generally, has typically been associated with a 'progressive' politics concerned with the struggle against oppression and inequity in all its forms. But the idea of children's rights can also be combined with the argument that children should be given increasing duties and responsibilities towards their parents or those they may affect or harm (as Andrew Bainham argues at Chapter 6).

The concept of children's rights, however, is unlike other magic terms such as community in so far as it openly supposes the existence of competing or countervailing interests (and rights) against which their rights need to be asserted. Much theoretical discussion and practical implementation indeed focuses on how to safeguard the primacy of the child's rights with respect to the possibly competing interests or rights of parents, carers, teachers, welfare professionals, or other representatives of the local communities to which the child belongs. Certainly the underlying assumption here is that these actors cannot simply be trusted without more to take care of children's rights. The role of the judge (and other figures such as the child advocate or *guardian ad litem*) is somehow to play these actors off against each other so as to give the child 'voice' - even if this causes difficulties for the smooth operations of the professionals (see the discussion by Ya'ir Ronen at Chapter 14).

The brings us to the common theme of this collection of papers, which is the potential conflict between children's rights and traditional values. If we take it that 'law begins where community ends' then, equally, treating children as autonomous, rights-bearing persons can also be seen to challenge those societies dedicated to maintaining traditional, often religiously based, values. Just because they have become signatories to the United Nations Convention does not mean that non-liberal polities will accept liberal interpretations of children's rights. But, even ostensibly liberal societies may include non-liberal cultures, and, in general, many, perhaps most, individual members of such societies still adhere to more traditionalist views of family roles. Not surprisingly therefore, the emergence of children's rights has gone together with the reassertion of parents' rights, with which they may not always be compatible.

Those articles in this volume which concentrate on the situation in Israel are especially troubled by the clash between children's rights and traditional values in a multi-cultural reality which includes both liberal and non-liberal societies, each of which has very different ideas about whether children should be considered as having rights.[9] But the complexities of the Israel situation include divisions not only between the religious and the secularists and between Arabs and Israelis but also between Arabs themselves. Thus the paper by Nadera Shalhoub-Kevorkian (at Chapter 13) describes how Palestinian girls who participated in the *intifada* suffered not only from a State which treated them as potential terrorists but also from their own traditional cultures which saw their entry into the public sphere as a threat. More generally, many of the other papers offer case-studies of how social and technological change confront traditional solutions enshrined in law. But it is not always made clear (perhaps because in practice the matter is often far from obvious) whether the authors think that it is judges or welfare professionals who are more attached to the traditional values which can obstruct the development of children's rights.

Children's Rights and Changing Contexts

The idea of children's rights can be intended to change the condition of children in dramatically contrasting social settings. If in poorer countries the problem may be exploitation of small children at work, in the West the problem is rather the extended and sometimes fruitless wait before finding satisfying work. If in Western countries the most common, though not the only, contexts in which children's rights are discussed regard the family and school, the institutions in which children pass most of their time, abroad, the issue is more likely to concern religious cultural practices such as female circumcision. Obviously, very different issues are - or should be - raised by, for example, efforts to end the use of children in carpet manufacture in Pakistan, as compared to ending the practice of female circumcision, or finding ways to guide or set limits to the discretion of judges, psychiatrists and social workers in their therapeutic or welfare interventions in family arrangements or children's lives. If the first case has to do with the economics of family survival, the second relates to persuading members of different cultural groups that their practices can harm children; the last often has to do with decisions in situations of uncertainty as for example where seeking the best outcome for a child whose parents decide to separate.

As if this were not already complex enough, arguments in favour of children's rights are now being adopted in the course of conflicts between different groups within multi-cultural liberal societies themselves. This is well-illustrated by the articles about tensions in Israeli society which represent the heart of this book. These discuss the hard choices which are thrown up when judges have to decide what is best for a child, one or both of whose parents belong to a minority culture (see the papers by Bilsky, Falk, and Kaplan, in this volume), or the even more controversial question of how far genuine multi-culturalism entails allowing national, religious or ethnic cultures to oppress their own members (see the papers on Ultra-Orthodox schooling in this volume by Goldstein, Kaplan, and Sebba and Shiffer). Can religious courts ever acknowledge that the 'best interests of the child' may clash with religious requirements? How far can and should a liberal state go in pressurising religious or other private schools to teach a core curriculum which includes respect for diversity? As this example suggests, we find ourselves here caught up in a battle between competing rights rather than simply between tradition and rights - on the one hand the right to autonomy claimed by or for the individual, on the other that claimed by the community. In the Israeli case - but this is perhaps not untypical - the struggle is also over which group(s) represent the soul of the country and whose practices should rather be considered most threatening to its survival as a moral community. In practice of course each side relies more on its political leverage than merely the strength of its arguments.

Children's rights supporters work to persuade states to intervene in families which fail to protect children (see Van Bueren at Chapter 2). But the difficulties in transferring principles established and developed in one context to other cultures can easily lead to charges of ethnocentrism, the claim that supposed universal principles are no more than the particularisms of the powerful. The spread of the new language of rights has in fact been described as an example of 'globalized localism',[10] which pays insufficient heed to the need for dialogue. The promoters of children's rights certainly see themselves as trying to fulfil Richard Rorty's project for liberal society as aiming 'to share some final vocabulary which can enable us to ask whether a fellow individual is in pain'.[11] They may concede, as does Van Bueren, that a culture of rights cannot be imposed but only brought about indirectly. But the concept of rights, never mind the substance of particular alleged rights, may often be alien and threatening to the many cultures which do not give the same theoretical importance as liberalism does to the claims of the individual as compared to those of the collectivity. These cultures include many in the Arab world, many of those which appeal to 'Asian values' and most of those nationalist or communist polities which were, or still are, organised as one-party states.

In some extreme cases the dangers of imposing ethnocentric values may seem less worthy of concern than the risks from which children need to be saved (though it is then all too easy to forget that there may still be 'costs' involved in such interventions). Thus particular attention is currently being given to the customary preferential feeding of male children, child marriage, or female circumcision, seen as a health-threatening practice. A number of difficult cases were described to me in the course of an interview which I conducted in 1987 with the then Ombudsman for Children in Jerusalem (an office based on that first invented in Oslo). He described being asked to arrange for reconstructive hymen operations to be carried out on both Jewish and Arab girls who otherwise ran great danger when getting married (some of these girls had lost their virginity at the hands of other family members). He also explained that he had been called in to protect children in Ultra-Orthodox schools who did not comply with school rules, including a case where a girl who wished to change school was threatened by the headmaster that he would make it impossible for her to find a marriage partner from the community.

It is arguable whether these or other similar dangers to children should be seen as essential rather than merely contingent expressions of the cultures concerned. It is clear that traditional cultures place a higher value on obedience to parents than on children's rights to assert their opposition. Every culture punishes according to its own definitions of non-conformity which are far from universal, but traditional cultures are particularly threatened by deliberate flouting of diversity. The undeniable fact that highly objectionable behaviour can flourish as part of traditional systems of value should not, however, be allowed to obscure the extent to which these same traditions may in many respects have something to teach us (as far as the problem of children's autonomy is concerned it is significant that we have abandoned the initiation ceremonies which mark the transition from childhood to adulthood in all traditional cultures). In any case the contrast between rights and traditional values can be overdrawn. Traditions can be 'invented' or reinvented, and the evolution of the liberal notion of individual rights is itself part of a tradition. Traditions are not and cannot be static;[12] if rights consciousness is to be integrated into different traditions a particularly important role can be played by 'immanent critique',[13] stimulated in part no doubt by contact with other cultures. Tradition is less to be identified with conservatism and more with the capacity to make the 'past live in the present'[14] - an essential element of social or cultural continuity. For many purposes it would be more useful to talk of different cultural traditions rather than traditional and non-traditional cultures.

Liberalism does not of course possess a monopoly on ideas of human dignity. It is one thing to show that autonomy is important, even more important than happiness, as shown by Nozick's 'thought experiment' in which he asks us to imagine whether we would be willing to be attached, once and for all, to a machine which provided us with all our desires.[15] But we may have become narcissistically over-attached to the idea of self-expression above all other values.[16] In practice choice often finds its cultural lowest common denominator in the spread of consumerism or the 'zapping' of television channels.

The Kantian idea of autonomy is a much more stringent conception than is conjured up by talking of maximising a child's control over her life-choices. Not least it belongs to a philosophy which is concerned to establish how the pursuit of one's own ends can make a place for the same pursuit by others.[17] But reference to other cultural traditions might nonetheless help us overcome the starkness of the Kantian alternative between heteronomy and autonomy (see Ze'ev Falk at Chapter 7). Take, for example, the Jewish tradition which stands behind some of the social conflicts discussed in this volume. For Levinas, the French Jewish philosopher whose ethical theory of the demands of the 'other' is increasingly influential in times of postmodern doubt over modernist ideologies, the Jewish world view stands opposed to the Greek/Western culture which is obsessed with 'the temptation of temptation' and the desire to experience choosing as an end in itself. He acknowledges that the only alternative to endlessly choosing to choose which our society can imagine is the dependent condition of childhood (a claim which sounds ironic in the context of the present discussion). But he proposes that we see 'whether it is possible to escape the temptation of temptation without either reverting to childhood or always violently restraining it'[18] by recognising that it may actually be possible to 'choose' heteronomy.

The plausibility of the liberal idea, of a political society based on freely choosing subjects, has in fact come under increasing criticism from communitarians such as Macintyre, Sandel, and Waltzer who emphasise the impossibility of separating individuals from their historically shaped identities as members of family, ethnic and other primary groups. Sebba and Shiffer, in their paper concerning the allegedly pernicious effects of ultra-orthodox education, rightly give careful consideration to this challenge to liberalism. They are mainly interested in arguing that the communitarian position does not justify schools ignoring the existence of other ways of life, particularly if this is done at state expense. They also criticise the unwillingness of most traditional cultures to tolerate the possibility of 'exit' by their members. Yet one could also question the plausibility of the typical 'liberal decision to bring children up so they can supposedly 'choose' later on between a religious or non-religious way of life.

On the other hand, for some writers the emphasis on individual rights is precisely the key to what is most unsound about liberal as compared to communitarian ways of organising society. Robert Cover, a highly original Yale Law Professor, mounted a sustained critique on societies which give rights talk so much centrality.[19] He contrasted a society based on the sovereignty of private ends, where individuals interrelate as potentially 'hostile others', relying ultimately on the state's monopoly of violence, with the sort of (perhaps idealised) community, or set of communities, tied together by reciprocal obligations where law unfolds as part of the working out of a common 'Nomos'. For Cover, rights - too often - only indicate a need rather than a solution because the members of society do not find it easy to know to whom they are addressed and by whom they will be satisfied; obligation, on the other hand, is always specific and always starts from the individual.

If there are serious problems in mobilising rights in cross-cultural contexts different, though not less intractable, problems arise in a second major context in which rights talk has been promoted. The claim here is that a stress on rights can improve the situation of children where there has been family breakdown or some other need for social intervention in their lives. The growing popularity of the concept of children's rights in this area has been seen as a reaction (or over-reaction) to earlier certainties concerning the capacity of welfare professionals to identify and secure the best interests of children. After all, in only one generation there have been drastic changes in the professional conventional wisdom over the appropriate practice to follow regarding maintaining contact with natural parents after adoption or with fathers after divorce. When faced with tragic choices involving separating couples, children given for adoption, or more recently, struggles arising from surrogacy contracts, judges have come to distrust the uncertainties of trying to predict 'the child's best interests'. By contrast, the idea of rights is supposed to sharpen consideration of the different parties whose interests can conflict and highlight the need to ask for and take into account the child's opinions.

A further alleged advantage of the concept of rights is its capacity to set definite limits to welfare interventions; in theory, rights could therefore be used to govern the threshold of intervention with therapeutic considerations taking over thereafter.[20] In the way they are actually used, however, it is often not clear whether it is judges or social workers who are better able to manipulate resort to rights for their purposes.[21] The fact that rules, whether generated by rights or any other general principles, always have to be interpreted and applied and that welfare professionals can be as skilful as others at exploiting the discretionary power that this involves, is regularly both forgotten and rediscovered.[22]

As long as judges cannot get to the 'facts' of these cases at first hand their need to rely on experts is not much reduced. Rights-talk may mark only a symbolic retreat from the 'normalising' role of welfare professionals. The move to rights-talk can help social workers avoid the need to guarantee the success of their therapeutic interventions.[23] Likewise, in the field of criminal justice, social and youth workers faced with the virtually impossible task of helping youngsters with little future tend to use rights talk to provide themselves with more manageable goals of damage-maintenance.[24]

Making Children's Rights Effective - and the Dangers of Doing So

The ambiguities which dog the definition of the concept of children's rights - many of which have already been noted - have numerous implications for any effort to enforce them. Where do children's rights begin and end? What about where children's rights conflict with the rights of other people (and it does not take long for opposing interests to be reformulated in these terms). Whatever their rights, the interests of parents and children are often fatally intertwined. Defining the individual child's right independently of the need for children to grow up in stable families and communities taxes the capacities of the best judges (see Bilsky at Chapter 9). What should we do where we have to choose the priority to give to some of a child's rights as against others she herself possesses? Should a child, for example, have a right that another person's body be checked for information which relates to her genetic identity (see O'Donovan at Chapter 12)? On the one hand, acknowledging that families or communities also have rights can make it easier for them to oppress those who depend on them. On the other, insisting that rights must always be individual perpetuates the enlightenment fallacy of offering emancipation only to individuals and never to groups.[25]

Many of these problems could be said to be generally applicable to all types of rights claim. They have to be tackled by careful legal drafting together with the fine tooling of judges' decision-making. What is meant by the 'primacy' which children are given in the United Nations Convention ? When is it legitimate to derogate from the fundamental rights now enshrined in Israel's Basic Law? Should the courts approve a teenage child's request to take a foreign holiday with a friend against her parents' wishes? When does a child born by artificial insemination have a right to check DNA material to discover the identity of her natural father? Judges offer different answers to these questions in different jurisdictions and the answers they give today may change tomorrow. Critical Legal Scholars would emphasise how much this means that adjudication - whether concerned with rights or otherwise - cannot offer any certainties; others would perhaps see this as valuable pragmatic flexibility.

On the other hand, some issues seem more specific to the question of children's rights. Children and adults cannot be treated as equal adversaries. Some even argue that children have the right not to be treated like adults, or as Douglas puts it in this volume, that they have the right to make mistakes. But can there be a right not to have responsibilities? Another set of problems arises from the fact that children almost always require others to interpret and assert their rights. Even if this is not in principle inconsistent with the idea of their actually having rights it certainly causes difficulties in practice given that those who must defend their rights are also often those from whom they have the right to be protected. It is also rather easy to rewrite even the most paternalistic goals as if they were children's rights, as in the 1994 statute of children's rights in Italy which includes the right to parents providing them with an 'ethical education'.[26]

Some argue that it is a mistake to think that children's rights can be made effective in the way hoped for by their proponents.[27] Apart from the difficulties, contingencies, and undesired side-effects of social interventions, it is said to be implausible to try to change society through mobilising the legal category of rights. King argues that there is no way of predicting whether the use of rights will advance children's welfare either in the international or domestic sphere. There are serious doubts about how far some governments really can (or want to) protect children through signing international conventions - for example where this would require interference in the economy. But, in addition, children's rights activists are accused of employing naive models of social change. King proposes instead drawing on the sociological theory of the distinguished German sociologist Niklas Luhman.[28] In highly differentiated modern societies, social complexity is sustained by the communications between the sub-systems.[29] But each of these can only regulate according to its operational codes, in essence regulating its own vision of the world. To understand the way social interventions using the language of rights can produce their effects we thus need to appreciate the potential for 'coupling' law, politics and economics. King suggests that law's function in particular is to control some of the side-effects of the difficulties of coordination between different sub-systems. As an example he suggests that law can at least solve social work's crisis of disappointing expectations by moving their aims nearer to those of law.[30] As long as they can show their interventions to be legally justifiable they will not be judged so much in terms of the outcomes they achieve. In general, like Teubner, he sees law as helping to deal with damaging 'fall-out' from other forms of social intervention.[31] But, it should be noted, there is no way of guaranteeing whether rights talk can be successful even in achieving this aim. It is just as likely that fashions in social policy may again soon change so as to relegitimise social work language at the expense of rights.

King is certainly correct in drawing our attention to the importance of 'law as communication';[32] rights talk can be seen less as a tool designed to achieve certain effects and more as an aspect of communication between discourses (and we might add between cultures). But the ambitious rhetoric used by children's rights proponents often conceals more modest goals than that of inducing social change. Few of the contributors to this volume (perhaps because of their legal backgrounds) even discuss the issue of how to ensure such change comes about. Some limit themselves to describing developments in the use of international conventions or international private law intended to deal with the problems of achieving legally acceptable cross-cultural agreements over what to do in cases of abduction or (more tricky) disputes over cross-cultural adoption.[33] They freely acknowledge that even success in these efforts would not necessarily reflect or lead to cultural convergence.

Apart from the difficulties of achieving children's rights we also need to ask whether or how far we should want this trend to proceed. Those who urge the use of this new vocabulary do not always look closely enough at what is lost in moves to children's rights. Why and when should we give rights to children? Are rights always good for them - and can everything that is good for children be expressed in terms of rights?

A danger of rights talk, as we have seen, could be its tendency to run too far ahead of practical problems of enforcement. It would be narrow-minded to assume that systems of law should always be framed in terms of wrongs and remedies, as the common law claims to be.[34] But civil law systems also have trouble in recognising children's rights as a species of what they call 'subjective rights'. And in countries where law and life are often out of touch rights talk can often serve to exaggerate this gulf. In some Latin legal cultures, for example, the expansion of formal rights often bears no relation to what is feasible, yet evidence that reality is out of line with the law is more likely to be seen as proving the need for an even more ambitious law rather than to re-think its applicability.[35] In Brazil, for example, a recent splendid statute of children's rights elaborates a series of positive and negative rights, but it does this in a context where hundreds of thousands of street children live daily at risk of death and injury, sometimes at the hands of the very police forces themselves who are supposedly the representatives of the state which has promulgated this statute.

A further problem with the extension of rights is the danger of the 'juridification' of social life[36] or what Habermas has called the 'colonisation of the lifeworld' of family and community.[37] Can society become too rights-conscious? How far do we want children in ordinary life to think of themselves as rights-bearers? If the bonds between parents and children are one of the few relationships to survive the increasing fragility of relationships between couples, do we really want to reshape them in terms of rights?

Using the language of rights involves trying to construe children's needs legally, and this carries numerous costs. Consider how little reference there is in all discussions of children's rights to the enormous influence, for good or ill, of peer-group pressures on the behaviour of young people. Nor can many other of the varied emotional and psychological factors affecting childhood be translated without loss into legal considerations or classified in terms of the dichotomies so necessary to legal adjudication. As contrasted with welfare terminology the language of rights has if anything more in common with the conceptual classifications of traditional religious legal systems (if not their substance) as they too seek to lay down general rules with cut-off points over which parent has responsibility at which age; when children must be asked their opinion and so on.

We also need to ask whether choosing rights for children is necessarily following the appropriate political strategy for advancing their interests. Turning political claims into law always carries some risk of losing momentum. For example, after the 'first generation' of feminists, the women's movement has become a lot more equivocal about the gains of even apparently successful legal campaigns.[38] By comparison with how much still needs to be done to help children in some parts of the world, the battle for rights could be considered not much more than pious conscience-saving, a form of symbolic small change for the desperately needy. Even where conditions for children are better, rights may be less useful than other more conventionally political ways of improving children's fortunes: fighting the cut-backs in welfare and the poverty which handicaps so many children's life chances; finding better ways to regulate bio-ethical technological innovations; and, not least, beginning to face the problem of justice between the generations, ranging from that raised by the problem of irreversible environmental damage to the enormous debt weighing on the young brought about by over-generous public pension provisions.

The Social Significance of Children's Rights

Children's rights may not be able to achieve all that we want from them but they seem to be an idea whose time has come. But why is this? The sort of 'Whig history' which rewrites the past as steady progress to the present might suggest that just as women have been emancipated (belatedly) from their status as the property of dominant males, so the same is now

330 Children's Rights and Traditional Values

happening to children who were previously regarded as the property of their parents (and see Bainham at Chapter 6). Children now 'own themselves' and have the right to make their own choices, as opposed to being seen as no more than the bearers of culture into the next generation (the view which still prevails in traditional cultures). The family - the last bastion of feudalism within capitalist liberal societies - has finally fallen to the logic of equal citizenship. On the other hand, and somewhat paradoxically, it would also be true to say that children in traditional societies are treated more like adults than they are in more modern societies. The problem of children's rights poses itself with particular force in our society because it is we who have 'invented' the status of childhood[39] as one of dependence and need of protection and removed children into the 'total institutions' of home and school.

From a sociological point of view the rise of children's rights is consistent with all the classical explanations of the social changes which characterise modernity. (Of course once mobilised by law and politics in a variety of cultures the idea itself takes on the potential to become a factor which helps bring about modernity.) This trend most obviously fits in with Maine's thesis of modernity as a process which marks the transformation in the political significance of the family, taking us from 'status to contract'.[40] As Tonnies explained, the breakdown of parental control itself forms part of simultaneous rise in power of both the state and the individual at the expense of 'secondary associations' such as the family.[41] And the decline in the importance of family has of course gone much further since these authors wrote their books. Even the role of mediating the outside world has become less essential when relationships are developed through television, travel, computers and so on.

The stress on individualism and personalisation (albeit not applied to children) is exactly the theme of Durkheim's explanation of the larger 'moral' presupposition and implications of the growth of the economic division of labour under capitalism.[42] As confirmed by Foucault's more recent socio-historical excursions, individualism here does not exactly mean freedom from social control. Rather it represents an obligation imposed on us by a society which develops through increasing economic specialisation and whose social order relies on reflexive self-control. Likewise, at a more banal level of analysis, children as potential choosing customers have a central place within the growth of 'consumer society' (one only has to think of the invention of 'teenagers' as a new market to be exploited). In other respects too, specific aspects of the campaign for children's rights belong to wider social developments. The emphasis on using law to protect children from as many harms as possible is an aspect of what Lawrence Friedman has characterised as the drive to 'Total Justice';[43] and the characterisation of children as victims is part of the spread of the victims' movement and the globalisation of criminal justice.[44]

However, if we consider the present period better characterised as one of postmodernity, the importance attached to children's rights could actually be considered as an example of the continued power of a relatively 'traditional' ideal belonging to modernity. Like many other legal ideals[45] rights talk may actually gloss over the extent of social change. In this case it may mask the extent to which society has become a set of sub-systems in which the individual psychic system has increasingly less autonomy[46] - what others have described as the 'de-centring of the subject' is a topic which can be noticed in literature but which law must continue to deny.[47] Children are thus given rights only when the concept has largely lost its social force. As O'Donovan suggests in this volume, even the most intimate of social bonds are being remade by technology. Given the fragmentation of paternity into genetic, legal and social elements, law's task, it is suggested, should be to give children the right to find out the 'truth' about their family relationships whilst making it clear that this does not necessarily have implications for how they are to live their affective relationships.

There are therefore multiple reasons why children are increasingly being interpolated as persons. But the ideal content of children's rights is of course more open to argument. Deciding what rights children can be said to have itself depends on how society conceives or constructs the idea of childhood, and this reflects the type of society we have, or want to have. Campaigns for the furtherance of children's rights are thus often a sign of disagreement over issues which do not just concern children - and this means that they are only more or less about children themselves. In this volume for example, the needs and rights of children point up problems as varied as what counts as success in creating a multi-cultural society, the prerogatives of the liberal state, differences between religious and secular conceptions of education, and the social implications of bio-technical engineering. Arguments over children's rights imply and reflect social, political and even epistemological choices between rights and welfare, liberalism and communitarianism, or universalism and relativism.

Our concerns about children are therefore also ways of worrying about ourselves. Just as our individual childhoods are constitutive of our personal identities, so is our collective image of childhood crucial to our social identity. The 'moral panics' over child abuse and paedophilia almost certainly reflect changes in our reactions to these offences more than they do any rise in the phenomenon. Why are we so much more worried now? As adult members of liberal societies - and providing we do not have even more urgent problems of survival - we too are caught up in the dialectic of autonomy and dependence. Whilst seeking to be ourselves as autonomous individuals we also know that it is only our relations with others which govern our emotional health, and provide us with any real sense of our selves. For the USA Critical Legal Scholars movement, the contradictions of modern law can be traced to the constant difficulties we find in knowing where to draw the line between ourselves and others, or between egoism and altruism. Other social commentators note that though we yearn for more intimacy in the roles we occupy in the world of work, we at the same time move to create impersonal rights in the spheres of intimacy.

Likewise, our uncertainty over whether the status of childhood is one to be pitied or celebrated can tell us a lot about the contradictions in our culture. We define childhood as a period of waiting to become a full person, but we are nostalgic both for its innocence and lack of responsibilities. We want to grant children control over their lives but we are worried if children grow up too quickly. Every step to adulthood (watching TV, receiving pocket money, going to school alone, using cigarettes) is fraught with this ambivalence. But at the same time, self-help books are now being written for children in order to help them see their busy parents' point of view - with 'latch-key children' being taught to value the independence this gives![48]

We are still far from having achieved the ideal for which Maria Montessori aimed, by which we would avoid what she called the 'adultism' of using adult standards to measure what was best for children, whilst at the same time treating children with full respect. Perhaps it is a mistake to start from the model of adults' rights - whether these be political, social, religious or economic - and then try to shape them to the measure of children? Perhaps we should rather make the effort to redesign our institutions and cities as if they were suited to children as a class of people in their own right - and see what advantages there may be also for us? (This is the approach used in some of Italy's world famous nursery schools such as those in Reggio-Emilia; a more general example is represented by the Rudolf Steiner schools). Some modern societies create the impression that dependence is necessarily incompatible with respect (or, in other terms, that the only way to earn respect is through independence). Yet in Italy the younger generation still tends to live at home into their 30s - and the word for 'child' is strictly limited to children aged less than ten.[49]

It would make practical choices regarding children much more straightforward if we could be certain that the discourse of rights was always part of the solution and never itself part of the problems we have been discussing. Certainly there is no denying the many values (some of them quite traditional!) which the grant of rights is intended to secure, whether this is protection from harm, greater welfare or empowerment. But, as we have seen, we must not beg the question whether this is the only way or best way of helping children; nor is increasing resort to the terminology of rights going to provide any easy way of deciding what to do when these values come into conflict.

Notes

[1]   MacCormick, D.N. (1982) 'Children's Rights: A Test-Case for Theories of Rights', in D.N. MacCormick, *Legal Right and Social Democracy*. Clarendon Press, pp. 154-166.

[2]   King, M. (1997) *A Better World for Children?* Routledge.

[3]   Maggioni, G. (1997) 'Cittadinanza Dei Bambini e Costruzione Sociale Del'Infanzia: introduzione', in G. Maggioni and C. Baraldi eds. (1997) *Cittadinanza Dei Bambini e Costruzione Sociale Del'Infanzia* Quattroventi pp. 7-46

[4]   Donzelot, J. (1980) *The Policing of Families: Welfare Versus the State* (trans. R. Hurley), Hutchinson.

[5]   Platt, A. (1969) *The Child Savers* University of Chicago Press.

[6]   Dworkin, R. (1977) *Taking Rights Seriously* Duckworth.

[7]   King, M. (1993) 'I diritti del bambino, ovvero la magia del diritto' *Sociologia del diritto* 3 pp. 25-44; Ronfani, P. (1997) 'L'interesse del minore: dato asiomatico o nozione magica' *Sociologia del diritto* xxiv 1 pp. 47-95.

[8]   Nelken, D. (1985) 'Community Involvement in Crime Control', *Current Legal Problems 1985* pp. 239-267 (revised version in L. Sebba (ed) *Social Control and Justice inside or outside the Law* (1996) Magnes Press pp. 235-277).

[9]   See the chapters in this volume by Falk, Goldstein, Kaplan, Sebba and Shiffer.

[10]   De Sousa Santos, B. (1995) *Toward a New Common Sense: Law, Science and Politics in the Paradigmatic Transition* Routledge; De Sousa Santos, B. (1997) 'Toward a Multicultural Conception of Human Rights', *Sociologia del diritto* xxiv 1 pp. 27-46.

[11]   Rorty, R. (1989) *Contingency, Irony and Solidarity* Cambridge University Press pp. 189-97.

[12] Shils, E. (1981) *Tradition* Faber; Kaplan, Chap. 4 above; Sebba and Shiffer, Chap. 10 above.

[13] An-na'im, A.A. (1990) *Toward an Islamic Reformation* Syracuse University Press.

[14] Krygier, M. (1986) 'Law as Tradition', *Law and Philosophy* 5: 237.

[15] Nozick, R. (1974) *Anarchy, State and Utopia* Blackwell.

[16] Lasch, C. (1978) *The Culture of Narcissism* W. W. Norton.

[17] Weinrib, E. (1995) *The Idea of Private Law* Harvard University Press.

[18] Levinas, E. (1990) *Nine Talmudic Readings* (trans. A. Aronowicz) Indiana University Press.

[19] Cover, R. (1987) 'Obligation: A Jewish Jurisprudence of the Social Order' 5 *Journal of Law and Religion* pp. 65-90.

[20] Nelken, D. (1980) 'Children's Hearings: The Way Forward', SCOLAG (Scottish Legal Action Group) pp. 144-149.

[21] Nelken, D. (1988) 'Social Work Contracts and Social Control', in R. Mathews (ed.) *Informal Justice*, Sage pp. 108-122; Nelken, D. (1989) 'Discipline and Punish: Some Notes on the Margin', in D. Nelken ed. *Marginal Criminal Justice: a special issue of the Howard Journal of Criminal Justice* pp. 245-254 (reprinted in S. Henry (ed) (1994) *Social Control: International Library of Essays in Criminology, Criminal Justice and Penology*, Dartmouth).

[22] Rose, N. (1986) 'Law, Rights and Psychiatry' in P. Miller and N. Rose (eds) *The Power of Psychiatry* Polity Press pp. 177-213.

[23] King, M. and Piper, C. (1990) *How the Law thinks about Children* Gower; King, supra n. 2; King, Chap. 1 in this volume.

[24] See Morrison, W. Chap. 16 above.

[25] Bauman, Z. (1989) *Modernity and the Holocaust* Polity.

[26] Ronfani supra n. 7.

[27] King, Chap. 1 above, and supra n. 2.

[28] King, op. cit. n. 2.

[29] Luhmann, N. (1982) *The Differentiation of Society* (trans. S. Holmes and C. Larmore), Columbia University Press.

[30] King op.cit. n. 2.

[31] Teubner, G. (1997) 'Altera Pars Audiatur: Law in the Collision of Discourses', in R. Rawlings ed. *Law, Society and Economy* Clarendon Press.

[32] Nelken, D. (1996) 'Law as Communication: Constituting the Field', in D. Nelken ed. *Law as Communication* Dartmouth pp. 3-24.

[33] See Duncan, W. Chap. 3 above; and Pearl, D. Chap. 5 above.

[34] See MacCormick supra n. 1.

[35] López-Aylon, S. (1995) 'Notes on Mexican Legal Culture' in D. Nelken (ed) *Legal Culture, Diversity and Globalization: a special issue of Social and Legal Studies* 4 1 pp. 477-493.

36 Teubner, G. (1987) *Juridification of Social Spheres: A Comparative Analysis in the areas of Labor, Corporate, Antitrust and Social Welfare Law* de Gruyter.

37 Habermas, J. (1987) *The Theory of Communicative Action, Volume 2: System and Lifeworld; A Critique of Functionalist Reason* Beacon Press

38 Smart, C. (1989) *Feminism and the Power of Law* Routledge.

39 Ariès, P. (1979) *Centuries of Childhood* Penguin.

40 Maine, H.S. (1917) *Ancient Law* Dent.

41 Tonnies, F. (1957) *Community and Society* (trans. C.P. Loomis) Michigan State University Press.

42 Durkheim, E. (1984) *The Division of Labour in Society* (trans. W.D. Halls) Macmillan.

43 Friedman, L. (1987) *Total Justice* Beacon Press.

44 Nelken, D. (1997) 'The Globalization of Crime and Criminal Justice: Prospects and Problems', in M. Freeman (ed) *Law at the End of the Century: Current Legal Problems Volume 50* Oxford University Press.

45 Nelken, D. (1982) 'Is there a Crisis in Law and Legal Ideology?' *Journal of Law and Society* pp. 177-189.

46 Luhmann supra n. 29.

47 Baker, B. (1991) 'Constructing Justice: Theories of the Subject in Law and Literature', *Minnesota Law Review* 75, 581.

48 Baraldi, C. (1997) 'L'eta dell'innocenza. Autonomia e cittadinanza dei bambini' in G. Maggioni, and C. Baraldi (eds) *Cittadinanza Dei Bambini e Costruzione Sociale Del'Infanzia* Quattroventi pp. 501-538.

49 Ibid.